DEPARTMENT OF THE ENVIRONMENT

National Dwelling and Housing Survey

London: Her Majesty's Stationery Office

ISBN 0 11 751382 2*

FOREWORD

by the Secretary of State for the Environment

I am pleased to contribute a foreword to this Report.

The variety of tables presented in the Report gives an indication of the wide range of information about the current housing situation which is now available as a result of the Survey. Data on these lines is particularly valuable when significant and fairly rapid changes in housing circumstances are happening and it is essential that our policies should suit the needs of the moment and that we should allocate our limited resources to the areas of the country where they will do most good.

I must thank all those who took part in the Survey for their co-operation and goodwill - without this it would have been impossible. It is particularly encouraging to note that in general those asked to help participated fully and there seems to be little doubt that the friendly confidential interview, lasting only a few minutes, has proved to be an acceptable way of collecting this kind of information.

One feature which deserves mention is the speed with which the Survey has been brought to a satisfactory conclusion. We need up-to-date as well as accurate and relevant information. This has been achieved only by the very close co-operation between my Department and the survey firms, which undertook the interviewing, the computing sub-contractors, and the GLC coding and fieldwork specialists.

The high response rate and general success which this major survey has achieved and the flexible tabulation system mean that housing policies can continue to be debated and developed with the background of good information readily available to all concerned. I am sure we can rely on continued help from the public as the Survey is now being extended to a further 200,000 households in other areas to improve our understanding of the range of housing conditions in England.

20. JUL. 1988

ACKNOWLEDGEMENT

The principal members of the Department of the Environment team responsible for the survey were Roger Sellwood, Chief Statistician, Dennis Roberts, Statistician, and Geoffrey Thomas, Consultant. The successful completion of the survey was due to the efforts of the staff of NOP Market Research Ltd, Research Surveys of Great Britain Ltd, Social and Community Planning Research, the GLC Survey Unit, Computer Aided Marketing Ltd, and the other members of the Unit at the Department.

The help of the members of the public who co-operated with the survey is gratefully acknowledged.

CONTENTS

CHAPTER 1. INTRODUCTION

1. In June 1977 the Secretary of State for the Environment and the Secretary of State for Wales presented to Parliament "Housing Policy: A Consultative Document" which was the outcome of a comprehensive review of housing policy in England and Wales. The starting point for the review was an assessment of the housing situation as it then was and recent changes in housing circumstances. That assessment, however, was deficient in various ways as the following extract from the Consultative Document records:-

> "A word of caution is necessary about what follows. We are better informed than every before, but we still do not have all the information we need. We now have up to date information on the condition of the housing stock from the House Condition Surveys 1976. But information on households and tenure is still based on the Census of 1971. Important changes have taken place since then but we can only make estimates of some of them. We need better and up to date information on such matters as the rate of household formation, changes in household composition, changes in the number of households sharing, vacant houses, and the composition and distribution of the private rented sector. We also need better information about differences between housing conditions in different areas. More up to date and comprehensive information will be obtained from a new National Housing Survey and a survey of vacant dwellings which will be launched later this year; and the Department of the Environment intend to establish a special Unit to analyse information about housing and to monitor progress."

2. Details of the National Housing Survey referred to in this extract were announced to Parliament on 6 July 1977 by the Minister for Housing and Construction. The Minister announced that the survey would provide up to date information on housing circumstances in England at national and regional level, and in the larger areas of housing stress. About 375,000 households would be interviewed. In each of the London Boroughs and in areas of housing stress outside London (listed below) sample sizes would average about 7,000 households. The areas outside London to be surveyed would be:

Newcastle
Sunderland
Gateshead
Sheffield
Bradford
Kirklees
Leeds
Wakefield
Bristol
Birmingham
Sandwell
Dudley
Liverpool
Manchester
Salford
Wigan

3. The survey as announced was designed to provide assessments of the current housing situation at regional and, in certain cases, local authority level. But, as noted in the extract from the Consultative Document, detailed information was also required on such topics as the private rented sector, households sharing a dwelling, and vacant properties. Detailed information on each of these topics could not be obtained in a single survey especially as the questions would be relevant to only a small section of the total population. More detailed studies of various topics were therefore made by follow-up surveys of households identified in the main survey as possessing specified characteristics.

4. The further studies carried out based on samples identified in the main survey were:-

    i.   A survey of the private rented sector: this was intended to provide up-to-date information about rents, rent allowances and condition of the stock in the various sub-sectors of the private rented sector.

    ii.   A survey of recent movers: this was the third movers survey (the two previous surveys were carried out in 1972 and 1974), and was designed to collect information on moves within and between tenures, reasons for moving, sources of finance for house purchase and so forth.

    iii. A survey of sharing and concealed households: this was designed to provide detailed information on sharing arrangements and the likely demand from sharing households for separate accommodation in the future.

5. These follow-up surveys were conducted by the Social Survey Division of the Office of Population Censuses and Surveys although fieldwork for the movers survey was contracted out to National Opinion Polls Market Research Limited. Steps were taken to ensure that no household was approached for more than one follow-up survey even though they might qualify for several. It is expected that reports on these surveys will be published in 1979.

6. A survey of vacant properties was also carried out by the Social Survey Division of the Office of Population Censuses and Surveys but in order to speed up the availability of results this was based on properties identified as vacant during fieldwork for the 1977 Labour Force Survey which was also conducted by OPCS. The report on this survey is also expected to be published in 1979.

EXTENSIONS TO NDHS

7. Following the successful completion of the main survey the Secretary of State for the Environment announced on 3 August 1978 that, since the National Dwelling and Housing Survey had already produced much valuable new information about housing conditions and the survey arrangements had worked well, the survey would be extended to cover certain additional areas, including the remaining Inner City Programme areas and a selection of others, to obtain more detailed information about the range of housing circumstances which exist. The areas in the extension to the survey are:

Barnsley
Bolton
Calderdale
Coventry
Doncaster
Eastbourne
Epping Forest
Epsom and Ewell
Kingston-upon-Hull
Leicester
Liverpool
Melton
Middlesbrough
North Tyneside
Norwich
Nottingham
Oldham
Plymouth

Portsmouth
Reading
Rochdale
Rotherham
Scarborough
Sevenoaks
Shepway
South Holland
South Oxfordshire
South Tyneside
Tameside
Taunton Dean
Three Rivers
Walsall
West Dorset
Wirral
Wolverhampton

8.   Interviewing for the extension has commenced and results should be available during the summer of 1979.

PART I

NATIONAL DWELLING AND HOUSING SURVEY: RESULTS

CHAPTER 2. TRENDS: 1971 TO 1977

DWELLINGS AND HOUSEHOLDS

1.   At end 1977 there were an estimated 17,224,000 dwellings in England of which 729,000 were vacant or second homes. The 16,495,000 occupied dwellings housed 16,824,000 households, 16,296,000 of whom each lived in a separate dwelling and 528,000 of whom lived in 199,000 shared dwellings. Of the 729,000 vacant dwellings or second homes, 127,000 were being converted or modernised at the time of the survey and thus were temporarily uninhabitable.

2.   Since 1971, the year of the latest Census of Population, some $1\frac{1}{4}$ million dwellings have been added to the housing stock and an additional 1 million households have been formed. The main effect of the net increase of 265,000 dwellings over households has been to reduce the level of sharing from 795,000 households to 528,000: the main reduction has been in sharing households containing more than one person for which the number has virtually halved from 365,000 to 187,000. The number of concealed households (married couple families and lone parent families living as part of other persons' households) has also been reduced from 392,000 to 253,000. These results are summarised in Table 2.1: more detailed notes on the derivation and comparability of these estimates are given in paragraphs 2.14 to 2.21.

3.   The regional distribution of dwellings and households is shown in Table 2.2. This shows that each region had a crude surplus of dwellings compared with households. Although the North had both the highest proportion of vacant dwellings and the largest proportionate crude surplus this simple relationship did not apply elsewhere. In particular, in Greater London as a whole a relatively high vacancy rate and a small crude surplus co-existed and within the area the highest borough vacancy rates often coincided with the largest crude deficits. The reasons for this are beyond the scope of this survey but the question will be examined in the light of data from other sources, such as the survey of vacant properties currently being conducted by the Office of Population Censuses and Surveys.

TABLE 2.1   DWELLINGS AND HOUSEHOLDS: 1971 AND 1977

Thousands

	April 1971	December 1977
Dwellings		
Total	15,970	17,224
Vacant and second homes	640	729
Shared	290	199
Households		
Total	15,835	16,824
Multi-person households sharing	365	187
One-person households sharing	430	341
Margin of dwellings over households (crude surplus)	135	400
Concealed households		
Married couple	245	149
Lone parent	147	104

TABLE 2.2   DWELLINGS AND HOUSEHOLDS BY REGION: 1977

Region	Total dwellings 000's	Vacant dwellings*		Households 000's	Crude surplus	
		000's	as % of all dwellings		000's	as % of all dwellings
North	1,176	61	5.2	1,120	55	4.7
Yorkshire/Humberside	1,785	69	3.9	1,741	44	2.5
East Midlands	1,417	55	3.9	1,371	46	3.2
East Anglia	699	32	4.6	678	21	3.0
South East	6,295	282	4.5	6,203	92	1.5
Greater London	2,669	129	4.8	2,660	9	0.4
Rest of South East	3,626	153	4.2	3,544	83	2.3
South West	1,629	76	4.7	1,583	46	2.8
West Midlands	1,831	65	3.6	1,792	39	2.1
North West	2,392	88	3.7	2,336	57	2.4
England	17,224	729	4.2	16,824	400	2.3

* Includes second homes.

LACK OF AMENITIES

4.   The number of households lacking exclusive use of at least one basic amenity (a WC inside the building, a fixed bath or shower, and a hot water supply) fell from 2,753,000 in 1971 to 1,445,000 by end 1977, a 48 per cent reduction. Similar percentage reductions occurred in the numbers of households lacking any one of these amenities (see Table 2.3).

5.   This evidence substantiates what was found in the 1976 English House Condition Survey where falls of 46 per cent and 41 per cent were estimated to have occurred in the number of dwellings lacking a fixed bath in a bathroom and an inside WC respectively during the period 1971-76. Precise comparisons between the two surveys are not possible because the House Condition Survey was based on dwellings, as distinct from households, and was conducted at a different time.

6.   Many of the households lacking exclusive use of basic amenities had at least shared use of such amenities. For example, of the 961,000 households lacking exclusive use of a fixed bath or shower, 504,000 had shared use of bath or shower, and of the 1,195,000 households lacking exclusive use of a WC inside the building 454,000 had shared use of this amenity.

7.   The numbers of households lacking amenities fell considerably faster between 1971 and end 1977 than the number sharing amenities: the number of households lacking inside WC and a fixed bath fell by 59 per cent and 66 per cent respectively whereas the numbers of households sharing these amenities fell by 13 per cent and 8 per cent respectively.

8

TABLE 2.3   LACK OF BASIC AMENITIES: 1971 AND 1977

Thousands

	April 1971	December 1977	% reduction 1971-1977
Households lacking exclusive use of:			
WC inside the building	2,350	1,195	49
Fixed bath or shower	1,871	961	49
Hot water supply	1,304	737	43
At least one basic amenity	2,753	1,445	48

DENSITY OF OCCUPATION

8.   Density of occupation can be measured in several ways. The traditional measure, used in recent Censuses of Population, has been the number of persons per room: in computing this measure bathrooms, toilets, small kitchens and rooms solely for business are excluded from the count of rooms. On this basis the number of households living at more than 1.5 persons per room is estimated to have been 73,000 at end 1977: a further 438,000 households were living at more than 1 person per room. Comparable figures for 1971 are 219,000 and 711,000 respectively.

9.   An alternative measure of overcrowding, which has no statutory force but which has been widely used in presenting survey results, is the bedroom standard. This prescribes a standard number of bedrooms required by households of varying composition. Full details of the standard are given on page 207. As with all such measures it is only an approximate one since, for example, it does not take into account size of bedrooms but assumes that all bedrooms can sleep two persons. Further, no allowance is made for regular visitors who are not members of the household.   In short, it is probably a better measure of over-occupancy by households below the standard than it is of under-occupancy by households above the standard.

10.   The number of households below the bedroom standard at end 1977 is estimated to have been 829,000, of which 102,000 were 2 or more bedrooms below the standard.   There are no equivalent figures from the 1971 Census of Population but the General Household Survey for 1971 indicated that some 960,000 households in England were then below the bedroom standard. One possible explanation for the apparent slower decline in the number of households living below the bedroom standard than that in the number living at over 1 person per room is that persons in the most crowded circumstances use for sleeping accommodation rooms intended for use other than as bedrooms and these rooms count as bedrooms in computing the bedroom standard. As the pressure on accommodation declines these rooms revert to other uses so the bedroom standard, as defined, is not improved.

TABLE 2.4   DENSITY OF OCCUPATION: 1971 AND 1977

Thousands

	1971	1977	% reduction 1971-1977
Households living at:			
Over 1 to 1½ persons per room	711	438	38
Over 1½ persons per room	219	73	67
Households living below the bedroom standard	960	829	14

TENURE

11.   The survey results confirm the continued growth in the 1970's of the owner-occupied, local authority and housing association tenures and the reduction in the number of households renting their accommodation in the private sector.   In Table 2.5 vacant dwellings in NDHS have been allocated tenures in the same way as Department of the Environment estimates based on the Census [however, in this table no deduction has been made in the 1971 figures for the 95,000 vacant properties not previously occupied as in Table 2.1 (see paragraph 2.19)].

12.   The number of owner-occupied dwellings increased by 1,315,000 between 1971 and 1977. Some of this increase was due to the sale of properties that were previously rented privately since there were only some 977,000 private sector dwellings completed in that period and some owner-occupied properties would have been demolished in that time. By way of contrast, the private rented sector contracted by 838,000 dwellings during that period part of which was accounted for by municipalisation. The increased activity of housing associations in the 1970's is shown by the near 50 per cent increase in the size of that sector.

13.   At end 1977 56.0 per cent of total dwelling stock was owner-occupied, 29.8 per cent was for rent from local authorities or new town corporations, 1.3 per cent was for rent from housing associations and 12.8 per cent was for rent from private landlords or provided rent-free: the equivalent percentages in 1971 were 51.9 per cent, 28.2 per cent, 1.0 per cent and 19.0 per cent respectively.

TABLE 2.5   TENURE OF DWELLINGS: 1971 AND 1977

Thousands

	April 1971	December 1977
Owner occupied	8,335	9,650
Rented from local authority or new town	4,530	5,137
Rented from housing association	155	230
Rented from private landlord and other tenures	3,045	2,207
Total dwellings	16,065	17,224

NOTES ON DERIVATION AND COMPARABILITY OF RESULTS

14.   Fieldwork for the survey was spread over a number of months so unlike a census of population the results do not relate to a single date. For the national sample fieldwork was concentrated in the last 3 months of 1977 and the early months of 1978: the results can therefore be taken to approximate to end 1977.

DWELLINGS

15.   The estimate of dwellings was derived from information supplied by respondents about their sharing arrangements, if any, with other households. Households were considered to be sharing a dwelling if they shared rooms (excluding bathrooms toilets and small kitchens) with another household, or if when moving between the rooms in their accommodation (excluding bathroom and toilet) they had to use a passageway to which other households had unrestricted access. Households in bedsits were also considered to be sharing a dwelling.

16.   At all properties in the survey where there were no sharing households each household was regarded as occupying a separate dwelling. At addresses where there were sharing households the number of dwellings was estimated by utilising information provided by respondents on the number of households with which they shared. (Further details of the procedure adopted are given in Notes and Definitions).

17.   As in the Census, caravans and non-permanent buildings were counted as dwellings only if they were the permanent residence of a household.

18.   The number of vacant dwellings was also estimated by using information on the extent of sharing at part occupied properties. Vacant household spaces in part-occupied dwellings did not count as vacant dwellings.

19.   The survey estimates of dwellings are not strictly comparable with the Department of the Environment's estimates based on the census for a variety of reasons. On the one hand in the 1971 Census some 95,000 dwellings in England were recorded as vacant not previously occupied. These properties were new buildings either still undergoing the final stages of construction or ready

11

for occupation but not yet occupied. From what is known about the housing market at that time it is thought that the majority of these properties would still have been under construction and therefore not immediately available for use. A better estimate of the stock of dwellings available for use in 1971 might therefore be some 95,000 less than the recorded census figure, and the number of vacant properties would be similarly reduced. This adjustment has been incorporated in the figures in Table 2.1 so the figures presented there are more comparable to those from NDHS where properties still under construction were excluded.

20.   On the other hand it is possible that NDHS slightly under-estimates the dwelling stock through two factors: first, properties that were boarded up or derelict have in the past been excluded from the housing stock because boarding up was usually a prelude to demolition. In recent years, however, there has been a tendency in some areas for most properties becoming vacant for an extended period to be boarded up even though there was no intention to demolish them. Many such properties would be regarded as part of the housing stock since with a minimum of work they could be returned to a habitable condition. In NDHS, as in previous censuses and surveys, no attempt was made to distinguish between derelict and boarded up properties that could easily be made habitable again and those that were likely to remain uninhabit-able or be demolished. In total 684 properties were recorded as derelict or boarded up in NDHS which yielded an estimate of some 137,000 such properties in England. Some of these might more reasonably be counted as vacant pro-perties rather than being excluded from the housing stock as they would have been treated according to the procedures followed in the 1971 Census and as they have been treated in NDHS.

21.   The second way by which NDHS may under-estimate the dwelling stock is through the treatment of properties that interviewers could not locate. When this situation arose further details of the locations were obtained from the Valuation Offices and fresh attempts were made to find the property. However, even these efforts failed to bring to light 624 addresses. In some instances failure to locate the property would have been caused through the property having been demolished but the interviewer failed to find anyone to confirm this: from information on rateable value and age of property it is estimated that this accounted for some 200 of the missing addresses. In other cases the property probably did exist but the interviewer simply could not find it. In the presentation of results here all such properties were ignored and assumed not to exist.

CHAPTER 3. THE PRESENT HOUSING POSITION

1.   In this Chapter we present some of the key cross-tabulations from the survey. There is enormous scope from such a survey to investigate a wide range of topics: and there is much interest in comparing and contrasting detailed results for different areas. In this volume, however, there is no room but to be selective.

2.   What have been included are a selection of cross tabulations of the major variables of interest at the present time, and details of the geographical spread of the incidence of most housing characteristics.

3.   The major topics covered in this chapter are differences between tenures, the housing characteristics of the major ethnic groups, the characteristics of households lacking basic amenities and households living below the bedroom standard, details of sharing and concealed households, a description of households registered on council house waiting lists, details of satisfaction with accommodation and area, the characteristics of households living off the ground floor, details of properties built at different periods, and a description of vacant properties.

HOUSING TENURES (TABLES 1-6)

4.   At end 1977 54 per cent of households were owner occupiers (31 per cent with the help of a mortgage or loan), 30 per cent rented their accommodation from local authorities or new town corporations, 1 per cent rented from housing associations, 11 per cent rented privately unfurnished, and 4 per cent rented their accommodation privately furnished.

Type and Size of Properties

5.   Most detached houses and most larger houses whether defined in terms of number of bedrooms or total number of rooms were owner occupied. Of 3 million households who live in detached houses, 2.6 million were owner occupiers: and of the 1.6 million houses and flats with 4 or more bedrooms, 1.3 million were owner occupied.

6.   Very few owner occupiers had only 1 bedroom - under 300,000 - which is largely explained by the small number of flats that were owner occupied. 3 bedroom houses were the most common type of owner occupied properties, and two out of three households buying their houses with a mortgage or loan were buying such properties.

7.   Properties rented from local authorities and new town corporations were almost exclusively semi-detached or terraced houses or purpose built flats or maisonettes. Almost all council properties had 3 bedrooms or less - fewer than 170,000 had 4 or more. 870,000 local authority tenants had 1 bedroom and there were more 1 bedroom lettings from local authorities than there were from private landlords and housing associations. Nevertheless 2.7 million households renting from local authorities contained only one or two persons.

8.   Properties rented from housing associations were predominantly flats - either purpose built or converted - and almost half contained only 1 bedroom.

9.   Unfurnished and furnished lettings in the private rented sector displayed very different characteristics. Furnished lettings were mainly parts of houses and contained only 1 bedroom but there was also a sprinkling of larger detached houses which were perhaps let while the owner occupier was temporarily away. Unfurnished lettings were the most diversified, consisting of a selection of all types of houses and flats and containing a wide spread of lettings of various sizes.

Type of Household

10.   The type and size of households, and age of heads of household for each tenure are shown in Tables 3 and 4. Taken as a whole the distribution of type of households in the owner occupied sector closely resembles that of households in all tenures but there are marked differences between households that own outright and those that are buying with a mortgage or loan. Almost one quarter of households owning outright were individuals aged 60 or over compared with just 1 per cent of households buying with a mortgage. Six out of ten households owning outright were elderly households containing one or two persons, whereas most owner occupiers buying with a mortgage were families, headed by someone aged between 25 and 54.

11.   Older households were more likely to be local authority tenants than were younger households, and large families were more likely to be local authority tenants than small families. Less than one quarter of households headed by a person aged under 45 rented from local authorities.

12.   Private unfurnished lettings were mainly occupied by households with a head aged 55 or over.

Density of Occupation

13.   Some 350,000 households in the local authority sector were below the bedroom standard compared with 300,000 owner occupiers below the standard. This is partly due to the small number of lettings from local authorities with 4 or more bedrooms. However, the higher proportion of local authority lettings designed for small households means that there were relatively few households with 2 or more rooms above the standard - 0.7 million compared with 2.7 million in the case of owner occupiers.

Employment Status and SEG of Head of Household

14.   The distribution of employment status of head of household by tenure is given in Tables 3 and 4. This shows that virtually all owner occupiers buying with a mortgage or loan were either employed or seeking work. By contrast over half of heads of household owning outright were wholly retired or housewives, as were over one-third of local authority tenants and households renting privately unfurnished. Heads of household renting furnished were predominantly either working full-time or students.

15.   Table 4 shows that owner occupation was the majority tenure among persons in professional and managerial occupations, other non-manual occupations and skilled manual occupations. But there is no clear cut relationship between occupation and tenure - overall some 40 per cent of owner occupiers were in manual occupations, these include one third of all semi skilled manual workers and a quarter of unskilled manual workers.

14

Provision of Amenities

16.   Properties being purchased with a mortgage or loan were the best provided with basic amenities: less than 75,000 lacked basic amenities. Council tenants were also well provided with basic amenities but 133,000 had no inside WC. The main groups lacking basic amenities were households owning outright and households renting privately unfurnished - 275,000 households owning outright lacked at least one basic amenity as did nearly 400,000 households that rented privately unfurnished.

17.   Sharing of amenities was concentrated amongst furnished lettings.

Main Form of Room Heating

18.   Although 53 per cent of households possessed central heating only 43 per cent of households said that central heating was their main form of room heating. So about 20 per cent of households with central heating did not use it as their main form of room heating. This occurred to varying degrees in all tenures.

19.   Owner occupiers with a mortgage were the most likely tenure to possess central heating and the majority of such households possessed a gas central heating system. This fuel was also most prevalent in other tenures although a large proportion of local authority and housing association tenants had electric central heating other than storage heaters, and storage heaters were common in houses owned outright.

20.   Where central heating was not the main form of room heating gas was again the most popular fuel in all tenures. Open fires were most common in properties owned outright, rented from local authorities and rented privately unfurnished.

ETHNIC MINORITIES (TABLES 7 AND 8)

21.   Respondents to the survey were shown a card listing the main ethnic groups in this country and asked to which of the groups listed each member of the household belonged. Less than one in a thousand respondents refused to answer this question but a few insisted on being recorded as British, English etc rather than one of the specific groups listed - White, West Indian and so forth. Overall less than 1 per cent of persons were recorded as "other (please state)": analysis of the details given indicates that many of these persons belonged to one of the groups listed. However, because there was insufficient information to recode most of these persons - often the only information recorded was English or British - no attempt has been made to do so in these results. The "other" category in tables 7 and 8 is thus very heterogeneous since it contains not only persons recorded as "other (please state)" but also persons recorded as "Chinese", "Other Asian", "Arab", and persons of "Mixed Origin".

22.   At present, because of the pattern and timing of migration, there are pronounced demographic differences between the main ethnic groups as shown in the types and sizes of households. For instance, 45 per cent of White heads of households were over 55, and 32 per cent of households were either older couples or older single persons living alone. The corresponding figures for West Indian households were 11 per cent and $2\frac{1}{2}$ per cent, and for Indian, Pakistani and Bangladeshi households were 11 per cent and 3 per cent. There were proportionally more large families in the ethnic minorities. Excluding the older households over 30 per cent of the West Indian households and 35 per cent of

the Indian, Pakistani and Bangladeshi households were large families, as against 13 per cent of White households. Consequently, the average size of households varied between the groups - 2.7 persons for White households, 3.7 for West Indian households and 4.3 for Indian, Pakistani and Bangladeshi households.

23. The economic status of the ethnic minority groups was also different which in part reflected the different age distributions. Of heads of households with identified socio-economic group, 3 per cent of West Indians and 17 per cent of Indians, Pakistanis and Bangladeshis were either professional or employers and managers, as against 23 per cent of Whites; and 42 per cent of West Indians and 37 per cent of Indians, Pakistanis and Bangladeshis were semi-skilled or unskilled manual workers, as against 21 per cent of Whites. West Indian, Indian, Pakistani or Bangladeshi heads of households were also more likely to be unemployed than Whites.

24. Tenure patterns were dissimilar. Nearly half of West Indian households rented from councils or housing associations, as against a third of White households and only a tenth of Indian, Pakistani and Bangladeshi households. Over two-thirds of Indian, Pakistani and Bangladeshi households were owner-occupiers as against one-third of West Indian households, and just over half of White households.

25. The ethnic minorities were on average less well housed than White households. One in five West Indian households, and one in three Indian, Pakistani and Bangladeshi households lived below the bedroom standard, compared with one in twenty White households. One in ten West Indian households and one in seven Indian, Pakistani and Bangladeshi households shared dwellings, compared with one in thirty six White households. One in seven West Indian households and one in four Indian, Pakistani and Bangladeshi households lacked sole use of all basic amenities, compared with one in twelve White households, and Indian, Pakistani and Bangladeshi households were twice as likely as White households not even to have shared access to at least one basic amenity.

26. In response to the question on satisfaction with accommodation over one quarter of West Indian households expressed a degree of dissatisfaction with their accommodation compared with 8 per cent of White households and 9 per cent of Indian, Pakistani and Bangladeshi households.

DENSITY OF OCCUPATION (TABLE 9)

27. Households living below the bedroom standard, almost by definition, tended to be large families. They did not, however live in smaller properties than other households: 65 per cent of households with 2 or more bedrooms below the standard had at least 3 bedrooms as did 50 per cent of households with 1 bedroom below the standard.

28. Households living below the bedroom standard generally considered they had too few rooms although as many as 40 per cent of such households said that they had the right number of rooms. Against this a substantial proportion of households with at least 2 bedrooms above the standard said that they had too many rooms: in absolute numbers there were more households with 2 or more rooms above the standard that said that they had too many rooms then there were households below the standard that said that they had too few rooms. However the properties of households that consider they have too many rooms may not be suitable for those that consider they have too few rooms.

USE OF BASIC AMENITIES (TABLES 10 AND 6)

29.   The majority of households lacking at least one of the basic amenities
(WC inside the building, fixed bath or shower, and piped hot water supply)
were elderly households: 30 per cent consisted of a single person aged 60
or over, and 24 per cent consisted of a couple at least one of whom was
aged 60 or over. Only 22 per cent of households lacking basic amenities were
headed by a person aged under 45.

30.   For the vast majority of these households lack of basic amenities was a
well established way of life: 68 per cent had lived in their accommodation for
10 years or longer and a further 10 per cent had lived in their accommodation
for at least 5 years. As noted previously the majority of these households
either owned their accommodation outright or rented it unfurnished.

31.   By contrast households sharing basic amenities were younger and more
transitory. 55 per cent of heads of households sharing amenities were aged
under 35 and 50 per cent had lived in their accommodation for less than 2
years. But in addition to this transitory group of sharers there was a hard
core of households sharing amenities that had been living in their present
accommodation for at least 10 years. Many of these would be found amongst
the elderly households that represented over one fifth of all households
sharing amenities.

32.   The North West region had the highest proportion and the largest number
of households lacking amenities: at end 1977 180,000 households in that
region still lacked at least one of the basic amenities. But Greater London
had by far the highest proportion of households sharing amenities, and consequently the lowest proportion of households having exclusive use of all
basic amenities.

SATISFACTION WITH ACCOMMODATION AND AREA (TABLES 11-14)

33.   Respondents to the survey were asked to indicate their degree of satisfaction with their accommodation and the area in general on the scale 'Very
Satisfied, Satisfied, Neither Satisfied nor Dissatisfied, Dissatisfied and
Very Dissatisfied'. No guidance was given to the respondent about what was
meant by the area and they were left to interpret this themselves as, for
example, the immediate vicinity, the block or the town.

34.   Most respondents expressed some degree of satisfaction with both their
accommodation and the area in which they lived. 82 per cent of respondents
were very satisfied or satisfied with their accommodation, and 80 per cent
were very satisfied or satisfied with the area.

35.   Degree of satisfaction with accommodation was related to the traditional
measures of adverse housing circumstances. Households in detached houses,
owner occupiers and households with central heating were most likely to be very
satisfied with their accommodation, and households lacking amenities and below
the bedroom standard were least likely to be satisfied with their accommodation.
However, only some 40 per cent of households with two or more bedrooms below the
bedroom standard said that they were less than satisfied with their accommodation,
a similar figure for households lacking at least one basic amenity. So physical
condition was by no means the only factor determining satisfaction with
accommodation.

36.   Only 10 per cent of owner occupiers said that they were less than satisfied with their accommodation; for all other tenures the equivalent proportions were around 25-30 per cent.

HOUSEHOLDS SHARING ACCOMMODATION (TABLE 15)

37.   Of the estimated 528,000 households sharing a dwelling at end 1977, 191,000 (36 per cent) lived in Greater London, representing 7 per cent of all households in London. In each of the other regions at most 3 per cent of households shared accommodation.

38.   Amongst the various types of sharing,households sharing rooms and households in bedsits exhibited similar characteristics. 60 per cent of such households consisted of one person aged under 60 (mostly aged under 35), and around 55 per cent had lived in their accommodation for less than two years. By way of contrast over half of households sharing circulation space or in self contained accommodation in a shared dwelling contained at least 2 persons and a similar proportion had lived in their accommodation for at least 5 years.

39.   Most respondents said that they were satisfied with their shared accommodation, but a lower than average proportion said they were very satisfied. Households sharing circulation space were more inclined to be dissatisfied with their accommodation and 15 per cent of these households were registered on a council house waiting list.

40.   More detailed information on households attitudes to sharing will be obtained from the follow up survey on sharing and concealed households conducted by the Office of Population Censuses and Surveys.

CONCEALED HOUSEHOLDS (TABLE 16)

41.   A concealed household is defined as a married couple with or without children, or a lone parent with child(ren) who form part of someone else's household. The majority of concealed households arise from a married couple or lone parent living with their parents or parents in law.

42.   It is estimated that at end 1977 there were 149,000 married couple concealed households and 104,000 lone parent concealed households. Table 16 shows the characteristics of the concealed households rather than the characteristics of the whole household ie host household plus concealed household.

43.   Two thirds of married couple concealed households were living with parents or in laws as were four out of five concealed lone parent households. In some cases the position was reversed with parents living with one of their children: Only 5 per cent of concealed married couple households and 8 per cent of concealed lone parent households lived with an unrelated person.

44.   In most cases lone parent households contained a dependent child. 79 per cent of these households consisted of one parent with one or two children under 16 and 3 per cent contained three or more children under 16. 70 per cent of concealed lone parents were under 35.

45.   Married couple concealed households were less likely to have children living with them: 41 per cent consisted solely of a couple both aged under 60,

and 17 per cent consisted of a couple at least one of whom was aged 60 or over. Almost half of heads of concealed married couple households were aged 35 or over.

46.   As might be expected households containing a concealed household were more likely than other households to be overcrowded. 47 per cent of households containing lone parent concealed households, and 28 per cent of households containing married couple concealed households were below the bedroom standard.

47.   Young married couples of Indian descent were more likely to live with parents or in laws. 15 per cent of all married couple concealed households were of Indian, Pakistani or Bangladeshi descent whereas this group represented only one per cent of all households.

COUNCIL HOUSE WAITING LISTS (TABLES 17-18)

48.   Respondents to the survey were asked whether they or any member of their household were on a council house waiting or transfer list, or new town corporation list. 5 per cent of households said that the head of household was on a list, 1 per cent said that another member of the household was on a list (in some of these households there would have been more than one other person), and a further 1 per cent said that both the head of household and another member of the household were on a list (although in some cases the respondent might simply have meant that a couple had their names on a list jointly for a tenancy.) Assuming that where the head of household and another person had their name on a list only two people had their names registered, leads to an estimate of 1.5 million persons registered on council house waiting lists.

49.   Half of all persons registered on a list were already in council accommodation: almost three-quarters of these were heads of household who would already be council tenants and must therefore have been registered on the transfer list. 13 per cent of heads of household registered were owner occupiers and 20 per cent of households where another member of the household was registered were owner occupiers.

50.   28 per cent of heads of household registered were in private rented unfurnished accommodation which represented one in six of all households in that tenure.

51.   Almost one quarter of households with head of household registered were elderly persons living alone, and 14 per cent were elderly couples.

52.   Overall only a small proportion of households suffering housing deprivation - for example lack of basic amenities, overcrowding or sharing - had members registered on the waiting list. But households living in poor conditions were more likely to have a member on the list compared to households occupying more acceptable dwellings.

53.   Households where someone other than the head of household had their name on the list were mainly large adult households or large families where it appears that the son or daughter was registered. Almost one third of these households were below the bedroom standard and 28 per cent contained concealed households.

19

54. West Indian households were more likely to be on a waiting list than households in other ethnic groups.

AGE OF PROPERTY/BUILDING (TABLE 19)

55. Fashions in type of property constructed in the past century can be readily traced in Table 19. Pre 1919 saw the eminence of the terraced house, many of the larger of which have now been converted into flats. In the inter war period one half of the properties built were semi-detached houses. After World War II the purpose built flat or maisonette became common: one in every six properties built between 1940 and 1964 were flats or maisonettes but nearly half were still semi-detached houses. In the period 1965 to 1977 detached houses, semi-detached houses, terraced houses and purpose built flats each represented about one quarter of new buildings.

56. Owner occupiers owned about 60 per cent of properties built in all periods other than that following World War II when priority was given to local authority housing. Very few local authority dwellings pre date World War I and some of those that do have been purchased more recently from other sectors.

57. Most privately rented accommodation was built before 1919 and this tenure still represented about one third of properties dating from that period.

58. Lack of basic amenities was closely related to age of property. Although most properties have now had all basic amenities installed as many as one in six households living in pre 1919 dwellings lacked at least one basic amenity.

LOWEST FLOOR OF ACCOMMODATION (TABLE 20)

59. 4 out of 5 households lived in houses and thus had street level or lower as their lowest floor of accommodation. In addition to these another 8 per cent of households living in flats or maisonettes or some other type of accommodation also lived on the ground floor or below. So only 12 per cent of households had all their rooms above the ground floor.

60. As with many aspects of housing London was different from all other regions: 32 per cent of households lived on the first floor or higher compared with 8 per cent in the rest of the country. And the concentration of off ground living in London was even more striking if one considered the higher levels. Nearly 60 per cent of households living on the 3rd floor or higher lived in London.

61. A high proportion of flats were occupied by one person households but a substantial proportion of flats, including those above the 9th floor, were occupied by small families containing children aged under 16. Few large families lived off the ground floor.

62. Although a comparatively high proportion of households living above the ground floor said they were dissatisfied with their accommodation, and a high proportion had their names on the council house waiting list, over 60 per cent of households said that they were satisfied or very satisfied with their accommodation; this applied even to households living above the 9th floor. This suggests that high rise flats are not universally unpopular with tenants.

VACANT PROPERTIES AND SECOND HOMES (TABLE 21)

63.   It is estimated that at end 1977 there were 789,000 vacant household spaces and second homes in England. After taking account of vacant household spaces in part vacant dwellings, and dwellings containing more than one vacant household space it is estimated that this was equivalent to 729,000 vacant dwellings or second homes. Of these 127,000 vacant dwellings were being modernised or converted at the time of the survey.

64.   From other sources it is estimated that the number of second homes in England stood at around 120,000. So the number of vacant dwellings (excluding those under-going conversion or modernisation) was around 480,000 at end 1977 or some 2.8 per cent of the stock of dwellings.

65.   Details of the characteristics of vacant household spaces are given in Table 21 together with comparative figures for all household spaces. This shows that vacant properties were likely to be old properties, pre-1919, and to have low rateable values. This agrees with the findings of the 1976 English House Condition Survey which also showed that vacant properties were likely to lack basic amenities. No comparable information on basic amenities is available from NDHS.

66.   More detailed information on vacant properties should be provided from the survey of vacant properties being conducted by the Office of Population Censuses and Surveys.

LIST OF TABLES

Region, London Borough and District Tables.

	Region	London Borough	District
Type of Accommodation	22	62	102
Lowest Floor of Accommodation	23	63	103
Household Size	24	64	104
Type of Household (1)	25	65	105
Type of Household (2)	26	66	106
Number of Rooms	27	67	107
Number of Bedrooms	28	68	108
Density of Occupation	29	69	109
Difference from Bedroom Standard	30	70	110
Households Sharing a Dwelling	31	71	111
Use of Basic Amenities	32	72	112
Use of Bath or Shower	33	73	113
Use of Hot Water Supply	34	74	114
Use of Flush Toilet	35	75	115
Type of Central Heating	36	76	116
Main Form of Room Heating	37	77	117
Tenure	38	78	118
Leasehold/Freehold Tenures	39	-	-
Households in Privately Rented Accommodation: Type of Landlord	40	79	119
Individual Private Landlords	41	80	120
Council House Waiting List	42	81	121
Satisfaction with Accommodation	43	82	122
Satisfaction with Area	44	83	123
Satisfaction with Number of Rooms	45	84	124
Satisfaction with Size of Rooms	46	85	125
Availability of Cars and Vans	47	86	126
Off-street Parking Provision	48	87	127
Age and Sex of Head of Household	49	88	128
Marital Status of Head of Household	50	89	129
Length of Residence of Head of Household	51	90	130
Employment Status of Head of Household	52	91	131

	Region	London Borough	District
Birthplace of Head of Household	53	92	132
Age and Sex of Private Household Population	54	93	133
Age of Private Household Population	55	94	134
Length of Residence of Persons	56	95	135
Employment Status of Persons aged 16 or over	57	96	136
Economically Active Persons: Socio-Economic Group	58	97	137
Birthplace of Persons	59	98	138
Ethnic Group of Persons	60	99	139
Type of Family	61	100	140
Dwellings, Vacant Dwellings and Households	(2.2)	101	141

TABLE 1.   Rateable Value, Type of Accommodation, Number of Rooms, Number of Bedrooms, and Bedroom standard:
Analysis by Tenure.

Percentages

	Owned outright	Owned with mortgage or loan	Rented from council	Rented from housing associa- tion	Privately rented		All households (= 100%) 000's
					un- furnished	furnished	
Rateable Value							
Up to £75	31.8	15.0	8.1	2.1	26.8	16.2	1,245
£76 - 100	26.0	18.5	25.8	1.6	21.9	6.2	1,168
£101 - 150	17.9	18.4	47.2	1.7	11.7	3.1	3,480
£151 - 200	19.3	29.7	41.1	1.1	7.4	1.4	4,110
£201 - 300	25.1	42.7	23.7	1.1	6.0	1.3	4,786
£301 - 400	32.3	51.3	7.4	0.9	5.9	2.2	1,196
£401 or over	32.9	40.0	2.9	0.7	19.4	4.1	675
Exempt or block address	12.3	20.4	18.8	4.0	25.5	19.0	164
Type of Accommodation							
Detached house	40.8	48.0	2.0	0.2	8.1	0.9	2,966
Semi-detached house	22.7	39.9	30.4	0.4	5.8	0.7	5,559
Terraced house	23.4	27.2	35.3	1.0	11.8	1.2	4,868
Purpose built flat/maisonette	6.0	6.6	71.6	4.3	10.0	1.5	1,989
Other flat/rooms	12.0	9.7	8.1	4.5	31.9	33.8	1,248
Other	36.3	13.1	6.7	1.4	37.4	5.1	194
Number of Rooms							
1	1.3	0.5	17.8	6.5	11.6	62.3	195
2	5.9	2.5	34.0	7.1	17.7	32.8	428
3	9.7	6.2	54.5	4.3	17.4	7.9	1,385
4	24.7	19.7	38.7	1.5	13.2	2.3	3,560
5	21.2	35.0	32.7	0.8	9.2	1.0	5,485
6	29.4	40.2	20.1	0.5	8.9	0.9	4,119
7 or more	32.0	52.2	5.2	0.3	8.8	1.5	1,652
Number of Bedrooms							
1	8.8	4.9	44.3	5.2	17.5	19.3	1,969
2	30.3	21.0	31.1	1.4	14.1	2.2	4,834
3	22.1	39.0	29.4	0.6	7.9	0.9	8,394
4	26.2	52.2	11.9	0.4	7.5	1.6	1,288
5 or more	31.8	48.3	3.2	0.5	13.1	3.2	339
Difference from Bedroom Standard							
2 or more below	12.1	21.7	45.7	2.0	12.4	6.0	102
1 below	11.4	23.8	40.8	1.5	13.4	9.1	727
Equal to standard	12.6	24.9	40.8	2.5	11.8	7.3	5,505
1 above	26.1	35.2	26.6	0.8	10.1	1.2	6,645
2 or more above	37.0	34.2	17.0	0.5	10.4	0.9	3,846
All households	23.4	31.0	29.8	1.3	10.9	3.5	16,824

26

TABLE 2. Tenure: Analysis by Rateable Value, Type of Accommodation, Number of Rooms, Number of Bedrooms, and Bedroom Standard

Percentages

	Owned outright	Owned with mortgage or loan	Rented from council	Rented from housing associa-tion	Privately rented unfurnished	furnished	All households
Rateable Value							
Up to £75	10.0	3.6	2.0	11.7	18.2	34.1	7.4
£76 - 100	7.7	4.1	6.0	8.5	14.0	12.1	6.9
£101 - 150	15.9	12.3	32.8	25.7	22.3	18.4	20.7
£151 - 200	20.1	23.4	33.8	20.3	16.6	10.0	24.4
£201 - 300	30.4	39.1	22.7	24.0	15.7	10.9	28.4
£301 - 400	9.7	11.7	1.7	4.8	3.9	4.5	7.1
£401 or over	5.6	5.1	0.4	2.1	7.1	4.7	4.0
Exempt or block address	0.5	0.6	0.6	2.9	2.3	5.2	1.0
Type of Accommodation							
Detached house	30.5	27.1	1.2	2.4	13.3	4.4	17.6
Semi-detached house	32.0	42.4	33.8	10.8	17.9	6.4	33.0
Terraced house	28.9	25.3	34.3	22.7	31.8	10.1	28.9
Purpose built flat/maisonette	3.0	2.5	28.4	38.0	11.0	5.2	11.8
Other flat/rooms	3.8	2.3	2.0	24.9	22.0	72.1	7.4
Other	1.8	0.5	0.3	1.2	4.0	1.7	1.2
Number of Rooms							
1	0.1	-	0.7	5.6	1.2	21.4	1.2
2	0.6	0.2	2.9	13.5	4.1	24.3	2.5
3	3.4	1.7	15.1	26.4	13.2	19.3	8.2
4	22.3	13.4	27.4	23.0	25.8	14.5	21.2
5	29.6	36.7	35.8	20.2	27.7	9.9	32.6
6	30.7	31.6	16.5	9.2	20.0	6.4	24.5
7 or more	13.4	16.4	1.7	1.9	8.0	4.2	9.8
Number of Bedrooms							
1	4.4	1.8	17.4	45.1	18.8	64.2	11.7
2	37.2	19.4	30.0	30.0	37.3	17.9	28.7
3	47.2	62.8	49.3	21.8	36.3	12.5	49.9
4	8.5	12.8	3.1	2.4	5.3	3.5	7.7
5 or more	2.7	3.1	0.2	0.7	2.4	1.9	2.0
Difference from Bedroom Standard							
2 or more below	0.3	0.4	0.9	0.9	0.7	1.0	0.6
1 below	2.1	3.3	5.9	5.0	5.3	11.4	4.3
Equal to standard	17.6	26.3	44.9	61.7	35.5	68.5	32.7
1 above	44.0	44.8	35.3	23.7	36.6	13.5	39.5
2 or more above	36.0	25.1	13.0	8.8	21.8	5.7	22.9
All households (= 100%) 000's	3,943	5,222	5,013	225	1,830	590	16,824

Percentages

	Owned outright	Owned with mortgage or loan	Rented from council	Rented from housing associa-tion	Privately rented		All households (= 100%) 000's
					un-furnished	furnished	
Type of Household							
One person aged under 60	16.8	19.5	23.0	2.4	14.2	24.1	1,063
Small adult household	14.1	46.4	21.2	0.9	11.2	6.2	2,576
Small family	7.6	55.6	25.8	1.0	8.2	1.8	3,475
Large family	8.8	43.1	39.5	0.8	7.0	0.8	1,543
Large adult household	23.0	33.5	32.5	0.7	8.5	1.9	2,875
Older small household	48.5	6.9	30.5	1.2	12.5	0.4	2,894
One person aged 60 or over	38.6	2.3	38.2	3.1	16.4	1.3	2,398
Number of Persons in Household							
1	32.0	7.6	33.4	2.9	15.8	8.3	3,461
2	31.9	25.3	26.7	1.1	11.9	3.2	5,603
3	18.7	39.6	29.6	1.0	9.1	2.0	2,884
4	10.7	53.5	26.3	0.7	7.4	1.4	2,981
5	10.0	46.3	34.1	0.6	7.5	1.5	1,217
6 or more	10.3	35.6	45.4	0.9	6.7	1.0	679
Age of Head of Household							
Under 25	2.5	29.2	23.9	1.8	14.7	27.9	796
25-34	3.7	56.5	22.4	1.2	9.6	6.6	2,990
35-44	9.4	55.3	24.1	0.9	8.0	2.3	2,690
45-54	18.2	39.7	31.3	0.8	8.6	1.5	2,903
55-64	33.7	17.4	36.2	1.2	10.5	1.0	3,030
65 or over	45.3	2.9	34.2	2.1	14.6	0.7	4,415
Employment Status of HoH							
Employed full time	14.4	46.4	25.1	1.0	9.6	3.5	10,500
Employed part time	36.6	11.3	33.4	1.5	14.1	3.0	541
Unemployed	15.7	14.2	50.2	1.3	10.6	8.0	586
Wholly retired	46.3	3.5	34.0	2.1	13.4	0.7	3,068
Housewife	38.7	3.8	40.6	2.3	13.7	0.9	1,574
Other	19.5	8.2	39.2	1.8	10.0	21.4	555
SEG of Head of Household							
Professional	22.3	62.8	3.7	0.9	5.4	4.8	861
Employers and managers	30.2	47.5	9.2	0.8	10.2	2.1	2,330
Other non-manual	24.9	38.9	18.6	1.6	11.3	4.7	2,993
Skilled manual	19.3	33.2	35.3	1.1	9.5	1.6	5,087
Semi-skilled manual	17.4	19.4	45.0	1.4	14.2	2.6	2,162
Unskilled manual	14.7	11.1	57.5	1.6	11.4	3.7	837
Other	32.2	8.1	37.6	2.0	12.6	7.4	2,555
All households	23.4	31.0	29.8	1.3	10.9	3.5	16,824

TABLE 4. Tenure: Analysis by Type of Household, Size of Household, Age of HoH, Employment Status of HoH, and Socio-economic Group of HoH.

Percentages

| | Owned outright | Owned with mortgage or loan | Rented from council | Rented from housing association | Privately rented | | All households |
					un-furnished	furnished	
Type of Household							
One person aged under 60	4.5	4.0	4.9	11.2	8.3	43.1	6.3
Small adult household	9.2	22.9	10.9	10.5	15.7	27.5	15.3
Small family	6.7	37.0	17.9	15.5	15.6	10.7	20.6
Large family	3.4	12.8	12.1	5.3	5.9	2.1	9.2
Large adult household	16.8	18.4	18.5	8.9	13.3	9.2	17.1
Older small household	35.7	3.8	17.5	15.7	19.8	1.9	17.2
One person aged 60 or over	23.6	1.1	18.2	32.9	21.5	5.5	14.3
No. of Persons in Household							
1	28.1	5.1	23.1	43.9	29.8	48.4	20.6
2	45.3	27.1	29.8	27.8	36.4	30.4	33.3
3	13.7	21.8	17.0	13.4	14.4	9.7	17.1
4	8.1	30.6	15.6	8.9	12.0	7.3	17.7
5	3.1	10.8	8.3	3.2	5.0	3.1	7.2
6 or more	1.8	4.6	6.2	2.8	2.5	1.1	4.0
Age of Head of Household							
Under 25	0.5	4.5	3.8	6.5	6.4	37.9	4.7
25-34	2.8	32.4	13.4	15.4	15.7	33.4	17.8
35-44	6.5	28.5	12.9	10.8	11.8	10.5	16.0
45-54	13.4	22.0	18.0	10.5	13.6	7.3	17.3
55-64	26.0	10.1	21.8	15.4	17.4	5.2	18.0
65 or over	50.9	2.5	30.1	41.3	35.2	5.7	26.2
Employment Status of HoH							
Employed full time	38.4	93.2	52.6	44.4	55.2	63.0	62.4
Employed part time	5.0	1.2	3.6	3.7	4.2	2.8	3.2
Unemployed	2.3	1.6	5.9	3.3	3.4	7.7	3.5
Wholly retired	36.1	2.1	20.8	28.0	22.4	3.9	18.2
Housewife	15.4	1.2	12.7	16.2	11.8	2.3	9.4
Other	2.7	0.9	4.3	4.5	3.0	20.3	3.3
SEG of Head of Household							
Professional	4.9	10.4	0.6	3.4	2.6	7.1	5.1
Employers and managers	17.9	21.2	4.3	8.4	13.0	8.2	13.8
Other non-manual	18.9	22.3	11.1	21.4	18.4	24.0	17.8
Skilled manual	24.9	32.4	35.9	24.6	26.5	13.6	30.3
Semi-skilled manual	9.6	8.0	19.5	13.2	16.8	9.8	12.9
Unskilled manual	3.1	1.8	9.6	6.0	5.2	5.1	5.0
Other	20.8	4.0	19.1	23.1	17.5	32.1	15.1
All households (= 100%) 000's	3,943	5,222	5,013	225	1,830	590	16,824

TABLE 5. Basic Amenities, Type of Central Heating, Main Form of Room Heating and Number of Cars and Vans: Analysis by Tenure.

Percentages

| | Owned outright | Owned with mortgage or loan | Rented from council | Rented from housing associa- tion | Privately rented | | All households (= 100%) 000's |
					un- furnished	furnished	
Basic Amenities							
Sole use of all	23.6	33.3	31.2	1.2	8.8	1.8	15,379
Some shared, none lacked	8.1	7.2	8.6	3.6	18.0	54.6	468
At least one lacked	28.3	7.4	18.0	1.6	39.7	4.6	977
Sole use of bath/shower	23.7	32.5	31.2	1.3	9.4	1.9	15,863
Shared use of bath/shower	8.0	6.5	8.5	3.0	19.0	55.0	504
No bath/shower	30.2	5.7	4.5	1.9	54.8	2.9	457
Sole use of inside WC	23.6	32.9	31.1	1.3	9.2	1.9	15,629
Shared use of inside WC	6.8	6.3	5.1	3.1	19.0	59.6	454
Use of outside WC only	28.2	7.8	19.1	1.3	41.3	2.4	695
No WC	41.1	6.8	4.3	0.5	43.5	3.7	46
Type of Central Heating							
No central heating	23.1	18.2	34.9	1.4	17.7	4.7	7,949
Solid fuel	24.4	32.3	36.4	0.3	5.9	0.7	984
Gas	21.3	50.5	22.1	0.9	2.9	2.2	5,067
Oil	32.4	43.5	12.5	1.4	7.7	2.5	903
Electric storage heaters	34.5	30.0	19.3	1.9	9.7	4.7	1,187
Other	12.1	20.0	56.9	4.1	4.4	2.5	734
Main Form of Room Heating							
Central heating	22.8	45.0	24.6	1.3	4.1	2.2	7,253
Open fire	28.6	13.7	36.0	0.7	19.6	1.4	2,483
Closed stove	34.3	14.4	35.4	0.5	14.6	0.8	400
Electric	22.8	17.2	29.3	2.2	18.0	10.5	2,103
Gas	21.4	26.7	34.1	1.4	13.0	3.4	4,351
Other	15.3	16.1	36.4	3.0	19.2	10.0	234
No.of Cars and Vans Available to Household							
0	23.4	10.9	44.6	2.2	13.8	5.1	7,092
1	23.3	42.8	21.3	0.8	9.3	2.5	7,763
2 or more	24.0	57.6	9.9	0.4	6.6	1.6	1,969
All households	23.4	31.0	29.8	1.3	10.9	3.5	16,824

TABLE 6. Tenure: Analysis by Basic Amenities, Type of Central Heating, Main Form of Room Heating, and Number of Cars and Vans.   Percentages

| | Owned outright | Owned with mortgage or loan | Rented from council | Rented from housing associa-tion | Privately rented | | All households |
					un-furnished	furnished	
Basic Amenities							
Sole use of all	92.1	98.0	95.7	85.6	74.2	49.0	91.4
Some shared, none lacked	1.0	0.6	0.8	7.4	4.6	43.3	2.8
At least one lacked	7.0	1.4	3.5	7.0	21.2	7.7	5.8
Sole use of bath/shower	95.5	98.9	98.7	89.6	81.1	51.3	94.3
Shared use of bath/shower	1.0	0.6	0.9	6.6	5.2	46.7	3.0
No bath/shower	3.5	0.5	0.4	3.7	13.6	2.0	2.7
Sole use of inside WC	93.8	98.4	96.9	89.7	78.5	51.5	92.9
Shared use of inside WC	0.8	0.5	0.5	6.3	4.7	45.4	2.7
Use of outside WC only	4.9	1.1	2.7	3.9	15.7	2.7	4.1
No WC	0.5	0.1	-	0.1	1.1	0.3	0.3
Type of Central Heating							
No central heating	46.5	27.8	55.4	48.4	77.1	63.0	47.2
Solid fuel	6.1	6.1	7.1	1.3	3.2	1.3	5.8
Gas	27.4	49.1	22.4	21.3	8.0	19.2	30.1
Oil	7.4	7.5	2.2	5.5	3.8	3.9	5.4
Electric storage heaters	10.4	6.8	4.6	10.1	6.3	9.5	7.1
Other	2.3	2.8	8.3	13.4	1.8	3.2	4.4
Main Form of Room Heating							
Central heating	41.9	62.5	35.6	40.8	16.3	27.7	43.1
Open fire	18.0	6.5	17.9	7.9	26.5	5.6	14.8
Closed stove	3.5	1.1	2.8	0.9	3.2	0.6	2.4
Electric	12.1	6.9	12.3	20.5	20.6	37.3	12.5
Gas	23.6	22.3	29.7	26.9	30.9	25.2	25.9
Other	0.9	0.7	1.7	3.1	2.5	3.6	1.4
No. of Cars and Vans Available to Household							
0	42.1	14.8	63.1	67.8	53.6	61.6	42.2
1	46.1	63.8	33.0	29.1	39.5	33.1	46.1
2 or more	11.8	21.4	3.8	3.1	7.0	5.3	11.7
All households (= 100%) 000's	3,943	5,222	5,013	225	1,830	590	16,824

31

TABLE 7. Ethnic Group of Head of Household: Analysis by Type of Household, Size of Household, Age of HoH, Employment Status of HoH, Socio-economic Group of HoH, and Birthplace.

Percentages

	Ethnic group of head of household					All households
	White	West Indian	African	Indian/ Pakistani/ Bangladeshi	Other	
Type of Household						
One person aged under 60	6.1	11.5	26.9	7.9	14.7	6.3
Small adult household	15.3	12.4	16.6	10.3	19.4	15.3
Small family	20.5	26.7	22.8	24.9	23.8	20.6
Large family	8.6	29.8	23.5	33.6	14.5	9.2
Large adult household	17.0	17.1	10.2	20.2	16.9	17.1
Older small household	17.7	1.3	-	2.1	6.6	17.2
One person aged 60 or over	14.7	1.2	-	1.0	4.2	14.3
Number of People in Household						
1	20.8	12.7	28.0	8.9	18.7	20.6
2	33.8	18.4	17.8	12.9	26.7	33.3
3	17.2	17.2	16.5	12.7	16.7	17.1
4	17.6	19.9	12.2	22.3	18.9	17.7
5	7.0	14.5	10.1	17.1	11.6	7.2
6 or more	3.6	17.3	15.4	26.0	7.4	4.0
Age of Head of Household						
Under 25	4.5	11.2	20.8	8.3	12.4	4.7
25-34	17.4	19.4	34.2	29.9	32.7	17.8
35-44	15.5	35.1	28.5	32.1	20.2	16.0
45-54	17.2	23.6	13.4	19.0	15.6	17.3
55-64	18.4	9.0	2.4	8.9	9.5	18.0
65 or over	27.0	1.7	0.7	1.8	9.6	26.2
Employment Status of HoH						
Employed full time	62.0	76.9	63.7	83.1	67.0	62.4
Employed part time	3.3	4.3	0.8	0.8	1.5	3.2
Unemployed	3.4	9.7	3.9	7.2	4.4	3.5
Wholly retired	18.8	1.9	0.7	2.2	7.2	18.2
Housewife	9.5	5.7	2.3	1.9	4.9	9.4
Other	3.1	1.5	28.6	4.8	15.1	3.3
SEG of Head of Household						
Professional	5.1	0.6	4.3	7.9	6.6	5.1
Employers and managers	14.1	2.1	3.8	7.5	13.1	13.8
Other non-manual	17.9	13.6	21.9	11.8	18.2	17.8
Skilled manual	30.4	35.3	20.7	28.8	20.4	30.3
Semi-skilled manual	12.6	26.1	10.6	22.9	13.5	12.9
Unskilled manual	4.9	10.9	3.0	11.2	4.3	5.0
Other	15.1	11.4	35.7	9.9	23.9	15.1
Birthplace of Head of Household						
United Kingdom	95.6	5.2	3.1	2.4	29.7	92.7
Not in United Kingdom	4.4	94.8	96.9	97.6	70.3	7.3
All households (= 100%) 000's	16,240	152	29	186	217	16,824

TABLE 8.   Ethnic Group of Head of Household: Analysis by Tenure, Basic Amenities, Age of Property, Bedroom Standard, Shared Dwelling and Satisfaction with Accommodation

Percentages

	Ethnic group of head of household					All households
	White	West Indian	African	Indian/ Pakistani/ Bangladeshi	Other	
Tenure						
Owned outright	23.8	4.5	5.0	17.0	14.8	23.4
Owned with mortgage/loan	30.8	31.4	17.6	52.9	33.5	31.0
Rented from council	30.0	45.2	29.0	10.1	18.0	29.8
Rented from HA	1.3	4.4	5.1	0.4	2.3	1.3
Rented privately unfurnished	11.0	6.9	11.9	6.9	12.0	10.9
Rented privately furnished	3.1	7.5	31.4	12.7	19.4	3.5
Basic Amenities						
Sole use of all	91.8	86.8	69.4	75.9	81.3	91.4
Some shared, none lacked	2.4	8.6	28.2	12.6	13.3	2.8
At least one lacked	5.8	4.6	2.4	11.5	5.4	5.8
Sole use of bath/shower	94.7	88.8	71.0	82.3	83.8	94.3
Shared use of bath/shower	2.6	9.8	29.0	13.4	13.7	3.0
No bath/shower	2.7	1.3	-	4.4	2.4	2.7
Age of Property/Building						
Pre 1919	26.6	46.8	58.9	61.7	39.7	27.3
1919-1939	23.8	15.3	16.2	20.1	25.0	23.7
1940-1964	27.0	18.6	12.9	9.6	19.0	26.7
1965 or later	22.6	19.3	12.0	8.5	16.3	22.3
Difference from Bedroom Standard						
2 or more below	0.5	2.2	2.3	8.3	2.6	0.6
1 below	3.9	16.1	14.0	21.2	9.3	4.3
Equal to standard	32.2	53.9	59.0	39.4	48.3	32.7
1 above	40.1	21.5	17.5	24.3	28.1	39.5
2 or more above	23.4	6.4	7.1	6.9	11.7	22.9
Sharing						
In shared dwelling	2.8	10.2	28.4	14.5	12.5	3.1
Not in shared dwelling	97.2	89.8	71.6	85.5	87.5	96.9
Satisfaction with Accommodation						
Very satisfied	37.6	13.6	17.1	21.4	25.2	37.0
Satisfied	45.2	44.2	52.1	59.8	49.7	45.4
Neutral	8.8	15.5	11.0	9.6	10.8	8.9
Dissatisfied	5.8	18.3	10.0	6.0	8.6	6.0
Very dissatisfied	2.5	8.4	9.8	3.2	5.7	2.7
All households (= 100%) 000's	16,240	152	29	186	217	16,824

33

TABLE 9.   Bedroom Standard: Analysis by Type of Household, Ethnic Group of HoH, Number of Bedrooms, Satisfaction with Number of Rooms, and Basic Amenities.

Percentages

	Difference from bedroom standard					All households
	2 or more below	1 below	Equal to standard	1 above	2 or more above	
Type of Household						
One person aged under 60	-	-	8.8	4.9	6.8	6.3
Small adult household	-	7.4	7.0	14.3	31.0	15.3
Small family	3.9	14.0	21.1	28.5	7.9	20.6
Large family	62.0	43.1	16.1	3.1	1.7	9.2
Large adult household	34.1	33.0	22.4	17.2	5.7	17.1
Older small household	-	2.5	9.7	18.8	28.6	17.2
One person aged 60 or over	-	-	14.9	13.3	18.3	14.3
Ethnic Group of HoH						
White	75.6	87.9	95.0	97.8	98.7	96.5
West Indian	3.2	3.4	1.5	0.5	0.3	0.9
Indian/Pakistani/Bangladeshi	15.0	5.4	1.3	0.7	0.3	1.1
Other	6.2	3.4	2.2	1.0	0.7	1.5
Number of Bedrooms						
1	9.4	18.4	33.2	-	-	11.7
2	25.8	31.1	28.4	45.5	-	28.7
3	52.4	45.7	35.5	47.6	75.2	49.9
4 or more	12.4	4.8	2.9	6.9	24.8	9.7
Satisfaction with No. of Rooms						
Too few	61.6	52.1	25.1	10.3	3.2	15.7
Too many	0.4	0.8	1.3	4.6	18.0	6.4
About right	37.9	47.1	73.7	85.0	78.7	77.9
Basic Amenities						
Sole use of all	84.9	85.6	87.6	93.7	94.2	91.4
Some shared, none lacked	3.3	5.9	6.8	0.5	0.3	2.8
At least one lacked	11.8	8.5	5.6	5.7	5.6	5.8
Sole use of bath/shower	91.0	90.2	90.2	96.7	97.0	94.3
Shared use of bath/shower	3.5	6.3	7.4	0.5	0.3	3.0
No bath/shower	5.5	3.5	2.4	2.8	2.8	2.7
Sole use of inside WC	87.4	87.9	89.7	94.9	95.3	92.9
Shared use of inside WC	3.5	5.9	6.7	0.4	0.2	2.7
Use of outside WC only	8.7	5.9	3.5	4.4	4.2	4.1
No WC	0.4	0.3	0.2	0.3	0.3	0.3
All households (= 100%) 000's	102	727	5,505	6,645	3,846	16,824

TABLE 10. Basic Amenities: Analysis by Type of Household, Age of HoH, Socio-economic Group of HoH, Length of Residence of HoH, and Ethnic Group of HoH.

Percentages

	Use of basic amenities			All households
	Sole use of all	Some shared, none lacked	At least one lacked	
Type of Household				
One person aged under 60	4.9	48.2	8.4	6.3
Small adult household	15.7	14.5	8.9	15.3
Small family	21.7	7.2	10.6	20.6
Large family	9.6	2.5	5.5	9.2
Large adult household	17.8	3.8	12.3	17.1
Older small household	17.1	4.9	24.3	17.2
One person aged 60 or over	13.1	18.9	30.1	14.3
Age of Head of Household				
Under 25	3.9	30.8	5.6	4.7
25-34	18.2	23.9	9.0	17.8
35-44	16.8	8.4	7.5	16.0
45-54	17.9	7.9	11.3	17.3
55-64	18.3	8.1	17.9	18.0
65 or over	25.0	20.8	48.7	26.2
SEG of Head of Household				
Professional	5.4	4.2	1.0	5.1
Employers and managers	14.7	6.7	4.0	13.8
Other non-manual	18.1	23.3	10.9	17.8
Skilled manual	30.6	16.6	31.4	30.3
Semi-skilled manual	12.5	12.9	18.7	12.9
Unskilled manual	4.6	6.2	9.8	5.0
Other	14.1	30.1	24.2	15.1
Length of Residence of HoH				
Under 1 year	10.1	36.2	6.9	10.6
1 year but under 2	7.9	14.1	4.6	7.9
2 years but under 3	9.0	11.9	5.1	8.9
3 years but under 5	10.2	8.4	5.0	9.8
5 years but under 10	19.5	11.5	10.4	18.7
10 years or longer	43.3	17.9	67.9	44.1
Ethnic Group of HoH				
White	97.0	84.2	95.9	96.5
West Indian	0.9	2.8	0.7	0.9
Indian/Pakistani/Bangladeshi	0.9	5.0	2.2	1.1
Other	1.3	7.9	1.3	1.5
All households (= 100%) 000's	15,379	468	977	16,824

TABLE 11. Type of Accommodation, Tenure, Type of Household, Bedroom Standard, Basic Amenities and Central Heating: Analysis by Satisfaction with Accommodation.

Percentages

| | Satisfaction with accommodation | | | | | All households (= 100%) 000's |
	Very satisfied	Satisfied	Neutral	Dis-satisfied	Very dis-satisfied	
Type of Accommodation						
Detached house	54.3	37.5	5.2	2.3	0.6	2,966
Semi-detached house	38.3	46.9	8.2	5.0	1.6	5,559
Terraced house	30.7	49.2	9.8	7.1	3.0	4,868
Purpose built flat/maisonette	30.1	43.7	11.0	9.2	6.0	1,989
Other flat/rooms	27.2	45.6	13.7	8.7	4.9	1,248
Other	33.1	44.8	10.6	8.2	3.3	194
Tenure						
Owned outright	49.0	42.1	5.5	2.5	0.8	3,943
Owned with mortgage/loan	44.2	45.6	6.5	3.2	0.6	5,222
Rented from council	25.9	48.0	11.8	9.7	4.6	5,013
Rented from HA	34.8	41.8	12.2	7.5	3.7	225
Rented privately unfurnished	26.2	44.6	13.0	10.1	6.1	1,830
Rented privately furnished	21.7	49.3	15.6	8.8	4.6	590
Type of Household						
One person aged under 60	31.5	48.0	11.6	6.2	2.7	1,063
Small adult household	38.8	45.8	8.6	4.8	2.0	2,576
Small family	34.9	45.3	9.5	7.1	3.3	3,475
Large family	30.2	45.4	10.8	8.7	4.9	1,543
Large adult household	35.5	46.9	9.3	5.9	2.4	2,875
Older small household	41.8	43.6	7.6	5.0	2.0	2,894
One person aged 60 or over	41.1	44.6	7.3	4.9	2.1	2,398
Difference from Bedroom Standard						
2 or more below	15.2	43.0	15.2	15.5	11.2	102
1 below	19.0	45.9	14.1	12.6	8.4	727
Equal to standard	30.8	46.9	10.7	7.9	3.7	5,505
1 above	39.2	45.8	8.4	4.8	1.8	6,645
2 or more above	46.4	42.5	6.2	3.6	1.3	3,846
Use of Basic Amenities						
Sole use of all	38.7	45.5	8.3	5.4	2.1	15,379
Some shared, none lacked	23.2	49.5	14.1	8.7	4.5	468
At least one lacked	17.2	42.9	15.4	13.7	10.8	977
Availability of Central Heating						
With central heating	45.6	42.7	6.5	3.8	1.3	8,875
No central heating	27.4	48.5	11.6	8.4	4.1	7,949
All households	37.0	45.4	8.9	6.0	2.7	16,824

TABLE 12. Satisfaction with Accommodation: Analysis by Type of Accommodation, Tenure, Type of Household, Bedroom Standard, Basic Amenities and Central Heating

Percentages

	Satisfaction with accommodation					All households
	Very satisfied	Satisfied	Neutral	Dis-satisfied	Very dis-satisfied	
Type of Accommodation						
Detached house	25.8	14.6	10.4	6.7	4.4	17.6
Semi-detached house	34.2	34.1	30.4	27.8	19.7	33.0
Terraced house	24.0	31.4	32.0	34.7	33.7	28.9
Purpose built flat/maisonette	9.6	11.4	14.6	18.3	27.0	11.8
Other flat/rooms	5.4	7.4	11.3	10.8	13.8	7.4
Other	1.0	1.1	1.4	1.6	1.5	1.2
Tenure						
Owned outright	31.0	21.7	14.5	10.0	7.1	23.4
Owned with mortgage/loan	37.1	31.2	22.5	16.4	7.1	31.0
Rented from council	20.9	31.5	39.3	48.2	52.4	29.8
Rented from HA	1.3	1.2	1.8	1.7	1.9	1.3
Rented privately unfurnished	7.7	10.7	15.8	18.4	25.1	10.9
Rented privately furnished	2.0	3.7	6.0	5.1	6.0	3.5
Type of Household						
One person aged under 60	5.4	6.7	8.2	6.6	6.4	6.3
Small adult household	16.1	15.4	14.8	12.3	11.5	15.3
Small family	19.5	20.6	22.0	24.5	25.6	20.6
Large family	7.5	9.2	11.1	13.3	17.0	9.2
Large adult household	16.4	17.7	17.8	17.0	15.3	17.1
Older small household	19.4	16.5	14.6	14.6	12.9	17.2
One person aged 60 or over	15.8	14.0	11.6	11.8	11.4	14.3
Difference from Bedroom Standard						
2 or more below	0.2	0.6	1.0	1.6	2.6	0.6
1 below	2.2	4.4	6.8	9.2	13.7	4.3
Equal to standard	27.1	33.8	39.2	43.5	46.4	32.7
1 above	41.8	39.9	37.0	32.1	26.3	39.5
2 or more above	28.6	21.4	15.9	13.7	11.0	22.9
Use of Basic Amenities						
Sole use of all	95.6	91.5	85.6	82.6	71.7	91.4
Some shared, none lacked	1.7	3.0	4.4	4.0	4.7	2.8
At least one lacked	2.7	5.5	10.0	13.4	23.5	5.8
Availability of Central Heating						
With central heating	65.0	49.6	38.6	33.9	26.6	52.8
No central heating	35.0	50.4	61.4	66.1	73.4	47.2
All households (= 100%) 000's	6,231	7,643	1,502	1,003	446	16,824

37

TABLE 13.   Tenure, Type of Household, Age of HoH, Socio-economic Group of HoH, and Number of Cars and Vans: Analysis by Satisfaction with Area.

Percentages

| | Satisfaction with area | | | | | All households (= 100%) 000's |
	Very satisfied	Satisfied	Neutral	Dis- satisfied	Very dis- satisfied	
Tenure						
Owned outright	44.0	39.8	7.1	6.6	2.5	3,943
Owned with mortgage/loan	39.5	43.2	8.8	6.7	1.8	5,222
Rented from council	28.2	47.9	8.7	9.9	5.3	5,013
Rented from HA	33.8	41.9	9.8	9.2	5.2	225
Privately rented unfurnished	33.7	45.4	8.2	8.0	4.8	1,830
Privately rented furnished	27.0	52.0	12.3	6.5	2.3	590
Type of Household						
One person aged under 60	30.4	47.5	11.0	8.0	3.0	1,063
Small adult household	35.5	44.1	9.3	7.8	3.3	2,576
Small family	35.0	43.3	9.4	8.4	3.9	3,475
Large family	32.7	45.4	8.8	8.6	4.6	1,543
Large adult household	35.1	45.7	8.2	7.9	3.1	2,875
Older small household	39.6	42.7	6.9	7.6	3.2	2,894
One person aged 60 or over	39.6	44.2	7.0	6.7	2.6	2,398
Age of Head of Household						
Under 25	25.8	48.0	12.3	9.2	4.7	796
25-34	32.5	45.4	9.9	8.2	4.0	2,990
35-44	36.0	44.0	9.0	8.0	3.0	2,690
45-54	35.7	44.5	8.4	8.1	3.3	2,903
55-64	37.2	42.9	8.2	8.1	3.6	3,030
65 or over	39.7	44.0	6.6	6.8	2.8	4,415
SEG of Head of Household						
Professional	44.5	39.6	8.9	5.7	1.2	861
Employers and managers	45.1	38.8	7.8	6.2	2.1	2,330
Other non-manual	37.1	42.7	9.3	7.8	3.1	2,993
Skilled manual	33.5	45.9	8.5	8.3	3.9	5,087
Semi-skilled manual	31.7	47.4	7.8	9.0	4.0	2,162
Unskilled manual	28.9	49.9	7.9	9.0	4.4	837
Other	34.9	45.1	8.5	7.8	3.7	2,555
No. of Cars and Vans Available to Household						
0	31.5	46.9	8.3	8.9	4.4	7,092
1	37.9	43.2	8.7	7.4	2.8	7,763
2 or more	45.4	39.5	8.0	5.4	1.7	1,969
All households	36.1	44.3	8.5	7.8	3.4	16,824

38

TABLE 14. Satisfaction with Area: Analysis by Tenure, Type of Household, Age of HoH, Socio-economic Group of HoH, and Number of Cars and Vans.

Percentages

	Satisfaction with area					All households
	Very satisfied	Satisfied	Neutral	Dis-satisfied	Very dis-satisfied	
Tenure						
Owned outright	28.6	21.0	19.7	19.8	17.1	23.4
Owned with mortgage/loan	34.0	30.3	32.4	26.8	16.2	31.0
Rented from council	23.3	32.2	30.7	37.9	46.6	29.8
Rented from HA	1.3	1.3	1.6	1.6	2.1	1.3
Rented privately unfurnished	10.2	11.1	10.5	11.1	15.4	10.9
Rented privately furnished	2.6	4.0	5.1	2.9	2.6	3.5
Type of Household						
One person aged under 60	5.3	6.8	8.3	6.5	5.6	6.3
Small adult household	15.1	15.3	16.8	15.2	15.0	15.3
Small family	20.1	20.2	22.9	22.1	24.0	20.6
Large family	8.3	9.4	9.6	10.1	12.4	9.2
Large adult household	16.7	17.6	16.6	17.3	15.5	17.1
Older small household	18.9	16.5	14.1	16.6	16.5	17.2
One person aged 60 or over	15.7	14.2	11.7	12.2	11.1	14.3
Age of Head of Household						
Under 25	3.4	5.1	6.9	5.6	6.6	4.7
25-34	16.0	18.2	20.9	18.6	20.9	17.8
35-44	16.0	15.9	17.0	16.4	14.3	16.0
45-54	17.1	17.3	17.1	17.8	17.0	17.3
55-64	18.6	17.4	17.5	18.7	19.1	18.0
65 or over	28.9	26.0	20.6	22.9	22.1	26.2
SEG of Head of Household						
Professional	6.3	4.6	5.4	3.8	1.9	5.1
Employers and managers	17.3	12.1	12.8	10.9	8.7	13.8
Other non-manual	18.3	17.1	19.6	17.7	16.3	17.8
Skilled manual	28.1	31.4	30.3	32.0	34.7	30.3
Semi-skilled manual	11.3	13.8	11.9	14.8	15.2	12.9
Unskilled manual	4.0	5.6	4.7	5.7	6.5	5.0
Other	14.7	15.4	15.3	15.1	16.8	15.1
No. of Cars and Vans Available to Household						
0	36.9	44.6	41.3	48.3	55.0	42.2
1	48.6	45.1	47.8	43.6	39.1	46.1
2 or more	14.6	10.3	11.0	8.1	5.9	11.7
All households (= 100%) 000's	6,068	7,453	1,423	1,315	566	16,824

39

TABLE 15. Sharing Households: Analysis by Type of Household, Age of HoH, Length of Residence of HoH, Size of Household, Council Waiting List and Satisfaction with Accommodation.

Percentages

	Sharing rooms	Sharing circulation space	Bedsit	Self-contained accommodation in shared dwelling	Self-contained accommodation not in shared dwelling	All households
Type of Household						
One person aged under 60	59.4	22.9	60.4	33.7	5.0	6.3
Small adult household	9.9	18.2	9.7	22.0	15.4	15.3
Small family	7.8	11.0	1.2	11.5	21.1	20.6
Large family	3.0	4.2	0.2	2.3	9.4	9.2
Large adult household	3.6	8.1	0.2	5.9	17.5	17.1
Older small household	3.6	11.4	0.2	10.4	17.6	17.2
One person aged 60 or over	12.7	24.2	28.1	14.1	14.1	14.3
Age of Head of Household						
Under 25	41.7	16.0	30.2	25.0	3.9	4.7
25-34	25.1	18.4	19.8	23.4	17.6	17.8
35-44	7.8	10.9	8.2	10.4	16.2	16.0
45-54	5.4	10.8	9.3	12.9	17.5	17.3
55-64	6.5	11.9	8.7	6.9	18.3	18.0
65 or over	13.6	32.0	23.8	21.4	26.4	26.2
Length of Residence of HoH						
Under 1 year	44.8	20.2	38.8	31.5	9.9	10.6
1 but under 2 years	15.1	9.5	15.3	7.2	7.7	7.9
2 but under 3 years	12.5	10.5	13.2	7.5	8.8	8.9
3 but under 5 years	6.6	8.0	11.7	12.7	9.8	9.8
5 but under 10 years	9.3	14.3	12.1	13.3	18.9	18.7
10 years or longer	11.7	37.5	9.0	27.9	44.8	44.1
Number of Persons in Household						
1	71.9	46.9	88.6	46.8	19.1	20.6
2	14.9	30.4	9.8	35.7	33.7	33.3
3 or more	13.2	22.7	1.6	17.5	47.2	46.1
Council House Waiting List						
Head of household registered	7.3	14.8	13.7	19.0	6.2	6.4
Head of household not registered	92.7	85.2	86.3	81.0	93.8	93.6
Satisfaction with Accommodation						
Very satisfied	22.4	27.3	19.3	19.2	37.5	37.0
Satisfied	53.9	41.4	39.6	46.8	45.4	45.4
Neutral	12.0	13.6	26.0	14.3	8.7	8.9
Dissatisfied	7.5	9.9	8.6	12.0	5.9	6.0
Very dissatisfied	4.2	7.8	6.5	7.6	2.5	2.7
All households (=100%) 000's	210	190	99	29	16,296	16,824

TABLE 16.   Concealed Households: Analysis by Type of Household, Age of HoH, Relationship to HoH, Ethnic Group of HoH, and Bedroom Standard.

Percentages

	Concealed married couple household	Concealed lone parent household
Type of Concealed Household		
Small adult family	41.4	10.8
Small family	30.7	79.0
Large family	5.1	3.3
Large adult family	6.1	2.0
Older small family	16.7	4.9
Age of Head of Concealed Household		
Under 25	22.5	33.8
26-34	29.1	35.9
35-44	13.6	16.8
45-54	13.1	6.9
55-64	7.5	4.0
65 or over	14.1	2.7
Relationship of Head of Concealed Household to Head of Household		
Child or child in law	67.7	78.5
Parent or parent in law	13.0	3.0
Brother or sister	5.6	5.7
Other relation	9.0	4.8
Unrelated	4.7	8.0
Ethnic Group of Head of Concealed Household		
White	80.8	92.0
West Indian	0.3	2.4
Indian/Pakistani/Bangladeshi	15.1	2.3
Other	3.8	3.3
Difference from Bedroom Standard		
2 or more below	8.6	14.2
1 below	19.2	32.9
Equal to standard	38.3	44.1
1 above	27.3	8.4
2 or more above	6.6	0.4
Total concealed households (=100%) 000's	149	104

TABLE 17. Council House Waiting List: Analysis by Tenure, Type of Household, Age of HoH, Length of Residence of HoH, and Ethnic Group of HoH.

Percentages

	Member of household registered on waiting list				All households
	Head of household	Other person	HoH and other person	No-one	
Tenure					
Owned outright	8.0	12.1	6.4	24.6	23.4
Owned with mortgage/loan	5.1	17.2	5.3	33.0	31.0
Rented from council	48.6	56.4	52.7	28.1	29.8
Rented from HA	2.4	1.7	2.9	1.3	1.3
Privately rented unfurnished	28.8	10.2	27.2	9.7	10.9
Privately rented furnished	7.1	2.4	5.5	3.3	3.5
Type of Household					
One person aged under 60	8.1	-	-	6.4	6.3
Small adult household	12.9	7.2	20.4	15.5	15.3
Small family	22.1	8.4	27.8	20.6	20.6
Large family	10.6	22.3	13.1	8.9	9.2
Large adult household	9.3	54.2	14.3	17.1	17.1
Older small household	14.2	7.9	24.4	17.4	17.2
One person aged 60 or over	22.8	-	-	14.2	14.3
Age of Head of Household					
Under 25	7.1	4.2	10.4	4.5	4.7
25-34	18.9	8.3	24.7	17.7	17.8
35-44	14.0	14.8	14.1	16.1	16.0
45-54	12.4	34.7	14.0	17.4	17.3
55-64	18.2	23.0	16.1	18.0	18.0
65 or over	29.5	15.0	20.7	26.3	26.2
Length of Residence of HoH					
Under 1 year	10.0	6.4	12.2	10.7	10.6
1 year but under 2	9.4	5.3	8.7	7.8	7.9
2 years but under 3	9.2	7.5	12.1	8.8	8.9
3 years but under 5	12.4	7.9	14.0	9.6	9.8
5 years but under 10	20.6	16.2	19.0	18.6	18.7
10 years or longer	38.5	56.7	34.1	44.4	44.1
Ethnic Group of HoH					
White	94.5	93.9	93.6	96.7	96.5
West Indian	2.4	2.7	1.8	0.8	0.9
Indian/Pakistani/Bangladeshi	1.3	1.9	1.7	1.1	1.1
Other	1.9	1.5	2.9	1.4	1.5
All households (= 100%) 000's	848	186	232	15,558	16,824

42

TABLE 18. Council House Waiting List: Analysis by Type of Accommodation, Basic Amenities, Bedroom Standard, Shared Dwellings, Concealed Households and Lowest Floor of Accommodation.

Percentages

	Member of household registered on waiting list				All households
	Head of household	Other person	HoH and other person	No-one	
Type of Accommodation					
Detached house	4.8	7.5	4.7	18.6	17.6
Semi-detached house	19.7	37.3	19.5	33.9	33.0
Terraced house	31.4	38.8	31.5	28.7	28.9
Purpose built flat/maisonette	26.7	10.0	27.2	10.8	11.8
Other flat/rooms	14.9	5.7	13.9	6.9	7.4
Other	2.6	0.7	3.3	1.1	1.2
Basic Amenities					
Sole use of all	80.3	90.7	85.3	92.1	91.4
Some shared, none lacked	4.8	2.1	3.2	2.7	2.8
At least one lacked	14.9	7.2	11.6	5.2	5.8
Difference from Bedroom Standard					
2 or more below	1.2	8.4	1.8	0.5	0.6
1 below	9.1	23.2	12.4	3.7	4.3
Equal to standard	41.1	41.5	40.7	32.0	32.7
1 above	32.5	23.2	32.1	40.2	39.5
2 or more above	16.1	3.8	13.0	23.6	22.9
Sharing					
In shared dwelling	6.2	2.2	4.4	3.0	3.1
Not in shared dwelling	93.8	97.8	95.6	97.0	96.9
Households containing:					
Married couple concealed household	0.2	16.3	1.2	0.7	0.9
Lone parent concealed household	0.7	11.4	2.1	0.5	0.6
No concealed household	99.1	72.2	96.7	98.9	98.5
Lowest floor of Accommodation					
Ground floor or below	73.0	89.1	70.1	89.2	88.2
1st floor	14.4	6.5	15.3	6.5	7.0
2nd floor	6.4	1.8	6.5	2.2	2.5
3rd floor	2.0	0.7	3.1	0.7	0.8
4th-9th floor	2.9	1.4	3.5	1.0	1.1
10th floor or higher	1.3	0.5	1.5	0.3	0.4
All households (= 100%) 000's	848	186	232	15,558	16,824

43

Percentages

	Age of property/building				All households
	Pre 1919	1919-1939	1940-1964	1965 or later	
Type of Accommodation					
Detached house	13.0	15.3	17.7	25.9	17.6
Semi-detached house	14.2	51.4	45.4	28.1	33.0
Terraced house	50.6	25.1	19.1	22.3	28.9
Purpose built flat/maisonette	3.0	5.1	16.5	22.3	11.8
Other flat/rooms	18.7	2.8	1.0	1.0	7.4
Other	0.4	0.2	0.3	0.4	1.2
Tenure					
Owned outright	33.9	29.0	17.4	13.3	23.4
Owned with mortgage/loan	27.6	31.4	26.2	46.1	31.0
Rented from council	4.4	30.3	52.0	35.4	29.8
Rented from HA	1.8	0.7	0.5	1.7	1.3
Privately rented unfurnished	24.2	7.2	3.2	2.7	10.9
Privately rented furnished	8.1	1.5	0.7	0.8	3.5
Basic Amenities					
Sole use of all	77.6	93.7	98.6	98.9	91.4
Some shared, none lacked	6.4	1.3	0.6	0.7	2.8
At least one lacked	16.0	4.9	0.8	0.4	5.8
Age of Head of Household					
Under 25	7.5	2.8	2.7	5.1	4.7
25-34	17.4	14.4	12.3	28.0	17.8
35-44	13.7	15.0	15.8	20.0	16.0
45-54	14.4	17.0	22.2	15.1	17.3
55-64	16.8	19.2	22.8	12.8	18.0
65 or over	30.2	31.6	24.3	19.0	26.2
All households (= 100%) 000's	4,601	3,991	4,484	3,748	16,824

TABLE 20.   Lowest Floor of Accommodation: Analysis by Type of Household, Length of Residence of HoH,
Council Waiting List and Satisfaction with Accommodation.   Percentages

	Lowest floor of accommodation						All households
	Ground floor or lower	1st floor	2nd floor	3rd floor	4th-9th floor	10th floor or higher	
Type of Household							
One person aged under 60	4.8	17.8	21.1	18.7	12.0	17.1	6.3
Small adult household	14.8	19.0	20.3	18.5	18.7	20.6	15.3
Small family	21.5	13.1	15.0	17.1	18.0	14.6	20.6
Large family	9.9	3.9	4.0	5.6	4.3	1.5	9.2
Large adult household	18.2	8.0	10.3	9.1	8.2	6.9	17.1
Older small household	17.6	13.6	13.8	14.5	15.4	14.4	17.2
One person aged 60 or over	13.2	24.8	15.5	16.5	23.5	25.0	14.3
Length of Residence of HoH							
Under 1 year	9.6	19.0	19.0	17.8	13.0	15.3	10.6
1 year but under 2	7.4	12.2	12.7	9.0	9.7	8.0	7.9
2 years but under 3	8.5	12.7	11.0	10.9	9.7	9.2	8.9
3 years but under 5	9.5	11.3	13.6	14.5	10.7	14.4	9.8
5 years but under 10	18.6	18.5	18.7	14.2	28.0	28.7	18.7
10 years or longer	46.4	26.3	25.0	33.6	28.9	24.5	44.1
Council House Waiting List							
Head of household registered	5.3	13.3	16.7	17.2	17.8	23.3	6.4
Head of household not registered	94.7	86.7	83.3	82.8	82.2	76.7	93.6
Satisfaction with Accommodation							
Very satisfied	38.3	29.6	25.5	22.2	25.3	27.7	37.0
Satisfied	45.6	45.1	43.6	45.1	42.4	36.1	45.4
Neutral	8.4	11.5	13.5	15.0	14.5	15.0	8.9
Dissatisfied	5.4	8.8	10.6	11.7	10.4	14.4	6.0
Very dissatisfied	2.2	5.0	6.8	6.1	7.5	6.8	2.7
All households (= 100%) 000's	14,831	1,186	419	141	185	62	16,824

TABLE 21   Vacant Properties and Second Homes: Analysis by Rateable Value, Type of Accommodation, Age of Property and Lowest Floor of Accommodation.

Percentages

	Vacant household spaces and second homes	All household spaces
Rateable Value		
Up to £75	20.4	8.0
£76-100	11.3	7.2
£101-125	11.2	9.3
£126-150	9.9	11.6
£151-200	17.4	24.3
£201-250	11.8	18.1
£251-300	6.1	10.1
Over £300	11.8	11.3
Type of Accommodation		
Detached house	15.5	17.7
Semi-detached house	17.5	32.3
Terraced house	29.8	28.8
Purpose built flat/maisonette	13.0	11.9
Other flat/rooms	19.4	7.9
Other	4.7	1.4
Age of Property/Building		
Pre 1919	56.1	28.5
1919-1939	17.2	23.5
1940-1964	12.3	26.1
1965 or later	14.4	22.0
Lowest Floor of Accommodation		
Below street level	3.8	1.9
Ground	73.9	85.8
1st floor	13.4	7.3
2nd floor	5.3	2.6
3rd floor or higher	3.6	2.4
Total household spaces (= 100%) 000's	789	17,613

TABLE 22 Type of Accommodation : Region

Thousands

Region	Type of accommodation						All household spaces
	Detached house	Semi-detached house	Terraced house	Purpose-built flat or maisonette	Other flat or rooms	Other	
North	143	466	398	134	34	8	1,182
Yorkshire/Humberside	250	678	644	151	75	18	1,817
East Midlands	414	590	298	66	41	18	1,427
East Anglia	186	248	183	45	38	11	710
South East	1,096	1,651	1,681	1,139	857	96	6,519
Greater London	133	505	768	806	557	41	2,809
Rest of South East	963	1,146	913	333	300	55	3,710
South West	467	448	453	122	150	27	1,666
West Midlands	306	733	515	195	89	26	1,865
North West	252	876	909	241	114	34	2,426
England	3,114	5,690	5,081	2,093	1,398	238	17,613

Percentages

Region	Type of accommodation						All household spaces
	Detached house	Semi-detached house	Terraced house	Purpose-built flat or maisonette	Other flat or rooms	Other	
North	12.1	39.4	33.7	11.3	2.9	0.6	100.0
Yorkshire/Humberside	13.8	37.3	35.5	8.3	4.1	1.0	100.0
East Midlands	29.0	41.4	20.9	4.6	2.9	1.3	100.0
East Anglia	26.2	34.9	25.8	6.3	5.3	1.5	100.0
South East	16.8	25.3	25.8	17.5	13.1	1.5	100.0
Greater London	4.7	18.0	27.3	28.7	19.8	1.4	100.0
Rest of South East	26.0	30.9	24.6	9.0	8.1	1.5	100.0
South West	28.0	26.9	27.2	7.3	9.0	1.6	100.0
West Midlands	16.4	39.3	27.6	10.4	4.8	1.4	100.0
North West	10.4	36.1	37.5	9.9	4.7	1.4	100.0
England	17.7	32.3	28.8	11.9	7.9	1.4	100.0

47

TABLE 23 Lowest Floor of Accommodation : Region

Region	Lowest floor of accommodation						All households
	Ground floor or lower	1st floor	2nd floor	3rd floor	4th-9th floor	10th floor or higher	
North	1,029	72	8	3	5	3	1,120
Yorkshire/Humberside	1,617	77	20	6	12	8	1,741
East Midlands	1,316	41	9	2	2	1	1,371
East Anglia	636	33	7	1	1	-	678
South East	5,023	649	270	109	123	30	6,203
Greater London	1,816	410	209	91	111	23	2,660
Rest of South East	3,207	239	61	18	12	7	3,544
South West	1,444	98	28	5	8	-	1,583
West Midlands	1,643	88	30	7	14	9	1,792
North West	2,123	128	47	8	18	11	2,336
England	14,831	1,186	419	141	185	62	16,824

Region	Lowest floor of accommodation						All households
	Ground floor or lower	1st floor	2nd floor	3rd floor	4th-9th floor	10th floor or higher	
North	91.9	6.4	0.7	0.2	0.5	0.3	100.0
Yorkshire/Humberside	92.9	4.5	1.1	0.3	0.7	0.5	100.0
East Midlands	96.0	3.0	0.7	0.2	0.1	-	100.0
East Anglia	93.8	4.8	1.0	0.2	0.1	0.1	100.0
South East	81.0	10.5	4.4	1.8	2.0	0.5	100.0
Greater London	68.3	15.4	7.9	3.4	4.2	0.8	100.0
Rest of South East	90.5	6.7	1.7	0.5	0.3	0.2	100.0
South West	91.2	6.2	1.7	0.3	0.5	-	100.0
West Midlands	91.7	4.9	1.7	0.4	0.8	0.5	100.0
North West	90.9	5.5	2.0	0.4	0.8	0.5	100.0
England	88.2	7.0	2.5	0.8	1.1	0.4	100.0

TABLE 24 Household Size : Region

Thousands

Region	Number of people in household						All households
	1	2	3	4	5	6 or more	
North	231	364	209	192	78	46	1,120
Yorkshire/Humberside	373	567	297	295	127	81	1.741
East Midlands	243	466	237	270	99	55	1,371
East Anglia	139	235	105	129	50	20	678
South East	1,319	2,108	1,009	1,097	439	230	6,203
Greater London	615	882	442	417	190	113	2,660
Rest of South East	704	1,227	567	680	249	117	3,544
South West	310	551	270	291	110	50	1,583
West Midlands	341	579	335	315	142	80	1,792
North West	504	732	421	392	172	116	2,336
England	3,461	5,603	2,884	2,981	1,217	679	16,824

Percentages

Region	Number of people in household						All households
	1	2	3	4	5	6 or more	
North	20.6	32.5	18.7	17.1	7.0	4.0	100.0
Yorkshire/Humberside	21.4	32.6	17.1	16.9	7.3	4.7	100.0
East Midlands	17.7	34.0	17.3	19.7	7.2	4.0	100.0
East Anglia	20.4	34.7	15.6	19.0	7.3	4.0	100.0
South East	21.3	34.0	18.3	17.7	7.1	3.7	100.0
Greater London	23.1	33.2	16.6	15.7	7.2	4.2	100.0
Rest of South East	19.9	34.6	16.0	19.2	7.0	3.3	100.0
South West	19.6	34.8	17.1	18.4	7.0	3.1	100.0
West Midlands	19.0	32.3	18.7	17.6	7.9	4.5	100.0
North West	21.6	31.3	18.0	16.8	7.4	5.0	100.0
England	20.6	33.3	17.1	17.7	7.2	4.0	100.0

TABLE 25 Type of Household : Region

Region	Married couple household	Lone parent household	One person aged under 60	One person aged 60 or over	Other house-hold	All households
North	784	73	58	173	32	1,120
Yorkshire/Humberside	1,200	107	103	270	61	1,741
East Midlands	1,015	78	54	189	35	1,371
East Anglia	476	38	44	95	25	678
South East	4,207	385	471	848	292	6,203
Greater London	1,688	199	250	365	158	2,660
Rest of South East	2,520	186	221	483	134	3,544
South West	1,120	88	80	230	65	1,583
West Midlands	1,285	118	102	239	48	1,792
North West	1,575	176	151	353	80	2,336
England	11,663	1,063	1,063	2,398	637	16,824

Region	Married couple household	Lone parent household	One person aged under 60	One person aged 60 or over	Other house-hold	All households
North	69.9	6.5	5.2	15.4	2.9	100.0
Yorkshire/Humberside	68.9	6.1	6.0	15.5	3.5	100.0
East Midlands	74.1	5.6	4.0	13.8	2.5	100.0
East Anglia	70.2	5.6	6.4	14.0	3.7	100.0
South East	67.8	6.2	7.6	13.7	4.7	100.0
Greater London	63.4	7.5	9.4	13.7	5.9	100.0
Rest of South East	71.1	5.2	6.2	13.6	3.8	100.0
South West	70.7	5.5	5.0	14.6	4.1	100.0
West Midlands	71.6	6.6	5.7	13.4	2.7	100.0
North West	67.4	7.5	6.5	15.1	3.4	100.0
England	69.3	6.3	6.3	14.3	3.8	100.0

TABLE 26 Type of Household : Region

Thousands

Region	One person h'hld	Small adult h'hld	Small family	Large family	Large adult h'hld	Older small h'hld	All households
North	231	169	238	98	199	186	1,120
Yorkshire/Humberside	373	256	356	172	284	300	1,741
East Midlands	243	226	310	129	232	231	1,371
East Anglia	139	104	143	57	109	126	678
South East	1,319	992	1,244	536	1,051	1,061	6,203
Greater London	615	439	487	234	471	414	2,660
Rest of South East	704	553	757	302	580	647	3,544
South West	310	239	336	133	259	305	1,583
West Midlands	341	276	381	183	322	288	1,792
North West	504	314	467	235	419	397	2,336
England	3,461	2,576	3,475	1,543	2,875	2,894	16,824

Percentages

Region	One person h'hld	Small adult h'hld	Small family	Large family	Large adult h'hld	Older small h'hld	All households
North	20.6	15.1	21.2	8.7	17.8	16.6	100.0
Yorkshire/Humberside	21.4	14.7	20.4	9.9	16.3	17.2	100.0
East Midlands	17.7	16.5	22.7	9.4	16.9	16.8	100.0
East Anglia	20.4	15.4	21.1	8.4	16.1	18.5	100.0
South East	21.3	16.0	20.1	8.6	16.9	17.1	100.0
Greater London	23.1	16.5	18.3	8.8	17.7	15.6	100.0
Rest of South East	19.9	15.6	21.4	8.5	16.4	18.3	100.0
South West	19.6	15.1	21.3	8.4	16.4	19.2	100.0
West Midlands	19.0	15.4	21.3	10.2	18.0	16.1	100.0
North West	21.6	13.4	20.0	10.1	17.9	17.0	100.0
England	20.6	15.3	20.6	9.2	17.1	17.2	100.0

TABLE 27 Number of Rooms : Region

Thousands

Region	Number of rooms								All households
	1	2	3	4	5	6	7	8 or more	
North	4	19	82	310	364	239	58	45	1,120
Yorkshire/Humberside	16	44	150	430	594	370	79	58	1,741
East Midlands	4	17	67	267	521	360	80	56	1,371
East Anglia	8	16	40	115	232	194	42	31	678
South East	109	224	641	1,317	1,804	1,448	392	267	6,203
Greater London	63	144	384	629	648	559	136	96	2,660
Rest of South East	46	80	257	688	1,156	889	256	171	3,544
South West	17	33	105	303	528	395	115	87	1,583
West Midlands	17	35	124	330	672	475	91	47	1,792
North West	21	40	175	489	770	638	126	76	2,336
England	195	428	1,385	3,560	5,485	4,119	984	668	16,824

Percentages

Region	Number of rooms								All households
	1	2	3	4	5	6	7	8 or more	
North	0.3	1.7	7.3	27.6	32.5	21.3	5.2	4.1	100.0
Yorkshire/Humberside	0.9	2.6	8.6	24.7	34.1	21.2	4.5	3.4	100.0
East Midlands	0.3	1.2	4.9	19.5	38.0	26.2	5.8	4.1	100.0
East Anglia	1.2	2.3	5.9	17.0	34.3	28.7	6.2	4.5	100.0
South East	1.8	3.6	10.3	21.2	29.1	23.4	6.3	4.3	100.0
Greater London	2.4	5.4	14.4	23.6	24.4	21.0	5.1	3.6	100.0
Rest of South East	1.3	2.3	7.2	19.4	32.6	25.1	7.2	4.8	100.0
South West	1.1	2.1	6.6	19.1	33.4	24.9	7.3	5.4	100.0
West Midlands	0.9	2.0	6.9	18.4	37.5	26.5	5.1	2.6	100.0
North West	0.9	1.7	7.5	20.9	33.0	27.3	5.4	3.3	100.0
England	1.2	2.5	8.2	21.2	32.6	24.5	5.8	4.0	100.0

TABLE 28 Number of Bedrooms : Region

Thousands

Region	Number of bedrooms						All households
	1	2	3	4	5	6 or more	
North	99	400	525	71	18	7	1,120
Yorkshire/Humberside	190	558	840	121	24	8	1,741
East Midlands	85	380	764	117	19	6	1,371
East Anglia	63	166	375	59	9	5	678
South East	975	1,724	2,828	539	99	37	6,203
Greater London	587	789	1,045	189	38	12	2,660
Rest of South East	388	935	1,783	351	62	24	3,544
South West	160	444	800	129	34	17	1,583
West Midlands	167	449	1,044	111	16	5	1,792
North West	231	712	1,217	141	23	12	2,336
England	1,969	4,834	8,394	1,288	244	96	16,824

Percentages

Region	Number of bedrooms						All households
	1	2	3	4	5	6 or more	
North	8.8	35.7	46.9	6.3	1.6	0.6	100.0
Yorkshire/Humberside	10.9	32.1	48.2	6.9	1.4	0.4	100.0
East Midlands	6.2	27.7	55.8	8.5	1.4	0.4	100.0
East Anglia	9.3	24.5	55.4	8.8	1.4	0.7	100.0
South East	15.7	27.8	45.6	8.7	1.6	0.6	100.0
Greater London	22.1	29.7	39.3	7.1	1.4	0.5	100.0
Rest of South East	11.0	26.4	50.3	9.9	1.7	0.7	100.0
South West	10.1	28.0	50.6	8.1	2.1	1.1	100.0
West Midlands	9.3	25.1	58.3	6.2	0.9	0.3	100.0
North West	9.9	30.5	52.1	6.1	1.0	0.5	100.0
England	11.7	28.7	49.9	7.7	1.4	0.6	100.0

TABLE 29 Density of Occupation : Region

Region	Persons per room					All households
	Less than $\frac{1}{2}$	$\frac{1}{2}$ to $\frac{3}{4}$	Over $\frac{3}{4}$ to 1	Over 1 to $1\frac{1}{2}$	Over $1\frac{1}{2}$	
North	436	461	190	32	3	1,120
Yorkshire/Humberside	675	681	318	58	9	1,741
East Midlands	567	529	240	33	3	1,371
East Anglia	288	254	125	10	2	678
South East	2,370	2,521	1,133	144	36	6,203
Greater London	915	1,124	515	80	26	2,660
Rest of South East	1,455	1,397	618	64	10	3,544
South West	673	607	268	31	5	1,583
West Midlands	700	680	352	53	7	1,792
North West	946	905	396	78	10	2,336
England	6,655	6,638	3,020	438	73	16,824

Region	Persons per room					All households
	Less than $\frac{1}{2}$	$\frac{1}{2}$ to $\frac{3}{4}$	Over $\frac{3}{4}$ to 1	Over 1 to $1\frac{1}{2}$	Over $1\frac{1}{2}$	
North	38.9	41.1	16.9	2.8	0.2	100.0
Yorkshire/Humberside	38.8	39.1	18.3	3.3	0.5	100.0
East Midlands	41.3	38.6	17.5	2.4	0.2	100.0
East Anglia	42.5	37.4	18.4	1.4	0.3	100.0
South East	38.2	40.6	18.3	2.3	0.6	100.0
Greater London	34.4	42.3	19.3	3.0	1.0	100.0
Rest of South East	41.1	39.4	17.4	1.8	0.3	100.0
South West	42.5	38.4	16.9	2.0	0.3	100.0
West Midlands	39.1	38.0	19.6	2.9	0.4	100.0
North West	40.5	38.7	17.0	3.4	0.4	100.0
England	39.6	39.5	17.9	2.6	0.5	100.0

TABLE 30 Difference from Bedroom Standard : Region

Thousands

Region	Difference from bedroom standard					All households
	2 or More Below	1 Below	Equal	1 Above	2 or More Above	
North	5	52	354	480	229	1,120
Yorkshire/Humberside	14	77	574	698	379	1,741
East Midlands	5	50	366	588	363	1,371
East Anglia	3	16	196	279	184	678
South East	37	274	2,240	2,302	1,349	6,203
Greater London	25	169	1,176	850	439	2,660
Rest of South East	12	105	1,064	1,452	910	3,544
South West	6	53	463	659	402	1,583
West Midlands	11	84	550	716	431	1,792
North West	20	122	763	922	508	2,336
England	102	727	5,505	6,645	3,846	16,824

Percentages

Region	Difference from bedroom standard					All households
	2 or More Below	1 Below	Equal	1 Above	2 or More Above	
North	0.5	4.6	31.6	42.9	20.5	100.0
Yorkshire/Humberside	0.8	4.4	33.0	40.1	21.7	100.0
East Midlands	0.3	3.6	26.7	42.9	26.5	100.0
East Anglia	0.4	2.3	28.9	41.2	27.2	100.0
South East	0.6	4.4	36.1	37.1	21.8	100.0
Greater London	1.0	6.4	44.2	32.0	16.5	100.0
Rest of South East	0.4	3.0	30.0	41.0	25.7	100.0
South West	0.4	3.3	29.2	41.6	25.4	100.0
West Midlands	0.6	4.7	30.7	40.0	24.1	100.0
North West	0.9	5.2	32.7	39.5	21.7	100.0
England	0.6	4.3	32.7	39.5	22.9	100.0

TABLE 31 Households Sharing a Dwelling : Region

Thousands

Region	Type of sharing					All households
	Sharing rooms	Sharing circulation space	Bedsit	Self contained accommodation		
				In shared dwelling	Not in shared dwelling	
North	3	2	3	-	1,112	1,120
Yorkshire/Humberside	21	6	9	1	1,704	1,741
East Midlands	6	6	2	1	1,356	1,371
East Anglia	7	7	5	-	658	678
South East	114	117	51	21	5,900	6,203
Greater London	60	84	29	18	2,468	2,660
Rest of South East	54	33	22	3	3,432	3,544
South West	16	23	9	2	1,533	1,583
West Midlands	23	13	6	1	1,748	1,792
North West	20	16	14	3	2,283	2,336
England	210	190	99	29	16,296	16,824

Percentages

Region	Type of sharing					All households
	Sharing rooms	Sharing circulation space	Bedsit	Self contained accommodation		
				In shared dwelling	Not in shared dwelling	
North	0.3	0.2	0.2	-	99.2	100.0
Yorkshire/Humberside	1.2	0.3	0.5	0.1	97.9	100.0
East Midlands	0.5	0.4	0.1	-	99.0	100.0
East Anglia	1.0	1.0	0.8	0.1	97.1	100.0
South East	1.8	1.9	0.8	0.3	95.1	100.0
Greater London	2.3	3.2	1.1	0.7	92.8	100.0
Rest of South East	1.5	0.9	0.6	0.1	96.8	100.0
South West	1.0	1.5	0.5	0.2	96.9	100.0
West Midlands	1.3	0.8	0.4	-	97.6	100.0
North West	0.9	0.7	0.6	0.1	97.7	100.0
England	1.2	1.1	0.6	0.2	96.9	100.0

TABLE 32 Use of Basic Amenities : Region

Thousands

Region	Use of basic amenities			All households
	Sole use of all	Some shared none lacked	At least one lacked	
North	1,057	9	54	1,120
Yorkshire/Humberside	1,602	32	107	1,741
East Midlands	1,268	14	89	1,371
East Anglia	623	17	38	678
South East	5,622	281	301	6,203
Greater London	2,328	176	156	2,660
Rest of South East	3,293	105	145	3,544
South West	1,454	35	94	1,583
West Midlands	1,644	33	114	1,792
North West	2,109	47	180	2,336
England	15,379	468	977	16,824

Percentages

Region	Use of basic amenities			All households
	Sole use of all	Some shared none lacked	At least one lacked	
North	94.4	0.8	4.9	100.0
Yorkshire/Humberside	92.0	1.8	6.2	100.0
East Midlands	92.5	1.0	6.5	100.0
East Anglia	91.9	2.5	5.6	100.0
South East	90.6	4.5	4.8	100.0
Greater London	87.5	6.6	5.9	100.0
Rest of South East	92.9	3.0	4.1	100.0
South West	91.9	2.2	6.0	100.0
West Midlands	91.8	1.9	6.4	100.0
North West	90.3	2.0	7.7	100.0
England	91.4	2.8	5.8	100.0

TABLE 33 Use of Bath or Shower : Region

Region	Use of bath or shower			All households
	Sole use	Shared use	None	
North	1,083	9	28	1,120
Yorkshire/Humberside	1,656	35	50	1,741
East Midlands	1,313	15	43	1,371
East Anglia	642	17	19	678
South East	5,766	292	145	6,203
Greater London	2,401	185	73	2,660
Rest of South East	3,364	107	72	3,544
South West	1,497	45	41	1,583
West Midlands	1,709	38	45	1,792
North West	2,196	52	88	2,336
England	15,863	504	457	16,824

Percentages

Region	Use of bath or shower			All households
	Sole use	Shared use	None	
North	96.7	0.8	2.5	100.0
Yorkshire/Humberside	95.1	2.0	2.9	100.0
East Midlands	95.8	1.1	3.1	100.0
East Anglia	94.7	2.5	2.8	100.0
South East	92.9	4.7	2.3	100.0
Greater London	90.3	7.0	2.7	100.0
Rest of South East	94.9	3.0	2.0	100.0
South West	94.6	2.8	2.6	100.0
West Midlands	95.4	2.1	2.5	100.0
North West	94.0	2.2	3.8	100.0
England	94.3	3.0	2.7	100.0

TABLE 34 Use of Hot Water Supply : Region

Thousands

Region	Use of hot water supply			All households
	Sole use	Shared use	None	
North	1,098	4	19	1,120
Yorkshire/Humberside	1,678	22	41	1,741
East Midlands	1,329	7	35	1,371
East Anglia	642	11	25	678
South East	5,889	159	155	6,203
Greater London	2,489	92	79	2,660
Rest of South East	3,400	67	77	3,544
South West	1,505	19	59	1,583
West Midlands	1,711	28	52	1,792
North West	2,233	27	76	2,336
England	16,087	275	462	16,824

Percentages

Region	Use of hot water supply			All households
	Sole use	Shared use	None	
North	98.0	0.3	1.7	100.0
Yorkshire/Humberside	96.4	1.3	2.3	100.0
East Midlands	96.9	0.5	2.6	100.0
East Anglia	94.7	1.6	3.6	100.0
South East	95.0	2.6	2.5	100.0
Greater London	93.6	3.4	3.0	100.0
Rest of South East	96.0	1.9	2.1	100.0
South West	95.1	1.2	3.7	100.0
West Midlands	95.5	1.5	2.9	100.0
North West	95.6	1.1	3.3	100.0
England	95.6	1.6	2.7	100.0

TABLE 35 Use of Flush Toilet : Region

Thousands

Region	Use of flush toilet				All households
	Sole use inside building	Shared use inside building	Use of outside WC only	None	
North	1,064	7	47	2	1,120
Yorkshire/Humberside	1,613	34	91	3	1,741
East Midlands	1,280	13	72	6	1,371
East Anglia	636	14	22	5	678
South East	5,752	260	181	10	6,203
Greater London	2,400	167	92	1	2,660
Rest of South East	3,352	93	89	9	3,544
South West	1,493	40	45	5	1,583
West Midlands	1,662	37	88	5	1,792
North West	2,129	49	149	10	2,336
England	15,629	454	695	46	16,824

Percentages

Region	Use of flush toilet				All households
	Sole use inside building	Shared use inside building	Use of outside WC only	None	
North	95.0	0.6	4.2	0.2	100.0
Yorkshire/Humberside	92.7	2.0	5.2	0.2	100.0
East Midlands	93.3	0.9	5.3	0.4	100.0
East Anglia	93.9	1.9	3.3	0.8	100.0
South East	92.7	4.2	2.9	0.2	100.0
Greater London	90.2	6.3	3.5	-	100.0
Rest of South East	94.6	2.6	2.5	0.3	100.0
South West	94.3	2.5	2.8	0.3	100.0
West Midlands	92.8	2.0	4.9	0.3	100.0
North West	91.1	2.0	6.4	0.4	100.0
England	92.9	2.7	4.1	0.3	100.0

TABLE 36 Type of Central Heating : Region

Thousands

Region	No central heating	Central heating fuel					All households
		Solid fuel	Gas	Oil	Electric storage heaters	Other *	
North	477	123	375	44	65	37	1,120
Yorkshire/Humberside	950	126	422	64	90	88	1,741
East Midlands	586	150	469	59	68	39	1,371
East Anglia	286	57	184	68	52	30	678
South East	2,748	250	2,064	389	472	280	6,203
Greater London	1,396	46	800	123	149	145	2,660
Rest of South East	1,352	204	1,264	266	323	135	3,544
South West	721	108	327	138	210	79	1,583
West Midlands	908	82	535	56	122	88	1,792
North West	1,273	87	690	85	108	93	2,336
England	7,949	984	5,067	903	1,187	734	16,824

Percentages

Region	No central heating	Central heating fuel					All households
		Solid fuel	Gas	Oil	Electric storage heaters	Other *	
North	42.5	10.9	33.5	4.0	5.8	3.3	100.0
Yorkshire/Humberside	54.6	7.2	24.3	3.7	5.2	5.0	100.0
East Midlands	42.7	10.9	34.2	4.3	5.0	2.9	100.0
East Anglia	42.2	8.5	27.2	10.0	7.7	4.4	100.0
South East	44.3	4.0	33.3	6.3	7.6	4.5	100.0
Greater London	52.5	1.7	30.1	4.6	5.6	5.5	100.0
Rest of South East	38.1	5.8	35.7	7.5	9.1	3.8	100.0
South West	45.5	6.8	20.7	8.7	13.2	5.1	100.0
West Midlands	50.7	4.6	29.8	3.1	6.8	4.9	100.0
North West	54.5	3.7	29.5	3.6	4.6	3.9	100.0
England	47.2	5.8	30.1	5.4	7.1	4.4	100.0

* Mainly other electric

61

Region	Main form of room heating						All households
	Central heating	Open fire	Closed stove	Electric	Gas	Other*	
North	520	297	14	70	212	7	1,120
Yorkshire/Humberside	617	376	17	148	578	5	1,741
East Midlands	619	301	45	81	319	7	1,371
East Anglia	331	128	21	59	127	11	678
South East	2,933	586	161	1,037	1,356	129	6,203
Greater London	1,098	125	49	616	703	68	2,660
Rest of South East	1,835	461	112	421	653	61	3,544
South West	669	296	75	251	257	36	1,583
West Midlands	687	217	30	212	624	22	1,792
North West	877	282	36	246	880	15	2,336
England	7,253	2,483	400	2,103	4,351	234	16,824

Percentages

Region	Main form of room heating						All households
	Central heating	Open fire	Closed stove	Electric	Gas	Other*	
North	46.4	26.5	1.2	6.3	18.9	0.7	100.0
Yorkshire/Humberside	35.4	21.6	1.0	8.5	33.2	0.2	100.0
East Midlands	45.1	21.9	3.3	5.9	23.2	0.6	100.0
East Anglia	48.9	19.0	3.1	8.7	18.7	1.6	100.0
South East	47.3	9.5	2.6	16.7	21.9	2.1	100.0
Greater London	41.3	4.7	1.8	23.2	26.4	2.5	100.0
Rest of South East	51.8	13.0	3.2	11.9	18.4	1.7	100.0
South West	42.2	18.7	4.7	15.8	16.2	2.2	100.0
West Midlands	38.3	12.1	1.7	11.8	34.8	1.3	100.0
North West	37.5	12.1	1.5	10.5	37.7	0.7	100.0
England	43.1	14.8	2.4	12.5	25.9	1.4	100.0

* Mainly oil or paraffin

TABLE 38   Tenure by Region

Thousands

Region	Owned out-right	Owned with mortgage or loan	Rented from council	Rented from housing associa-tion	Rented privately		All households
					un-furnished	furnished	
North	215	283	467	18	125	13	1,120
Yorkshire/Humberside	399	503	587	13	196	43	1,741
East Midlands	323	455	407	9	156	20	1,371
East Anglia	187	197	184	9	75	25	678
South East	1,329	1,977	1,706	117	733	340	6,203
Greater London	442	733	831	87	366	200	2,660
Rest of South East	887	1,244	875	30	367	140	3,544
South West	493	484	367	16	160	63	1,583
West Midlands	382	575	624	21	155	35	1,792
North West	614	748	670	23	229	51	2,336
England	3,943	5,222	5,013	225	1,830	590	16,824

Percentages

Region	Owned out-right	Owned with mortgage or loan	Rented from council	Rented from housing associa-tion	Rented privately		All households
					un-furnished	furnished	
North	19.2	25.2	41.7	1.6	11.2	1.2	100.0
Yorkshire/Humberside	22.9	28.9	33.7	0.7	11.3	2.5	100.0
East Midlands	23.6	33.2	29.7	0.7	11.4	1.5	100.0
East Anglia	27.7	29.1	27.2	1.3	11.1	3.7	100.0
South East	21.4	31.9	27.5	1.9	11.8	5.5	100.0
Greater London	16.6	27.6	31.3	3.3	13.8	7.5	100.0
Rest of South East	25.0	35.1	24.7	0.8	10.4	3.9	100.0
South West	31.2	30.6	23.1	1.0	10.1	4.0	100.0
West Midlands	21.3	32.1	34.9	1.2	8.7	1.9	100.0
North West	26.3	32.0	28.7	1.0	9.8	2.2	100.0
England	23.4	31.0	29.8	1.3	10.9	3.5	100.0

63

TABLE 39 Leasehold/Freehold Tenures : Region

Thousands

Region	Owned leasehold	Owned freehold	All owner-occupiers
North	95	403	498
Yorkshire/Humberside	106	796	902
East Midlands	23	755	778
East Anglia	10	374	384
South East	314	2,992	3,306
Greater London	183	992	1,175
Rest of South East	129	2,002	2,131
South West	91	886	977
West Midlands	188	769	957
North West	564	798	1,362
England	1,391	7,773	9,165

Percentages

Region	Owned leasehold	Owned freehold	All owner-occupiers
North	19.0	81.0	100.0
Yorkshire/Humberside	11.8	88.2	100.0
East Midlands	2.9	97.1	100.0
East Anglia	2.5	97.5	100.0
South East	9.5	90.5	100.0
Greater London	15.6	84.4	100.0
Rest of South East	6.1	93.9	100.0
South West	9.3	90.7	100.0
West Midlands	19.6	80.4	100.0
North West	41.4	58.6	100.0
England	15.1	84.9	100.0

64

TABLE 40 Households in Privately Rented Accommodation: Type of Landlord : Region

Thousands

Region	Type of landlord						All households privately renting
	Property company	Employer-company	Employer-person	Relative	Other person	Other	
North	10	18	14	11	71	13	138
Yorkshire/Humberside	21	42	17	11	125	23	239
East Midlands	15	34	17	7	91	12	176
East Anglia	7	17	12	3	53	8	100
South East	187	115	68	58	560	83	1,073
Greater London	143	45	21	24	298	34	566
Rest of South East	44	70	47	34	262	49	507
South West	16	32	18	16	119	22	224
West Midlands	25	29	11	13	103	8	190
North West	53	27	7	13	158	22	281
England	335	315	166	133	1,281	192	2,421

Percentages

Region	Type of landlord						All households privately renting
	Property company	Employer-company	Employer-person	Relative	Other person	Other	
North	7.5	13.0	10.4	8.0	51.4	9.7	100.0
Yorkshire/Humberside	8.8	17.8	7.1	4.4	52.5	9.5	100.0
East Midlands	8.7	19.2	9.9	4.0	51.4	6.9	100.0
East Anglia	6.6	16.7	11.7	3.5	53.4	8.1	100.0
South East	17.4	10.8	6.4	5.5	52.2	7.8	100.0
Greater London	25.2	8.0	3.8	4.3	52.6	6.1	100.0
Rest of South East	8.7	13.9	9.3	6.7	51.7	9.7	100.0
South West	7.1	14.5	8.2	7.2	53.4	9.7	100.0
West Midlands	1.5	17.6	6.6	7.6	61.8	4.9	100.0
North West	18.9	9.6	2.6	4.8	56.4	7.8	100.0
England	13.8	13.0	6.8	5.5	52.9	7.9	100.0

TABLE 41 Individual Private Landlords : Region

Thousands

Region	Households renting from individual*			All households renting from individual
	Resident landlord sharing space	Resident landlord not sharing space	No resident landlord	
North	1	4	91	97
Yorkshire/Humberside	7	4	142	153
East Midlands	3	2	110	115
East Anglia	6	4	59	69
South East	66	60	562	687
Greater London	39	37	268	344
Rest of South East	27	23	294	343
South West	13	16	125	154
West Midlands	9	3	114	127
North West	9	6	164	179
England	114	99	1,366	1,579

Percentages

Region	Households renting from individual*			All households renting from individual
	Resident landlord sharing space	Resident landlord not sharing space	No resident landlord	
North	1.1	4.3	94.5	100.0
Yorkshire/Humberside	4.6	2.4	93.0	100.0
East Midlands	2.4	1.6	95.9	100.0
East Anglia	8.1	6.2	85.7	100.0
South East	9.6	8.6	81.8	100.0
Greater London	11.4	10.6	77.9	100.0
Rest of South East	7.8	6.6	85.6	100.0
South West	8.4	10.3	81.2	100.0
West Midlands	7.4	2.6	90.0	100.0
North West	4.9	3.5	91.5	100.0
England	7.2	6.3	86.5	100.0

* Employer, relative or other person

66

TABLE 42 Persons Registered on Council House Waiting List : Region

Thousands

Region	Member of household registered				All households
	Head of household	Other person	HoH and other person	No one	
North	80	12	17	1,012	1,120
Yorkshire/Humberside	109	23	28	1,581	1,741
East Midlands	64	20	18	1,269	1,371
East Anglia	23	7	9	638	678
South East	313	65	85	5,741	6,203
Greater London	173	27	55	2,405	2,660
Rest of South East	140	38	30	3,336	3,544
South West	59	15	21	1,489	1,583
West Midlands	90	21	30	1,650	1,792
North West	111	23	23	2,179	2,336
England	848	186	232	15,558	16,824

Percentages

Region	Member of household registered				All households
	Head of household	Other person	HoH and other person	No one	
North	7.1	1.1	1.5	90.3	100.0
Yorkshire/Humberside	6.2	1.3	1.6	90.8	100.0
East Midlands	4.7	1.4	1.3	92.6	100.0
East Anglia	3.4	1.1	1.3	94.2	100.0
South East	5.1	1.0	1.4	92.5	100.0
Greater London	6.5	1.0	2.1	90.4	100.0
Rest of South East	4 0	1.1	0.9	94.1	100.0
South West	3.7	1.0	1.3	94.0	100.0
West Midlands	5.0	1.2	1.7	92.1	100.0
North West	4.8	1.0	1.0	93.3	100.0
England	5 0	1.1	1.4	92.5	100.0

67

TABLE 43 Satisfaction with Accommodation : Region

Thousands

Region	Satisfaction with accommodation					All households
	Very satisfied	Satisfied	Neutral	Dissatis-fied	Very dissatis-fied	
North	421	497	105	69	28	1,120
Yorkshire/Humberside	606	802	161	120	52	1,741
East Midlands	508	630	124	78	31	1,371
East Anglia	290	302	50	26	9	678
South East	2,294	2,846	558	346	160	6,203
Greater London	799	1,287	275	195	104	2,660
Rest of South East	1,495	1,559	283	151	56	3,544
South West	702	654	129	72	27	1,583
West Midlands	591	869	168	117	46	1,792
North West	818	1,042	208	175	93	2,336
England	6,231	7,643	1,502	1,003	446	16,824

Percentages

Region	Satisfaction with accommodation					All households
	Very satisfied	Satisfied	Neutral	Dissatis-fied	Very dissatis-fied	
North	37.6	44.4	9.3	6.2	2.5	100.0
Yorkshire/Humberside	34.8	46.1	9.2	6.9	3.0	100.0
East Midlands	37.1	46.0	9.0	5.7	2.3	100.0
East Anglia	42.9	44.6	7.3	3.9	1.3	100.0
South East	37.0	45.9	9.0	5.6	2.6	100.0
Greater London	30.0	48.4	10.3	7.3	3.9	100.0
Rest of South East	42.2	44.0	8.0	4.3	1.6	100.0
South West	44.3	41.3	8.1	4.6	1.7	100.0
West Midlands	33.0	48.5	9.4	6.5	2.6	100.0
North West	35.0	44.6	8.9	7.5	4.0	100.0
England	37.0	45.4	8.9	6.0	2.7	100.0

TABLE 44 Satisfaction with Area : Region

Thousands

Region	Satisfaction with area					All households
	Very satisfied	Satisfied	Neutral	Dissatis-fied	Very dissatis-fied	
North	445	492	80	75	27	1,120
Yorkshire/Humberside	640	777	131	137	55	1,741
East Midlands	530	616	102	89	34	1,371
East Anglia	290	285	53	40	10	678
South East	2,047	2,778	609	530	237	6,203
Greater London	617	1,283	309	299	151	2,660
Rest of South East	1,430	1,495	300	231	86	3,544
South West	753	612	100	89	29	1,583
West Midlands	586	840	160	146	60	1,792
North West	775	1,053	187	208	113	2,336
England	6,068	7,453	1,423	1,315	566	16,824

Percentages

Region	Satisfaction with area					All households
	Very satisfied	Satisfied	Neutral	Dissatis-fied	Very dissatis-fied	
North	39.8	43.9	7.1	6.7	2.4	100.0
Yorkshire/Humberside	36.8	44.6	7.6	7.9	3.2	100.0
East Midlands	38.7	44.9	7.4	6.5	2.5	100.0
East Anglia	42.8	42.1	7.8	5.9	1.5	100.0
South East	33.0	44.8	9.8	8.5	3.8	100.0
Greater London	23.2	48.3	11.6	11.3	5.7	100.0
Rest of South East	40.4	42.2	8.5	6.5	2.4	100.0
South West	47.6	38.7	6.3	5.6	1.9	100.0
West Midlands	32.7	46.9	8.9	8.1	3.4	100.0
North West	33.2	45.1	8.0	8.9	4.8	100.0
England	36.1	44.3	8.5	7.8	3.4	100.0

TABLE 45 Satisfaction with Number of Rooms : Region

Thousands

| Region | Satisfaction with number of rooms | | | All households |
	Too few	Too many	About right	
North	149	75	896	1,120
Yorkshire/Humberside	261	113	1,367	1,741
East Midlands	203	103	1,064	1,371
East Anglia	97	41	540	678
South East	1,107	350	4,747	6,203
Greater London	510	152	1,998	2,660
Rest of South East	597	198	2,749	3,544
South West	232	92	1,259	1,583
West Midlands	234	132	1,425	1,792
North West	353	168	1,815	2,336
England	2,637	1,074	13,113	16,824

Percentages

| Region | Satisfaction with number of rooms | | | All households |
	Too few	Too many	About right	
North	13.3	6.7	80.0	100.0
Yorkshire/Humberside	15.0	6.5	78.5	100.0
East Midlands	14.8	7.5	77.6	100.0
East Anglia	14.2	6 1	79.7	100.0
South East	17.8	5.6	76.5	100.0
Greater London	19.2	5.7	75.1	100.0
Rest of South East	16.9	5.6	77.6	100.0
South West	14.7	5.8	79.5	100.0
West Midlands	13.1	7.4	79.6	100.0
North West	15.1	7.2	77.7	100.0
England	15.7	6.4	77.9	100.0

70

TABLE 46 Satisfaction with Size of Rooms : Region

Region	Satisfaction with size of rooms				All households
	All or some too small	All or some too large	All about right	Some too large, others too small	
North	172	22	902	24	1,120
Yorkshire/Humberside	297	32	1,383	28	1,741
East Midlands	240	24	1,081	26	1,371
East Anglia	113	9	541	15	678
South East	1,272	80	4,751	101	6,203
Greater London	589	37	1,993	41	2,660
Rest of South East	683	43	2,758	60	3,544
South West	235	22	1,299	27	1,583
West Midlands	326	28	1,404	34	1,792
North West	416	42	1,827	51	2,336
England	3,071	259	13,190	304	16,824

Percentages

Region	Satisfaction with size of rooms				All households
	All or some too small	All or some too large	All about right	Some too large, others too small	
North	15.4	2 0	80.5	2.1	100.0
Yorkshire/Humberside	17.0	1.8	79.5	1.6	100.0
East Midlands	17.5	1.8	78.8	1.9	100.0
East Anglia	16.7	1.3	79.9	2.1	100.0
South East	20.5	1.3	76.6	1.6	100.0
Greater London	22.2	1.4	74.9	1.5	100.0
Rest of South East	19.3	1.2	77.8	1.7	100.0
South West	14.9	1.4	82.1	1.7	100.0
West Midlands	18.2	1.6	78.4	1.9	100.0
North West	17.8	1.8	78.2	2.2	100.0
England	18.3	1.5	78.4	1.8	100.0

TABLE 47 Availability of Cars and Vans : Region

Thousands

Region	Number of cars and vans available to household				All households
	0	1	2	3 or more	
North	550	468	88	15	1,120
Yorkshire/Humberside	864	731	129	17	1,741
East Midlands	531	663	159	18	1,371
East Anglia	241	346	79	11	678
South East	2,461	2,933	706	103	6,203
Greater London	1,280	1,141	208	30	2,660
Rest of South East	1,181	1,792	498	73	3,544
South West	547	818	195	24	1,583
West Midlands	741	836	191	24	1,792
North West	1,159	972	182	22	2,336
England	7,092	7,763	1,733	236	16,824

Percentages

Region	Number of cars and vans available to household				All households
	0	1	2	3 or more	
North	49.1	41.8	7.9	1.3	100.0
Yorkshire/Humberside	49.6	42.0	7.4	1.0	100.0
East Midlands	38.7	48.4	11.6	1.3	100.0
East Anglia	35.5	51.0	11.7	1.6	100.0
South East	39.7	47.3	11.4	1.7	100.0
Greater London	48.1	42.9	7.8	1.1	100.0
Rest of South East	33.3	50.6	14.1	2.1	100.0
South West	34.6	51.7	12.3	1.5	100.0
West Midlands	41.4	46.7	10.7	1.3	100.0
North West	49.6	41.6	7.8	0.9	100.0
England	42.2	46.1	10.3	1.4	100.0

TABLE 48 Off-street Parking Provision for Households With Cars or Vans : Region

Thousands

Region	Off-street parking provision			All households with car or van
	For all cars and vans	For some cars and vans	None	
North	469	9	92	570
Yorkshire/Humberside	715	15	147	877
East Midlands	726	16	98	840
East Anglia	377	9	50	437
South East	2,804	118	821	3,743
Greater London	809	54	517	1,380
Rest of South East	1,995	64	304	2,363
South West	869	20	147	1,036
West Midlands	912	18	120	1,051
North West	906	26	245	1,177
England	7,780	232	1,721	9,732

Percentages

Region	Off-street parking provision			All households with car or van
	For all cars and vans	For some cars and vans	None	
North	82.3	1.6	16.1	100.0
Yorkshire/Humberside	81.5	1.7	16.8	100.0
East Midlands	86.4	1.9	11.6	100.0
East Anglia	86.4	2.1	11.5	100.0
South East	74.9	3.1	21.9	100.0
Greater London	58.6	3.9	37.4	100.0
Rest of South East	84.4	2.7	12.9	100.0
South West	83.9	1.9	14.2	100.0
West Midlands	86.8	1.7	11.4	100.0
North West	76.9	2.2	20.8	100.0
England	79.9	2.4	17.7	100.0

TABLE 49 Age and Sex of Head of Household : Region

Thousands

Region	Age and sex of head of household								All heads of household
	Male				Female				
	16-29	30-44	45-64	65 or over	16-29	30-44	45-59	60 or over	
North	124	254	336	164	9	23	45	165	1,120
Yorkshire/Humberside	202	393	514	244	26	31	66	267	1,741
East Midlands	159	344	425	187	14	21	42	179	1,371
East Anglia	79	165	191	108	8	14	25	88	678
South East	734	1,468	1,760	861	132	147	243	857	6,203
Greater London	320	603	749	343	80	81	119	365	2,660
Rest of South East	414	865	1,011	518	52	66	124	492	3,544
South West	174	356	459	258	22	26	56	232	1,583
West Midlands	204	437	559	251	23	37	59	222	1,792
North West	257	503	684	337	35	54	104	361	2,336
England	1,933	3,921	4,929	2,410	270	352	639	2,371	16,824

Percentages

Region	Age and sex of head of household								All heads of household
	Male				Female				
	16-29	30-44	45-64	65 or over	16-29	30-44	45-59	60 or over	
North	11.1	22.7	30.0	14.7	0.8	2.0	4.0	14.8	100.0
Yorkshire/Humberside	11.6	22.6	29.5	14.0	1.5	1.8	3.8	15.3	100.0
East Midlands	11.6	25.1	31.0	13.6	1.0	1.6	3.0	13.1	100.0
East Anglia	11.7	24.3	28.1	15.9	1.3	2.0	3.7	13.0	100.0
South East	11.8	23.7	28.4	13.9	2.1	2.4	3.9	13.8	100.0
Greater London	12.0	22.7	28.2	12.9	3.0	3.0	4.5	13.7	100.0
Rest of South East	11.7	24.4	28.5	14.6	1.5	1.9	3.5	13.9	100.0
South West	11.0	22.5	29.0	16.3	1.4	1.7	3.5	14.6	100.0
West Midlands	11.4	24.4	31.2	14.0	1.3	2.0	3.3	12.4	100.0
North West	11.0	21.6	29.3	14.4	1.5	2.3	4.5	15.4	100.0
England	11.5	23.3	29.3	14.3	1.6	2.1	3.8	14.1	100.0

TABLE 50 Marital Status of Head of Household : Region

Region	Marital status					All heads of household
	Single	Married	Divorced	Widowed	Separated	
North	84	785	32	205	14	1,120
Yorkshire/Humberside	141	1,207	51	312	30	1,741
East Midlands	84	1,018	32	218	18	1,371
East Anglia	64	477	21	106	10	678
South East	702	4,230	213	952	107	6,203
Greater London	385	1,700	98	421	56	2,660
Rest of South East	317	2,530	115	531	51	3,544
South West	133	1,123	44	262	21	1,583
West Midlands	132	1,291	52	286	31	1,792
North West	193	1,577	76	451	39	2,336
England	1,533	11,708	522	2,793	269	16,824

Percentages

Region	Marital status					All heads of household
	Single	Married	Divorced	Widowed	Separated	
North	7.5	70.1	2.8	18.3	1.3	100.0
Yorkshire/Humberside	8.1	69.3	3.0	17.9	1.7	100.0
East Midlands	6.1	74.3	2.4	15.9	1.3	100.0
East Anglia	9.4	70.4	3.1	15.7	1.4	100.0
South East	11.3	68.2	3.4	15.3	1.7	100.0
Greater London	14.5	63.9	3.7	15.8	2.1	100.0
Rest of South East	8.9	71.4	3.3	15.0	1.4	100.0
South West	8.4	70.9	2.8	16.5	1.3	100.0
West Midlands	7.4	72.0	2.9	16.0	1.7	100.0
North West	8.2	67.5	3.2	19.3	1.7	100.0
England	9.1	69.6	3.1	16.6	1.6	100.0

TABLE 51   Length of Residence of Head of Household: Region

Thousands

Region	Length of residence (years)						All heads of household
	Under 1	1 but under 2	2 but under 3	3 but under 5	5 but under 10	10 or over	
North	117	95	98	104	206	501	1,120
Yorkshire/Humberside	160	129	149	168	333	802	1,741
East Midlands	133	95	126	127	262	629	1,371
East Anglia	76	56	64	66	130	286	678
South East	734	540	586	636	1,149	2,559	6,203
Greater London	330	222	238	277	453	1,140	2,660
Rest of South East	404	318	348	359	696	1,419	3,544
South West	186	131	132	146	310	678	1,583
West Midlands	174	132	145	185	325	832	1,792
North West	211	153	194	218	434	1,126	2,336
England	1,789	1,329	1,495	1,650	3,148	7,413	16,824

Percentages

Region	Length of residence (years)						All heads of household
	Under 1	1 but under 2	2 but under 3	3 but under 5	5 but under 10	10 or over	
North	10.4	8.5	8.8	9.3	18.4	44.7	100.0
Yorkshire/Humberside	9.2	7.4	8.6	9.7	19.1	46.1	100.0
East Midlands	9.7	6.9	9.2	9.3	19.1	45.9	100.0
East Anglia	11.3	8.3	9.5	9.7	19.1	42.1	100.0
South East	11.8	8.7	9.4	10.3	18.5	41.3	100.0
Greater London	12.4	8.3	8.9	10.4	17.0	42.9	100.0
Rest of South East	11.4	9.0	9.8	10.1	19.6	40.0	100.0
South West	11.7	8.3	8.3	9.2	19.6	42.8	100.0
West Midlands	9.7	7.3	8.1	10.3	18.1	46.4	100.0
North West	9.0	6.5	8.3	9.3	18.6	48.2	100.0
England	10.6	7.9	8.9	9.8	18.7	44.1	100.0

TABLE 52 Employment Status of Head of Household : Region

Thousands

Region	Employment status						All heads of household
	Employed		Unem-ployed	Wholly retired	House-wife	Other	
	Full time	Part time					
North	665	25	46	201	139	46	1,120
Yorkshire/Humberside	1,042	52	65	332	179	72	1,741
East Midlands	904	37	37	232	125	37	1,371
East Anglia	423	23	21	129	62	21	678
South East	3,994	222	183	1,080	544	182	6,203
Greater London	1,727	92	90	464	203	85	2,660
Rest of South East	2,267	130	93	616	341	97	3,544
South West	938	47	60	320	168	50	1,583
West Midlands	1,163	57	70	316	140	45	1,792
North West	1,373	78	104	460	217	103	2,336
England	10,500	541	586	3,068	1,574	555	16,824

Percentages

Region	Employment status						All heads of household
	Employed		Unem-ployed	Wholly retired	House-wife	Other	
	Full time	Part time					
North	59.3	2.2	4.2	17.9	12.4	4.1	100.0
Yorkshire/Humberside	59.8	3.0	3.8	19.0	10.3	4.1	100.0
East Midlands	65.9	2.7	2.7	16.9	9.1	2.7	100.0
East Anglia	62.4	3.3	3.0	19.0	9.1	3.2	100.0
South East	64.4	3.6	2.9	17.4	8.8	2.9	100.0
Greater London	64.9	3.4	3.4	17.4	7.6	3.2	100.0
Rest of South East	64.0	3.7	2.6	17.4	9.6	2.7	100.0
South West	59.2	3.0	3.8	20.2	10.6	3.2	100.0
West Midlands	64.9	3.2	3.9	17.6	7.8	2.6	100.0
North West	58.8	3.4	4.4	19.7	9.3	4.4	100.0
England	62.4	3.2	3.5	18.2	9.4	3.3	100.0

77

TABLE 53 Birthplace of Head of Household : Region

Thousands

| Region | Birthplace | | All heads of household |
	United Kingdom	Not in United Kingdom	
North	1,103	17	1,120
Yorkshire/Humberside	1,664	77	1,741
East Midlands	1,317	54	1,371
East Anglia	639	39	678
South East	5,478	725	6,203
Greater London	2,165	495	2,660
Rest of South East	3,313	230	3,544
South West	1,521	62	1,583
West Midlands	1,660	132	1,792
North West	2,221	115	2,336
England	15,604	1,220	16,824

Percentages

| Region | Birthplace | | All heads of household |
	United Kingdom	Not in United Kingdom	
North	98.5	1.5	100.0
Yorkshire/Humberside	95.6	4.4	100.0
East Midlands	96.0	4.0	100.0
East Anglia	94.3	5.7	100.0
South East	88.3	11.7	100.0
Greater London	81.4	18.6	100.0
Rest of South East	93.5	6.5	100.0
South West	96.1	3.9	100.0
West Midlands	92.6	7.4	100.0
North West	95.1	4.9	100.0
England	92.7	7.3	100.0

Table 5.4 Age and Sex of Private Household Population : Region

Thousands

Region	Age of males					All males
	0-14	15-29	30-44	45-64	65 or over	
North	352	331	281	352	173	1,489
Yorkshire/Humberside	559	523	430	542	258	2,312
East Midlands	466	406	377	443	195	1,886
East Anglia	207	199	178	200	116	899
South East	1,842	1,884	1,610	1,833	918	8,089
Greater London	741	855	679	785	368	3,429
Rest of South East	1,101	1,029	931	1,048	550	4,660
South West	502	418	392	480	276	2,068
West Midlands	618	538	482	587	266	2,491
North West	740	708	559	726	360	3,093
England	5,285	5,008	4,309	5,163	2,562	22,327

Thousands

Region	Age of females					All females
	0-14	15-29	30-44	45-59	60 or over	
North	319	316	287	296	339	1,556
Yorkshire/Humberside	533	507	430	428	541	2,439
East Midlands	421	397	382	340	395	1,935
East Anglia	197	186	175	155	208	922
South East	1,739	1,855	1,606	1,492	1,877	8,569
Greater London	715	852	670	637	773	3,648
Rest of South East	1,024	1,003	936	855	1,104	4,921
South West	435	441	386	396	531	2,189
West Midlands	546	536	475	447	510	2,516
North West	718	680	578	596	753	3,326
England	4,908	4,920	4,319	4,150	5,154	23,452

TABLE 55 Age of Private Household Population : Region

Thousands

Region	Age of private household population					All persons
	0-14	15-29	30-44	45-59/64*	60/65 or over*	
North	670	647	568	648	512	3,045
Yorkshire/Humberside	1,092	1,030	860	970	799	4,751
East Midlands	886	804	759	782	590	3,821
East Anglia	404	385	353	356	324	1,821
South East	3,581	3,740	3,216	3,326	2,795	16,658
Greater London	1,456	1,708	1,349	1,423	1,141	7,077
Rest of South East	2,125	2,032	1,867	1,903	1,654	9,582
South West	937	859	778	877	807	4,257
West Midlands	1,164	1,075	958	1,034	776	5,007
North West	1,458	1,388	1,137	1,322	1,113	6,418
England	10,193	9,928	8,629	9,313	7,716	45,779

Percentages

Region	Age of private household population					All persons
	0-14	15-29	30-44	45-59/64*	60/65 or over*	
North	22.1	21.3	18.6	21.3	16.8	100.0
Yorkshire/Humberside	23.0	21.7	18.1	20.4	16.8	100.0
East Midlands	23.2	21.0	19.9	20.5	15.4	100.0
East Anglia	22.2	21.1	19.4	19.5	17.8	100.0
South East	21.5	22.4	19.3	20.0	16.8	100.0
Greater London	20.6	24.1	19.1	20.1	16.1	100.0
Rest of South East	22.2	21.2	19.5	19.8	17.2	100.0
South West	22.0	20.2	18.3	20.6	19.0	100.0
West Midlands	23.2	21.5	19.1	20.6	15.5	100.0
North West	22.7	21.6	17.7	20.6	17.3	100.0
England	22.2	21.6	18.8	20.4	16.9	100.0

* 59 for females, 64 for males.

TABLE 56 Length of Residence : Region

Region	Length of residence (years)						All persons
	Under 1	1 but under 2	2 but under 3	3 but under 5	5 but under 10	10 or over	
North	368	277	297	317	628	1,160	3,045
Yorkshire/Humberside	502	389	461	512	1,027	1,858	4,751
East Midlands	431	290	378	421	817	1,485	3,821
East Anglia	235	168	175	196	388	659	1,821
South East	2,203	1,560	1,669	1,879	3,428	5,919	16,658
Greater London	974	625	680	816	1,377	2,604	7,077
Rest of South East	1,229	935	989	1,063	2,051	3,315	9,582
South West	598	386	393	420	907	1,553	4,257
West Midlands	557	409	446	585	1,032	1,978	5,007
North West	664	468	604	694	1,372	2,616	6,418
England	5,556	3,948	4,423	5,024	9,599	17,228	45,779

Region	Length of residence (years)						All persons
	Under 1	1 but under 2	2 but under 3	3 but under 5	5 but under 10	10 or over	
North	12.1	9.1	9.7	10.4	20.6	38.1	100.0
Yorkshire/Humberside	10.6	8.2	9.7	10.8	21.6	39.1	100.0
East Midlands	11.3	7.6	9.9	11.0	21.4	38.9	100.0
East Anglia	12.9	9.2	9.6	10.8	21.3	36.2	100.0
South East	13.2	9.4	10.0	11.3	20.6	35.5	100.0
Greater London	13.8	8.8	9.6	11.5	19.5	36.8	100.0
Rest of South East	12.8	9.8	10.3	11.1	21.4	34.6	100.0
South West	14.0	9.1	9.2	9.9	21.3	36.5	100.0
West Midlands	11.1	8.2	8.9	11.7	20.6	39.5	100.0
North West	10.3	7.3	9.4	10.8	21.4	40.8	100.0
England	12.1	8.6	9.7	11.0	21.0	37.6	100.0

TABLE 57 Employment Status : Region

Region	Employment status						All persons aged 16 or over
	Employed						
	Full time	Part time	Unem-ployed	Retired	House-wife	Other	
North	1,093	218	103	229	553	125	2,321
Yorkshire/Humberside	1,696	382	118	407	768	210	3,581
East Midlands	1,476	307	72	281	599	129	2,864
East Anglia	663	163	42	158	297	65	1,388
South East	6,481	1,329	335	1,352	2,579	719	12,795
Greater London	2,926	525	159	600	959	338	5,507
Rest of South East	3,555	804	176	752	1,620	381	7,288
South West	1,469	330	112	386	791	170	3,258
West Midlands	1,909	397	145	391	729	184	3,755
North West	2,346	479	212	598	918	304	4,857
England	17,134	3,604	1,139	3,802	7,234	1,905	34,818

Region	Employment status						All persons aged 16 or over
	Employed						
	Full time	Part time	Unem-ployed	Retired	House-wife	Other	
North	47.1	9.4	4.5	9.9	23.8	5.4	100.0
Yorkshire/Humberside	47.3	10.7	3.3	11.4	21.5	5.9	100.0
East Midlands	51.5	10.7	2.5	9.8	20.9	4.4	100.0
East Anglia	47.8	11.7	3.1	11.4	21.4	4.7	100.0
South East	50.7	10.4	2.6	10.6	20.2	5.6	100.0
Greater London	53.1	9.5	2.9	10.9	17.4	6.2	100.0
Rest of South East	48.8	11.0	2.4	10.3	22.2	5.2	100.0
South West	45.1	10.1	3.4	11.8	24.3	5.2	100.0
West Midlands	50.9	10.6	3.9	10.4	19.4	4.9	100.0
North West	48.3	9.9	4.4	12.3	18.9	6.3	100.0
England	49.2	10.4	3.3	10.9	20.8	5.5	100.0

TABLE 58 Economically Active Persons: Socio-economic group : Region

Thousands

Region	Socio-economic group						All economically active persons
	Profl/ emplr/ mngr	Other non- manual	Skilled manual	Semi- skilled manual	Un- skilled manual	Other	
North	195	415	385	263	113	42	1,414
Yorkshire/Humberside	276	602	666	428	158	65	2,196
East Midlands	265	527	571	343	99	52	1,855
East Anglia	132	258	221	167	54	35	868
South East	1,512	2,832	1,868	1,269	415	249	8,145
Greater London	615	1,344	801	544	195	111	3,610
Rest of South East	897	1,488	1,067	725	220	138	4,535
South West	300	565	500	354	127	64	1,911
West Midlands	318	665	748	495	162	63	2,451
North West	392	907	813	596	230	99	3,038
England	3,390	6,774	5,773	3,914	1,358	668	21,877

Percentages

Region	Socio-economic group						All economically active persons
	Profl/ emplr/ mngr	Other non- manual	Skilled manual	Semi- skilled manual	Un- skilled manual	Other	
North	13.8	29.4	27.2	18.6	8.0	3.0	100.0
Yorkshire/Humberside	12.6	27.4	30.3	19.5	7.2	3.0	100.0
East Midlands	14.3	28.4	30.8	18.5	5.3	2.8	100.0
East Anglia	15.2	29.8	25.5	19.2	6.3	4.1	100.0
South East	18.6	34.8	22.9	15.6	5.1	3.1	100.0
Greater London	17.0	37.2	22.2	15.1	5.4	3.1	100.0
Rest of South East	19.8	32.8	23.5	16.0	4.9	3.0	100.0
South West	15.7	29.6	26.2	18.5	6.7	3.3	100.0
West Midlands	13.0	27.1	30.5	20.2	6.6	2.6	100.0
North West	12.9	29.9	26.8	19.6	7.6	3.2	100.0
England	15.5	31.0	26.4	17.9	6.2	3.1	100.0

TABLE 59 Birthplace : Region

Region	Birthplace		All persons
	United Kingdom	Not in United Kingdom	
North	3,000	46	3,045
Yorkshire/Humberside	4,564	187	4,751
East Midlands	3,685	136	3,821
East Anglia	1,712	109	1,821
South East	14,919	1,740	16,658
Greater London	5,903	1,174	7,077
Rest of South East	9,016	566	9,582
South West	4,095	162	4,257
West Midlands	4,698	309	5,007
North West	6,153	266	6,418
England	42,827	2,952	45,779

Region	Birthplace		All persons
	United Kingdom	Not in United Kingdom	
North	98.5	1.5	100.0
Yorkshire/Humberside	96.1	3.9	100.0
East Midlands	96.4	3.6	100.0
East Anglia	94.0	6.0	100.0
South East	89.6	10.4	100.0
Greater London	83.4	16.6	100.0
Rest of South East	94.1	5.9	100.0
South West	96.2	3.8	100.0
West Midlands	93.8	6.2	100.0
North West	95.9	4.1	100.0
England	93.6	6.4	100.0

TABLE 60 Ethnic Group : Region

Thousands

Region	Ethnic group					All persons
	White	West Indian	African	Indian/ Pakistani/ Bangladeshi	Other	
North	3,023	-	-	5	17	3,045
Yorkshire/Humberside	4,592	28	2	85	44	4,751
East Midlands	3,723	33	1	28	36	3,821
East Anglia	1,769	10	5	16	22	1,821
South East	15,443	324	59	381	450	16,658
Greater London	6,097	281	52	308	338	7,077
Rest of South East	9,346	43	7	73	112	9,582
South West	4,208	12	3	5	30	4,257
West Midlands	4,665	93	3	175	71	5,007
North West	6,244	19	7	86	63	6,418
England	43,670	518	80	780	732	45,779

Percentages

Region	Ethnic group					All persons
	White	West Indian	African	Indian/ Parkistani/ Bangladeshi	Other	
North	99.3	-	-	0.2	0.6	100.0
Yorkshire/Humberside	96.7	0.6	-	1.8	0.9	100.0
East Midlands	97.4	0.9	-	0.7	0.9	100.0
East Anglia	97.1	0.5	0.3	0.9	1.2	100.0
South East	92.7	1.9	0.4	2.3	2.7	100.0
Greater London	86.2	4.0	0.7	4.4	4.8	100.0
Rest of South East	97.5	0.5	0.1	0.8	1.2	100.0
South West	98.8	0.3	0.1	0.1	0.7	100.0
West Midlands	93.2	1.9	0.1	3.4	1.4	100.0
North West	97.3	0.3	0.1	1.4	1.0	100.0
England	95.4	1.1	0.2	1.8	1.6	100.0

85

TABLE 61 Type of Family: Region

Region	Main married couple	Main lone parent	One person HoH	Concealed married couple	Concealed lone parent	One person not HoH	All families
North	784	73	263	7	5	70	1,203
Yorkshire/Humberside	1,200	107	434	14	15	122	1,892
East Midlands	1,015	78	278	10	6	75	1,462
East Anglia	476	38	164	4	2	49	734
South East	4,207	385	1,611	56	34	584	6,877
Greater London	1,688	199	773	31	20	310	3,020
Rest of South East	2,520	186	838	25	14	274	3,857
South West	1,120	88	375	16	10	132	1,742
West Midlands	1,285	118	389	18	14	110	1,933
North West	1,575	176	585	24	19	171	2,549
England	11,663	1,063	4,098	149	104	1,314	18,392

Percentages

Region	Main married couple	Main lone parent	One person HoH	Concealed married couple	Concealed lone parent	One person not HoH	All families
North	65.2	6.1	21.9	0.6	0.5	5.8	100.0
Yorkshire/Humberside	63.4	5.7	22.9	0.7	0.8	6.5	100.0
East Midlands	69.5	5.3	19.0	0.7	0.4	5.2	100.0
East Anglia	64.9	5.2	22.3	0.6	0.3	6.7	100.0
South East	61.2	5.6	23.4	0.8	0.5	8.5	100.0
Greater London	55.9	6.6	25.6	1.0	0.7	10.3	100.0
Rest of South East	65.3	4.8	21.7	0.6	0.4	7.1	100.0
South West	64.3	5.0	21.5	0.9	0.6	7.6	100.0
West Midlands	66.4	6.1	20.1	0.9	0.7	5.7	100.0
North West	61.8	6.9	22.9	0.9	0.7	6.7	100.0
England	63.4	5.8	22.3	0.8	0.6	7.1	100.0

LONDON   BOROUGH   AND   DISTRICT   TABLES

TABLE 62A Type of Accommodation: London Borough

London Borough	Type of accommodation						All household spaces
	Detached house	Semi-detached house	Terraced house	Purpose-built flat or maisonette	Other flat or rooms	Other	
City of London	-	-	0.1	2.5	0.1	0.3	2.9
Barking	0.4	4.4	39.1	12.5	1.4	0.5	58.5
Barnet	13.6	38.6	20.8	26.1	16.1	1.1	116.2
Bexley	4.8	40.0	20.0	12.1	1.7	1.6	80.1
Brent	3.3	25.3	18.8	22.7	28.9	1.6	100.7
Bromley	20.0	36.1	27.0	18.7	11.3	1.8	114.9
Camden	1.3	2.1	7.6	35.4	39.3	1.6	87.3
Croydon	14.1	31.1	39.9	18.8	16.5	1.6	122.0
Ealing	4.0	21.5	35.4	25.7	21.1	0.9	108.6
Enfield	4.5	24.7	41.8	20.0	8.2	1.3	100.6
Greenwich	2.1	15.8	28.0	27.1	8.7	0.8	82.4
Hackney	0.4	1.4	12.8	42.6	20.5	1.5	79.3
Hammersmith	0.3	1.5	15.5	23.0	32.3	1.0	73.7
Haringey	1.3	4.1	34.6	19.5	27.6	1.0	88.0
Harrow	8.1	31.0	17.2	12.3	6.2	0.4	75.3
Havering	9.3	37.3	26.5	12.1	2.0	1.0	88.2
Hillingdon	11.9	32.9	21.1	15.5	3.4	0.8	85.6
Hounslow	2.3	25.4	19.9	18.1	10.0	1.1	76.7
Islington	0.3	0.8	11.6	33.1	27.3	1.6	74.8
Kensington & Chelsea	0.6	1.0	8.4	27.7	40.0	1.3	78.8
Kingston-upon-Thames	6.4	19.6	10.1	11.7	6.8	0.8	55.4
Lambeth	1.6	5.3	19.1	46.3	39.8	1.2	113.3
Lewisham	2.1	9.4	33.7	28.9	24.3	1.7	100.1
Merton	2.4	10.2	32.5	13.4	8.0	1.4	67.9
Newham	0.5	1.7	44.4	23.4	12.2	1.7	83.9
Redbridge	2.8	18.8	42.9	12.0	10.6	1.1	88.3
Richmond	5.3	17.3	19.8	16.0	13.0	1.0	72.4
Southwark	1.4	2.8	14.3	53.7	19.3	1.5	92.8
Sutton	7.0	20.2	17.8	14.8	4.3	0.5	64.5
Tower Hamlets	0.6	0.3	5.5	46.5	4.6	0.9	58.4
Waltham Forest	1.3	9.7	44.6	20.0	12.4	1.5	89.5
Wandsworth	1.6	6.5	29.2	42.4	30.9	1.9	112.4
Westminster	0.8	0.8	8.3	52.2	41.8	1.8	105.7
Greater London	136.4	497.6	768.3	806.8	550.6	39.8	2799.2

TABLE 62B Type of Accommodation: London Borough

Percentages

London Borough	Type of accommodation						All household spaces
	Detached house	Semi-detached house	Terraced house	Purpose-built flat or maisonette	Other flat or rooms	Other	
City of London	-	0.4	2.1	84.5	2.1	10.7	100.0
Barking	0.8	7.6	66.9	21.4	2.5	0.9	100.0
Barnet	11.7	33.2	17.9	22.5	13.9	1.0	100.0
Bexley	5.9	49.9	24.9	15.2	2.1	2.0	100.0
Brent	3.3	25.1	18.7	22.6	28.7	1.6	100.0
Bromley	17.4	31.4	23.5	16.3	9.8	1.5	100.0
Camden	1.5	2.4	8.7	40.6	45.0	1.8	100.0
Croydon	11.6	25.5	32.7	15.4	13.5	1.3	100.0
Ealing	3.7	19.8	32.6	23.7	19.5	0.8	100.0
Enfield	4.5	24.6	41.6	19.9	8.2	1.3	100.0
Greenwich	2.5	19.2	33.9	32.8	10.6	1.0	100.0
Hackney	0.5	1.8	16.2	53.8	25.9	1.9	100.0
Hammersmith	0.4	2.1	21.0	31.2	43.8	1.4	100.0
Haringey	1.4	4.7	39.3	22.1	31.3	1.1	100.0
Harrow	10.7	41.2	22.9	16.3	8.2	0.6	100.0
Havering	10.6	42.3	30.1	13.7	2.3	1.1	100.0
Hillingdon	13.8	38.4	24.7	18.1	4.0	0.9	100.0
Hounslow	3.0	33.1	25.9	23.6	13.0	1.4	100.0
Islington	0.4	1.0	15.6	44.3	36.5	2.2	100.0
Kensington & Chelsea	0.7	1.2	10.6	35.1	50.7	1.6	100.0
Kingston-upon-Thames	11.6	35.4	18.2	21.1	12.3	1.4	100.0
Lambeth	1.4	4.7	16.9	40.9	35.1	1.0	100.0
Lewisham	2.1	9.3	33.7	28.9	24.3	1.7	100.0
Merton	3.6	14.9	47.8	19.7	11.8	2.1	100.0
Newham	0.6	2.1	52.9	28.0	14.5	2.0	100.0
Redbridge	3.2	21.3	48.6	13.6	12.0	1.3	100.0
Richmond	7.4	23.9	27.3	22.1	17.9	1.4	100.0
Southwark	1.6	3.0	15.4	57.8	20.7	1.6	100.0
Sutton	10.8	31.4	27.5	22.9	6.6	0.7	100.0
Tower Hamlets	1.0	0.5	9.4	79.8	7.8	1.5	100.0
Waltham Forest	1.4	10.9	49.8	22.4	13.9	1.6	100.0
Wandsworth	1.4	5.8	26.0	37.7	27.5	1.6	100.0
Westminster	0.8	0.8	7.9	49.3	39.6	1.7	100.0
Greater London	4.9	17.8	27.4	29.1	19.5	1.4	100.0

TABLE 63A Lowest Floor of Accommodation : London Borough

Thousands

London borough	Lowest floor of accommodation						All households
	Ground floor or lower	1st floor	2nd floor	3rd floor	4th-9th floor	10th floor or higher	
City of London	0.2	0.4	0.2	0.3	1.1	0.2	2.5
Barking	47.7	3.7	2.7	0.4	1.6	0.9	57.0
Barnet	86.8	16.9	5.6	1.2	1.3	0.1	111.9
Bexley	67.8	6.7	1.7	0.5	1.1	0.5	78.2
Brent	65.6	18.9	6.1	1.7	1.7	1.0	95.1
Bromley	93.5	12.0	4.3	0.6	0.6	0.1	111.2
Camden	32.0	18.7	14.8	6.3	6.8	1.1	79.7
Croydon	98.3	12.7	4.8	1.0	1.3	0.1	118.2
Ealing	79.4	15.2	5.2	1.5	1.6	0.4	103.4
Enfield	79.8	10.1	3.5	0.9	1.7	1.4	97.4
Greenwich	57.2	11.0	5.0	2.6	3.2	0.6	79.6
Hackney	33.1	14.4	9.7	6.4	6.9	2.2	72.6
Hammersmith	34.8	15.8	7.4	4.2	3.9	0.7	66.7
Haringey	54.8	16.7	7.3	1.9	1.7	0.6	83.0
Harrow	63.1	7.7	2.2	0.2	0.1	-	73.2
Havering	77.5	5.3	1.9	0.2	0.7	0.3	86.0
Hillingdon	72.0	8.6	2.2	0.1	0.2	0.1	83.2
Hounslow	56.1	9.9	4.3	1.3	1.2	0.8	73.6
Islington	29.7	15.5	11.1	4.4	4.9	1.1	66.7
Kensington & Chelsea	33.4	13.9	9.1	7.7	5.7	0.7	70.5
Kingston-upon-Thames	42.6	6.9	2.8	0.7	0.5	0.1	53.6
Lambeth	50.9	27.8	13.1	6.0	5.9	0.9	104.8
Lewisham	62.9	17.0	7.7	2.3	2.8	0.9	93.7
Merton	53.1	8.3	2.7	0.8	0.7	-	65.5
Newham	55.2	11.5	6.2	1.3	3.0	2.3	79.6
Redbridge	72.1	8.7	3.2	0.5	0.5	0.1	85.1
Richmond	53.4	10.0	3.9	1.3	0.5	0.1	69.1
Southwark	38.6	17.4	13.1	6.0	8.8	2.0	85.9
Sutton	51.7	7.7	2.5	0.7	0.7	0.1	63.3
Tower Hamlets	19.0	9.3	11.6	5.1	7.6	2.4	55.1
Waltham Forest	66.0	12.4	3.1	1.1	1.9	1.3	85.9
Wandsworth	59.2	23.8	9.3	4.8	7.0	1.5	105.8
Westminster	30.5	18.2	15.2	11.8	14.1	1.2	91.0
Greater London	1818.3	413.0	203.6	85.9	101.2	26.1	2648.2

90

TABLE 63B Lowest Floor of Accommodation : London Borough

Percentages

London borough	Lowest floor of accommodation						All households
	Ground floor or lower	1st floor	2nd floor	3rd floor	4th-9th floor	10th floor or higher	
City of London	8.5	14.4	9.2	13.7	44.9	9.2	100.0
Barking	83.7	6.6	4.7	0.7	2.8	1.6	100.0
Barnet	77.7	15.1	5.0	1.0	1.2	0.1	100.0
Bexley	86.6	8.5	2.1	0.7	1.4	0.6	100.0
Brent	69.0	19.9	6.4	1.8	1.8	1.1	100.0
Bromley	83.1	10.8	3.9	0.6	0.5	0.1	100.0
Camden	40.1	23.5	18.6	8.0	8.5	1.4	100.0
Croydon	83.1	10.7	4.1	0.8	1.1	0.1	100.0
Ealing	76.9	14.7	5.1	1.4	1.5	0.4	100.0
Enfield	81.9	10.4	3.6	0.9	1.7	1.4	100.0
Greenwich	71.9	13.8	6.3	3.2	4.1	0.7	100.0
Hackney	45.6	19.8	13.4	8.8	9.5	3.0	100.0
Hammersmith	52.2	23.6	11.1	6.2	5.8	1.1	100.0
Haringey	66.1	20.1	8.8	2.3	2.0	0.7	100.0
Harrow	86.2	10.5	3.0	0.3	0.1	-	100.0
Havering	90.1	6.2	2.2	0.3	0.8	0.4	100.0
Hillingdon	86.4	10.4	2.6	0.1	0.3	0.1	100.0
Hounslow	76.2	13.4	5.8	1.7	1.7	1.1	100.0
Islington	44.5	23.2	16.6	6.6	7.4	1.6	100.0
Kensington & Chelsea	47.3	19.8	12.8	10.9	8.1	1.0	100.0
Kingston-upon-Thames	79.5	12.8	5.3	1.2	1.0	0.2	100.0
Lambeth	48.6	26.5	12.5	5.7	5.7	0.9	100.0
Lewisham	67.1	18.1	8.2	2.5	3.0	1.0	100.0
Merton	81.0	12.6	4.1	1.1	1.1	-	100.0
Newham	69.4	14.5	7.8	1.7	3.8	2.9	100.0
Redbridge	84.7	10.2	3.8	0.5	0.6	0.2	100.0
Richmond	77.2	14.5	5.7	1.9	0.7	0.1	100.0
Southwark	44.9	20.2	15.2	7.0	10.2	2.4	100.0
Sutton	81.6	12.1	3.9	1.2	1.1	0.1	100.0
Tower Hamlets	34.5	16.8	21.1	9.3	13.9	4.4	100.0
Waltham Forest	76.9	14.4	3.7	1.3	2.2	1.6	100.0
Wandsworth	56.0	22.5	8.8	4.6	6.7	1.4	100.0
Westminster	33.5	20.0	16.7	13.0	15.5	1.3	100.0
Greater London	68.6	15.6	7.7	3.2	3.8	1.0	100.0

TABLE 64A Household size : London Borough

London borough	Number of people in household						All households
	1	2	3	4	5	6 or more	
City of London	1.3	0.7	0.3	0.2	-	-	2.5
Barking	10.7	19.9	10.4	9.5	4.2	2.3	57.0
Barnet	22.2	36.4	20.5	19.3	8.7	4.7	111.9
Bexley	12.2	27.7	13.9	16.1	6.0	2.4	78.2
Brent	21.2	28.8	15.8	15.0	8.3	6.1	95.1
Bromley	21.5	37.7	20.0	20.8	8.0	3.3	111.2
Camden	28.4	26.5	10.7	8.2	4.0	2.0	79.7
Croydon	23.9	38.4	20.2	21.0	9.3	5.4	118.2
Ealing	20.8	34.7	18.4	16.1	7.3	6.1	103.4
Enfield	19.5	31.9	16.5	18.1	7.5	3.8	97.4
Greenwich	17.1	26.1	13.4	13.0	6.1	4.0	79.6
Hackney	18.7	22.5	11.6	9.4	5.8	4.5	72.6
Hammersmith	21.7	20.8	9.9	7.7	3.8	2.8	66.7
Haringey	20.1	27.0	13.2	12.5	6.0	4.2	83.0
Harrow	14.2	24.7	12.8	13.2	5.6	2.6	73.2
Havering	12.2	28.6	16.4	19.6	6.6	2.7	86.0
Hillingdon	14.3	29.0	14.7	15.8	6.5	2.9	83.2
Hounslow	15.6	24.5	13.0	12.1	5.5	3.0	73.6
Islington	20.3	19.7	10.7	9.0	4.1	3.0	66.7
Kensington & Chelsea	28.9	21.3	8.5	6.6	3.0	2.2	70.5
Kingston-upon-Thames	12.9	18.7	8.5	8.7	3.3	1.5	53.6
Lambeth	30.3	33.1	15.9	13.4	6.3	5.8	104.8
Lewisham	21.3	29.5	17.4	14.1	6.7	4.6	93.7
Merton	14.1	23.2	11.1	10.7	4.2	2.2	65.5
Newham	17.8	25.0	12.9	12.2	5.8	5.9	79.6
Redbridge	16.4	28.6	15.0	15.2	6.3	3.7	85.1
Richmond	18.5	24.9	10.5	9.9	3.8	1.5	69.1
Southwark	22.7	28.1	14.6	11.1	6.1	3.3	85.9
Sutton	12.7	22.5	10.8	11.2	4.3	1.8	63.3
Tower Hamlets	13.7	17.7	9.5	7.6	3.5	3.1	55.1
Waltham Forest	17.9	29.8	15.2	13.7	5.4	3.9	85.9
Wandsworth	25.7	35.3	15.9	16.5	7.7	4.7	105.8
Westminster	37.6	28.2	11.8	7.6	3.3	2.5	91.0
Greater London	626.2	871.5	439.9	415.0	183.0	112.5	2648.2

TABLE 64B Household size : London Borough

| London borough | Number of people in household | | | | | | All households |
	1	2	3	4	5	6 or more	
City of London	52.7	27.4	11.5	6.9	0.8	0.7	100.0
Barking	18.7	35.0	18.3	16.7	7.3	3.9	100.0
Barnet	19.9	32.6	18.3	17.3	7.8	4.2	100.0
Bexley	15.5	35.4	17.8	20.5	7.6	3.0	100.0
Brent	22.2	30.2	16.6	15.7	8.7	6.4	100.0
Bromley	19.3	33.9	18.0	18.7	7.2	2.9	100.0
Camden	35.6	33.2	13.4	10.3	5.0	2.5	100.0
Croydon	20.2	32.5	17.1	17.8	7.9	4.6	100.0
Ealing	20.1	33.6	17.8	15.5	7.0	5.9	100.0
Enfield	20.1	32.8	16.9	18.6	7.7	3.9	100.0
Greenwich	21.5	32.8	16.8	16.3	7.7	5.0	100.0
Hackney	25.8	31.0	16.0	12.9	8.0	6.2	100.0
Hammersmith	32.6	31.2	14.9	11.6	5.7	4.1	100.0
Haringey	24.2	32.5	15.9	15.1	7.2	5.0	100.0
Harrow	19.4	33.8	17.5	18.1	7.6	3.6	100.0
Havering	14.2	33.3	19.1	22.7	7.6	3.0	100.0
Hillingdon	17.2	34.9	17.6	19.0	7.8	3.5	100.0
Hounslow	21.2	33.2	17.7	16.4	7.4	4.0	100.0
Islington	30.4	29.6	16.0	13.5	6.1	4.4	100.0
Kensington & Chelsea	40.9	30.3	12.0	9.4	4.3	3.1	100.0
Kingston-upon-Thames	24.1	34.9	15.9	16.2	6.2	2.8	100.0
Lambeth	28.9	31.6	15.2	12.8	6.0	5.5	100.0
Lewisham	22.7	31.5	18.6	15.1	7.1	5.0	100.0
Merton	21.5	35.4	16.9	16.4	6.5	3.4	100.0
Newham	22.3	31.4	16.2	15.3	7.3	7.5	100.0
Redbridge	19.3	33.5	17.6	17.8	7.4	4.3	100.0
Richmond	26.7	36.0	15.2	14.4	5.5	2.2	100.0
Southwark	26.5	32.7	17.0	12.9	7.1	3.9	100.0
Sutton	20.0	35.5	17.1	17.7	6.9	2.9	100.0
Tower Hamlets	24.8	32.1	17.3	13.7	6.4	5.7	100.0
Waltham Forest	20.9	34.7	17.7	15.9	6.3	4.5	100.0
Wandsworth	24.3	33.4	15.0	15.6	7.2	4.5	100.0
Westminster	41.3	30.9	12.9	8.3	3.7	2.8	100.0
Greater London	23.6	32.9	16.6	15.7	6.9	4.2	100.0

TABLE 65A Type of Household : London Borough

London Borough	Married couple household	Lone parent household	One person aged under 60	One person aged 60 or over	Other household	All households
City of London	0.9	0.1	1.2	0.1	0.1	2.5
Barking	40.7	4.6	2.4	8.2	1.0	57.0
Barnet	75.7	8.1	9.4	12.8	5.8	111.9
Bexley	59.2	4.8	3.2	9.0	2.1	78.2
Brent	59.2	8.2	10.9	10.3	6.5	95.1
Bromley	78.1	7.2	7.6	13.9	4.4	111.2
Camden	36.1	5.9	15.3	13.0	9.4	79.7
Croydon	82.3	7.8	9.2	14.7	4.2	118.2
Ealing	68.0	7.9	9.1	11.7	6.7	103.4
Enfield	68.1	5.8	6.1	13.5	3.9	97.4
Greenwich	54.1	6.1	5.0	12.0	2.3	79.6
Hackney	40.7	8.7	8.2	10.6	4.5	72.6
Hammersmith	32.0	6.2	10.6	11.1	6.8	66.7
Haringey	51.3	6.4	9.6	10.5	5.2	83.0
Harrow	51.2	4.6	5.3	8.9	3.3	73.2
Havering	66.8	4.9	3.4	8.8	2.2	86.0
Hillingdon	60.8	5.5	4.6	9.7	2.6	83.2
Hounslow	48.3	5.5	6.2	9.4	4.2	73.6
Islington	34.7	6.4	9.5	10.8	5.3	66.7
Kensington & Chelsea	26.8	4.7	19.2	9.7	10.2	70.5
Kingston-upon-Thames	35.2	3.2	5.2	7.7	2.3	53.6
Lambeth	56.1	10.8	15.3	15.0	7.6	104.8
Lewisham	58.7	9.1	8.1	13.2	4.6	93.7
Merton	43.7	4.3	5.2	8.9	3.4	65.5
Newham	52.3	6.3	5.9	11.9	3.2	79.6
Redbridge	59.6	5.5	6.2	10.2	3.6	85.1
Richmond	41.5	4.7	7.2	11.2	4.5	69.1
Southwark	49.9	9.2	7.7	15.1	4.1	85.9
Sutton	44.2	4.4	4.6	8.1	2.1	63.3
Tower Hamlets	32.1	5.8	5.0	8.7	3.6	55.1
Waltham Forest	59.3	5.6	5.7	12.2	3.0	85.9
Wandsworth	64.0	8.3	10.6	15.0	7.9	105.8
Westminster	38.4	6.0	20.3	17.3	9.0	91.0
Greater London	1670.1	202.5	262.9	363.3	149.4	2648.2

TABLE 65B Type of Household : London Borough

London Borough	Married couple household	Lone parent household	One person aged under 60	One person aged 60 or over	Other household	All households
City of London	37.6	4.4	49.2	3.5	5.4	100.0
Barking	71.5	8.0	4.3	14.4	1.8	100.0
Barnet	67.7	7.3	8.4	11.5	5.2	100.0
Bexley	75.7	6.2	4.1	11.5	2.6	100.0
Brent	62.2	8.7	11.4	10.8	6.9	100.0
Bromley	70.2	6.5	6.8	12.5	4.0	100.0
Camden	45.3	7.4	19.2	16.3	11.8	100.0
Croydon	69.6	6.6	7.8	12.4	3.5	100.0
Ealing	65.8	7.6	8.8	11.3	6.5	100.0
Enfield	69.9	6.0	6.2	13.9	4.0	100.0
Greenwich	68.0	7.6	6.3	15.1	2.9	100.0
Hackney	56.0	11.9	11.3	14.5	6.2	100.0
Hammersmith	47.9	9.3	15.8	16.7	10.2	100.0
Haringey	61.7	7.8	11.6	12.6	6.3	100.0
Harrow	70.0	6.2	7.2	12.2	4.4	100.0
Havering	77.6	5.7	3.9	10.2	2.5	100.0
Hillingdon	73.0	6.6	5.6	11.6	3.1	100.0
Hounslow	65.6	7.4	8.4	12.8	5.8	100.0
Islington	51.9	9.6	14.2	16.2	8.0	100.0
Kensington & Chelsea	38.1	6.6	27.2	13.7	14.4	100.0
Kingston-upon-Thames	65.7	5.9	9.7	14.3	4.3	100.0
Lambeth	53.5	10.3	14.6	14.3	7.3	100.0
Lewisham	62.6	9.7	8.6	14.1	5.0	100.0
Merton	66.7	6.6	7.9	13.6	5.2	100.0
Newham	65.7	7.9	7.4	14.9	4.1	100.0
Redbridge	70.0	6.5	7.3	12.0	4.2	100.0
Richmond	60.1	6.7	10.5	16.3	6.5	100.0
Southwark	58.1	10.7	8.9	17.5	4.8	100.0
Sutton	69.8	6.9	7.2	12.8	3.3	100.0
Tower Hamlets	58.2	10.5	9.0	15.8	6.5	100.0
Waltham Forest	69.0	6.6	6.7	14.2	3.5	100.0
Wandsworth	60.5	7.9	10.0	14.2	7.4	100.0
Westminster	42.1	6.6	22.3	19.0	9.9	100.0
Greater London	63.1	7.6	9.9	13.7	5.6	100.0

TABLE 66A Type of Household: London Borough

Thousands

London Borough	One person household	Small adult household	Small family	Large family	Large adult household	Older small household	All households
City of London	1.3	0.5	0.2	-	0.3	0.2	2.5
Barking	10.7	8.7	10.7	4.8	11.4	10.7	57.0
Barnet	22.2	16.1	19.9	9.7	24.7	19.2	111.9
Bexley	12.2	13.4	17.6	6.7	14.6	13.8	78.2
Brent	21.2	13.7	16.1	10.2	20.3	13.7	95.1
Bromley	21.5	19.3	22.6	8.6	21.6	17.7	111.2
Camden	28.4	15.7	10.1	4.3	11.7	9.6	79.7
Croydon	23.9	19.8	23.7	11.6	21.6	17.6	118.2
Ealing	20.8	17.7	18.8	10.0	20.0	16.0	103.4
Enfield	19.5	14.5	19.3	9.0	18.7	16.3	97.4
Greenwich	17.1	12.1	15.3	7.9	14.1	13.2	79.6
Hackney	18.7	10.1	13.3	8.4	11.4	10.7	72.6
Hammersmith	21.7	11.3	9.4	4.9	10.8	8.7	66.7
Haringey	20.1	14.2	14.4	7.3	15.2	11.9	83.0
Harrow	14.2	11.5	14.1	6.2	14.4	12.8	73.2
Havering	12.2	14.9	19.7	7.3	18.7	13.2	86.0
Hillingdon	14.3	13.9	17.3	7.2	16.1	14.5	83.2
Hounslow	15.6	12.5	14.6	6.2	13.7	11.0	73.6
Islington	20.3	10.2	10.8	5.1	12.0	8.4	66.7
Kensington & Chelsea	28.9	13.6	8.2	3.4	9.8	6.6	70.5
Kingston-upon-Thames	12.9	8.5	10.1	3.6	8.8	9.7	53.6
Lambeth	30.3	17.2	16.6	9.4	17.1	14.3	104.8
Lewisham	21.3	13.7	17.3	9.1	18.0	14.3	93.7
Merton	14.1	11.4	11.6	5.3	11.8	11.3	65.5
Newham	17.8	11.6	14.1	9.2	14.4	12.6	79.6
Redbridge	16.4	14.4	16.2	7.6	17.3	13.2	85.1
Richmond	18.5	12.9	11.1	4.0	11.2	11.5	69.1
Southwark	22.7	13.0	15.0	6.9	15.0	13.4	85.9
Sutton	12.7	11.3	13.2	4.7	10.9	10.6	63.3
Tower Hamlets	13.7	8.4	9.7	5.2	9.9	8.3	55.1
Waltham Forest	17.9	13.5	17.7	7.5	13.8	15.4	85.9
Wandsworth	25.7	16.7	18.1	9.2	18.6	17.5	105.8
Westminster	37.6	15.7	10.0	4.3	12.2	11.1	91.0
Greater London	626.2	432.1	476.7	224.8	479.7	408.8	2648.2

96

TABLE 66B Type of Household: London Borough

London borough	One person household	Small adult household	Small family	Large family	Large adult household	Older small household	All households
City of London	52.7	21.0	9.2	-	10.4	6.7	100.0
Barking	18.7	15.2	18.8	8.5	20.0	18.7	100.0
Barnet	19.9	14.4	17.8	8.7	22.1	17.2	100.0
Bexley	15.5	17.1	22.5	8.6	18.6	17.7	100.0
Brent	22.2	14.4	16.9	10.7	21.3	14.4	100.0
Bromley	19.3	17.3	20.3	7.7	19.4	15.9	100.0
Camden	35.6	19.7	12.6	5.4	14.7	12.0	100.0
Croydon	20.2	16.8	20.0	9.8	18.2	14.9	100.0
Ealing	20.1	17.2	18.2	9.6	19.4	15.5	100.0
Enfield	20.1	14.9	19.8	9.2	19.2	16.7	100.0
Greenwich	21.5	15.2	19.2	9.9	17.7	16.5	100.0
Hackney	25.8	13.9	18.3	11.6	15.7	14.7	100.0
Hammersmith	32.6	16.9	14.0	7.4	16.1	13.0	100.0
Haringey	24.2	17.1	17.3	8.8	18.3	14.3	100.0
Harrow	19.4	15.7	19.3	8.5	19.6	17.5	100.0
Havering	14.2	17.3	22.9	8.4	21.8	15.4	100.0
Hillingdon	17.2	16.7	20.7	8.6	19.3	17.4	100.0
Hounslow	21.2	17.0	19.8	8.5	18.6	14.9	100.0
Islington	30.4	15.2	16.2	7.6	18.0	12.5	100.0
Kensington & Chelsea	40.9	19.3	11.7	4.9	13.9	9.3	100.0
Kingston-upon-Thames	24.1	15.9	18.8	6.7	16.4	18.1	100.0
Lambeth	28.9	16.4	15.9	8.9	16.3	13.6	100.0
Lewisham	22.7	14.7	18.5	9.7	19.2	15.3	100.0
Merton	21.5	17.4	17.7	8.1	18.1	17.2	100.0
Newham	22.3	14.5	17.7	11.5	18.1	15.8	100.0
Redbridge	19.3	16.9	19.0	8.9	20.3	15.5	100.0
Richmond	26.7	18.6	16.1	5.8	16.2	16.6	100.0
Southwark	26.5	15.1	17.5	8.0	17.4	15.6	100.0
Sutton	20.0	17.8	20.8	7.4	17.2	16.8	100.0
Tower Hamlets	24.8	15.2	17.6	9.5	17.9	15.0	100.0
Waltham Forest	20.9	15.8	20.6	8.7	16.1	17.9	100.0
Wandsworth	24.3	15.8	17.1	8.7	17.6	16.5	100.0
Westminster	41.3	17.3	11.0	4.7	13.4	12.2	100.0
Greater London	23.6	16.3	18.0	8.5	18.1	15.4	100.0

Thousands

| London Borough | Number of Rooms | | | | | | | | All households |
	1	2	3	4	5	6	7	8 or more	
City of London	0.3	0.4	0.7	0.6	0.2	0.3	–	0.0	2.5
Barking	0.1	1.1	6.2	17.9	21.6	8.8	0.8	0.4	57.0
Barnet	2.2	4.3	11.1	25.1	23.6	27.1	10.6	7.8	111.9
Bexley	0.1	0.6	5.0	16.7	25.6	24.8	3.9	1.5	78.2
Brent	4.1	6.1	13.5	20.8	18.3	23.1	6.0	3.1	95.1
Bromley	1.0	3.0	9.5	21.5	28.4	33.0	8.7	6.2	111.2
Camden	6.7	11.6	19.2	19.7	12.2	5.1	2.6	2.6	79.7
Croydon	1.8	3.9	10.2	22.7	28.3	36.3	9.3	5.7	118.2
Ealing	2.6	5.3	12.5	23.0	23.7	28.2	4.8	3.1	103.4
Enfield	0.7	2.1	9.2	19.5	27.7	29.3	5.6	3.2	97.4
Greenwich	0.6	2.6	11.3	19.1	22.9	16.6	4.3	2.3	79.6
Hackney	2.6	6.7	16.4	21.5	16.0	5.4	2.5	1.5	72.6
Hammersmith	3.9	7.3	17.0	16.6	11.4	6.6	2.3	1.6	66.7
Haringey	3.0	5.6	13.8	19.1	17.1	15.5	5.5	3.5	83.0
Harrow	0.6	1.6	5.9	12.9	16.9	27.0	5.2	2.9	73.2
Havering	0.2	0.8	4.8	17.7	33.5	24.3	3.3	1.4	86.0
Hillingdon	0.7	2.1	6.2	20.6	26.3	21.8	3.5	2.0	83.2
Hounslow	1.3	3.3	8.5	17.7	18.5	19.5	3.3	1.5	73.6
Islington	3.8	7.5	17.2	17.9	12.3	4.5	2.0	1.5	66.7
Kensington & Chelsea	8.6	10.4	16.1	15.4	8.8	4.3	3.0	3.9	70.5
Kingston-upon-Thames	1.1	1.4	5.2	10.9	13.4	16.5	3.4	1.7	53.6
Lambeth	4.5	10.1	21.7	28.1	21.2	11.5	4.2	3.4	104.8
Lewisham	1.5	4.6	13.7	26.5	21.2	18.5	5.1	2.6	93.7
Merton	0.9	2.1	5.8	13.4	17.3	20.3	3.4	2.3	65.5
Newham	1.2	2.3	13.3	19.5	25.2	13.6	3.4	1.0	79.6
Redbridge	1.5	3.0	6.4	14.7	23.2	26.8	6.2	3.4	85.1
Richmond	1.8	3.1	7.9	15.2	16.5	15.0	5.4	4.2	69.1
Southwark	1.1	5.6	20.5	27.7	18.4	7.6	3.0	2.0	85.9
Sutton	0.6	1.5	5.3	15.0	16.8	17.2	4.1	2.9	63.3
Tower Hamlets	1.0	3.6	12.0	19.6	14.6	3.4	0.5	0.4	55.1
Waltham Forest	1.2	2.8	10.7	20.3	24.5	20.7	4.2	1.5	85.9
Wandsworth	3.6	5.5	18.0	30.7	20.8	16.6	6.3	4.3	105.8
Westminster	8.1	13.3	23.9	21.8	13.3	5.6	1.9	3.2	91.0
Greater London	72.8	145.0	378.4	629.2	640.3	555.1	138.5	88.8	2648.2

TABLE 67B Number of Rooms : London Borough

London borough	Number of rooms								All households
	1	2	3	4	5	6	7	8 or more	
City of London	12.7	15.9	26.7	24.6	8.6	10.2	-	1.3	100.0
Barking	0.2	2.0	10.8	31.5	37.8	15.5	1.5	0.6	100.0
Barnet	2.0	3.8	9.9	22.4	21.1	24.3	9.5	6.9	100.0
Bexley	0.2	0.8	6.3	21.3	32.7	31.7	5.0	1.9	100.0
Brent	4.3	6.4	14.2	21.9	19.3	24.3	6.3	3.3	100.0
Bromley	0.9	2.7	8.5	19.3	25.5	29.6	7.8	5.6	100.0
Camden	8.4	14.5	24.1	24.7	15.3	6.4	3.3	3.3	100.0
Croydon	1.5	3.3	8.7	19.2	24.0	30.7	7.8	4.8	100.0
Ealing	2.5	5.1	12.1	22.3	23.0	27.3	4.6	3.0	100.0
Enfield	0.7	2.2	9.5	20.0	28.5	30.1	5.8	3.3	100.0
Greenwich	0.7	3.3	14.2	23.9	28.8	20.8	5.4	2.9	100.0
Hackney	3.5	9.2	22.6	29.7	22.0	7.4	3.4	2.1	100.0
Hammersmith	5.9	10.9	25.5	24.9	17.1	9.9	3.5	2.3	100.0
Haringey	3.6	6.7	16.6	23.0	20.6	18.7	6.6	4.2	100.0
Harrow	0.9	2.2	8.1	17.6	23.2	36.9	7.1	4.0	100.0
Havering	0.2	0.9	5.6	20.6	38.9	28.3	3.8	1.6	100.0
Hillingdon	0.8	2.5	7.4	24.8	31.6	26.2	4.3	2.4	100.0
Hounslow	1.7	4.5	11.5	24.0	25.2	26.4	4.5	2.1	100.0
Islington	5.7	11.3	25.8	26.8	18.4	6.7	3.0	2.3	100.0
Kensington & Chelsea	12.1	14.8	22.8	21.9	12.5	6.2	4.2	5.5	100.0
Kingston-upon-Thames	2.1	2.5	9.7	20.3	25.0	30.8	6.4	3.2	100.0
Lambeth	4.3	9.7	20.7	26.8	20.2	11.0	4.0	3.2	100.0
Lewisham	1.6	5.0	14.6	28.2	22.7	19.7	5.5	2.8	100.0
Merton	1.3	3.3	8.9	20.4	26.5	31.0	5.1	3.5	100.0
Newham	1.6	2.9	16.7	24.5	31.7	17.1	4.3	1.2	100.0
Redbridge	1.7	3.5	7.6	17.2	27.3	31.4	7.2	4.0	100.0
Richmond	2.6	4.5	11.5	21.9	23.9	21.7	7.9	6.1	100.0
Southwark	1.2	6.5	23.9	32.3	21.4	8.8	3.5	2.4	100.0
Sutton	0.9	2.3	8.3	23.7	26.5	27.2	6.5	4.6	100.0
Tower Hamlets	1.9	6.6	21.8	35.6	26.5	6.1	0.9	0.6	100.0
Waltham Forest	1.4	3.3	12.5	23.6	28.6	24.1	4.9	1.7	100.0
Wandsworth	3.4	5.2	17.0	29.1	19.6	15.7	6.0	4.0	100.0
Westminster	8.9	14.6	26.2	23.9	14.6	6.2	2.1	3.5	100.0
Greater London	2.8	5.5	14.3	23.8	24.2	21.0	5.2	3.4	100.0

TABLE 68A Number of Bedrooms : London Borough

Thousands

London Borough	Number of bedrooms						All households
	1	2	3	4	5	6 or more	
City of London	1.5	0.6	0.2	0.1	-	-	2.5
Barking	6.2	21.7	27.8	1.1	0.1	-	57.0
Barnet	17.8	29.0	47.1	13.7	3.5	0.7	111.9
Bexley	5.3	22.1	44.7	5.4	0.7	0.1	78.2
Brent	24.1	24.0	37.6	7.9	1.2	0.3	95.1
Bromley	14.1	29.2	52.4	12.4	2.3	0.8	111.2
Camden	35.0	25.1	13.2	4.5	1.2	0.7	79.7
Croydon	16.4	31.4	56.5	11.3	2.1	0.5	118.2
Ealing	20.8	27.8	47.0	6.2	1.1	0.6	103.4
Enfield	12.7	23.4	53.7	6.3	1.1	0.2	97.4
Greenwich	14.2	22.8	35.6	6.2	0.6	0.2	79.6
Hackney	23.4	24.7	19.1	4.2	0.9	0.2	72.6
Hammersmith	26.1	21.4	14.3	3.7	0.9	0.3	66.7
Haringey	23.9	25.4	25.3	6.7	1.4	0.3	83.0
Harrow	8.3	16.5	40.6	6.8	0.8	0.3	73.2
Havering	6.1	22.2	52.7	4.4	0.6	0.1	86.0
Hillingdon	8.4	25.4	44.1	4.5	0.8	0.1	83.2
Hounslow	12.7	22.0	34.3	3.9	0.6	0.2	73.6
Islington	25.9	21.4	14.6	3.6	0.8	0.3	66.7
Kensington & Chelsea	31.9	21.3	10.3	4.5	1.4	1.2	70.5
Kingston-upon-Thames	8.0	14.2	26.4	4.0	0.8	0.2	53.6
Lambeth	35.5	33.6	26.1	7.3	1.7	0.5	104.8
Lewisham	21.9	29.5	34.7	7.1	1.0	0.3	93.7
Merton	9.1	18.3	33.1	3.6	0.9	0.4	65.5
Newham	17.3	24.8	33.1	3.8	0.4	0.1	79.6
Redbridge	11.7	17.2	47.8	7.2	1.1	0.2	85.1
Richmond	13.5	20.9	25.4	7.3	1.6	0.4	69.1
Southwark	26.1	30.8	22.2	5.6	0.9	0.4	85.9
Sutton	7.5	18.5	30.5	5.4	1.1	0.3	63.3
Tower Hamlets	14.2	21.9	16.3	2.5	0.1	0.1	55.1
Waltham Forest	15.2	25.6	40.0	4.4	0.6	0.1	85.9
Wandsworth	26.8	38.1	30.5	8.0	1.7	0.7	105.8
Westminster	45.0	27.2	13.0	3.7	1.4	0.7	91.0
Greater London	586.0	777.7	1050.1	187.2	35.6	11.6	2648.2

TABLE 68B Number of Bedrooms : London Borough

Percentages

London borough	Number of bedrooms						All households
	1	2	3	4	5	6 or more	
City of London	62.1	24.8	9.8	2.7	-	0.7	100.0
Barking	11.0	38.0	48.8	2.0	0.2	-	100.0
Barnet	15.9	25.9	42.1	12.2	3.2	0.7	100.0
Bexley	6.8	28.2	57.1	6.8	0.9	0.1	100.0
Brent	25.3	25.2	39.6	8.4	1.3	0.3	100.0
Bromley	12.7	26.2	47.1	11.2	2.1	0.7	100.0
Camden	44.0	31.5	16.6	5.6	1.5	0.9	100.0
Croydon	13.9	26.6	47.8	9.6	1.8	0.4	100.0
Ealing	20.1	26.9	45.4	6.0	1.0	0.6	100.0
Enfield	13.0	24.0	55.1	6.5	1.1	0.2	100.0
Greenwich	17.8	28.6	44.7	7.8	0.8	0.3	100.0
Hackney	32.3	34.1	26.3	5.8	1.3	0.3	100.0
Hammersmith	39.1	32.1	21.4	5.6	1.3	0.5	100.0
Haringey	28.8	30.6	30.5	8.0	1.7	0.4	100.0
Harrow	11.3	22.5	55.4	9.3	1.1	0.3	100.0
Havering	7.1	25.8	61.3	5.1	0.7	0.1	100.0
Hillingdon	10.1	30.5	53.0	5.4	0.9	0.2	100.0
Hounslow	17.3	29.8	46.6	5.2	0.8	0.2	100.0
Islington	38.9	32.1	21.9	5.4	1.3	0.4	100.0
Kensington & Chelsea	45.3	30.1	14.6	6.3	2.0	1.6	100.0
Kingston-upon-Thames	14.9	26.4	49.2	7.5	1.5	0.5	100.0
Lambeth	33.9	32.1	24.9	6.9	1.6	0.5	100.0
Lewisham	22.4	31.4	37.1	7.6	1.1	0.3	100.0
Merton	13.9	28.0	50.5	5.5	1.4	0.6	100.0
Newham	21.7	31.2	41.6	4.8	0.6	0.2	100.0
Redbridge	13.8	20.2	56.1	8.4	1.3	0.2	100.0
Richmond	19.6	30.2	36.7	10.5	2.3	0.6	100.0
Southwark	30.4	35.8	25.8	6.5	1.1	0.4	100.0
Sutton	11.9	29.3	48.2	8.5	1.7	0.4	100.0
Tower Hamlets	25.7	39.6	29.5	4.6	0.3	0.3	100.0
Waltham Forest	17.7	29.8	46.6	5.1	0.7	0.1	100.0
Wandsworth	25.3	36.0	28.8	7.6	1.6	0.7	100.0
Westminster	49.5	29.9	14.3	4.1	1.5	0.8	100.0
Greater London	22.1	29.4	39.7	7.1	1.3	0.4	100.0

Thousands

London Borough	Persons per room					All households
	Less than $\frac{1}{2}$	$\frac{1}{2}$ to $\frac{3}{4}$	Over $\frac{3}{4}$ to 1	Over 1 to $1\frac{1}{2}$	Over $1\frac{1}{2}$	
City of London	0.7	1.4	0.4	-	-	2.5
Barking	19.3	23.0	12.4	2.1	0.3	57.0
Barnet	41.2	47.5	19.1	3.2	0.8	111.9
Bexley	29.8	32.2	14.8	1.4	0.1	78.2
Brent	27.8	39.2	22.7	3.9	1.5	95.1
Bromley	45.0	47.6	16.5	2.0	0.2	111.2
Camden	21.0	37.2	18.0	2.0	1.6	79.7
Croydon	45.7	48.6	20.4	2.9	0.7	118.2
Ealing	34.1	43.4	20.7	3.9	1.4	103.4
Enfield	38.5	38.2	17.6	2.7	0.5	97.4
Greenwich	28.6	31.6	16.4	2.8	0.2	79.6
Hackney	17.4	31.9	17.9	4.2	1.1	72.6
Hammersmith	20.1	27.4	14.1	3.4	1.7	66.7
Haringey	26.4	35.7	17.8	2.4	0.8	83.0
Harrow	29.7	31.3	10.8	1.2	0.2	73.2
Havering	30.8	34.7	18.5	1.8	0.2	86.0
Hillingdon	29.5	34.3	17.1	2.0	0.3	83.2
Hounslow	25.3	31.0	14.7	2.1	0.4	73.6
Islington	16.2	29.6	16.6	3.2	1.2	66.7
Kensington & Chelsea	21.4	29.2	15.3	2.2	2.5	70.5
Kingston-upon-Thames	23.4	20.9	8.3	0.7	0.3	53.6
Lambeth	29.6	45.3	23.6	5.0	1.3	104.8
Lewisham	29.9	41.4	18.1	3.6	0.7	93.7
Merton	26.7	26.7	10.6	1.3	0.2	65.5
Newham	26.7	29.8	18.0	4.3	0.8	79.6
Redbridge	32.6	34.8	15.6	1.9	0.3	85.1
Richmond	30.5	28.0	9.4	0.9	0.4	69.1
Southwark	24.6	40.1	17.8	3.0	0.4	85.9
Sutton	25.5	26.6	10.1	1.1	-	63.3
Tower Hamlets	14.3	24.4	12.3	3.0	1.1	55.1
Waltham Forest	31.3	35.1	16.2	2.8	0.5	85.9
Wandsworth	33.1	46.1	21.5	4.2	0.9	105.8
Westminster	28.0	40.3	18.5	2.3	1.9	91.0
Greater London	904.7	1114.2	521.8	83.3	24.1	2648.2

Percentages

London borough	Persons per room					All households
	Less than $\frac{1}{2}$	$\frac{1}{2}$ to $\frac{3}{4}$	Over $\frac{3}{4}$ to 1	Over 1 to $1\frac{1}{2}$	Over $1\frac{1}{2}$	
City of London	26.7	56.4	16.9	-	-	100.0
Barking	33.8	40.4	21.7	3.6	0.5	100.0
Barnet	36.9	42.5	17.1	2.9	0.7	100.0
Bexley	38.1	41.2	18.9	1.8	0.1	100.0
Brent	29.2	41.2	23.9	4.1	1.6	100.0
Bromley	40.5	42.8	14.8	1.8	0.2	100.0
Camden	26.3	46.7	22.6	2.4	2.0	100.0
Croydon	38.6	41.1	17.2	2.5	0.6	100.0
Ealing	33.0	41.9	20.0	3.8	1.3	100.0
Enfield	39.5	39.2	18.0	2.7	0.5	100.0
Greenwich	36.0	39.7	20.6	3.5	0.2	100.0
Hackney	24.0	44.0	24.7	5.7	1.6	100.0
Hammersmith	30.1	41.1	21.1	5.1	2.6	100.0
Haringey	31.8	43.0	21.4	2.9	0.9	100.0
Harrow	40.6	42.7	14.7	1.7	0.2	100.0
Havering	35.8	40.3	21.5	2.1	0.2	100.0
Hillingdon	35.5	41.2	20.6	2.4	0.3	100.0
Hounslow	34.4	42.2	20.0	2.8	0.6	100.0
Islington	24.2	44.3	24.9	4.8	1.8	100.0
Kensington & Chelsea	30.4	41.4	21.7	3.0	3.5	100.0
Kingston-upon-Thames	43.7	38.9	15.5	1.3	0.5	100.0
Lambeth	28.2	43.3	22.5	4.8	1.2	100.0
Lewisham	31.9	44.2	19.3	3.8	0.7	100.0
Merton	40.8	40.8	16.1	2.0	0.3	100.0
Newham	33.6	37.4	22.6	5.4	1.0	100.0
Redbridge	38.3	40.8	18.3	2.2	0.3	100.0
Richmond	44.1	40.5	13.6	1.3	0.6	100.0
Southwark	28.7	46.7	20.7	3.5	0.4	100.0
Sutton	40.3	42.0	15.9	1.8	0.1	100.0
Tower Hamlets	26.0	44.3	22.3	5.4	2.0	100.0
Waltham Forest	36.4	40.9	18.9	3.3	0.6	100.0
Wandsworth	31.3	43.6	20.3	4.0	0.8	100.0
Westminster	30.8	44.2	20.3	2.5	2.1	100.0
Greater London	34.2	42.1	19.7	3.1	0.9	100.0

TABLE 70A Difference from Bedroom Standard : London Borough

Thousands

London Borough	Difference from bedroom standard					All households
	2 or more below	1 below	Equal	1 above	2 or more above	
City of London	-	0.1	1.9	0.5	-	2.5
Barking	0.3	2.9	22.2	22.6	9.0	57.0
Barnet	1.0	6.2	41.4	36.8	26.5	111.9
Bexley	0.2	2.2	23.6	33.6	18.7	78.2
Brent	1.7	9.2	44.5	25.6	14.0	95.1
Bromley	0.4	3.9	36.1	42.4	28.4	111.2
Camden	0.8	6.6	49.1	17.7	5.5	79.7
Croydon	0.7	5.6	43.0	41.5	27.4	118.2
Ealing	1.4	7.6	43.8	32.8	17.7	103.4
Enfield	0.6	4.5	35.0	34.3	23.1	97.4
Greenwich	0.4	3.8	34.2	26.6	14.6	79.6
Hackney	1.0	6.6	42.7	18.0	4.2	72.6
Hammersmith	1.2	7.2	38.2	15.0	5.1	66.7
Haringey	0.9	6.9	42.3	23.3	9.7	83.0
Harrow	0.4	2.7	23.3	27.8	19.0	73.2
Havering	0.3	3.2	27.3	36.1	19.2	86.0
Hillingdon	0.4	3.1	29.8	32.6	17.3	83.2
Hounslow	0.7	3.9	31.3	24.7	12.9	73.6
Islington	0.8	6.4	41.3	14.9	3.3	66.7
Kensington & Chelsea	0.9	7.3	40.6	15.3	6.4	70.5
Kingston-upon-Thames	0.1	1.8	17.9	20.4	13.4	53.6
Lambeth	1.2	9.8	57.8	26.4	9.7	104.8
Lewisham	0.8	6.7	43.6	29.8	12.9	93.7
Merton	0.3	2.7	22.7	25.3	14.5	65.5
Newham	1.3	6.9	37.6	22.8	11.0	79.6
Redbridge	0.5	3.5	29.2	30.2	21.6	85.1
Richmond	0.2	3.0	25.4	24.3	16.2	69.1
Southwark	0.6	5.6	49.5	22.8	7.3	85.9
Sutton	0.2	2.0	20.7	25.2	15.2	63.3
Tower Hamlets	0.9	4.2	30.0	16.5	3.6	55.1
Waltham Forest	0.8	4.4	35.2	29.7	15.7	85.9
Wandsworth	0.8	8.4	53.1	31.1	12.4	105.8
Westminster	1.0	7.6	58.8	18.0	5.7	91.0
Greater London	22.9	166.4	1172.8	844.6	441.5	2648.2

Percentages

London borough	Difference from bedroom standard					All households
	2 or more below	1 below	Equal	1 above	2 or more above	
City of London	-	2.2	75.8	20.1	1.9	100.0
Barking	0.5	5.1	38.9	39.6	15.9	100.0
Barnet	0.9	5.6	37.0	32.9	23.7	100.0
Bexley	0.2	2.8	30.1	43.0	23.9	100.0
Brent	1.8	9.7	46.8	26.9	14.8	100.0
Bromley	0.4	3.5	32.5	38.1	25.5	100.0
Camden	1.0	8.3	61.6	22.2	6.9	100.0
Croydon	0.6	4.8	36.4	35.1	23.1	100.0
Ealing	1.3	7.4	42.4	31.8	17.2	100.0
Enfield	0.6	4.6	35.9	35.2	23.7	100.0
Greenwich	0.6	4.8	42.9	33.5	18.3	100.0
Hackney	1.4	9.1	58.9	24.8	5.8	100.0
Hammersmith	1.8	10.7	57.2	22.6	7.7	100.0
Haringey	1.0	8.3	50.9	28.0	11.7	100.0
Harrow	0.6	3.7	31.8	38.0	26.0	100.0
Havering	0.3	3.7	31.7	42.0	22.3	100.0
Hillingdon	0.5	3.7	35.8	39.2	20.8	100.0
Hounslow	1.0	5.3	42.6	33.5	17.6	100.0
Islington	1.2	9.6	62.0	22.3	4.9	100.0
Kensington & Chelsea	1.3	10.3	57.5	21.7	9.1	100.0
Kingston-upon-Thames	0.2	3.4	33.3	38.1	25.0	100.0
Lambeth	1.2	9.3	55.1	25.2	9.2	100.0
Lewisham	0.8	7.1	46.6	31.8	13.8	100.0
Merton	0.5	4.1	34.7	38.6	22.2	100.0
Newham	1.7	8.6	47.3	28.6	13.8	100.0
Redbridge	0.6	4.2	34.3	35.5	25.4	100.0
Richmond	0.3	4.3	36.8	35.2	23.5	100.0
Southwark	0.7	6.5	57.6	26.6	8.5	100.0
Sutton	0.3	3.2	32.7	39.8	24.0	100.0
Tower Hamlets	1.6	7.7	54.4	29.9	6.5	100.0
Waltham Forest	0.9	5.1	41.0	34.6	18.3	100.0
Wandsworth	0.7	7.9	50.2	29.4	11.7	100.0
Westminster	1.1	8.3	64.6	19.7	6.2	100.0
Greater London	0.9	6.3	44.3	31.9	16.7	100.0

Thousands

London borough	Type of sharing					All households
	Sharing rooms	Sharing circulation space	Bedsit	Self-contained accommodation in shared dwelling	not in shared dwelling	
City of London	-	-	-	-	2.4	2.5
Barking	0.2	0.1	-	-	56.8	57.0
Barnet	2.5	2.5	1.3	0.3	105.2	111.9
Bexley	0.2	0.3	0.1	0.1	77.6	78.2
Brent	3.9	5.2	2.4	0.6	83.1	95.1
Bromley	1.2	1.6	0.5	0.1	107.8	111.2
Camden	1.8	4.7	4.0	1.4	68.0	79.7
Croydon	2.2	1.4	1.1	0.2	113.3	118.2
Ealing	4.8	2.8	1.0	0.5	94.2	103.4
Enfield	1.6	1.8	0.2	0.2	93.5	97.4
Greenwich	1.2	1.4	0.2	0.2	76.7	79.6
Hackney	1.5	3.6	1.7	1.2	64.5	72.6
Hammersmith	2.5	4.9	2.4	1.0	56.0	66.7
Haringey	2.3	5.5	2.0	0.9	72.3	83.0
Harrow	1.4	0.8	0.2	-	70.8	73.2
Havering	0.5	0.5	0.1	-	85.0	86.0
Hillingdon	1.0	0.4	0.3	-	81.6	83.2
Hounslow	1.7	1.5	0.6	0.2	69.6	73.6
Islington	1.9	4.9	1.9	1.4	56.6	66.7
Kensington & Chelsea	4.7	1.6	4.4	0.2	59.6	70.5
Kingston-upon-Thames	0.9	0.7	0.8	0.1	51.1	53.6
Lambeth	5.4	5.9	2.6	1.4	89.5	104.8
Lewisham	2.3	3.8	0.7	0.6	86.3	93.7
Merton	0.6	1.3	0.5	0.1	63.0	65.5
Newham	1.1	2.6	0.6	0.7	74.5	79.6
Redbridge	1.3	1.8	0.9	0.4	80.9	85.1
Richmond	1.3	2.0	1.1	0.3	64.5	69.1
Southwark	1.3	2.1	0.3	0.5	81.7	85.9
Sutton	0.8	0.7	0.3	0.1	61.5	63.3
Tower Hamlets	0.6	0.7	0.3	0.2	53.3	55.1
Waltham Forest	0.9	1.6	0.6	0.3	82.4	85.9
Wandsworth	2.0	5.7	2.2	0.9	94.9	105.8
Westminster	3.8	2.9	4.6	0.3	79.3	91.0
Greater London	59.4	77.3	39.7	14.4	2457.3	2648.2

Percentages

London borough	Type of sharing					All households
	Sharing rooms	Sharing circulation space	Bedsit	Self-contained accommodation in shared dwelling	not in shared dwelling	
City of London	-	0.7	-	-	99.3	100.0
Barking	0.3	0.1	-	-	99.4	100.0
Barnet	2.3	2.3	1.2	0.3	94.0	100.0
Bexley	0.2	0.4	0.1	0.1	99.2	100.0
Brent	4.0	5.5	2.5	0.6	87.3	100.0
Bromley	1.1	1.4	0.5	0.1	96.9	100.0
Camden	2.2	5.8	5.0	1.7	85.2	100.0
Croydon	1.9	1.2	0.9	0.2	95.8	100.0
Ealing	4.7	2.7	1.0	0.5	91.1	100.0
Enfield	1.6	1.9	0.2	0.2	96.0	100.0
Greenwich	1.5	1.7	0.2	0.3	96.3	100.0
Hackney	2.1	4.9	2.3	1.7	88.9	100.0
Hammersmith	3.7	7.3	3.5	1.5	83.9	100.0
Haringey	2.8	6.7	2.4	1.1	87.0	100.0
Harrow	1.9	1.1	0.3	0.1	96.6	100.0
Havering	0.6	0.5	0.1	-	98.7	100.0
Hillingdon	1.2	0.5	0.3	-	97.9	100.0
Hounslow	2.3	2.0	0.8	0.3	94.6	100.0
Islington	2.9	7.3	2.9	2.0	84.8	100.0
Kensington & Chelsea	6.7	2.3	6.2	0.3	84.4	100.0
Kingston-upon-Thames	1.7	1.4	1.5	0.2	95.3	100.0
Lambeth	5.1	5.7	2.5	1.3	85.4	100.0
Lewisham	2.4	4.0	0.7	0.7	92.1	100.0
Merton	0.9	2.0	0.8	0.1	96.2	100.0
Newham	1.5	3.3	0.8	0.9	93.6	100.0
Redbridge	1.5	2.1	1.0	0.4	95.0	100.0
Richmond	1.9	2.8	1.5	0.4	93.2	100.0
Southwark	1.5	2.5	0.3	0.6	95.1	100.0
Sutton	1.2	1.1	0.5	0.1	97.1	100.0
Tower Hamlets	1.0	1.3	0.6	0.4	96.7	100.0
Waltham Forest	1.0	1.9	0.7	0.4	96.0	100.0
Wandsworth	1.9	5.4	2.1	0.9	89.8	100.0
Westminster	4.2	3.2	5.0	0.4	87.1	100.0
Greater London	2.2	2.9	1.5	0.5	92.8	100.0

Thousands

London borough	Use of basic amenities			All households
	Sole use of all	Some shared, none lacked	At least one lacked	
City of London	2.4	-	-	2.5
Barking	54.9	0.3	1.8	57.0
Barnet	102.1	6.3	3.5	111.9
Bexley	75.4	0.6	2.3	78.2
Brent	80.2	11.6	3.3	95.1
Bromley	104.6	2.9	3.7	111.2
Camden	65.9	9.6	4.2	79.7
Croydon	107.7	5.5	5.0	118.2
Ealing	90.0	8.3	5.1	103.4
Enfield	89.7	3.2	4.5	97.4
Greenwich	71.6	1.7	6.3	79.6
Hackney	58.5	7.5	6.5	72.6
Hammersmith	49.2	8.9	8.6	66.7
Haringey	66.3	10.2	6.6	83.0
Harrow	69.8	2.6	0.8	73.2
Havering	83.3	0.9	1.7	86.0
Hillingdon	80.4	1.7	1.1	83.2
Hounslow	66.2	4.0	3.5	73.6
Islington	52.6	8.2	6.0	66.7
Kensington & Chelsea	56.4	11.6	2.6	70.5
Kingston-upon-Thames	49.5	2.5	1.7	53.6
Lambeth	82.3	14.1	8.3	104.8
Lewisham	81.9	6.4	5.5	93.7
Merton	60.0	2.1	3.5	65.5
Newham	58.6	3.4	17.5	79.6
Redbridge	77.6	3.9	3.6	85.1
Richmond	61.0	4.1	4.1	69.1
Southwark	74.7	3.4	7.9	85.9
Sutton	60.2	1.8	1.2	63.3
Tower Hamlets	48.1	0.8	6.1	55.1
Waltham Forest	71.5	2.6	11.8	85.9
Wandsworth	88.0	8.5	9.3	105.8
Westminster	73.2	11.2	6.6	91.0
Greater London	2313.7	170.3	164.1	2648.2

TABLE 72B   Use of Basic Amenities :   London Borough

Percentages

London borough	Use of basic amenities			All households
	Sole use of all	Some shared, none lacked	At least one lacked	
City of London	98.6	0.7	0.7	100.0
Barking	96.5	0.5	3.1	100.0
Barnet	91.2	5.6	3.1	100.0
Bexley	96.3	0.8	2.9	100.0
Brent	84.3	12.3	3.5	100.0
Bromley	94.0	2.6	3.3	100.0
Camden	82.8	12.0	5.2	100.0
Croydon	91.1	4.6	4.3	100.0
Ealing	87.0	8.0	5.0	100.0
Enfield	92.2	3.3	4.6	100.0
Greenwich	89.9	2.2	7.9	100.0
Hackney	80.6	10.4	9.0	100.0
Hammersmith	73.8	13.4	12.9	100.0
Haringey	79.8	12.2	7.9	100.0
Harrow	95.3	3.5	1.1	100.0
Havering	96.8	1.2	2.0	100.0
Hillingdon	96.5	2.1	1.4	100.0
Hounslow	89.9	5.3	4.7	100.0
Islington	78.8	12.2	8.9	100.0
Kensington & Chelsea	80.0	16.4	3.6	100.0
Kingston-upon-Thames	92.3	4.5	3.1	100.0
Lambeth	78.6	12.5	7.9	100.0
Lewisham	87.3	6.8	5.8	100.0
Merton	91.6	3.1	5.3	100.0
Newham	73.7	4.3	22.0	100.0
Redbridge	91.1	4.6	4.2	100.0
Richmond	88.1	5.9	5.9	100.0
Southwark	86.9	3.9	9.2	100.0
Sutton	95.1	2.9	1.9	100.0
Tower Hamlets	87.4	1.5	11.1	100.0
Waltham Forest	83.3	3.1	13.7	100.0
Wandsworth	83.2	8.0	8.8	100.0
Westminster	80.5	12.2	7.3	100.0
Greater London	87.4	6.4	6.2	100.0

TABLE 73A Use of Bath or Shower : London Borough

Thousands

| London Borough | Use of bath or shower | | | All households |
	Sole use	Shared use	None	
City of London	2.4	-	-	2.5
Barking	56.4	0.3	0.2	57.0
Barnet	104.2	6.8	0.8	111.9
Bexley	76.6	0.6	1.1	78.2
Brent	81.4	12.3	1.4	95.1
Bromley	106.4	2.9	1.9	111.2
Camden	66.9	10.2	2.6	79.7
Croydon	109.8	5.9	2.6	118.2
Ealing	92.5	8.7	2.2	103.4
Enfield	91.9	3.4	2.0	97.4
Greenwich	74.4	1.9	3.3	79.6
Hackney	60.4	8.0	4.1	72.6
Hammersmith	51.8	9.5	5.3	66.7
Haringey	69.2	11.0	2.9	83.0
Harrow	70.4	2.5	0.3	73.2
Havering	84.5	1.0	0.6	86.0
Hillingdon	81.3	1.7	2.0	83.2
Hounslow	67.9	4.2	1.5	73.6
Islington	54.6	8.5	3.6	66.7
Kensington & Chelsea	57.7	11.5	1.3	70.5
Kingston-upon-Thames	50.2	2.6	0.8	53.6
Lambeth	85.4	15.3	4.0	104.8
Lewisham	84.0	6.9	2.8	93.7
Merton	61.2	2.2	2.0	65.5
Newham	66.8	3.9	8.8	79.6
Redbridge	80.2	4.2	0.8	85.1
Richmond	62.8	4.3	2.0	69.1
Southwark	77.6	3.5	4.8	85.9
Sutton	61.2	1.7	0.4	63.3
Tower Hamlets	50.0	1.0	4.1	55.1
Waltham Forest	76.6	3.1	6.2	85.9
Wandsworth	91.7	8.9	5.2	105.8
Westminster	75.3	12.0	3.7	91.0
Greater London	2384.1	180.5	83.6	2648.1

110

TABLE 73B Use of Bath or Shower : London Borough

Percentages

London borough	Use of bath or shower			All households
	Sole use	Shared use	None	
City of London	98.6	0.7	0.7	100.0
Barking	99.1	0.5	0.4	100.0
Barnet	93.2	6.1	0.8	100.0
Bexley	97.9	0.7	1.4	100.0
Brent	85.6	12.9	1.5	100.0
Bromley	95.7	2.6	1.7	100.0
Camden	84.0	12.7	3.3	100.0
Croydon	92.8	5.0	2.2	100.0
Ealing	89.5	8.4	2.1	100.0
Enfield	94.4	3.5	2.1	100.0
Greenwich	93.4	2.4	4.2	100.0
Hackney	83.3	11.1	5.7	100.0
Hammersmith	77.7	14.3	8.0	100.0
Haringey	83.3	13.2	3.5	100.0
Harrow	96.2	3.5	0.3	100.0
Havering	98.2	1.2	0.7	100.0
Hillingdon	97.7	2.1	0.2	100.0
Hounslow	92.3	5.7	2.0	100.0
Islington	81.8	12.7	5.4	100.0
Kensington & Chelsea	81.8	16.3	1.9	100.0
Kingston-upon-Thames	93.7	4.9	1.4	100.0
Lambeth	81.6	14.6	3.8	100.0
Lewisham	89.6	7.4	3.0	100.0
Merton	93.5	3.3	3.1	100.0
Newham	84.0	4.9	11.1	100.0
Redbridge	94.2	4.9	0.9	100.0
Richmond	90.8	6.2	2.9	100.0
Southwark	90.3	4.1	5.6	100.0
Sutton	96.7	2.7	0.6	100.0
Tower Hamlets	90.7	1.9	7.4	100.0
Waltham Forest	89.2	3.6	7.2	100.0
Wandsworth	86.7	8.4	4.9	100.0
Westminster	82.8	13.1	4.1	100.0
Greater London	90.0	6.8	3.2	100.0

Thousands

London Borough	Use of hot water supply			All households
	Sole use	Shared use	None	
City of London	2.4	-	-	2.5
Barking	55.9	0.2	0.8	57.0
Barnet	106.9	3.1	1.8	111.9
Bexley	76.8	0.3	1.1	78.2
Brent	87.2	5.7	2.2	95.1
Bromley	107.3	1.6	2.3	111.2
Camden	74.2	3.1	2.5	79.7
Croydon	113.0	3.0	2.3	118.2
Ealing	95.7	5.8	1.9	103.4
Enfield	92.8	2.2	2.4	97.4
Greenwich	75.7	1.3	2.6	79.6
Hackney	66.8	2.6	3.2	72.6
Hammersmith	56.6	5.0	5.1	66.7
Haringey	76.2	3.4	3.5	83.0
Harrow	71.0	1.9	0.3	73.2
Havering	84.2	0.8	1.1	86.0
Hillingdon	81.5	1.3	0.4	83.2
Hounslow	69.1	2.7	1.8	73.6
Islington	60.0	3.2	3.5	66.7
Kensington & Chelsea	63.1	5.8	1.6	70.5
Kingston-upon-Thames	51.2	1.7	0.7	53.6
Lambeth	93.8	7.1	3.8	104.8
Lewisham	87.8	3.4	2.5	93.7
Merton	62.4	1.1	1.9	65.5
Newham	69.8	2.4	7.4	79.6
Redbridge	81.4	1.9	1.9	85.1
Richmond	65.4	1.7	2.0	69.1
Southwark	80.8	1.7	3.5	85.9
Sutton	61.8	0.9	0.6	63.3
Tower Hamlets	50.5	0.6	3.9	55.1
Waltham Forest	79.2	1.7	4.9	85.9
Wandsworth	97.3	3.9	4.6	105.8
Westminster	80.6	5.8	4.6	91.0
Greater London	2478.4	86.9	82.8	2648.2

Percentages

London borough	Use of hot water supply			All households
	Sole use	Shared use	None	
City of London	99.3	0.7	-	100.0
Barking	98.2	0.4	1.4	100.0
Barnet	95.6	2.8	1.6	100.0
Bexley	98.2	0.4	1.4	100.0
Brent	91.7	6.0	2.3	100.0
Bromley	96.5	1.5	2.1	100.0
Camden	93.0	3.9	3.1	100.0
Croydon	95.6	2.5	1.9	100.0
Ealing	92.5	5.6	1.9	100.0
Enfield	95.3	2.2	2.5	100.0
Greenwich	95.1	1.7	3.2	100.0
Hackney	92.1	3.5	4.4	100.0
Hammersmith	84.8	7.5	7.6	100.0
Haringey	91.7	4.1	4.2	100.0
Harrow	97.0	2.6	0.4	100.0
Havering	97.8	0.9	1.2	100.0
Hillingdon	97.9	1.6	0.5	100.0
Hounslow	93.9	3.7	2.4	100.0
Islington	89.9	4.8	5.3	100.0
Kensington & Chelsea	89.5	8.3	2.2	100.0
Kingston-upon-Thames	95.4	3.2	1.4	100.0
Lambeth	89.6	6.8	3.6	100.0
Lewisham	93.7	3.6	2.7	100.0
Merton	95.4	1.7	3.0	100.0
Newham	87.7	3.0	9.3	100.0
Redbridge	95.6	2.2	2.2	100.0
Richmond	94.6	2.5	2.9	100.0
Southwark	94.0	2.0	4.0	100.0
Sutton	97.7	1.4	0.9	100.0
Tower Hamlets	91.7	1.2	7.2	100.0
Waltham Forest	92.3	2.0	5.7	100.0
Wandsworth	92.0	3.7	4.4	100.0
Westminster	88.5	6.4	5.1	100.0
Greater London	93.6	3.3	3.1	100.0

TABLE 75A Use of Flush Toilet : London Borough

London Borough	Use of a flush toilet				All households
	Sole use inside building	Shared use inside building	Use of outside WC only	None	
City of London	2.4	-	-	-	2.5
Barking	55.8	0.3	0.9	-	57.0
Barnet	104.2	5.8	1.8	-	111.9
Bexley	76.0	0.5	1.7	-	78.2
Brent	83.6	10.5	1.0	-	95.1
Bromley	106.3	2.6	2.3	0.1	111.2
Camden	68.3	10.4	1.0	-	79.7
Croydon	109.3	5.5	3.4	-	118.2
Ealing	92.3	7.9	2.9	0.2	103.4
Enfield	91.5	2.9	2.9	-	97.4
Greenwich	73.4	1.5	4.6	0.1	79.6
Hackney	62.0	7.2	3.1	0.1	72.6
Hammersmith	53.6	9.5	3.5	0.1	66.7
Haringey	70.6	9.4	3.0	0.1	83.0
Harrow	70.4	2.3	0.5	-	73.2
Havering	84.0	1.0	0.9	0.1	86.0
Hillingdon	80.8	1.5	0.9	-	83.2
Hounslow	67.6	3.8	2.2	-	73.6
Islington	55.7	9.3	1.7	-	66.7
Kensington & Chelsea	58.1	11.6	0.7	-	70.5
Kingston-upon-Thames	50.0	2.4	1.2	-	53.6
Lambeth	86.4	14.4	3.8	0.1	104.8
Lewisham	84.1	6.2	3.4	0.1	93.7
Merton	61.8	2.0	1.6	0.1	65.5
Newham	61.6	3.5	14.4	0.1	79.6
Redbridge	79.5	3.6	2.0	0.1	85.1
Richmond	62.7	3.8	2.7	-	69.1
Southwark	78.9	3.1	3.8	-	85.9
Sutton	60.9	1.6	0.7	-	63.3
Tower Hamlets	50.9	1.4	2.7	0.1	55.1
Waltham Forest	75.0	2.3	8.5	0.1	85.9
Wandsworth	92.3	8.4	5.1	-	105.8
Westminster	76.9	12.9	1.2	-	91.0
Greater London	2387.2	169.2	90.2	1.6	2648.2

114

TABLE 75B Use of Flush Toilet : London Borough

| London borough | Use of flush toilet | | | | All households |
	Sole use inside building	Shared use inside building	Use of outside wc only	None	
City of London	99.3	0.7	-	-	100.0
Barking	97.9	0.5	1.6	-	100.0
Barnet	93.2	5.2	1.6	-	100.0
Bexley	97.1	0.6	2.2	-	100.0
Brent	87.9	11.0	1.1	-	100.0
Bromley	95.6	2.3	2.0	0.1	100.0
Camden	85.7	13.1	1.1	-	100.0
Croydon	92.5	4.6	2.9	-	100.0
Ealing	89.3	7.7	2.8	0.2	100.0
Enfield	94.0	3.0	3.0	-	100.0
Greenwich	92.2	1.8	5.7	0.2	100.0
Hackney	85.5	10.1	4.3	0.1	100.0
Hammersmith	80.4	14.2	5.2	0.2	100.0
Haringey	85.0	11.3	3.6	0.1	100.0
Harrow	96.2	3.1	0.7	-	100.0
Havering	97.6	1.2	1.1	0.1	100.0
Hillingdon	97.1	1.9	1.1	-	100.0
Hounslow	91.9	5.1	3.0	-	100.0
Islington	83.4	14.0	2.6	0.1	100.0
Kensington & Chelsea	82.4	16.5	1.0	-	100.0
Kingston-upon-Thames	93.2	4.6	2.2	-	100.0
Lambeth	82.5	13.8	3.6	0.1	100.0
Lewisham	89.8	6.6	3.5	0.1	100.0
Merton	94.4	3.1	2.4	0.1	100.0
Newham	77.4	4.4	18.1	0.1	100.0
Redbridge	93.4	4.2	2.4	0.1	100.0
Richmond	90.7	5.4	3.9	-	100.0
Southwark	91.9	3.6	4.5	-	100.0
Sutton	96.2	2.6	1.2	-	100.0
Tower Hamlets	92.4	2.5	5.0	0.1	100.0
Waltham Forest	87.3	2.8	9.9	0.1	100.0
Wandsworth	87.2	7.9	4.8	-	100.0
Westminster	84.5	14.1	1.4	-	100.0
Greater London	90.1	6.4	3.4	0.1	100.0

TABLE 76A Type of Central Heating : London Borough

Thousands

London borough	Central heating fuel						All households
	No central heating	Solid fuel	Gas	Oil	Electric storage-heaters	Other	
City of London	0.2	-	0.1	0.2	-	2.0	2.5
Barking	38.7	1.1	10.5	0.5	3.6	2.6	57.0
Barnet	42.4	1.7	50.2	3.9	9.2	4.5	111.9
Bexley	35.1	2.9	31.5	1.0	4.0	3.8	78.2
Brent	46.8	1.2	27.9	4.0	8.3	6.8	95.1
Bromley	41.6	2.9	51.7	4.3	7.8	2.9	111.2
Camden	39.8	0.3	21.3	9.9	4.6	3.8	79.7
Croydon	58.9	2.9	39.7	2.7	8.3	5.8	118.2
Ealing	53.3	2.1	30.7	5.1	7.7	4.6	103.4
Enfield	44.9	2.6	33.7	2.1	6.1	7.9	97.4
Greenwich	46.1	1.2	20.5	2.1	3.6	6.1	79.6
Hackney	46.7	0.2	9.5	6.8	3.2	6.1	72.6
Hammersmith	46.5	0.1	13.3	1.9	2.6	2.6	66.7
Haringey	52.3	0.8	17.4	4.5	5.2	2.8	83.0
Harrow	27.7	1.4	33.4	2.3	5.2	3.3	73.2
Havering	35.9	3.6	38.4	1.2	4.3	2.7	86.0
Hillingdon	33.9	3.3	34.9	1.5	7.0	2.6	83.2
Hounslow	35.6	2.2	24.0	4.1	4.9	2.7	73.6
Islington	37.8	0.2	18.9	4.4	2.5	3.0	66.7
Kensington & Chelsea	33.3	0.1	19.8	9.2	5.1	3.0	70.5
Kingston-upon-Thames	23.6	1.6	20.4	1.5	4.2	2.2	53.6
Lambeth	68.5	0.7	19.8	5.3	4.7	5.7	104.8
Lewisham	59.3	0.8	21.6	1.9	5.0	5.2	93.7
Merton	35.6	1.3	21.9	1.1	3.6	2.0	65.5
Newham	51.9	1.0	13.0	0.4	4.1	9.2	79.6
Redbridge	39.5	2.4	34.2	1.3	5.0	2.6	85.1
Richmond	30.5	1.4	25.9	2.4	6.2	2.8	69.1
Southwark	53.9	0.2	11.4	6.7	4.4	9.3	85.9
Sutton	23.7	1.4	26.3	2.6	4.5	4.6	63.3
Tower Hamlets	32.5	0.1	9.1	6.5	1.9	5.0	55.1
Waltham Forest	56.3	1.3	16.7	2.6	6.8	2.1	85.9
Wandsworth	63.1	0.6	27.5	6.2	4.1	4.2	105.8
Westminster	46.9	0.5	16.2	13.2	4.7	9.5	91.0
Greater London	1382.7	44.2	791.6	123.5	162.6	143.6	2648.2

116

TABLE 76B Type of Central Heating : London Borough

Percentages

London borough	Central heating fuel						All households
	No central heating	Solid fuel	Gas	Oil	Electric storage-heaters	Other	
City of London	8.8	-	3.3	6.9	1.3	79.7	100.0
Barking	67.9	2.0	18.4	0.9	6.3	4.6	100.0
Barnet	37.9	1.5	44.9	3.5	8.2	4.0	100.0
Bexley	44.9	3.7	40.2	1.3	5.1	4.8	100.0
Brent	49.2	1.3	29.3	4.2	8.8	7.2	100.0
Bromley	37.4	2.6	46.5	3.9	7.0	2.6	100.0
Camden	49.9	0.4	26.7	12.5	5.8	4.7	100.0
Croydon	49.8	2.4	33.6	2.3	7.0	4.8	100.0
Ealing	51.5	2 0	29.7	4.9	7.4	4.4	100.0
Enfield	46.1	2.7	34.6	2.1	6.3	8.1	100.0
Greenwich	57.8	1.4	25.7	2.7	4.5	7.7	100.0
Hackney	64.4	0.3	13.1	9.4	4.4	8.4	100.0
Hammersmith	69.8	0.2	19.9	2.9	4.0	3.3	100.0
Haringey	63.0	1.0	21.0	5.4	6.2	3.4	100.0
Harrow	37.8	1.9	45.6	3.1	7.1	4.5	100.0
Havering	41.7	4.2	44.6	1.5	5.0	3.1	100.0
Hillingdon	40.8	3.9	42.0	1.8	8.4	3.2	100.0
Hounslow	48.5	3.0	32.5	5.5	6.7	3.7	100.0
Islington	56.6	0.3	28.3	6.5	3.7	4.5	100.0
Kensington & Chelsea	47.2	0.2	28.1	13.0	7.3	4.3	100.0
Kingston-upon-Thames	44.1	3.1	38.1	2.9	7.8	4.1	100.0
Lambeth	65.4	0.7	18.9	5.1	4.4	5.5	100.0
Lewisham	63.3	0.9	23.1	2.0	5.3	5.6	100.0
Merton	54.4	2.0	33.3	1.7	5.5	3.0	100.0
Newham	65.2	1.2	16.3	0.5	5.2	11.5	100.0
Redbridge	46.4	2.8	40.3	1.6	5.9	3.0	100.0
Richmond	44.1	2.0	37.4	3.5	8.9	4.1	100.0
Southwark	62.8	0.3	13.2	7.7	5.2	10.8	100.0
Sutton	37.5	2.3	41.6	4.1	7.2	7.3	100.0
Tower Hamlets	58.9	0.2	16.5	11.8	3.4	9.1	100.0
Waltham Forest	65.6	1.5	19.5	3.1	7.9	2.5	100.0
Wandsworth	59.7	0.6	26.0	5.8	3.9	4.0	100.0
Westminster	51.6	0.6	17.8	14.5	5.1	10.5	100.0
Greater London	52.2	1.7	29.9	4.7	6.1	5.4	100.0

117

TABLE 77A Main Form of Room Heating: London Borough

Thousands

London borough	Main form of room heating						All households
	Central heating	Open fire	Closed stove	Electric	Gas	Other	
City of London	2.1	-	-	0.3	-	-	2.5
Barking	15.9	4.0	0.8	8.4	26.7	1.2	57.0
Barnet	60.3	4.8	3.3	22.3	19.2	2.0	111.9
Bexley	37.0	4.2	2.6	10.8	22.8	0.9	78.2
Brent	42.8	2.9	1.4	23.9	20.9	3.2	95.1
Bromley	58.2	4.9	3.3	15.9	27.4	1.5	111.2
Camden	35.9	2.0	0.5	23.4	13.7	4.1	79.7
Croydon	49.7	5.6	2.7	22.3	36.1	1.8	118.2
Ealing	43.2	6.0	2.9	24.3	24.5	2.5	103.4
Enfield	45.6	4.6	2.5	16.6	26.7	1.4	97.4
Greenwich	27.7	5.0	1.8	13.9	29.8	1.4	79.6
Hackney	21.0	2.7	0.1	23.1	19.6	6.1	72.6
Hammersmith	17.0	2.6	0.6	23.1	19.0	4.4	66.7
Haringey	26.3	3.9	1.0	23.7	24.0	4.0	83.0
Harrow	41.4	2.9	2.2	11.2	14.6	0.9	73.2
Havering	46.3	4.7	2.7	8.9	22.1	1.2	86.0
Hillingdon	43.0	4.6	3.1	11.7	19.6	1.1	83.2
Hounslow	33.4	5.3	1.8	12.5	18.9	1.6	73.6
Islington	25.5	1.9	0.3	19.5	16.1	3.3	66.7
Kensington & Chelsea	34.7	0.9	0.1	18.8	14.1	1.9	70.5
Kingston-upon-Thames	26.5	2.7	1.6	10.6	11.6	0.6	53.6
Lambeth	28.3	3.6	0.7	35.2	31.4	5.6	104.8
Lewisham	28.2	4.6	1.0	22.4	35.0	2.5	93.7
Merton	25.4	3.3	1.7	13.4	20.7	1.0	65.5
Newham	23.7	7.3	1.9	16.3	27.4	3.0	79.6
Redbridge	40.5	4.2	1.7	14.9	22.3	1.7	85.1
Richmond	34.2	3.3	1.8	13.4	15.2	1.3	69.1
Southwark	26.6	4.0	0.6	26.0	26.5	2.2	85.9
Sutton	32.5	2.4	1.3	9.2	17.3	0.6	63.3
Tower Hamlets	18.6	3.9	0.3	15.8	13.5	3.0	55.1
Waltham Forest	24.7	6.5	1.4	22.7	27.2	3.4	85.9
Wandsworth	37.2	5.4	1.6	27.7	30.2	3.5	105.8
Westminster	38.8	1.4	0.4	30.0	17.4	3.1	91.0
Greater London	1092.2	126.3	50.1	591.8	711.7	76.0	2648.2

118

TABLE 77B Main Form of Room Heating: London Borough

Percentages

London borough	Main form of room heating						All households
	Central heating	Open fire	Closed stove	Electric	Gas	Other	
City of London	87.3	-	0.6	11.4	0.7	-	100.0
Barking	27.9	7.0	1.4	14.7	46.9	2.2	100.0
Barnet	53.9	4.3	2.9	19.9	17.1	1.8	100.0
Bexley	47.3	5.4	3.3	13.7	29.1	1.1	100.0
Brent	45.0	3.0	1.5	25.1	21.9	3.4	100.0
Bromley	52.3	4.4	3.0	14.3	24.7	1.3	100.0
Camden	45.1	2.5	0.7	29.3	17.2	5.2	100.0
Croydon	42.0	4.7	2.3	18.8	30.5	1.6	100.0
Ealing	41.8	5.8	2.8	23.5	23.7	2.4	100.0
Enfield	46.8	4.7	2.6	17.0	27.4	1.5	100.0
Greenwich	34.9	6.3	2.1	17.5	37.5	1.8	100.0
Hackney	28.9	3.7	0.2	31.9	27.0	8.3	100.0
Hammersmith	25.5	3.9	0.8	34.7	28.5	6.6	100.0
Haringey	31.7	4.7	1.2	28.6	28.9	4.9	100.0
Harrow	56.5	4.0	3.1	15.3	19.9	1.2	100.0
Havering	53.8	5.5	3.1	10.4	15.7	1.4	100.0
Hillingdon	51.7	5.6	3.8	14.1	23.6	1.3	100.0
Hounslow	45.5	7.1	2.5	17 0	25.7	2.1	100.0
Islington	38.2	2.9	0.5	29.3	24.1	5.0	100.0
Kensington & Chelsea	49.2	1.3	0.2	26.6	20.0	2.7	100.0
Kingston-upon-Thames	49.4	5.1	2.9	19.8	21.6	1.1	100.0
Lambeth	27.0	3.4	0.7	33.6	29.9	5.3	100.0
Lewisham	30.0	4.9	1.1	23.9	37.4	2.7	100.0
Merton	38.8	5.0	2.7	20.5	31.5	1.5	100.0
Newham	29.8	9.2	2.4	20.4	34.4	3.7	100.0
Redbridge	47.6	4.9	1.9	17.5	26.1	1.9	100.0
Richmond	49.5	4.8	2.5	19.3	22.0	1.8	100.0
Southwark	31.0	4.6	0.7	30.2	30.8	2.6	100.0
Sutton	51.3	3.8	2.1	14.5	27.3	0.8	100.0
Tower Hamlets	33.8	7.0	0.6	28.7	24.5	5.3	100.0
Waltham Forest	28.7	7.6	1.7	26.4	31.6	4.0	100.0
Wandsworth	35.2	5.1	1.5	26.2	28.6	3.4	100.0
Westminster	42.7	1.5	0.5	32.7	19.2	3.4	100.0
Greater London	41.2	4.8	1.9	22.3	26.9	2.9	100.0

TABLE 78A Tenure: London Borough

Thousands

London borough	Owned out-right	Owned with mort-gage	Rented from council	Rented from housing association	Rented privately unfur-nished	fur-nished	All households
City of London	-	-	2.0	-	0.4	0.1	2.5
Barking	5.2	9.9	39.7	0.1	1.9	0.3	57.0
Barnet	28.6	37.0	21.4	1.6	13.9	9.4	111.9
Bexley	20.0	35.0	16.0	1.0	5.4	0.9	78.2
Brent	18.0	29.7	19.4	2.4	14.1	11.6	95.1
Bromley	25.6	47.8	20.7	2.1	10.7	4.3	111.2
Camden	7.0	10.3	26.2	4.2	16.7	15.3	79.7
Croydon	25.7	47.1	23.2	1.8	15.6	4.9	118.2
Ealing	19.2	36.8	21.3	3.1	13.9	9.1	103.4
Enfield	23.3	38.6	22.5	1.0	10.0	2.0	97.4
Greenwich	11.5	18.0	36.9	2.9	8.9	1.5	79.6
Hackney	3.8	5.8	40.7	4.4	11.6	6.2	72.6
Hammersmith	6.8	9.7	19.0	4.4	16.4	10.4	66.7
Haringey	11.6	20.4	23.0	2.9	15.2	10.0	83.0
Harrow	19.2	34.1	9.8	0.8	6.6	2.7	73.2
Havering	19.0	39.8	21.1	0.6	5.1	0.6	86.0
Hillingdon	15.9	30.6	25.8	1.0	7.4	2.5	83.2
Hounslow	13.8	23.5	21.6	1.7	8.2	4.9	73.6
Islington	4.2	5.9	33.1	4.4	11.4	7.8	66.7
Kensington & Chelsea	11.0	9.4	9.0	7.5	14.5	19.2	70.5
Kingston-upon-Thames	15.2	19.8	7.8	0.5	7.2	3.1	53.6
Lambeth	9.9	13.0	42.0	5.2	21.0	13.7	104.8
Lewisham	10.3	20.2	41.3	3.9	12.9	5.2	93.7
Merton	15.1	24.1	14.1	1.1	8.6	2.5	65.5
Newham	10.9	17.6	31.3	2.1	14.8	2.9	79.6
Redbridge	21.7	36.4	14.4	1.3	7.5	3.8	85.1
Richmond	16.9	23.2	10.2	1.3	11.7	5.9	69.1
Southwark	4.9	6.5	54.7	5.6	11.2	3.0	85.9
Sutton	14.8	27.0	13.3	1.3	5.4	1.5	63.3
Tower Hamlets	0.6	0.6	44.3	2.3	5.7	1.6	55.1
Waltham Forest	16.9	27.3	20.5	1.9	16.7	2.5	85.9
Wandsworth	13.5	20.4	36.8	5.1	21.2	8.8	105.8
Westminster	8.2	6.6	26.1	10.1	24.8	15.3	91.0
Greater London	447.9	731.5	809.6	89.5	376.3	193.3	2648.2

TABLE 78B Tenure: London Borough

Percentages

London borough	Owned out-right	Owned with mort-gage	Rented from council	Rented from housing association	Rented privately unfur-nished	fur-nished	All households
City of London	-	1.3	79.8	-	16.1	2.8	100.0
Barking	9.1	17.4	69.7	0.2	3.3	0.4	100.0
Barnet	25.6	33.1	19.2	1.4	12.5	8.4	100.0
Bexley	25.6	44.7	20.4	1.2	6.9	1.2	100.0
Brent	18.9	31.2	20.4	2.5	14.8	12.2	100.0
Bromley	23.0	43.0	18.6	1.9	9.7	3.8	100.0
Camden	8.8	12.9	32.9	5.3	20.9	19.2	100.0
Croydon	21.7	39.8	19.6	1.5	13.2	4.2	100.0
Ealing	18.5	35.6	20.6	3.0	13.5	8.8	100.0
Enfield	23.9	39.7	23.1	1.0	10.2	2.1	100.0
Greenwich	14.4	22.6	46.3	3.6	11.2	1.9	100.0
Hackney	5.3	8.0	56.0	6.1	16.0	8.6	100.0
Hammersmith	10.2	14.5	28.5	6.7	24.5	15.7	100.0
Haringey	13.9	24.5	27.7	3.5	18.3	12.0	100.0
Harrow	26.3	46.6	13.4	1.1	9.0	3.6	100.0
Havering	22.0	46.2	24.5	0.7	5.9	0.7	100.0
Hillingdon	19.1	36.8	30.9	1.2	8.9	3.0	100.0
Hounslow	18.7	32.0	29.3	2.3	11.2	6.6	100.0
Islington	6.3	8.8	49.7	6.5	17.1	11.7	100.0
Kensington & Chelsea	15.5	13.3	12.8	10.6	20.5	27.2	100.0
Kingston-upon-Thames	28.4	36.9	14.6	0.8	13.4	5.8	100.0
Lambeth	9.5	12.4	40.1	5.0	20.0	13.1	100.0
Lewisham	10.9	21.5	44.1	4.2	13.7	5.6	100.0
Merton	23.0	36.8	21.5	1.7	13.1	3.8	100.0
Newham	13.7	22.1	39.3	2.6	18.6	3.7	100.0
Redbridge	25.5	42.8	16.9	1.5	8.8	4.5	100.0
Richmond	24.5	33.6	14.7	1.9	16.9	8.5	100.0
Southwark	5.8	7.5	63.7	6.6	13.0	3.4	100.0
Sutton	23.4	42.6	21.1	2.0	8.5	2.4	100.0
Tower Hamlets	1.2	1.2	80.4	4.1	10.3	2.9	100.0
Waltham Forest	19.7	31.9	23.8	2.2	19.5	2.9	100.0
Wandsworth	12.8	19.3	34.8	4.9	20.0	8.2	100.0
Westminster	9.0	7.2	28.7	11.0	27.2	16.9	100.0
Greater London	16.9	27.6	30.6	3.4	14.2	7.3	100.0

TABLE 79A   Households in Privately Rented Accommodation: Type of Landlord by London Borough

Thousands

London Borough	Type of landlord						All households privately renting
	Property company	Employer-company	Employer-person	Relative	Other person	Other	
City of London	0.1	0.3	-	-	-	-	0.5
Barking	0.5	0.4	0.1	0.1	1.0	0.1	2.1
Barnet	5.7	2.8	1.0	1.1	11.3	1.4	23.3
Bexley	1.7	0.7	0.4	0.4	2.9	0.3	6.3
Brent	5.2	1.4	0.6	1.1	16.8	0.6	25.7
Bromley	2.9	1.8	0.5	0.9	8.2	0.8	15.0
Camden	8.8	1.9	1.1	0.5	17.4	2.3	32.0
Croydon	4.6	2.0	0.8	0.9	11.3	0.9	20.5
Ealing	4.4	1.5	0.7	1.6	13.9	1.0	23.0
Enfield	2.6	1.1	0.6	0.6	6.2	0.9	12.0
Greenwich	3.6	1.2	0.2	0.4	4.2	0.7	10.4
Hackney	3.9	0.8	0.3	0.6	11.1	1.2	17.8
Hammersmith	7.4	1.1	0.5	0.8	15.9	1.0	26.8
Haringey	4.7	0.9	0.5	1.0	17.4	0.7	25.2
Harrow	2.4	0.9	0.4	0.5	4.4	0.7	9.2
Havering	1.4	0.8	0.4	0.3	2.4	0.3	5.7
Hillingdon	2.8	2.6	0.5	0.3	3.3	0.4	9.9
Hounslow	3.0	1.1	0.3	0.6	7.3	0.8	13.1
Islington	2.7	1.3	0.3	0.8	11.5	2.4	19.2
Kensington & Chelsea	12.1	2.1	1.5	0.9	16.0	1.0	33.7
Kingston-upon-Thames	2.1	1.4	0.6	0.4	5.5	0.3	10.3
Lambeth	7.2	1.4	0.5	1.2	21.1	3.2	34.6
Lewisham	4.1	1.4	0.5	0.9	10.6	0.7	18.1
Merton	3.4	0.7	0.2	0.5	5.7	0.6	11.1
Newham	4.0	1.2	0.1	0.6	11.3	0.5	17.8
Redbridge	2.1	0.9	0.5	0.6	6.6	0.6	11.3
Richmond	4.3	1.2	1.0	0.8	9.5	0.8	17.5
Southwark	3.0	1.6	0.2	0.4	7.9	1.0	14.2
Sutton	1.4	0.8	0.2	0.4	3.4	0.7	6.9
Tower Hamlets	1.4	1.6	0.1	0.1	2.8	1.2	7.2
Waltham Forest	7.5	0.8	0.4	0.8	8.8	0.8	19.2
Wandsworth	7.3	1.2	0.4	1.1	17.9	2.1	30.0
Westminster	17.5	3.3	2.3	0.9	13.1	3.0	40.1
Greater London	145.8	44.0	17.8	22.1	306.8	33.2	569.6

122

Table 79B Households in Privately Rented Accommodation:
        Type of Landlord : London Borough

Percentages

London Borough	Type of landlord						All households privately renting
	Property company	Employer-company	Employer-person	Relative	Other person	Other	
City of London	14.0	74.8	-	-	4.1	7.1	100.0
Barking	24.7	18.0	3.0	6.0	45.4	2.9	100.0
Barnet	24.6	11.8	4.2	4.5	48.6	6.2	100.0
Bexley	26.3	10.9	6.0	5.9	46.0	4.9	100.0
Brent	20.3	5.5	2.5	4.2	65.3	2.2	100.0
Bromley	19.1	11.7	3.3	6.1	54.4	5.3	100.0
Camden	27.5	6.0	3.4	1.6	54.4	7.1	100.0
Croydon	22.4	9.9	4.1	4.2	55.1	4.3	100.0
Ealing	19.2	6.4	3.1	6.9	60.2	4.3	100.0
Enfield	21.9	8.9	4.8	5.3	51.4	7.8	100.0
Greenwich	34.6	11.7	2.4	3.9	40.4	7.0	100.0
Hackney	22.1	4.4	1.5	3.3	62.1	6.6	100.0
Hammersmith	27.6	4.1	1.9	3.0	59.5	3.9	100.0
Haringey	18.5	3.4	2.1	3.8	69.3	3.0	100.0
Harrow	26.5	9.3	3.8	5.4	47.3	7.7	100.0
Havering	24.4	14.4	7.1	5.8	42.3	6.1	100.0
Hillingdon	28.3	25.8	4.9	3.1	33.5	4.4	100.0
Hounslow	23.2	8.1	2.6	4.3	55.6	6.1	100.0
Islington	14.0	7.0	1.8	4.3	60.3	12.7	100.0
Kensington & Chelsea	36.0	6.2	4.5	2.7	47.5	3.0	100.0
Kingston-upon-Thames	20.8	13.2	5.6	4.3	53.0	2.9	100.0
Lambeth	20.7	4.2	1.5	3.5	61.0	9.1	100.0
Lewisham	22.9	7.6	2.6	4.9	58.4	3.6	100.0
Merton	30.3	6.0	2.2	4.1	51.7	5.6	100.0
Newham	22.6	6.6	0.8	3.2	63.9	3.0	100.0
Redbridge	18.3	8.3	4.2	5.2	58.8	5.2	100.0
Richmond	24.5	6.6	5.6	4.6	54.3	4.3	100.0
Southwark	21.1	11.4	1.4	2.9	56.1	7.2	100.0
Sutton	20.4	11.1	3.2	6.5	48.8	10.0	100.0
Tower Hamlets	18.9	22.0	1.6	1.6	38.7	17.1	100.0
Waltham Forest	39.1	4.4	2.3	4.2	45.7	4.3	100.0
Wandsworth	24.4	4.1	1.3	3.6	59.8	6.9	100.0
Westminster	43.7	8.2	5.7	2.3	32.7	7.4	100.0
Greater London	25.6	7.7	3.1	3.9	53.9	5.8	100.0

123

TABLE 80A   Individual Private Landlords: London Borough

Thousands

London Borough	Households renting from individual *			All households renting from individual
	Resident landlord sharing space	Resident landlord not sharing space	No resident landlord	
City of London	-	-	-	-
Barking	0.1	-	1.0	1.1
Barnet	1.5	1.1	10.8	13.4
Bexley	0.2	0.1	3.4	3.7
Brent	3.0	1.8	13.7	18.5
Bromley	0.7	0.6	8.3	9.6
Camden	2.0	2.7	14.4	19.0
Croydon	1.3	1.1	10.7	13.0
Ealing	2.8	1.8	11.5	16.2
Enfield	0.9	0.2	6.2	7.4
Greenwich	0.5	0.4	3.9	4.9
Hackney	1.5	1.0	9.4	11.9
Hammersmith	1.8	2.0	13.4	17.2
Haringey	2.2	1.6	15.0	18.9
Harrow	0.7	0.4	4.1	5.2
Havering	0.2	-	2.9	3.1
Hillingdon	0.3	0.2	3.7	4.1
Hounslow	0.9	0.8	6.5	8.2
Islington	1.9	1.9	8.9	12.7
Kensington & Chelsea	2.1	3.5	12.8	18.4
Kingston-upon-Thames	0.6	0.4	5.4	6.5
Lambeth	3.2	2.4	17.3	22.9
Lewisham	1.9	1.2	8.8	11.9
Merton	0.5	0.5	5.5	6.4
Newham	0.9	0.4	10.7	12.0
Redbridge	0.9	0.6	6.2	7.7
Richmond	1.1	1.3	8.9	11.3
Southwark	1.2	0.7	6.6	8.5
Sutton	0.4	0.3	3.4	4.1
Tower Hamlets	0.2	0.1	2.7	3.0
Waltham Forest	0.9	0.5	8.6	10.0
Wandsworth	2.4	1.4	15.5	19.4
Westminster	1.4	2.2	12.7	16.3
Greater London	40.4	33.3	273.0	346.7

* employer, relative or other person

124

TABLE 80B Individual Private Landlords: London Borough

Percentages

London borough	Households renting from individual *			All households renting from individual
	Resident landlord sharing space	Resident landlord not sharing space	No resident landlord	
City of London	-	-	100.0	100.0
Barking	9.5	-	90.5	100.0
Barnet	11.0	8.2	80.7	100.0
Bexley	4.1	3.3	92.5	100.0
Brent	16.2	9.8	74.0	100.0
Bromley	7.8	6.1	86.1	100.0
Camden	10.3	14.1	75.6	100.0
Croydon	9.7	8.2	82.1	100.0
Ealing	17.4	11.4	71.1	100.0
Enfield	12.7	2.8	84.5	100.0
Greenwich	10.0	9.2	80.8	100.0
Hackney	12.5	8.2	79.2	100.0
Hammersmith	10.2	11.8	78.0	100.0
Haringey	11.8	8.7	79.5	100.0
Harrow	13.7	6.9	79.4	100.0
Havering	7.1	1.6	91.4	100.0
Hillingdon	6.6	3.7	89.7	100.0
Hounslow	11.1	9.6	79.3	100.0
Islington	14.9	14.7	70.4	100.0
Kensington & Chelsea	11.3	19.0	69.7	100.0
Kingston-upon-Thames	9.6	6.5	83.9	100.0
Lambeth	14.0	10.4	75.6	100.0
Lewisham	16.0	10.1	73.9	100.0
Merton	7.5	7.5	85.0	100.0
Newham	7.7	3.7	88.6	100.0
Redbridge	11.7	7.4	80.8	100.0
Richmond	10.0	11.6	78.5	100.0
Southwark	14.3	7.8	77.8	100.0
Sutton	9.5	7.3	83.2	100.0
Tower Hamlets	6.5	4.2	89.2	100.0
Waltham Forest	9.4	5.0	85.6	100.0
Wandsworth	12.3	7.4	80.3	100.0
Westminster	8.6	13.4	78.0	100.0
Greater London	11.6	9.6	78.7	100.0

* employer, relative or other person

125

TABLE 81A   Person Registered on Council House Waiting List: London Borough

Thousands

London borough	Member of household registered				All households
	Head of household	Other person	HoH and other person	No one	
City of London	0.1	0.1	-	2.3	2.5
Barking	2.9	1.3	0.8	52.1	57.0
Barnet	4.5	1.0	1.6	105.6	111.9
Bexley	3.2	0.5	0.1	74.4	78.2
Brent	5.7	1.4	2.1	85.9	95.1
Bromley	4.3	0.4	0.8	105.7	111.2
Camden	6.8	0.9	3.3	68.7	79.7
Croydon	3.6	0.5	1.8	112.4	118.2
Ealing	5.1	1.3	1.8	95.2	103.4
Enfield	4.2	1.0	1.2	90.9	97.4
Greenwich	4.4	1.2	4.7	69.3	79.6
Hackney	10.0	0.9	4.3	57.3	72.6
Hammersmith	6.6	0.8	1.4	57.8	66.7
Haringey	5.5	0.7	0.9	75.9	83.0
Harrow	1.6	0.5	0.5	70.6	73.2
Havering	3.1	0.6	0.9	81.4	86.0
Hillingdon	3.9	0.9	1.3	77.1	83.2
Hounslow	4.1	1.1	0.6	67.8	73.6
Islington	7.8	1.0	2.6	55.3	66.7
Kensington & Chelsea	3.4	0.5	1.2	65.4	70.5
Kingston-upon-Thames	1.2	0.1	0.6	51.6	53.6
Lambeth	11.4	1.3	4.1	88.0	104.8
Lewisham	8.5	1.3	2.6	81.3	93.7
Merton	2.1	0.4	0.9	62.1	65.5
Newham	8.2	0.9	1.3	69.2	79.6
Redbridge	3.1	0.7	0.8	80.5	85.1
Richmond	3.1	0.4	0.4	65.3	69.1
Southwark	9.2	1.3	5.4	70.0	85.9
Sutton	2.5	0.3	0.5	60.0	63.3
Tower Hamlets	9.7	1.0	3.5	40.9	55.1
Waltham Forest	3.8	0.9	1.1	80.1	85.9
Wandsworth	9.1	1.0	1.9	93.8	105.8
Westminster	6.5	0.6	1.6	82.4	91.0
Greater London	169.3	26.8	56.6	2395.4	2648.2

126

TABLE 81B Persons registered on Council House Waiting List: London Borough

Percentages

| London borough | Member of household registered | | | | All households |
	Head of household	Other person	HoH and other person	No one	
City of London	3.5	3.0	1.4	92.1	100.0
Barking	5.2	2.2	1.2	91.4	100.0
Barnet	4.0	0.9	1.4	93.7	100.0
Bexley	4.1	0.6	0.2	95.1	100.0
Brent	6.0	1.4	2.2	90.4	100.0
Bromley	3.8	0.4	0.7	95.1	100.0
Camden	8.6	1.1	4.1	86.2	100.0
Croydon	3.0	0.4	1.5	95.0	100.0
Ealing	4.9	1.3	1.7	92.1	100.0
Enfield	4.3	1.0	1.2	93.4	100.0
Greenwich	5.6	1.5	5.9	87.0	100.0
Hackney	13.8	1.3	5.9	79.0	100.0
Hammersmith	10.0	1.2	2.2	86.7	100.0
Haringey	6.6	0.9	1.1	91.4	100.0
Harrow	2.2	0.7	0.6	96.5	100.0
Havering	3.6	0.7	1.0	94.6	100.0
Hillingdon	4.7	1.1	1.5	92.6	100.0
Hounslow	5.6	1.6	0.8	92.1	100.0
Islington	11.7	1.6	3.9	82.8	100.0
Kensington & Chelsea	4.8	0.7	1.8	92.7	100.0
Kingston-upon-Thames	2.3	0.2	1.1	96.3	100.0
Lambeth	10.9	1.2	3.9	84.0	100.0
Lewisham	9.0	1.4	2.8	86.8	100.0
Merton	3.1	0.6	1.4	94.9	100.0
Newham	10.3	1.1	1.6	87.0	100.0
Redbridge	3.7	0.8	1.0	94.6	100.0
Richmond	4.5	0.5	0.5	94.4	100.0
Southwark	10.7	1.5	6.3	81.5	100.0
Sutton	3.9	0.5	0.8	94.7	100.0
Tower Hamlets	17.7	1.8	6.4	74.1	100.0
Waltham Forest	4.4	1.1	1.3	93.2	100.0
Wandsworth	8.6	0.9	1.8	88.6	100.0
Westminster	7.1	0.6	1.7	90.5	100.0
Greater London	6.4	1.0	2.1	90.5	100.0

127

TABLE 82A Satisfaction with Accommodation: London Borough

Thousands

London Borough	Satisfaction with accommodation					All households
	Very satisfied	Satisfied	Neutral	Dis-satisfied	Very dis-satisfied	
City of London	0.8	1.3	0.2	0.1	-	2.5
Barking	12.3	32.7	6.3	4.0	1.6	57.0
Barnet	39.1	53.5	11.4	5.3	2.5	111.9
Bexley	28.3	38.3	7.4	3.0	1.2	78.2
Brent	24.0	49.5	11.2	7.0	3.5	95.1
Bromley	44.0	49.4	10.0	5.7	2.1	111.2
Camden	21.0	35.0	11.0	7.9	4.8	79.7
Croydon	43.7	54.2	10.8	6.5	3.1	118.2
Ealing	26.5	54.9	11.3	7.4	3.2	103.4
Enfield	35.5	46.0	9.3	4.6	1.9	97.4
Greenwich	25.2	38.0	7.8	5.8	2.8	79.6
Hackney	10.3	32.1	12.1	11.0	7.0	72.6
Hammersmith	17.1	28.4	9.6	7.1	4.5	66.7
Haringey	17.2	44.1	11.0	7.6	3.1	83.0
Harrow	23.7	38.0	6.6	3.9	1.0	73.2
Havering	33.3	40.2	7.4	3.3	1.8	86.0
Hillingdon	30.2	39.1	7.7	4.5	1.7	83.2
Hounslow	27.3	32.2	7.5	4.8	1.9	73.6
Islington	14.2	29.8	10.1	7.6	5.0	66.7
Kensington & Chelsea	23.3	31.8	8.5	4.5	2.4	70.5
Kingston-upon-Thames	19.8	26.2	4.3	2.5	0.9	53.6
Lambeth	24.2	48.5	12.9	11.6	7.5	104.8
Lewisham	26.4	43.7	10.4	8.4	4.8	93.7
Merton	22.6	31.2	6.8	3.7	1.3	65.5
Newham	14.1	42.7	8.8	9.7	4.3	79.6
Redbridge	28.7	40.8	9.1	5.1	1.4	85.1
Richmond	25.7	32.3	6.5	3.1	1.5	69.1
Southwark	15.8	42.2	11.3	10.8	5.9	85.9
Sutton	23.4	30.3	5.8	2.8	1.1	63.3
Tower Hamlets	8.9	24.0	8.2	7.7	6.3	55.1
Waltham Forest	25.1	41.5	10.0	6.3	3.0	85.9
Wandsworth	27.1	50.2	14.8	9.1	4.5	105.8
Westminster	23.7	42.4	11.5	8.9	4.5	91.0
Greater London	782.5	1264.6	297.6	201.2	102.3	2648.2

TABLE 82B Satisfaction with Accommodation: London Borough

Percentages

London Borough	Satisfaction with accommodation					All households
	Very satisfied	Satisfied	Neutral	Dis-satisfied	Very dis-satisfied	
City of London	34.3	53.0	6.9	4.4	1.4	100.0
Barking	21.6	57.4	11.1	7.0	2.9	100.0
Barnet	34.9	47.9	10.2	4.8	2.3	100.0
Bexley	36.2	49.0	9.5	3.8	1.5	100.0
Brent	25.2	52.0	11.7	7.3	3.7	100.0
Bromley	39.6	44.4	9.0	5.1	1.9	100.0
Camden	26.4	44.0	13.7	9.9	6.0	100.0
Croydon	37.0	45.9	9.1	5.5	2.6	100.0
Ealing	25.7	53.1	10.9	7.2	3.1	100.0
Enfield	36.5	47.3	9.6	4.7	2.0	100.0
Greenwich	31.7	47.8	9.8	7.2	3.5	100.0
Hackney	14.2	44.3	16.6	15.2	9.7	100.0
Hammersmith	25.6	42.6	14.4	10.7	6.8	100.0
Haringey	20.7	53.1	13.3	9.1	3.7	100.0
Harrow	32.4	51.9	9.0	5.3	1.4	100.0
Havering	38.8	46.7	8.6	3.8	2.1	100.0
Hillingdon	36.3	47.0	9.2	5.5	2.0	100.0
Hounslow	37.1	43.7	10.2	6.5	2.6	100.0
Islington	21.3	44.6	15.1	11.4	7.5	100.0
Kensington & Chelsea	33.0	45.2	12.0	6.4	3.4	100.0
Kingston-upon-Thames	37.0	48.8	8.0	4.6	1.6	100.0
Lambeth	23.1	46.3	12.3	11.1	7.2	100.0
Lewisham	28.1	46.7	11.1	9.0	5.1	100.0
Merton	34.4	47.6	10.3	5.6	2.1	100.0
Newham	17.7	53.7	11.0	12.2	5.4	100.0
Redbridge	33.8	47.9	10.7	6.0	1.7	100.0
Richmond	37.2	46.7	9.3	4.5	2.2	100.0
Southwark	18.4	49.1	13.1	12.5	6.9	100.0
Sutton	36.9	47.8	9.2	4.4	1.7	100.0
Tower Hamlets	16.1	43.6	14.9	14.0	11.4	100.0
Waltham Forest	29.2	48.4	11.6	7.3	3.5	100.0
Wandsworth	25.6	47.5	14.0	8.6	4.3	100.0
Westminster	26.0	46.6	12.6	9.8	5.0	100.0
Greater London	29.5	47.8	11.2	7.6	3.9	100.0

Thousands

London Borough	Satisfaction with area					All households
	Very satisfied	Satisfied	Neutral	Dis- satisfied	Very dis- satisfied	
City of London	0.6	0.9	0.6	0.3	-	2.5
Barking	8.4	32.5	7.2	6.4	2.6	57.0
Barnet	36.0	52.7	12.3	7.8	3.1	111.9
Bexley	21.4	38.5	8.8	7.0	2.5	78.2
Brent	13.6	46.2	14.9	12.7	7.7	95.1
Bromley	41.1	49.7	10.2	7.6	2.7	111.2
Camden	27.2	35.1	8.4	6.3	2.8	79.7
Croydon	33.1	54.6	13.3	12.3	5.0	118.2
Ealing	17.9	54.4	11.8	13.7	5.5	103.4
Enfield	30.0	45.1	10.0	9.0	3.2	97.4
Greenwich	22.6	37.5	8.2	7.6	3.8	79.6
Hackney	3.9	26.7	11.9	17.3	12.8	72.6
Hammersmith	14.3	30.5	9.2	8.4	4.4	66.7
Haringey	11.5	40.9	13.7	12.0	4.9	83.0
Harrow	20.2	37.0	8.8	5.6	1.5	73.2
Havering	28.4	39.1	9.1	6.6	2.7	86.0
Hillingdon	25.2	39.6	8.4	7.6	2.5	83.2
Hounslow	19.6	32.7	9.3	7.8	4.1	73.6
Islington	10.8	34.1	8.6	8.7	4.5	66.7
Kensington & Chelsea	24.3	30.0	6.9	6.0	3.3	70.5
Kingston-upon-Thames	18.8	25.3	4.8	3.7	1.1	53.6
Lambeth	14.4	45.0	16.1	17.6	11.7	104.8
Lewisham	16.9	46.3	11.7	12.6	6.2	93.7
Merton	18.3	31.7	8.0	5.6	1.9	65.5
Newham	5.2	40.4	10.9	14.8	8.3	79.6
Redbridge	21.2	41.8	10.9	8.6	2.7	85.1
Richmond	30.9	29.2	4.7	3.1	1.2	69.1
Southwark	10.5	42.2	10.8	14.4	8.1	85.9
Sutton	18.6	31.2	6.6	5.0	2.0	63.3
Tower Hamlets	5.6	24.7	7.4	10.0	7.4	55.1
Waltham Forest	17.4	42.4	11.0	10.4	4.7	85.9
Wandsworth	21.1	50.8	14.9	13.1	5.8	105.8
Westminster	27.0	44.2	8.9	8.0	3.0	91.0
Greater London	636.1	1253.1	318.1	297.2	143.7	2648.2

130

TABLE 83B Satisfaction with Area: London Borough

Percentages

London borough	Satisfaction with area					All households
	Very satisfied	Satisfied	Neutral	Dissatisfied	Very dissatis- fied	
City of London	24.6	38.1	22.8	13.3	1.3	100.0
Barking	14.7	57.0	12.6	11.2	4.5	100.0
Barnet	32.2	47.1	11.0	7.0	2.8	100.0
Bexley	27.4	49.2	11.3	8.9	3.2	100.0
Brent	14.3	48.6	15.7	13.3	8.1	100.0
Bromley	36.9	44.7	9.2	6.8	2.4	100.0
Camden	34.2	44.0	10.5	7.8	3.5	100.0
Croydon	28.0	46.1	11.2	10.4	4.2	100.0
Ealing	17.4	52.6	11.4	13.3	5.3	100.0
Enfield	30.9	46.4	10.3	9.2	3.3	100.0
Greenwich	28.4	47.1	10.2	9.5	4.8	100.0
Hackney	5.3	36.8	16.5	23.8	17.7	100.0
Hammersmith	21.4	45.7	13.7	12.5	6.6	100.0
Haringey	13.8	49.3	16.5	14.4	5.9	100.0
Harrow	27.6	50.6	12.0	7.6	2.1	100.0
Havering	33.1	45.5	10.6	7.7	3.2	100.0
Hillingdon	30.2	47.6	10.0	9.2	3.0	100.0
Hounslow	26.7	44.5	12.6	10.7	5.6	100.0
Islington	16.2	51.1	13.0	13.0	6.8	100.0
Kensington & Chelsea	34.5	42.6	9.8	8.5	4.6	100.0
Kingston-upon-Thames	35.1	47.1	8.9	6.9	2.0	100.0
Lambeth	13.8	43.0	15.3	16.8	11.1	100.0
Lewisham	18.0	49.4	12.5	13.4	6.7	100.0
Merton	28.0	48.4	12.2	8.5	2.9	100.0
Newham	6.5	50.8	13.7	18.5	10.4	100.0
Redbridge	24.9	49.1	12.8	10.0	3.1	100.0
Richmond	44.7	42.3	6.9	4.5	1.7	100.0
Southwark	12.2	49.1	12.5	16.7	9.4	100.0
Sutton	29.4	49.3	10.4	7.9	3.1	100.0
Tower Hamlets	10.2	44.8	13.4	18.2	13.4	100.0
Waltham Forest	20.2	49.4	12.9	12.1	5.5	100.0
Wandsworth	19.9	48.0	14.1	12.4	5.5	100.0
Westminster	29.7	48.5	9.8	8.8	3.3	100.0
Greater London	24.0	47.3	12.0	11.2	5.4	100.0

TABLE 84A Satisfaction with Number of Rooms: London Borough

Thousands

London Borough	Satisfaction with number of rooms			All households
	Too few	Too many	About right	
City of London	0.6	-	1.9	2.5
Barking	8.6	3.1	45.2	57.0
Barnet	19.5	7.1	85.4	111.9
Bexley	13.6	3.9	60.8	78.2
Brent	17.6	4.1	73.5	95.1
Bromley	20.5	6.2	84.4	111.2
Camden	22.3	3.6	53.8	79.7
Croydon	22.9	6.7	88.7	118.2
Ealing	20.1	5.1	78.2	103.4
Enfield	16.0	6.4	74.9	97.4
Greenwich	14.1	5.1	60.4	79.6
Hackney	15.7	5.1	51.7	72.6
Hammersmith	15.9	3.4	47.4	66.7
Haringey	17.2	5.0	60.9	83.0
Harrow	12.2	3.8	57.2	73.2
Havering	13.8	4.5	67.8	86.0
Hillingdon	15.6	3.6	64.1	83.2
Hounslow	13.8	4.1	55.6	73.6
Islington	14.3	3.0	49.4	66.7
Kensington & Chelsea	16.5	1.9	52.2	70.5
Kingston-upon-Thames	9.6	2.3	41.7	53.6
Lambeth	24.0	6.1	74.7	104.8
Lewisham	17.0	6.0	70.7	93.7
Merton	11.4	4.3	49.8	65.5
Newham	13.5	6.2	59.9	79.6
Redbridge	14.5	5.5	65.2	85.1
Richmond	13.1	3.9	52.2	69.1
Southwark	16.2	5.5	64.2	85.9
Sutton	11.1	3.2	48.9	63.3
Tower Hamlets	11.0	4.3	39.8	55.1
Waltham Forest	13.7	5.5	66.6	85.9
Wandsworth	22.5	7.1	76.2	105.8
Westminster	23.7	3.4	63.9	91.0
Greater London	512.1	149.0	1987.1	2648.2

TABLE 84B Satisfaction with Number of Rooms: London Borough

Percentages

London borough	Satisfaction with number of rooms			All households
	Too few rooms	Too many rooms	About the right number	
City of London	24.0	-	76.0	100.0
Barking	15.1	5.5	79.4	100.0
Barnet	17.4	6.3	76.3	100.0
Bexley	17.4	5.0	77.7	100.0
Brent	18.5	4.3	77.2	100.0
Bromley	18.5	5.6	75.9	100.0
Camden	28.0	4.5	67.4	100.0
Croydon	19.3	5.7	75.0	100.0
Ealing	19.4	5.0	75.6	100.0
Enfield	16.4	6.6	76.9	100.0
Greenwich	17.7	6.4	75.9	100.0
Hackney	21.7	7.1	71.2	100.0
Hammersmith	23.9	5.0	71.1	100.0
Haringey	20.7	6.0	73.3	100.0
Harrow	16.6	5.2	78.2	100.0
Havering	16.0	5.2	78.8	100.0
Hillingdon	18.7	4.3	77.0	100.0
Hounslow	18.8	5.5	75.6	100.0
Islington	21.4	4.6	74.0	100.0
Kensington & Chelsea	23.3	2.6	74.0	100.0
Kingston-upon-Thames	18.0	4.3	77.7	100.0
Lambeth	22.9	5.8	71.3	100.0
Lewisham	18.2	6.4	75.4	100.0
Merton	17.4	6.5	76.1	100.0
Newham	17.0	7.7	75.3	100.0
Redbridge	17.0	6.4	76.6	100.0
Richmond	18.9	5.6	75.5	100.0
Southwark	18.8	6.4	74.8	100.0
Sutton	17.6	5.1	77.3	100.0
Tower Hamlets	20.0	7.8	72.2	100.0
Waltham Forest	16.0	6.4	77.6	100.0
Wandsworth	21.3	6.7	72.0	100.0
Westminster	26.0	3.8	70.2	100.0
Greater London	19.3	5.6	75.0	100.0

TABLE 85A Satisfaction with Size of Rooms: London Borough

Thousands

London Borough	Satisfaction with size of rooms				All households
	All or some too small	All or some too large	All about right	Some too large, others too small	
City of London	0.4	-	2.0	-	2.5
Barking	16.1	0.3	39.8	0.7	57.0
Barnet	23.7	1.6	83.8	2.8	111.9
Bexley	20.4	0.6	56.4	0.8	78.2
Brent	18.4	1.1	74.7	1.0	95.1
Bromley	22.6	1.4	85.7	1.5	111.2
Camden	19.0	2.1	75.7	1.0	79.7
Croydon	25.4	2.0	88.7	2.1	118.2
Ealing	22.3	1.3	78.1	1.8	103.4
Enfield	19.1	1.3	75.4	1.5	97.4
Greenwich	19.8	0.9	57.4	1.4	79.6
Hackney	19.2	1.9	50.6	0.8	72.6
Hammersmith	14.3	1.1	49.9	1.4	66.7
Haringey	14.3	1.5	65.5	1.7	83.0
Harrow	16.2	0.6	55.1	1.3	73.2
Havering	18.0	0.7	65 9	1.4	86.0
Hillingdon	20.3	0.6	61.3	1.1	83.2
Hounslow	16.6	0.9	54.8	1.2	73.6
Islington	14.7	1.3	49.8	0.9	66.7
Kensington & Chelsea	13.9	0.8	54.9	0.9	70.5
Kingston-upon-Thames	11.2	0.6	41.3	0.5	53.6
Lambeth	24.3	2.2	75.3	2.9	104.8
Lewisham	17.1	1.9	73.2	1.6	93.7
Merton	14.0	0.5	49.9	1.0	65.5
Newham	15.4	0.9	62.6	0.7	79.6
Redbridge	17.5	1.4	64.7	1.6	85.1
Richmond	12.4	0.8	54.0	1.9	69.1
Southwark	20.9	1.3	62.8	0.9	85.9
Sutton	13.5	0.6	48.2	0.9	63.3
Tower Hamlets	14.3	0.8	39.0	1.0	55.1
Waltham Forest	17.9	1.1	65.9	1.1	85.9
Wandsworth	21.1	1.5	80.7	2.4	105.8
Westminster	20.2	1.5	67.3	2.0	91.0
Greater London	574.6	37.1	1992.4	43.9	2648.2

134

TABLE 85B Satisfaction with Size of Rooms: London Borough

London borough	Satisfaction with the size of rooms				All households
	All or some too small	All or some too large	All about right	Some too large others too small	
City of London	16.6	1.3	81.5	0.6	100.0
Barking	28.3	0.6	69.8	1.2	100.0
Barnet	21.2	1.4	74.9	2.5	100.0
Bexley	26.1	0.8	72.0	1.1	100.0
Brent	19.3	1.2	78.5	1.0	100.0
Bromley	20.3	1.2	77.1	1.4	100.0
Camden	23.8	2.6	72.3	1.3	100.0
Croydon	21.5	1.7	75.0	1.8	100.0
Ealing	21.6	1.2	75.5	1.7	100.0
Enfield	19.6	1.4	77.5	1.6	100.0
Greenwich	24.9	1.2	72.2	1.8	100.0
Hackney	26.4	2.7	69.8	1.1	100.0
Hammersmith	21.4	1.7	74.9	2.1	100.0
Haringey	17.3	1.8	78.9	2.0	100.0
Harrow	22.2	0.8	75.3	1.8	100.0
Havering	20.9	0.8	76.6	1.7	100.0
Hillingdon	24.3	0.7	73.6	1.3	100.0
Hounslow	22.6	1.3	74.4	1.7	100.0
Islington	22.0	2.0	74.6	1.4	100.0
Kensington & Chelsea	19.8	1.2	77.9	1.2	100.0
Kingston-upon-Thames	21.0	1.2	77.0	0.9	100.0
Lambeth	23.2	2.1	71.9	2.8	100.0
Lewisham	18.2	2.0	78.1	1.7	100.0
Merton	21.5	0.8	76.1	1.6	100.0
Newham	19.3	1.2	78.6	0.9	100.0
Redbridge	20.5	1.6	76.0	1.9	100.0
Richmond	18.0	1.1	78.1	2.8	100.0
Southwark	24.3	1.5	73.1	1.1	100.0
Sutton	21.4	0.9	76.2	1.5	100.0
Tower Hamlets	26.0	1.5	70.7	1.8	100.0
Waltham Forest	20.8	1.2	76.7	1.2	100.0
Wandsworth	20.0	1.4	76.3	2.3	100.0
Westminster	22.2	1.6	74.0	2.1	100.0
Greater London	21.7	1.4	75.2	1.7	100.0

135

TABLE 86A Availability of Cars and Vans: London Borough

| London Borough | Number of cars and vans available to household | | | | All households |
	0	1	2	3 or more	
City of London	1.2	1.1	0.1	-	2.5
Barking	29.5	23.4	2.7	0.6	57.0
Barnet	40.3	52.9	15.4	2.6	111.9
Bexley	26.2	42.9	7.8	1.4	78.2
Brent	46.8	40.5	6.5	1.3	95.1
Bromley	34.4	57.2	17.4	2.2	111.2
Camden	48.4	27.2	3.5	0.6	79.7
Croydon	44.4	59.6	12.6	1.6	118.2
Ealing	45.3	48.3	8.7	1.1	103.4
Enfield	37.8	47.8	10.3	1.5	97.4
Greenwich	38.8	35.9	4.5	0.4	79.6
Hackney	48.9	21.7	1.8	0.2	72.6
Hammersmith	42.4	20.9	2.9	0.5	66.7
Haringey	45.0	32.9	4.5	0.6	83.0
Harrow	23.5	38.8	9.5	1.4	73.2
Havering	26.8	47.7	10.3	1.2	86.0
Hillingdon	26.1	45.0	10.6	1.6	83.2
Hounslow	28.9	36.1	7.5	1.1	73.6
Islington	44.6	20.0	1.9	0.3	66.7
Kensington & Chelsea	40.4	24.9	4.4	0.8	70.5
Kingston-upon-Thames	19.7	27.6	5.7	0.7	53.6
Lambeth	65.7	34.4	4.0	0.7	104.8
Lewisham	49.5	38.5	4.9	0.7	93.7
Merton	26.4	32.6	5.8	0.6	65.5
Newham	45.9	30.9	2.4	0.3	79.6
Redbridge	29.9	43.5	10.4	1.4	85.1
Richmond	26.3	33.9	8.1	0.9	69.1
Southwark	54.7	28.4	2.6	0.3	85.9
Sutton	20.6	34.3	7.4	1.1	63.3
Tower Hamlets	39.2	14.8	1.0	0.2	55.1
Waltham Forest	42.4	38.1	4.8	0.6	85.9
Wandsworth	55.6	43.6	5.9	0.6	105.8
Westminster	59.6	26.3	4.6	0.6	91.0
Greater London	1254.8	1153.1	210.6	29.7	2648.2

136

TABLE 86B Availability of Cars and Vans: London Borough

Percentages

London Borough	Number of cars and vans available to household				All households
	0	1	2	3 or more	
City of London	49.2	45.1	5.8	-	100.0
Barking	51.7	42.4	4.8	1.1	100.0
Barnet	36.1	47.8	13.8	2.3	100.0
Bexley	33.5	54.8	9.9	1.8	100.0
Brent	49.2	42.6	6.9	1.4	100.0
Bromley	31.0	51.4	15.6	2.0	100.0
Camden	60.7	34.1	4.4	0.8	100.0
Croydon	37.6	50.4	10.7	1.4	100.0
Ealing	43.8	46.7	8.4	1.0	100.0
Enfield	38.8	49.1	10.6	1.6	100.0
Greenwich	48.7	45.1	5.7	0.5	100.0
Hackney	67.4	29.9	2.4	0.3	100.0
Hammersmith	63.5	31.4	4.3	0.8	100.0
Haringey	54.2	39.7	5.4	0.7	100.0
Harrow	32.1	53.0	12.9	1.9	100.0
Havering	31.2	55.4	12.0	1.4	100.0
Hillingdon	31.4	54.0	12.7	1.9	100.0
Hounslow	39.3	49.1	10.1	1.5	100.0
Islington	66.8	29.9	2.9	0.4	100.0
Kensington & Chelsea	57.3	35.4	6.3	1.1	100.0
Kingston-upon-Thames	36.7	51.5	10.6	1.2	100.0
Lambeth	62.7	32.8	3.8	0.7	100.0
Lewisham	52.8	41.1	5.3	0.8	100.0
Merton	40.4	49.8	8.9	1.0	100.0
Newham	57.7	38.9	3.1	0.4	100.0
Redbridge	35.1	51.1	12.2	1.7	100.0
Richmond	38.0	49.0	11.7	1.3	100.0
Southwark	63.7	33.0	3.0	0.3	100.0
Sutton	32.5	54.1	11.6	1.7	100.0
Tower Hamlets	71.0	26.8	1.8	0.3	100.0
Waltham Forest	49.4	44.3	5.5	0.7	100.0
Wandsworth	52.6	41.2	5.6	0.6	100.0
Westminster	65.4	28.9	5.0	0.7	100.0
Greater London	47.4	43.5	8.0	1.1	100.0

137

Thousands

London Borough	Off street parking provision			All households with car or van
	Yes for all cars or vans	Yes for some cars or vans	None	
City of London	1.2	-	-	1.2
Barking	12.8	1.2	13.5	27.5
Barnet	48.5	3.4	19.7	71.6
Bexley	42.8	1.8	7.5	52.1
Brent	29.5	1.8	17.0	48.3
Bromley	60.1	3.2	13.5	76.8
Camden	11.1	0.8	19.4	31.3
Croydon	49.3	3.0	21.6	73.8
Ealing	31.4	2.8	23.8	58.1
Enfield	37.5	2.5	19.6	59.6
Greenwich	23.5	1.4	15.8	40.8
Hackney	10.5	0.3	12.9	23.7
Hammersmith	6.3	0.3	17.7	24.3
Haringey	11.4	1.1	25.4	38.0
Harrow	38.0	2.1	9.5	49.7
Havering	46.6	2.0	10.5	59.2
Hillingdon	45.2	2.7	9.2	57.2
Hounslow	28.8	2.1	13.8	44.7
Islington	8.6	0.4	13.1	22.2
Kensington & Chelsea	8.4	1.1	20.6	30.1
Kingston-upon-Thames	25.4	1.1	7.5	34.0
Lambeth	15.8	0.8	22.5	39.1
Lewisham	21.5	1.3	21.4	44.2
Merton	22.1	1.7	15.2	39.0
Newham	9.9	0.7	23.0	33.6
Redbridge	37.1	3.2	15.0	55.3
Richmond	25.4	1.8	15.7	42.9
Southwark	17.1	0.6	13.7	31.3
Sutton	32.8	1.9	8.0	42.7
Tower Hamlets	7.9	0.2	7.7	15.9
Waltham Forest	21.9	1.5	20.1	43.5
Wandsworth	17.8	1.5	30.9	50.2
Westminster	15.7	0.8	14.9	31.4
Greater London	822.1	51.6	519.7	1393.4

TABLE 87B   Off Street Parking Provision for Households With Car or Van: London Borough

Percentages

London borough	Off street parking provision			All households with car or van
	For all cars and vans	For some cars and vans	None	
City of London	96.3	1.3	2.5	100.0
Barking	46.6	4.2	49.2	100.0
Barnet	67.8	4.7	27.5	100.0
Bexley	82.2	3.4	14.4	100.0
Brent	61.1	3.8	35.1	100.0
Bromley	78.2	4.2	17.6	100.0
Camden	35.6	2.4	62.0	100.0
Croydon	66.8	4.0	29.3	100.0
Ealing	54.1	4.9	41.0	100.0
Enfield	62.9	4.2	32.9	100.0
Greenwich	57.7	3.5	38.8	100.0
Hackney	44.1	1.2	54.6	100.0
Hammersmith	25.9	1.2	72.9	100.0
Haringey	30.0	3.0	66.9	100.0
Harrow	76.5	4.3	19.2	100.0
Havering	78.8	3.4	17.7	100.0
Hillingdon	79.1	4.8	16.1	100.0
Hounslow	64.5	4.7	30.9	100.0
Islington	38.8	2.0	59.2	100.0
Kensington & Chelsea	28.0	3.7	68.3	100.0
Kingston-upon-Thames	74.6	3.3	22.1	100.0
Lambeth	40.3	2.1	57.7	100.0
Lewisham	48.7	3.0	48.3	100.0
Merton	56.7	4.4	38.9	100.0
Newham	29.6	2.0	68.4	100.0
Redbridge	67.0	5.8	27.2	100.0
Richmond	59.3	4.3	36.5	100.0
Southwark	54.5	1.8	43.7	100.0
Sutton	76.8	4.4	18.8	100.0
Tower Hamlets	49.9	1.7	48.4	100.0
Waltham Forest	50.4	3.4	46.2	100.0
Wandsworth	35.5	2.9	61.6	100.0
Westminster	50.1	2.6	47.3	100.0
Greater London	59.0	3.7	37.3	100.0

TABLE 88A Age and Sex of Head of Household   London Borough

Thousands

London borough	Male				Females				All heads of household
	16-29	30-44	45-64	65 or over	16-29	30-44	45-59	60 or over	
City of London	0.5	0.5	0.7	0.1	0.2	0.2	0.1	0.1	2.5
Barking	5.9	11.1	18.7	8.7	0.5	0.9	2.5	8.5	57.0
Barnet	11.0	24.7	33.7	17.6	2.5	2.9	5.9	13.5	111.9
Bexley	8.3	20.2	25.2	11.0	0.7	1.6	2.1	9.1	78.2
Brent	11.2	22.8	27.1	11.2	4.4	3.5	4.3	10.6	95.1
Bromley	11.5	25.5	36.0	14.2	1.5	2.4	5.1	14.9	111.2
Camden	11.2	16.1	17.0	8.6	4.5	5.3	4.2	12.7	79.7
Croydon	14.2	29.6	35.1	13.9	2.7	2.7	4.5	15.5	118.2
Ealing	13.4	25.0	29.9	13.3	2.5	3.0	4.3	12.0	103.4
Enfield	9.8	23.6	29.2	14.0	1.4	2.3	3.3	13.7	97.4
Greenwich	9.5	16.3	23.8	11.1	1.7	2.3	3.3	11.8	79.6
Hackney	8.8	14.5	18.5	9.1	3.5	3.8	3.8	10.5	72.6
Hammersmith	9.1	12.5	14.7	8.5	4.3	3.5	3.3	10.8	66.7
Haringey	11.1	20.7	20.6	10.7	3.3	2.8	3.5	10.4	83.0
Harrow	7.3	18.0	22.4	10.3	1.0	1.8	3.0	9.2	73.2
Havering	9.2	22.8	30.4	9.6	0.8	1.3	2.9	9.1	86.0
Hillingdon	8.4	20.9	26.9	11.5	1.4	1.6	2.8	9.7	83.2
Hounslow	8.9	17.2	21.2	9.4	2.4	2.2	2.6	9.6	73.6
Islington	7.7	13.3	18.2	7.5	3.2	3.1	3.5	10.3	66.7
Kensington & Chelsea	10.5	15.6	13.8	5.7	6.6	4.9	4.5	8.9	70.5
Kingston-upon-Thames	5.7	12.8	14.6	7.5	1.1	1.4	2.4	8.2	53.6
Lambeth	14.2	20.2	26.6	12.2	6.4	4.8	5.1	15.2	104.8
Lewisham	10.1	19.1	26.3	12.9	2.9	3.7	4.1	13.7	93.7
Merton	6.8	15.1	19.8	9.0	1.1	1.4	3.0	9.3	65.5
Newham	10.9	16.2	23.5	10.6	1.5	2.0	3.3	11.7	79.6
Redbridge	9.3	20.0	27.2	11.0	1.6	2.1	3.6	10.2	85.1
Richmond	6.7	15.7	18.2	9.7	1.8	2.6	3.3	11.1	69.1
Southwark	9.7	14.1	25.9	11.4	2.9	3.2	4.3	14.3	85.9
Sutton	6.8	15.5	18.0	8.8	0.8	1.8	2.7	8.8	63.3
Tower Hamlets	6.2	9.8	16.9	7.5	1.9	1.6	3.1	8.3	55.2
Waltham Forest	10.6	20.0	24.3	13.0	1.4	1.7	3.0	11.9	85.9
Wandsworth	11.5	24.2	28.5	14.9	3.7	3.6	5.0	14.4	105.8
Westminster	11.2	17.3	21.5	10.3	5.3	4.6	5.6	15.2	91.0
Greater London	307.9	591.1	754.3	344.4	81.8	87.1	118.2	363.3	2648.2

140

TABLE 88B Age and sex of Head of Household: London Borough

Percentages

London borough	Males				Females				All heads of household
	16-29	30-44	45-64	65 or over	16-29	30-44	45-59	60 or over	
City of London	19.0	21.5	29.1	4.6	8.4	9.9	4.0	3.5	100.0
Barking	10.4	19.5	32.9	15.3	1.0	1.6	4.4	14.9	100.0
Barnet	9.9	22.1	30.2	15.8	2.2	2.6	5.3	12.1	100.0
Bexley	10.7	25.8	32.2	14.0	0.9	2.1	2.7	11.6	100.0
Brent	11.8	24.0	28.5	11.7	4.7	3.6	4.5	11.2	100.0
Bromley	10.3	23.0	32.4	12.8	1.3	2.2	4.6	13.4	100.0
Camden	14.0	20.2	21.3	10.8	5.7	6.7	5.3	16.0	100.0
Croydon	12.0	25.1	29.6	11.7	2.3	2.3	3.8	13.1	100.0
Ealing	12.9	24.2	28.9	12.9	2.5	2.9	4.1	11.6	100.0
Enfield	10.1	24.3	30.0	14.4	1.4	2.4	3.4	14.1	100.0
Greenwich	11.9	20.4	29.8	14.0	2.1	2.9	4.1	14.8	100.0
Hackney	12.2	20.0	25.4	12.6	4.8	5.3	5.3	14.4	100.0
Hammersmith	13.6	18.8	22.0	12.7	6.5	5.3	5.0	16.2	100.0
Haringey	13.2	24.9	24.8	12.8	4.0	3.4	4.3	12.6	100.0
Harrow	10.0	24.7	30.6	14.0	1.4	2.5	4.2	12.6	100.0
Havering	10.7	26.5	35.4	11.1	0.9	1.5	3.4	10.5	100.0
Hillingdon	10.0	25.1	32.3	13.9	1.7	1.9	3.4	11.6	100.0
Hounslow	12.1	23.4	28.8	12.7	3.3	3.0	3.6	13.0	100.0
Islington	11.5	20.0	27.2	11.2	4.9	4.6	5.2	15.4	100.0
Kensington & Chelsea	14.9	22.1	19.5	8.0	9.3	7.0	6.4	12.7	100.0
Kingston-upon-Thames	10.6	23.9	27.2	14.0	2.1	2.6	4.4	15.2	100.0
Lambeth	13.5	19.3	25.4	11.6	6.2	4.6	4.9	14.5	100.0
Lewisham	11.8	20.4	28.1	13.8	3.1	3.9	4.4	14.6	100.0
Merton	10.3	23.1	30.2	13.7	1.7	2.2	4.5	14.2	100.0
Newham	13.7	20.4	29.6	13.3	1.8	2.5	4.1	14.7	100.0
Redbridge	11.0	23.5	32.0	12.9	1.9	2.5	4.3	12.0	100.0
Richmond	9.7	22.7	26.3	14.0	2.7	3.8	4.7	16.1	100.0
Southwark	11.3	16.4	30.2	13.2	3.4	3.8	5.0	16.7	100.0
Sutton	10.8	24.4	28.5	13.9	1.4	2.8	4.2	13.9	100.0
Tower Hamlets	11.2	17.8	30.6	13.5	3.4	2.9	5.6	15.0	100.0
Waltham Forest	12.3	23.3	28.3	15.1	1.7	2.0	3.5	13.9	100.0
Wandsworth	10.8	22.9	26.9	14.1	3.5	3.4	4.8	13.6	100.0
Westminster	12.3	19.0	23.6	11.3	5.9	5.1	6.2	16.6	100.0
Greater London	11.6	22.3	28.5	13.0	3.1	3.3	4.5	13.7	100.0

Thousands

London Borough	Marital status					All heads of household
	Single	Married	Divorced	Widowed	Separated	
City of London	0.9	1.0	0.3	–	0.2	2.5
Barking	2.3	40.8	1.5	11.5	0.9	57.0
Barnet	15.0	75.9	3.6	15.9	1.5	111.9
Bexley	4.5	59.1	2.2	11.3	1.1	78.2
Brent	17.3	59.9	3.2	12.9	1.9	95.1
Bromley	10.5	78.6	3.7	16.6	1.7	111.2
Camden	25.4	36.9	4.2	11.1	2.1	79.7
Croydon	13.0	82.5	3.6	16.6	2.6	118.2
Ealing	15.1	68.5	3.3	14.6	1.8	103.4
Enfield	9.1	68.2	2.7	15.9	1.5	97.4
Greenwich	6.9	54.2	3.2	13.8	1.4	79.6
Hackney	12.7	41.5	4.0	11.6	2.7	72.6
Hammersmith	17.6	32.4	3.1	11.0	2.5	66.7
Haringey	15.3	51.6	3.1	10.9	2.1	83.0
Harrow	6.8	51.7	2.2	11.4	1.1	73.2
Havering	4.2	66.8	2.1	11.8	1.1	86.0
Hillingdon	5.7	60.8	2.6	12.7	1.4	83.2
Hounslow	9.5	48.7	2.5	11.3	1.5	73.6
Islington	14.8	35.3	2.8	11.7	2.2	66.7
Kensington & Chelsea	29.0	28.2	4.0	7.3	2.0	70.5
Kingston-upon-Thames	7.2	35.4	1.7	8.6	0.8	53.6
Lambeth	23.7	56.9	4.8	15.7	3.6	104.8
Lewisham	12.5	59.1	4.2	15.3	2.6	93.7
Merton	7.7	43.8	2.2	10.7	1.1	65.5
Newham	8.9	52.4	2.5	14.2	1.6	79.6
Redbridge	8.8	60.0	2.9	11.6	1.7	85.1
Richmond	11.4	41.5	3.0	11.9	1.3	69.1
Southwark	12.6	50.2	3.5	16.7	2.9	85.9
Sutton	5.8	44.0	2.3	10.1	1.1	63.3
Tower Hamlets	7.6	33.3	2.1	10.4	1.7	55.1
Waltham Forest	8.3	59.8	2.7	13.6	1.5	85.9
Wandsworth	17.6	64.5	4.7	16.6	2.4	105.8
Westminster	30.5	39.5	4.9	13.7	2.5	91.0
Greater London	398.2	1683.1	99.4	409.3	58.1	2648.2

TABLE 89B Marital Status of Head of Household: London Borough

Percentages

| London borough | Marital status of head of household | | | | | All households |
	Single	Married	Divorced	Widowed	Separated	
City of London	37.4	39.4	14.1	1.4	7.6	100.0
Barking	4.0	71.7	2.6	20.2	1.6	100.0
Barnet	13.4	67.9	3.2	14.2	1.3	100.0
Bexley	5.8	75.6	2.8	14.5	1.4	100.0
Brent	18.1	63.0	3.3	13.6	2.0	100.0
Bromley	9.5	70.7	3.3	15.0	1.5	100.0
Camden	31.9	46.2	5.2	14.0	2.6	100.0
Croydon	11.0	69.8	3.1	14.0	2.2	100.0
Ealing	14.6	66.3	3.2	14.1	1.8	100.0
Enfield	9.3	70.0	2.8	16.3	1.5	100.0
Greenwich	8.7	68.1	4.1	17.4	1.8	100.0
Hackney	17.5	57.2	5.5	16.0	3.7	100.0
Hammersmith	26.4	48.7	4.7	16.5	3.7	100.0
Haringey	18.5	62.1	3.8	13.1	2.6	100.0
Harrow	9.3	70.6	3.1	15.5	1.5	100.0
Havering	4.9	77.6	2.4	13.7	1.3	100.0
Hillingdon	6.9	73.1	3.1	15.3	1.7	100.0
Hounslow	12.9	66.2	3.4	15.3	2.1	100.0
Islington	22.2	52.9	4.2	17.5	3.2	100.0
Kensington & Chelsea	41.2	40.0	5.7	10.3	2.9	100.0
Kingston-upon-Thames	13.4	66.0	3.1	16.1	1.5	100.0
Lambeth	22.7	54.3	4.6	15.0	3.4	100.0
Lewisham	13.4	63.1	4.4	16.4	2.7	100.0
Merton	11.7	66.9	3.3	16.3	1.7	100.0
Newham	11.2	65.9	3.1	17.8	2.0	100.0
Redbridge	10.3	70.5	3.4	13.7	2.0	100.0
Richmond	16.5	60.1	4.3	17.2	1.9	100.0
Southwark	14.7	58.4	4.1	19.4	3.4	100.0
Sutton	9.1	69.5	3.6	16.0	1.8	100.0
Tower Hamlets	13.8	60.4	3.9	18.9	3.0	100.0
Waltham Forest	9.7	69.6	3.1	15.9	1.7	100.0
Wandsworth	16.6	60.9	4.4	15.7	2.3	100.0
Westminster	33.5	43.4	5.3	15.0	2.7	100.0
Greater London	15.0	63.6	3.8	15.5	2.2	100.0

Thousands

| London Borough | Length of residence (years) | | | | | | All heads of households |
	Under 1	1 but under 2	2 but under 3	3 but under 5	5 but under 10	10 or over	
City of London	0.6	0.3	0.3	0.5	0.5	0.1	2.5
Barking	3.5	2.3	4.9	5.0	9.5	31.8	57.0
Barnet	11.5	8.5	9.2	9.4	21.3	52.0	111.9
Bexley	6.3	5.3	6.0	7.8	13.3	39.5	78.2
Brent	13.0	8.5	10.9	9.3	16.2	37.2	95.1
Bromley	11.2	8.2	11.0	10.7	19.9	50.2	111.2
Camden	14.4	8.4	8.6	8.6	13.8	26.0	79.7
Croydon	13.3	9.2	12.6	10.9	20.3	52.0	118.2
Ealing	13.2	9.0	10.8	9.7	16.4	44.3	103.4
Enfield	7.1	6.5	8.7	9.9	17.0	48.2	97.4
Greenwich	9.1	6.8	7.6	7.7	13.4	35.0	79.6
Hackney	9.6	7.6	8.6	7.8	13.8	25.0	72.6
Hammersmith	9.2	6.3	7.0	6.3	10.8	27.0	66.7
Haringey	10.5	7.0	9.7	10.0	15.5	30.3	83.0
Harrow	6.6	5.0	6.5	7.2	13.4	34.5	73.2
Havering	6.3	5.3	7.8	7.6	15.2	43.7	86.0
Hillingdon	8.2	6.1	8.0	8.2	13.3	39.5	83.2
Hounslow	8.9	6.6	7.3	6.7	11.2	32.9	73.6
Islington	11.5	7.5	7.2	7.8	12.5	20.1	66.7
Kensington & Chelsea	15.7	8.4	8.9	7.5	11.0	19.2	70.5
Kingston-upon-Thames	5.7	3.8	5.3	5.6	9.4	23.7	53.6
Lambeth	15.0	10.3	12.1	11.7	17.5	38.2	104.8
Lewisham	11.5	8.8	9.7	8.5	15.6	39.6	93.7
Merton	6.3	4.1	5.1	5.6	12.1	32.4	65.5
Newham	7.8	5.9	6.8	8.7	13.2	37.2	79.6
Redbridge	7.6	6.2	6.6	8.7	14.9	41.2	85.1
Richmond	8.5	5.9	6.6	6.2	11.6	30.4	69.1
Southwark	10.5	7.9	9.6	8.3	15.9	33.7	85.9
Sutton	6.5	5.2	6.4	6.3	11.8	27.0	63.3
Tower Hamlets	8.2	4.7	5.8	5.8	11.1	19.5	55.1
Waltham Forest	7.1	5.5	7.3	7.7	14.9	43.3	85.9
Wandsworth	11.5	7.6	8.8	10.1	21.0	46.9	105.8
Westminster	14.3	8.2	12.8	11.3	16.3	28.1	91.0
Greater London	310.4	216.9	264.3	263.1	463.3	1130.1	2648.2

TABLE 90B   Length of Residence of Head of Household: London Borough

Percentages

| London Borough | Length of residence (years) | | | | | | All heads of household |
	Under 1	1 but under 2	2 but under 3	3 but under 5	5 but under 10	10 or over	
City of London	25.6	12.1	13.8	21.0	21.9	5.6	100.0
Barking	6.1	4.1	8.6	8.8	16.6	55.8	100.0
Barnet	10.3	7.6	8.2	8.4	19.0	46.5	100.0
Bexley	8.1	6.7	7.7	10.0	17.0	50.5	100.0
Brent	13.6	8.9	11.5	9.8	17.0	39.1	100.0
Bromley	10.1	7.4	9.9	9.6	17.9	45.1	100.0
Camden	18.0	10.5	10.8	10.8	17.3	32.6	100.0
Croydon	11.3	7.8	10.6	9.2	17.1	44.0	100.0
Ealing	12.8	8.7	10.4	9.4	15.9	42.9	100.0
Enfield	7.3	6.6	8.9	10.1	17.5	49.5	100.0
Greenwich	11.4	8.6	9.6	9.7	16.8	44.0	100.0
Hackney	13.3	10.5	11.9	10.8	19.1	34.5	100.0
Hammersmith	13.8	9.4	10.6	9.5	16.2	40.6	100.0
Haringey	12.7	8.5	11.7	12.0	18.6	36.5	100.0
Harrow	9.0	6.8	8.9	9.8	18.3	47.2	100.0
Havering	7.3	6.2	9.1	8.8	17.7	50.8	100.0
Hillingdon	9.8	7.3	9.6	9.8	16.0	47.5	100.0
Hounslow	12.2	8.9	9.9	9.1	15.2	44 7	100.0
Islington	17.3	11.2	10.8	11.7	18.8	30.2	100.0
Kensington & Chelsea	22.3	11.8	12.3	10.7	15.6	27.3	100.0
Kingston-upon-Thames	10.6	7.2	10.0	10.5	17.5	44.3	100.0
Lambeth	14.3	9.8	11.5	11.1	16.7	36.5	100.0
Lewisham	12.3	9.4	10.3	9.1	16.6	42.3	100.0
Merton	9.6	6.2	7.8	8.6	18.4	49.5	100.0
Newham	9.8	7.4	8.6	10.9	6.6	6.7	100.0
Redbridge	8.9	7.3	7.8	10.2	17.4	48.4	100.0
Richmond	12.3	8.5	9.5	9.0	16.7	43.9	100.0
Southwark	12.2	9.2	11.2	9.6	18.6	39.2	100.0
Sutton	10.3	8.2	10.1	10.0	18.7	42.7	100.0
Tower Hamlets	14.9	8.5	10.5	10.6	20.1	35.4	100.0
Waltham Forest	8.3	6.4	8.5	9.0	17.4	50.5	100.0
Wandsworth	10.9	7.2	8.3	9.5	19.8	44.3	100.0
Westminster	15.8	9.0	14.1	12.4	17.9	30.8	100.0
Greater London	11.7	8.2	10.0	9.9	17.5	42.7	100.0

Thousands

London borough	Employment status						All heads of household
	Employed full time	part time	Unemployed	Wholly retired	House-wife	Other	
City of London	2.3	-	-	0.1	-	-	2.5
Barking	34.7	1.3	1.7	10.2	7.6	1.4	57.0
Barnet	74.6	4.6	2.1	18.7	8.5	3.4	111.9
Bexley	53.8	2.1	1.7	13.6	5.8	1.2	78.2
Brent	65.3	2.1	3.4	14.7	5.9	3.8	95.1
Bromley	75.2	3.5	3.0	17.8	9.9	1.8	111.2
Camden	49.4	3.9	3.4	13.5	4.2	5.4	79.7
Croydon	82.3	3.8	3.2	16.9	10.0	2.1	118.2
Ealing	70.3	2.9	2.9	17.8	6.4	3.1	103.4
Enfield	64.8	3.6	2.3	16.8	7.6	2.3	97.4
Greenwich	50.1	2.6	2.8	15.6	6.7	1.7	79.6
Hackney	41.8	3.6	4.6	12.8	5.8	3.9	72.5
Hammersmith	40.0	2.8	3.0	12.6	4.8	3.5	66.7
Haringey	53.7	2.3	2.8	15.6	4.7	3.9	83.0
Harrow	50.3	2.1	1.3	12.3	6.3	1.0	73.2
Havering	62.1	2.1	1.8	11.9	6.8	1.3	86.0
Hillingdon	58.0	2.4	1.6	13.8	6.3	1.2	83.2
Hounslow	49.9	2.3	1.9	12.4	5.3	1.7	73.6
Islington	40.1	3.3	3.6	11.5	4.9	3.4	66.7
Kensington & Chelsea	46.0	3.4	2.4	8.5	4.6	5.5	70.5
Kingston-upon-Thames	35.4	1.6	0.9	8.9	5.7	1.1	53.6
Lambeth	64.3	3.6	5.3	20.0	6.3	5.3	104.8
Lewisham	58.4	3.0	3.2	17.7	7.9	3.5	93.7
Merton	43.6	1.9	1.5	11.8	5.1	1.5	65.5
Newham	48.7	1.9	3.9	13.7	8.4	3.1	79.6
Redbridge	58.1	2.7	2.5	13.9	6.3	1.8	85.1
Richmond	44.3	3.1	1.3	12.7	5.9	1.8	69.1
Southwark	49.9	3.7	4.7	18.7	5.5	3.5	85.9
Sutton	42.4	2.4	1.1	11.3	5.2	0.9	63.3
Tower Hamlets	31.5	1.8	4.1	9.8	5.5	2.4	55.1
Waltham Forest	55.1	2.7	2.1	17.7	6.4	1.9	85.9
Wandsworth	66.3	3.9	4.2	21.1	6.5	3.9	105.8
Westminster	56.2	4.6	3.4	15.4	5.9	5.5	91.0
Greater London	1718.8	91.7	87.6	459.5	202.8	87.7	2648.2

TABLE 91B Employment Status of Head of Household : London Borough

London borough	Employment Status						All heads of household
	Employed						
	full time	part time	Unem- ployed	Wholly retired	House- wife	Other	
City of London	92.0	1.2	0.6	4.1	1.4	0.6	100.0
Barking	61.0	2.4	3.0	17.9	13.4	2.4	100.0
Barnet	66.7	4.1	1.9	16.7	7.6	3.1	100.0
Bexley	68.8	2.7	2.2	17.4	7.4	1.5	100.0
Brent	68.6	2.2	3.6	15.4	6.2	4.1	100.0
Bromley	67.7	3.2	2.7	16.0	8.9	1.6	100.0
Camden	62.0	4.9	4.3	16.9	5.2	6.7	100.0
Croydon	69.6	3.2	2.7	14.3	8.4	1.8	100.0
Ealing	68.0	2.8	2.8	17.2	6.2	3.0	100.0
Enfield	66.5	3.7	2.3	17.3	7.8	2.4	100.0
Greenwich	63.0	3.3	3.6	19.6	8.5	2.2	100.0
Hackney	57.6	4.9	6.3	17.7	8.1	5.5	100.0
Hammersmith	60.0	4.2	4.5	18.8	7.2	5.2	100.0
Haringey	64.7	2.7	3.4	18.8	5.7	4.7	100.0
Harrow	68.7	2.8	1.7	16.8	8.6	1.4	100.0
Havering	72.2	2.5	2.1	13.8	7.9	1.6	100.0
Hillingdon	69.7	2.9	1.9	16.5	7.6	1.5	100.0
Hounslow	67.9	3.1	2.7	16.9	7.2	2.3	100.0
Islington	60.0	5.0	5.4	17.2	7.3	5.1	100.0
Kensington & Chelsea	65.3	4.9	3.5	12.0	6.6	7.8	100.0
Kingston-upon-Thames	66.1	2.9	1.6	16.6	10.7	2.1	100.0
Lambeth	61.4	3.4	5.1	19.1	6.0	5.0	100.0
Lewisham	62.3	3.2	3.4	18.9	8.4	3.7	100.0
Merton	66.7	2.9	2.3	18.0	7.8	2.3	100.0
Newham	61.1	2.4	4.9	17.2	10.5	3.9	100.0
Redbridge	68.2	3.2	2.9	16.3	7.4	2.1	100.0
Richmond	64.0	4.5	1.9	18.4	8.5	2.6	100.0
Southwark	58.1	4.3	5.4	21.7	6.4	4.1	100.0
Sutton	66.9	3.8	1.7	17.9	8.2	1.5	100.0
Tower Hamlets	57.2	3.2	7.6	17.7	10.0	4.4	100.0
Waltham Forest	64.1	3.1	2.4	20.7	7.4	2.3	100.0
Wandsworth	62.6	3.7	4.0	19.9	6.2	3.7	100.0
Westminster	61.7	5.1	3.8	16.9	6.5	6.1	100.0
Greater London	64.9	3.5	3.4	17.4	7.7	3.3	100.0

Thousands

London Borough	Birthplace		All heads of household
	In United Kingdom	Not in United Kingdom	
City of London	2.1	0.4	2.5
Barking	53.9	3.1	57.0
Barnet	86.5	25.4	111.9
Bexley	74.4	3.8	78.2
Brent	55.5	39.6	95.1
Bromley	103.9	7.3	111.2
Camden	55.4	24.3	79.7
Croydon	101.9	16.3	118.2
Ealing	73.3	30.1	103.4
Enfield	83.5	13.9	97.4
Greenwich	71.4	8.2	79.6
Hackney	49.1	23.5	72.6
Hammersmith	46.7	20.0	66.7
Haringey	57.7	25.4	83.0
Harrow	61.5	11.7	73.2
Havering	82.6	3.4	86.0
Hillingdon	75.5	7.8	83.2
Hounslow	60.2	13.3	73.6
Islington	48.0	18.7	66.7
Kensington & Chelsea	44.8	25.7	70.5
Kingston-upon-Thames	48.6	5.0	53.6
Lambeth	76.5	28.2	104.8
Lewisham	78.7	15.0	93.7
Merton	56.4	9.1	65.5
Newham	65.3	14.3	79.6
Redbridge	75.5	9.7	85.1
Richmond	60.7	8.4	69.1
Southwark	70.4	15.6	85.9
Sutton	58.3	5.0	63.3
Tower Hamlets	44.8	10.3	55.1
Waltham Forest	74.5	11.4	85.9
Wandsworth	83.5	22.3	105.8
Westminster	59.8	31.3	91.0
Greater London	2140.9	507.3	2648.2

TABLE 92B Birthplace of Head of Household: London Borough

Percentages

| London borough | Birthplace of head of household | | All heads of households |
	United Kingdom	Not in United Kingdom	
City of London	84.1	15.9	100.0
Barking	94.5	5.5	100.0
Barnet	77.3	22.7	100.0
Bexley	95.1	4.9	100.0
Brent	58.3	41.7	100.0
Bromley	93.4	6.6	100.0
Camden	69.5	30.5	100.0
Croydon	86.2	13.8	100.0
Ealing	70.9	29.1	100.0
Enfield	85.7	14.3	100.0
Greenwich	89.7	10.3	100.0
Hackney	67.7	32.3	100.0
Hammersmith	70.0	30.0	100.0
Haringey	69.4	30.6	100.0
Harrow	84.0	16.0	100.0
Havering	96.0	4.0	100.0
Hillingdon	90.7	9.3	100.0
Hounslow	81.9	18.1	100.0
Islington	72.0	28.0	100.0
Kensington & Chelsea	63.6	36.4	100.0
Kingston-upon-Thames	90.7	9.3	100.0
Lambeth	73.1	26.9	100.0
Lewisham	84.0	16.0	100.0
Merton	86.1	13.9	100.0
Newham	82.0	18.0	100.0
Redbridge	88.6	11.4	100.0
Richmond	87.9	12.1	100.0
Southwark	81.9	18.1	100.0
Sutton	92.1	7.9	100.0
Tower Hamlets	81.3	18.7	100.0
Waltham Forest	86.8	13.2	100.0
Wandsworth	78.9	21.1	100.0
Westminster	65.7	34.3	100.0
Greater London	80.8	19.2	100.0

TABLE 93A   Age and Sex of Private Household Population: London Borough

Thousands

| London Borough | Age of Males | | | | | All males |
	0-14	15-29	30-44	45-64	65 or over	
City of London	0.3	0.7	0.6	0.7	0.1	2.4
Barking	16.4	17.4	12.6	19.5	9.2	75.0
Barnet	30.2	35.5	27.8	35.6	18.7	147.8
Bexley	25.2	22.9	22.0	26.4	11.6	108.1
Brent	28.1	35.2	25.9	28.7	12.6	130.5
Bromley	32.3	32.9	27.8	37.2	15.3	145.5
Camden	14.6	24.7	18.8	18.2	9.0	85.4
Croydon	38.1	36.9	32.4	36.4	14.8	158.6
Ealing	30.6	36.5	28.3	32.0	14.4	141.7
Enfield	28.9	28.3	26.7	30.4	14.8	129.2
Greenwich	25.1	25.4	18.2	24.9	11.7	105.4
Hackney	23.1	25.1	16.6	19.7	9.5	94.0
Hammersmith	14.5	22.7	15.2	15.8	8.9	77.2
Haringey	23.9	28.5	22.9	21.9	11.3	108.5
Harrow	21.5	21.3	19.6	23.2	11.1	96.6
Havering	28.8	27.5	24.7	31.3	10.3	122.6
Hillingdon	25.6	25.3	23.1	27.9	12.3	114.1
Hounslow	21.1	23.2	19.7	22.6	10.2	96.7
Islington	16.3	21.2	16.0	19.2	8.0	80.7
Kensington & Chelsea	10.5	22.4	17.5	14.5	6.0	70.9
Kingston-upon-Thames	13.9	13.9	14.1	15.3	7.9	65.0
Lambeth	28.5	35.4	23.3	28.1	12.9	128.2
Lewisham	27.3	30.4	21.8	27.9	13.9	121.3
Merton	17.8	18.6	16.9	20.7	9.6	83.6
Newham	26.4	30.1	18.5	25.2	11.2	111.4
Redbridge	26.1	27.0	22.3	28.1	12.0	115.4
Richmond	14.6	17.4	17.6	19.1	10.1	78.8
Southwark	22.5	26.2	16.9	27.5	11.9	105.0
Sutton	17.4	17.7	16.8	18.9	9.4	80.3
Tower Hamlets	16.0	19.1	11.8	18.3	7.8	73.0
Waltham Forest	26.1	26.0	22.3	25.7	13.5	113.5
Wandsworth	30.1	33.2	27.3	30.4	16.1	137.0
Westminster	13.0	24.7	20.2	22.4	10.7	91.1
Greater London	734.7	833.3	666.2	793.6	366.8	3394.6

150

TABLE 93B Age and Sex of Private Household Population: London Borough

Thousands

London Borough	Age of females					All females
	0-14	15-29	30-44	45-59	60 or over	
City of London	0.1	0.7	0.5	0.4	0.3	2.0
Barking	15.3	17.3	12.5	16.7	18.4	80.2
Barnet	29.4	35.6	30.6	30.9	33.9	160.3
Bexley	23.3	22.2	22.6	20.2	22.5	110.8
Brent	27.3	36.5	26.5	22.9	24.5	137.7
Bromley	29.9	31.5	29.8	31.3	32.8	155.2
Camden	12.9	26.2	18.7	14.6	21.6	93.9
Croydon	35.3	38.9	32.2	29.7	32.8	168.8
Ealing	28.1	36.0	27.3	25.0	28.4	144.8
Enfield	28.4	28.9	26.5	24.0	30.8	138.6
Greenwich	23.5	25.0	19.4	20.6	24.3	112.7
Hackney	22.5	26.0	17.3	15.9	20.3	102.0
Hammersmith	14.0	22.9	15.0	12.5	19.4	83.8
Haringey	21.1	29.7	22.3	17.2	22.7	113.0
Harrow	19.3	21.6	20.8	19.1	22.6	103.4
Havering	25.7	26.2	24.8	25.6	22.1	124.4
Hillingdon	23.6	25.4	22.9	21.6	23.3	116.9
Hounslow	20.0	25.2	18.9	17.3	20.8	102.2
Islington	15.7	21.9	16.0	15.3	18.2	87.0
Kensington & Chelsea	11.3	26.7	17.3	12.0	14.5	81.8
Kingston-upon-Thames	13.0	14.3	13.6	12.6	18.2	71.6
Lambeth	27.1	37.2	23.8	22.9	28.4	139.5
Lewisham	26.5	31.0	23.5	22.8	28.6	132.3
Merton	15.9	18.1	16.9	16.7	20.8	88.4
Newham	23.7	27.6	18.6	19.6	23.6	113.2
Redbridge	23.4	25.7	23.2	22.6	24.6	119.4
Richmond	14.7	19.3	17.5	15.7	22.2	89.4
Southwark	21.1	27.3	18.9	21.1	26.5	114.9
Sutton	16.9	18.1	17.5	16.1	19.1	87.7
Tower Hamlets	15.1	17.6	11.5	13.8	15.8	73.8
Waltham Forest	24.7	25.7	20.9	19.8	26.7	117.8
Wandsworth	26.2	33.9	26.8	23.0	32.5	142.4
Westminster	13.9	25.9	18.5	18.2	25.0	101.6
Greater London	689.0	845.8	673.3	637.5	766.2	3611.7

151

TABLE 94A   Age of Private Household Population: London Borough

Thousands

London borough	All Persons					All persons
	0-14	15-29	30-44	45-59/64 *	60/65 *or over	
City of London	0.4	1.4	1.1	1.2	0.4	4.4
Barking	31.7	34.7	25.1	36.2	27.5	155.2
Barnet	59.6	71.0	58.5	66.4	52.6	308.1
Bexley	48.5	45.1	44.6	46.5	34.2	218.9
Brent	55.4	71.7	52.5	51.6	37.1	268.2
Bromley	62.2	64.4	57.6	68.5	48.1	300.7
Camden	27.5	50.9	37.5	32.8	30.6	179.3
Croydon	73.4	75.7	64.6	66.1	47.6	327.4
Ealing	58.7	72.6	55.6	57.0	42.8	286.5
Enfield	57.3	57.2	53.2	54.4	45.6	267.8
Greenwich	48.6	50.4	37.6	45.5	36.0	218.2
Hackney	45.6	51.1	33.9	35.5	29.8	196.0
Hammersmith	28.5	45.6	30.2	28.4	28.3	161.0
Haringey	45.0	58.2	45.2	39.1	34.0	221.5
Harrow	40.8	42.9	40.4	42.2	33.7	200.0
Havering	54.5	53.6	49.5	56.9	32.4	247.0
Hillingdon	49.2	50.7	46.0	49.5	35.5	231.0
Hounslow	41.1	48.4	38.6	39.8	31.1	199.0
Islington	31.9	43.1	32.0	34.5	26.2	167.7
Kensington & Chelsea	21.8	49.1	34.8	26.5	20.5	152.8
Kingston-upon-Thames	26.9	28.1	27.6	27.9	26.1	136.6
Lambeth	55.6	72.6	47.1	51.0	41.3	267.7
Lewisham	53.8	61.4	45.3	50.8	42.4	253.6
Merton	33.8	36.7	33.8	37.4	30.4	172.0
Newham	50.1	57.7	37.1	44.9	34.7	224.5
Redbridge	49.5	52.7	45.4	50.7	36.5	234.8
Richmond	29.2	36.7	35.1	34.8	32.3	168.2
Southwark	43.6	53.5	35.8	48.6	38.4	219.9
Sutton	34.3	35.8	34.3	35.0	28.6	168.0
Tower Hamlets	31.0	36.8	23.3	32.1	23.6	146.8
Waltham Forest	50.8	51.7	43.2	45.5	40.2	231.3
Wandsworth	56.3	67.1	54.1	53.4	48.6	279.5
Westminster	26.9	50.7	38.7	40.7	35.7	192.7
Greater London	1423.7	1678.9	1340.0	1431.1	1132.9	7006.3

* 59 for females, 64 for males

152

TABLE 94B   Age of Private Household Population: London Borough

Percentages

London Borough	All Persons					All persons
	0-14	15-29	30-44	45-59/64*	60/65* or over	
City of London	8.2	31.5	24.6	26.8	9.0	100.0
Barking	20.5	22.4	16.2	23.3	17.7	100.0
Barnet	19.3	23.0	18.9	21.6	17.1	100.0
Bexley	22.1	20.6	20.4	21.2	15.6	100.0
Brent	20.7	26.7	19.6	19.2	13.8	100.0
Bromley	20.7	21.4	19.2	22.8	16.0	100.0
Camden	15.3	28.4	20.9	18.3	17.0	100.0
Croydon	22.4	23.2	19.7	20.2	14.5	100.0
Ealing	20.5	25.4	19.4	19.9	14.9	100.0
Enfield	21.4	21.4	19.9	20.4	17.0	100.0
Greenwich	22.3	23.1	17.3	20.8	16.5	100.0
Hackney	23.3	26.1	17.3	18.1	15.3	100.0
Hammersmith	17.7	28.3	18.8	17.6	17.6	100.0
Haringey	20.3	26.3	20.4	17.7	15.4	100.0
Harrow	20.4	21.4	20.2	21.1	16.9	100.0
Havering	22.1	21.7	20.0	23.1	13.2	100.0
Hillingdon	21.3	21.9	19.9	21.5	15.4	100.0
Hounslow	20.7	24.4	19.4	20.0	15.6	100.0
Islington	19.0	25.7	19.1	20.6	15.6	100.0
Kensington & Chelsea	14.3	32.2	22.8	17.4	13.4	100.0
Kingston-upon-Thames	19.7	20.5	20.2	20.4	19.1	100.0
Lambeth	20.7	27.1	17.6	19.1	15.4	100.0
Lewisham	21.2	24.2	17.9	20.0	16.8	100.0
Merton	19.7	21.3	19.6	21.7	17.7	100.0
Newham	22.4	25.7	16.5	19.9	15.5	100.0
Redbridge	21.1	22.4	19.4	21.5	15.6	100.0
Richmond	17.4	21.9	20.9	20.7	19.2	100.0
Southwark	19.8	24.3	16.3	22.1	17.4	100.0
Sutton	20.4	21.3	20.4	20.9	17.0	100.0
Tower Hamlets	21.2	25.0	15.8	21.9	16.1	100.0
Waltham Forest	22.0	22.3	18.6	19.7	17.3	100.0
Wandsworth	20.2	24.0	19.4	19.1	17.4	100.0
Westminster	14.0	26.2	20.1	21.1	18.5	100.0
Greater London	20.3	24.0	19.1	20.4	16.1	100.0

* 59 for females, 64 for males

153

TABLE 95A Length of Residence: London Borough

Thousands

London Borough	Length of residence (years)						All persons
	Under 1	1 but under 2	2 but under 3	3 but under 5	5 but under 10	10 or over	
City of London	1.3	0.4	0.6	0.9	0.8	0.4	4.4
Barking	11.7	7.9	15.2	15.4	29.8	75.2	155.2
Barnet	37.8	26.5	27.0	29.5	65.3	122.0	308.1
Bexley	20.4	17.1	17.8	24.5	44.2	95.0	218.9
Brent	39.3	25.8	31.8	29.3	51.8	90.3	268.2
Bromley	36.8	24.5	30.6	31.0	61.4	116.4	300.7
Camden	36.7	20.6	19.8	18.9	32.1	51.2	179.3
Croydon	42.0	26.7	36.7	33.6	64.9	123.4	327.4
Ealing	40.7	27.0	31.4	29.3	52.1	106.0	286.5
Enfield	24.2	20.3	26.4	30.1	54.2	112.6	267.8
Greenwich	27.2	21.0	22.8	24.4	41.1	81.6	218.2
Hackney	28.2	23.2	24.7	21.4	41.9	56.5	196.0
Hammersmith	26.0	15.0	17.4	15.8	29.2	57.6	161.0
Haringey	28.4	18.6	28.3	30.5	45.2	70.5	221.5
Harrow	21.0	14.0	19.4	22.0	43.4	80.3	200.0
Havering	21.9	17.2	24.2	25.9	49.3	108.5	247.0
Hillingdon	25.1	19.5	24.3	25.0	41.3	95.7	231.0
Hounslow	27.9	18.2	20.7	21.1	35.3	75.8	199.0
Islington	31.3	19.9	18.2	19.8	33.8	44.7	167.7
Kensington & Chelsea	37.1	19.7	20.3	16.1	23.4	36.1	152.8
Kingston-upon-Thames	16.1	10.6	14.7	15.4	26.7	53.1	136.6
Lambeth	39.7	28.3	29.8	33.9	51.3	84.7	267.7
Lewisham	34.1	25.2	27.4	25.3	47.4	94.3	253.6
Merton	19.1	11.9	14.8	17.9	36.1	72.2	172.0
Newham	25.0	19.5	22.2	27.6	44.3	86.1	224.6
Redbridge	24.2	18.5	19.5	26.5	47.7	98.4	234.8
Richmond	24.7	15.0	16.6	15.7	31.4	64.8	168.2
Southwark	29.2	22.0	25.5	24.1	44.8	74.3	220.0
Sutton	20.1	14.5	17.1	18.4	35.4	62.5	168.0
Tower Hamlets	25.2	13.8	17.0	17.2	30.3	43.3	146.8
Waltham Forest	22.5	16.8	22.8	25.2	46.6	97.4	231.3
Wandsworth	34.4	19.7	24.8	30.2	63.9	106.6	279.5
Westminster	33.5	18.3	28.9	26.0	35.1	50.9	192.7
Greater London	912.7	617.0	738.6	768.1	1381.8	2588.1	7006.3

TABLE 95B Length of Residence: London Borough

London Borough	Length of residence						All persons
	Under 1	1 but under 2	2 but under 3	3 but under 5	5 but under 10	10 or over	
City of London	29.1	8.9	13.4	21.2	19.3	8.0	100.0
Barking	7.6	5.1	9.8	10.0	19.2	48.4	100.0
Barnet	12.3	8.6	8.8	9.6	21.2	39.6	100.0
Bexley	9.3	7.8	8.2	11.2	20.2	43.4	100.0
Brent	14.6	9.6	11.9	10.9	19.3	33.7	100.0
Bromley	12.2	8.1	10.2	10.3	20.4	38.7	100.0
Camden	20.4	11.5	11.0	10.6	17.9	28.6	100.0
Croydon	12.8	8.2	11.2	10.3	19.8	37.7	100.0
Ealing	14.2	9.4	11.0	10.2	18.2	37.0	100.0
Enfield	9.0	7.6	9.9	11.3	20.2	42.0	100.0
Greenwich	12.5	9.6	10.5	11.2	18.8	37.4	100.0
Hackney	14.4	11.8	12.6	10.9	21.4	28.8	100.0
Hammersmith	16.2	9.3	10.8	9.8	18.1	35.8	100.0
Haringey	12.8	8.4	12.8	13.8	20.4	31.8	100.0
Harrow	10.5	7.0	9.7	11.0	21.7	40.1	100.0
Havering	8.9	7.0	9.8	10.5	20.0	43.9	100.0
Hillingdon	10.9	8.5	10.5	10.8	17.9	41.4	100.0
Hounslow	14.0	9.1	10.4	10.6	17.7	38.1	100.0
Islington	18.7	11.8	10.9	11.8	20.1	26.7	100.0
Kensington & Chelsea	24.3	12.9	13.3	10.6	15.3	23.6	100.0
Kingston-upon-Thames	11.8	7.8	10.7	11.2	19.6	38.9	100.0
Lambeth	14.8	10.6	11.1	12.7	19.2	31.6	100.0
Lewisham	13.4	9.9	10.8	10.0	18.7	37.2	100.0
Merton	11.1	6.9	8.6	10.4	21.0	42.0	100.0
Newham	11.1	8.7	9.9	12.3	19.7	38.3	100.0
Redbridge	10.3	7.9	8.3	11.3	20.3	41.9	100.0
Richmond	14.7	8.9	9.9	9.3	18.6	38.5	100.0
Southwark	13.3	10.0	11.6	11.0	20.4	33.8	100.0
Sutton	11.9	8.6	10.2	10.9	21.1	37.2	100.0
Tower Hamlets	17.2	9.4	11.6	11.7	20.7	29.5	100.0
Waltham Forest	9.7	7.3	9.8	10.9	20.2	42.1	100.0
Wandsworth	12.3	7.0	8.9	10.8	22.8	38.1	100.0
Westminster	17.4	9.5	15.0	13.5	18.2	26.4	100.0
Greater London	13.0	8.8	10.5	11.0	19.7	36.9	100.0

TABLE 96A Employment Status: London Borough

London Borough	Employment status						All persons aged 16 or over
	Employed						
	full time	part time	Un- employed	Wholly retired	House- wife	Other	
City of London	3.0	0.4	0.1	0.2	0.2	0.1	4.0
Barking	58.5	10.9	3.3	12.4	30.5	5.3	120.8
Barnet	126.8	24.0	4.8	23.8	46.9	17.7	244.1
Bexley	88.1	16.7	3.1	17.0	35.1	6.6	166.6
Brent	117.3	15.1	7.1	20.2	31.1	17.5	208.3
Bromley	122.6	23.7	5.6	22.4	47.9	11.7	233.8
Camden	82.8	11.7	6.3	16.7	18.6	13.7	149.8
Croydon	134.5	25.5	6.0	21.0	47.7	13.7	248.5
Ealing	125.4	19.4	6.0	24.7	32.8	14.3	222.5
Enfield	107.2	22.4	4.0	21.6	40.0	11.0	206.2
Greenwich	85.7	16.9	5.3	19.9	30.5	7.8	166.1
Hackney	72.8	12.8	7.8	16.8	23.7	12.6	146.6
Hammersmith	70.1	10.2	5.7	15.7	17.9	10.5	130.0
Haringey	93.7	12.5	5.6	21.5	25.5	14.1	172.9
Harrow	82.9	13.2	2.9	15.7	33.0	8.2	156.0
Havering	101.1	20.0	3.7	15.4	40.3	7.5	187.9
Hillingdon	96.2	20.8	3.4	17.4	32.0	8.3	178.1
Hounslow	85.6	15.1	3.9	16.3	25.2	8.4	154.6
Islington	70.6	12.8	6.3	14.9	18.3	10.4	133.1
Kensington & Chelsea	73.3	9.0	4.5	10.2	18.0	14.0	129.0
Kingston-upon-Thames	56.3	10.4	1.6	10.9	23.2	5.4	107.8
Lambeth	112.1	17.2	9.5	25.4	27.9	15.0	207.3
Lewisham	101.4	19.3	6.5	23.3	32.3	12.4	195.2
Merton	72.2	13.2	2.9	15.5	24.6	7.5	135.8
Newham	87.6	13.3	7.5	16.8	35.4	10.0	170.5
Redbridge	97.2	16.6	4.6	18.2	35.7	9.7	182.1
Richmond	72.9	12.9	2.6	16.3	24.2	8.0	137.0
Southwark	88.7	17.9	7.8	23.7	24.0	10.6	172.6
Sutton	68.0	14.5	2.4	14.4	25.2	6.2	130.8
Tower Hamlets	56.9	10.5	6.4	12.8	19.7	6.7	112.9
Waltham Forest	89.4	19.1	4.3	23.5	32.6	8.2	177.0
Wandsworth	116.1	17.6	8.0	28.0	34.0	14.9	218.5
Westminster	88.6	11.7	6.2	18.8	23.9	14.2	163.5
Greater London	2905.7	507.2	165.8	591.2	957.7	342.1	5469.8

156

Percentages

London Borough	Employment Status						All persons aged 16 or over
	Employed						
	full time	part time	Un - employed	Wholly retired	Housewife	Other	
City of London	76.6	8.8	2.6	4.2	5.9	2.0	100.0
Barking	48.4	9.0	2.7	10.2	25.2	4.4	100.0
Barnet	52.0	9.8	2.0	9.8	19.2	7.3	100.0
Bexley	52.9	10.0	1.8	10.2	21.0	4.0	100.0
Brent	56.3	7.3	3.4	9.7	14.9	8.5	100.0
Bromley	52.4	10.1	2.5	9.6	20.5	5.0	100.0
Camden	55.3	7.8	4.1	11.1	12.4	9.1	100.0
Croydon	54.1	10.3	2.3	8.5	19.2	5.4	100.0
Ealing	56.4	8.7	2.7	11.1	14.7	6.4	100.0
Enfield	52.0	10.9	1.9	10.5	19.4	5.3	100.0
Greenwich	51.6	10.2	3.2	12.0	18.4	4.7	100.0
Hackney	49.6	8.7	5.4	11.5	16.2	8.6	100.0
Hammersmith	53.9	7.8	4.4	12.1	13.8	8.0	100.0
Haringey	54.2	7.2	3.2	12.4	14.8	8.1	100.0
Harrow	53.2	8.5	1.8	10.0	21.2	5.3	100.0
Havering	53.8	10.6	2.0	8.2	21.4	4.0	100.0
Hillingdon	54.0	11.7	1.9	9.8	18.0	4.7	100.0
Hounslow	55.4	9.8	2.5	10.5	16.3	5.4	100.0
Islington	53.0	9.6	4.6	11.2	13.7	7.8	100.0
Kensington & Chelsea	56.8	6.9	3.5	7.9	14.0	10.7	100.0
Kingston-upon-Thames	52.2	9.7	1.5	10.1	21.5	5.1	100.0
Lambeth	54.1	8.3	4.5	12.3	13.5	7.3	100.0
Lewisham	51.9	9.9	3.4	12.0	16.5	6.4	100.0
Merton	53.1	9.7	2.2	11.4	18.1	5.5	100.0
Newham	51.4	7.8	4.4	9.8	20.8	5.8	100.0
Redbridge	53.4	9.1	2.6	10.0	19.6	5.3	100.0
Richmond	53.3	9.4	1.9	11.9	17.7	5.8	100.0
Southwark	51.4	10.4	4.5	13.7	13.9	6.1	100.0
Sutton	52.0	11.2	1.9	11.0	19.2	4.8	100.0
Tower Hamlets	50.4	9.3	5.7	11.3	17.4	5.8	100.0
Waltham Forest	50.5	10.8	2.4	13.3	18.4	4.6	100.0
Wandsworth	53.1	8.0	3.7	12.8	15.5	6.7	100.0
Westminster	54.2	7.2	3.8	11.5	14.6	8.7	100.0
Greater London	53.1	9.3	3.1	10.8	17.5	6.2	100.0

TABLE 97A Socio-economic Group: London Borough

Thousands

London Borough	Socio-economic group						All persons economically active
	Professional employers and managers	Other non-manual	Skilled manual	Semi-skilled manual	Unskilled manual	Other	
City of London	1.6	1.2	0.3	0.3	-	-	3.5
Barking	5.3	22.1	22.3	15.6	5.4	2.0	72.7
Barnet	39.9	60.0	29.4	16.9	4.9	4.6	155.6
Bexley	17.7	44.5	25.6	12.9	4.9	2.4	107.9
Brent	21.3	52.2	30.4	23.6	7.2	4.8	139.5
Bromley	38.9	63.1	26.0	15.0	4.9	4.0	151.8
Camden	24.1	40.8	15.4	12.3	5.4	2.9	100.9
Croydon	34.5	68.3	33.9	18.6	6.7	4.1	166.1
Ealing	24.4	55.3	35.1	23.6	7.8	4.7	150.8
Enfield	22.4	47.4	32.5	22.5	4.7	4.2	133.6
Greenwich	13.2	40.7	25.7	17.2	7.8	3.3	108.0
Hackney	7.8	28.5	25.7	20.4	7.6	3.5	93.4
Hammersmith	14.7	31.9	16.4	13.9	5.7	3.4	85.9
Haringey	16.7	40.2	25.8	20.0	5.2	3.8	111.8
Harrow	23.6	43.1	18.2	9.6	2.1	2.5	99.1
Havering	19.7	49.3	31.1	16.5	5.7	2.5	124.8
Hillingdon	20.5	45.1	28.4	16.9	5.6	3.8	120.3
Hounslow	16.3	39.4	24.3	17.1	5.2	2.4	104.7
Islington	10.8	30.3	20.9	16.3	7.8	3.5	89.6
Kensington & Chelsea	26.3	33.5	9.9	11.2	3.2	2.7	86.8
Kingston-upon-Thames	16.1	28.0	12.0	6.8	2.4	3.0	68.3
Lambeth	17.8	53.6	29.3	21.1	10.5	6.5	138.8
Lewisham	15.9	48.9	30.5	18.9	9.1	3.9	127.2
Merton	16.9	36.6	19.4	10.6	3.0	1.7	88.3
Newham	8.2	34.7	29.1	23.4	10.3	2.7	108.4
Redbridge	24.7	48.2	25.4	13.5	3.7	2.9	118.5
Richmond	23.0	37.3	14.1	8.7	2.8	2.6	88.5
Southwark	10.7	39.8	27.7	20.7	12.5	2.8	114.3
Sutton	18.6	34.0	18.3	9.2	2.7	2.2	85.0
Tower Hamlets	4.6	19.9	20.8	16.7	9.0	2.7	73.8
Waltham Forest	14.0	40.5	31.8	19.2	4.9	2.4	112.7
Wandsworth	20.4	56.3	32.7	20.2	8.5	3.6	141.7
Westminster	26.2	40.1	13.7	15.2	6.2	5.2	106.5
Greater London	616.9	1354.6	782.2	524.6	193.1	107.3	3578.7

158

TABLE 97B Socio-economic Group: London Borough

London Borough	Socio-economic group						All persons economically active
	Profes-sional/ employer/ manager	Other non-manual	Skilled manual	Semi-skilled manual	Un-skilled manual	Other	
City of London	45.1	35.7	7.3	9.5	1.3	1.0	100.0
Barking	7.3	30.4	30.7	21.5	7.4	2.7	100.0
Barnet	25.6	38.5	18.9	10.9	3.1	3.0	100.0
Bexley	16.4	41.2	23.7	11.9	4.5	2.2	100.0
Brent	15.3	37.4	21.8	16.9	5.1	3.5	100.0
Bromley	25.6	41.5	17.1	9.8	3.2	2.6	100.0
Camden	23.9	40.4	15.2	12.2	5.3	2.9	100.0
Croydon	20.8	41.1	20.4	11.2	4.0	2.5	100.0
Ealing	16.2	36.7	23.2	15.6	5.2	3.1	100.0
Enfield	16.8	35.4	24.3	16.8	3.5	3.1	100.0
Greenwich	12.2	37.7	23.8	16.0	7.2	3.1	100.0
Hackney	8.3	30.5	27.5	21.8	8.1	3.8	100.0
Hammersmith	17.2	37.1	19.1	16.1	6.6	3.9	100.0
Haringey	15.0	36.0	23.1	17.9	4.7	3.4	100.0
Harrow	23.9	43.5	18.4	9.6	2.1	2.5	100.0
Havering	15.8	39.5	24.9	13.2	4.6	2.0	100.0
Hillingdon	17.1	37.5	23.6	14.0	4.6	3.2	100.0
Hounslow	15.5	37.7	23.3	16.3	5.0	2.3	100.0
Islington	12.1	33.8	23.4	18.2	8.7	3.9	100.0
Kensington & Chelsea	30.3	38.6	11.4	12.9	3.7	3.1	100.0
Kingston-upon-Thames	23.6	41.0	17.5	10.0	3.5	4.4	100.0
Lambeth	12.8	38.6	21.1	15.2	7.6	4.7	100.0
Lewisham	12.5	38.5	24.0	14.9	7.1	3.1	100.0
Merton	19.2	41.5	22.0	12.0	3.4	2.0	100.0
Newham	7.6	32.0	26.8	21.6	9.5	2.5	100.0
Redbridge	20.9	40.7	21.4	11.4	3.1	2.5	100.0
Richmond	26.0	42.2	15.9	9.8	3.2	2.9	100.0
Southwark	9.4	34.9	24.3	18.1	10.9	2.5	100.0
Sutton	21.9	40.0	21.6	10.9	3.2	2.5	100.0
Tower Hamlets	6.2	27.0	28.2	22.7	12.2	3.7	100.0
Waltham Forest	12.4	35.9	28.2	17.1	4.3	2.1	100.0
Wandsworth	14.4	39.7	23.1	14.3	6.0	2.5	100.0
Westminster	24.6	37.6	12.9	14.2	5.8	4.9	100.0
Greater London	17.2	37.9	21.9	14.7	5.4	3.0	100.0

TABLE 98A Birthplace: London Borough

Thousands

| London Borough | Birthplace | | All persons |
	United Kingdom	Not in United Kingdom	
City of London	3.5	0.9	4.4
Barking	148.1	7.1	155.2
Barnet	244.7	63.4	308.1
Bexley	209.0	9.9	218.9
Brent	170.4	97.9	268.2
Bromley	281.8	18.8	300.7
Camden	129.8	49.5	179.3
Croydon	286.4	41.0	327.4
Ealing	209.9	76.6	286.5
Enfield	234.7	33.1	267.8
Greenwich	199.4	18.7	218.2
Hackney	146.4	49.6	196.0
Hammersmith	119.5	41.5	161.0
Haringey	162.8	58.7	221.5
Harrow	168.6	31.3	200.0
Havering	238.5	8.5	247.0
Hillingdon	210.7	20.2	231.0
Hounslow	164.2	34.8	199.0
Islington	128.2	39.5	167.7
Kensington & Chelsea	100.9	51.9	152.8
Kingston-upon-Thames	124.9	11.7	136.6
Lambeth	208.7	59.0	267.7
Lewisham	220.3	33.4	253.6
Merton	148.9	23.0	172.0
Newham	185.0	39.5	224.5
Redbridge	209.4	25.4	234.8
Richmond	148.9	19.2	168.2
Southwark	188.1	31.9	220.0
Sutton	156.4	11.6	168.0
Tower Hamlets	122.3	24.5	146.8
Waltham Forest	202.4	28.9	231.3
Wandsworth	227.2	52.3	279.5
Westminster	131.1	61.6	192.7
Greater London	5832.2	1174.1	7006.3

TABLE 98B Birthplace : London Borough

| London borough | Birthplace | | All persons |
	United Kingdom	Not in United Kingdom	
City of London	80.5	19.5	100.0
Barking	95.4	4.6	100.0
Barnet	79.4	20.6	100.0
Bexley	95.5	4.5	100.0
Brent	63.5	36.5	100.0
Bromley	93.7	6.3	100.0
Camden	72.4	27.6	100.0
Croydon	87.5	12.5	100.0
Ealing	73.3	26.7	100.0
Enfield	87.7	12.3	100.0
Greenwich	91.4	8.6	100.0
Hackney	74.7	25.3	100.0
Hammersmith	74.2	25.8	100.0
Haringey	73.5	26.5	100.0
Harrow	84.3	15.7	100.0
Havering	96.6	3.4	100.0
Hillingdon	91.2	8.8	100.0
Hounslow	82.5	17.5	100.0
Islington	76.5	23.5	100.0
Kensington & Chelsea	66.0	34.0	100.0
Kingston-upon-Thames	91.5	8.5	100.0
Lambeth	78.0	22.0	100.0
Lewisham	86.8	13.2	100.0
Merton	86.6	13.4	100.0
Newham	82.4	17.6	100.0
Redbridge	89.2	10.8	100.0
Richmond	88.6	11.4	100.0
Southwark	85.5	14.5	100.0
Sutton	93.1	6.9	100.0
Tower Hamlets	83.3	16.7	100.0
Waltham Forest	87.5	12.5	100.0
Wandsworth	81.3	18.7	100.0
Westminster	68.0	32.0	100.0
Greater London	83.2	16.8	100.0

TABLE 99A Ethnic Group: London Borough

Thousands

London borough	Ethnic Group					All persons
	White	West Indian	African	Indian/ Bangladeshi/ Pakistani	Other	
City of London	3.9	-	-	-	0.4	4.4
Barking	148.9	0.4	0.1	3.1	2.8	155.2
Barnet	264.5	2.3	2.0	15.3	24.0	308.1
Bexley	210.8	0.8	0.5	2.6	4.2	218.9
Brent	180.0	30.3	6.8	34.5	16.6	268.2
Bromley	290.4	2.5	0.4	1.4	6.0	300.7
Camden	157.8	3.2	1.6	3.7	13.1	179.3
Croydon	291.3	9.3	1.9	10.8	14.1	327.4
Ealing	216.2	11.2	2.4	43.5	13.2	286.5
Enfield	243.6	6.1	1.5	5.1	11.5	267.8
Greenwich	202.2	3.9	1.0	7.2	3.8	218.2
Hackney	140.1	26.3	5.2	6.7	17.8	196.0
Hammersmith	132.9	12.3	1.7	3.2	10.8	161.0
Haringey	164.5	23.8	3.0	8.1	22.1	221.5
Harrow	174.1	2.0	0.9	12.1	10.8	200.0
Havering	242.3	0.8	0.3	1.4	2.2	247.0
Hillingdon	217.0	1.7	0.2	7.3	4.9	231.0
Hounslow	168.1	2.1	1.1	18.6	9.2	199.0
Islington	139.1	8.8	1.9	3.2	14.8	167.7
Kensington & Chelsea	129.9	3.6	2.6	2.1	14.7	152.8
Kingston-upon-Thames	130.8	0.3	0.3	2.1	3.2	136.6
Lambeth	204.1	32.2	9.2	6.3	15.9	267.7
Lewisham	215.9	21.5	3.2	2.1	10.9	253.6
Merton	151.6	3.5	0.6	6.3	10.0	172.0
Newham	172.9	14.3	3.3	24.0	10.0	224.5
Redbridge	213.6	3.2	0.4	10.3	7.3	234.8
Richmond	160.6	0.4	0.1	1.6	5.5	168.2
Southwark	185.8	18.3	3.1	3.5	9.5	220.1
Sutton	162.1	0.5	0.1	1.7	3.5	168.0
Tower Hamlets	119.1	6.5	2.2	11.2	7.8	146.8
Waltham Forest	192.6	9.9	2.3	13.9	12.7	231.3
Wandsworth	227.7	19.5	4.3	11.8	16.1	279.5
Westminster	159.1	8.2	1.4	3.1	20.9	192.7
Greater London	6014.7	289.1	65.3	287.6	349.5	7006.3

TABLE 99B Ethnic Group: London Borough

Percentages

| London borough | Ethnic Group | | | | | All persons |
	White	West Indian	African	Indian/ Bangladeshi/ Pakistani	Other	
City of London	89.2	0.4	0.3	-	10.0	100.0
Barking	96.0	0.2	0.1	2.0	1.7	100.0
Barnet	85.8	0.8	0.7	4.9	7.8	100.0
Bexley	96.3	0.4	0.2	1.2	1.9	100.0
Brent	67.2	11.3	2.5	12.9	6.2	100.0
Bromley	96.6	0.8	0.1	0.4	2.1	100.0
Camden	88.0	1.8	0.9	2.1	7.5	100.0
Croydon	88.9	2.8	0.6	3.3	4.3	100.0
Ealing	75.5	3.9	0.8	15.2	4.6	100.0
Enfield	91.0	2.3	0.6	1.9	4.3	100.0
Greenwich	92.7	1.8	0.4	3.3	1.8	100.0
Hackney	71.5	13.4	2.7	3.4	9.1	100.0
Hammersmith	82.6	7.7	1.1	2.0	6.8	100.0
Haringey	74.3	10.8	1.3	3.6	10.0	100.0
Harrow	87.1	1.0	0.4	6.1	5.4	100.0
Havering	98.2	0.3	0.1	0.5	0.8	100.0
Hillingdon	93.9	0.7	0.1	3.1	1.9	100.0
Hounslow	84.4	1.0	0.5	9.4	4.5	100.0
Islington	83.0	5.2	1.1	1.9	8.7	100.0
Kensington & Chelsea	85.0	2.4	1.7	1.3	9.5	100.0
Kingston-upon-Thames	95.7	0.2	0.2	1.5	2.5	100.0
Lambeth	76.2	12.0	3.4	2.4	6.0	100.0
Lewisham	85.1	8.5	1.3	0.8	4.2	100.0
Merton	88.1	2.1	0.4	3.6	5.8	100.0
Newham	77.0	6.4	1.5	10.7	4.5	100.0
Redbridge	91.0	1.4	0.2	4.4	3.1	100.0
Richmond	95.4	0.3	0.1	1.0	3.2	100.0
Southwark	84.4	8.3	1.4	1.5	4.3	100.0
Sutton	96.6	0.3	0.1	1.1	2.1	100.0
Tower Hamlets	81.1	4.4	1.5	7.7	5.3	100.0
Waltham Forest	83.2	4.3	1.0	6.0	5.5	100.0
Wandsworth	81.5	7.0	1.5	4.2	5.9	100.0
Westminster	82.6	4.3	0.7	1.6	10.9	100.0
Greater London	85.9	4.1	0.9	4.1	5.0	100.0

TABLE 100A Family Type : London Borough

Thousands

London borough	Main married couple	Main lone parent	One person HoH	Concealed married couple	Concealed lone parent	One person not HoH	All families
City of London	0.9	0.1	1.4	-	-	0.2	2.7
Barking	40.7	4.6	11.7	0.4	0.3	2.4	60.1
Barnet	75.7	8.1	28.0	1.6	0.8	14.9	129.2
Bexley	59.2	4.8	14.2	0.5	0.3	4.7	83.7
Brent	59.2	8.2	27.7	2.2	0.9	15.2	113.5
Bromley	78.1	7.2	25.9	0.9	0.4	9.2	121.7
Camden	36.1	5.9	37.8	0.6	0.3	16.8	97.4
Croydon	82.3	7.8	28.1	1.0	0.6	8.5	128.3
Ealing	68.0	7.9	27.5	2.1	0.6	13.7	119.8
Enfield	68.1	5.8	23.5	1.5	0.6	8.3	107.7
Greenwich	54.1	6.1	19.4	0.5	0.4	5.5	86.0
Hackney	40.7	8.7	23.2	0.9	0.8	7.9	82.2
Hammersmith	32.0	6.2	28.5	0.7	0.4	13.6	81.4
Haringey	51.3	6.4	25.3	1.3	0.6	10.9	95.8
Harrow	51.2	4.6	17.4	1.0	0.4	7.8	82.3
Havering	66.8	4.9	14.3	0.6	0.3	5.1	92.1
Hillingdon	60.8	5.5	16.9	0.8	0.5	5.5	90.0
Hounslow	48.3	5.5	19.8	1.3	0.5	9.3	84.6
Islington	34.7	6.4	25.7	1.0	0.3	9.8	77.9
Kensington & Chelsea	26.8	4.7	39.0	0.4	0.3	19.0	90.3
Kingston-upon-Thames	35.2	3.2	15.2	0.5	0.2	4.9	59.2
Lambeth	56.1	10.8	37.9	1.0	1.0	13.6	120.3
Lewisham	58.7	9.1	25.9	0.9	0.5	10.1	105.2
Merton	43.7	4.3	17.4	0.7	0.3	6.6	73.1
Newham	52.3	6.3	21.0	1.8	0.7	6.7	88.8
Redbridge	59.6	5.5	20.0	1.2	0.4	8.2	94.9
Richmond	41.5	4.7	22.9	0.4	0.3	8.4	78.3
Southwark	49.9	9.2	26.8	1.0	0.5	7.3	94.7
Sutton	44.2	4.4	14.7	0.5	0.3	4.2	68.3
Tower Hamlets	32.1	5.8	17.2	0.6	0.4	7.0	63.1
Waltham Forest	59.3	5.6	20.9	1.1	0.5	6.5	93.9
Wandsworth	64.0	8.3	33.5	1.1	0.5	15.9	123.3
Westminster	38.4	6.0	46.6	0.5	0.3	15.3	107.1
Greater London	1670.1	202.5	775.6	30.4	14.9	303.3	2996.7

TABLE 100B Family Type: London Borough

London borough	Main married couple	Main lone parent	One person HoH	Concealed married couple	Concealed lone parent	One person not HoH	All families
City of London	34.4	4.0	53.2	-	-	8.5	100.0
Barking	67.8	7.6	19.5	0.6	0.5	4.0	100.0
Barnet	58.6	6.3	21.7	1.3	0.6	11.6	100.0
Bexley	70.7	5.8	17.0	0.6	0.4	5.6	100.0
Brent	52.2	7.3	24.4	2.0	0.8	13.4	100.0
Bromley	64.2	5.9	21.3	0.8	0.3	7.6	100.0
Camden	37.1	6.0	38.7	0.6	0.3	17.3	100.0
Croydon	64.2	6.1	21.9	0.8	0.5	6.6	100.0
Ealing	56.8	6.6	23.0	1.7	0.5	11.5	100.0
Enfield	63.2	5.4	21.8	1.4	0.5	7.7	100.0
Greenwich	62.9	7.0	22.6	0.6	0.5	6.3	100.0
Hackney	49.5	10.5	28.3	1.1	1.0	9.6	100.0
Hammersmith	39.2	7.7	35.0	0.9	0.5	16.7	100.0
Haringey	53.5	6.7	26.4	1.3	0.6	11.4	100.0
Harrow	62.2	5.5	21.2	1.2	0.5	9.4	100.0
Havering	72.5	5.3	15.6	0.7	0.3	5.6	100.0
Hillingdon	67.5	6.1	18.8	0.9	0.5	6.1	100.0
Hounslow	57.1	6.5	23.4	1.5	0.5	11.0	100.0
Islington	44.5	8.2	33.0	1.3	0.4	12.6	100.0
Kensington & Chelsea	29.7	5.2	43.2	0.5	0.3	21.1	100.0
Kingston-upon-Thames	59.5	5.4	25.7	0.8	0.4	8.3	100.0
Lambeth	46.6	9.0	31.5	0.8	0.8	11.3	100.0
Lewisham	55.8	8.6	24.7	0.8	0.5	9.6	100.0
Merton	59.8	5.9	23.9	0.9	0.5	9.0	100.0
Newham	58.9	7.1	23.7	2.1	0.8	7.5	100.0
Redbridge	62.9	5.8	21.1	1.2	0.4	8.6	100.0
Richmond	53.1	6.0	29.3	0.5	0.3	10.8	100.0
Southwark	52.7	9.7	28.3	1.0	0.5	7.7	100.0
Sutton	64.7	6.4	21.6	0.7	0.4	6.2	100.0
Tower Hamlets	50.8	9.2	27.3	0.9	0.7	11.1	100.0
Waltham Forest	63.1	6.0	22.3	1.1	0.5	7.0	100.0
Wandsworth	51.9	6.7	27.2	0.9	0.4	12.9	100.0
Westminster	35.8	5.6	43.6	0.4	0.3	14.3	100.0
Greater London	55.7	6.8	25.9	1.0	0.5	10.1	100.0

TABLE 101   Dwellings, Vacant Dwellings and Households: London Borough

Thousands

London Borough	Total dwellings 000's	Vacant dwellings*		Households 000's	Crude surplus	
		000's	as % of all dwellings		000's	as % of all dwellings
City of London	2.9	0.5	16.3	2.5	0.5	15.9
Barking	58.3	1.4	2.5	57.0	1.3	2.2
Barnet	112.0	3.9	3.5	111.9	0.2	0.2
Bexley	79.8	1.8	2.3	78.2	1.6	2.0
Brent	92.7	4.5	4.8	95.1	2.5**	2.7**
Bromley	112.9	3.6	3.2	111.2	1.7	1.5
Camden	80.4	6.6	8.1	79.7	0.7	0.8
Croydon	118.9	3.5	2.9	118.2	0.7	0.6
Ealing	102.0	4.4	4.3	103.4	1.4**	1.4**
Enfield	98.2	3.0	3.1	97.4	0.8	0.8
Greenwich	80.7	2.6	3.2	79.6	1.1	1.4
Hackney	73.3	5.6	7.6	72.6	0.8	1.0
Hammersmith	65.7	5.6	8.6	66.7	1.0**	1.5**
Haringey	80.9	4.3	5.3	83.0	2.1**	2.6**
Harrow	73.9	2.0	2.7	73.2	0.7	0.9
Havering	87.5	2.0	2.3	86.0	1.5	1.7
Hillingdon	84.2	2.0	2.3	83.2	1.0	1.2
Hounslow	74.5	3.0	4.1	73.6	0.9	1.2
Islington	67.3	6.6	9.9	66.7	0.6	0.9
Kensington & Chelsea	70.8	6.9	9.7	70.5	0.3	0.4
Kingston-upon-Thames	53.8	1.5	2.8	53.6	0.1	0.3
Lambeth	102.4	7.0	6.8	104.8	2.4**	2.3**
Lewisham	95.2	5.5	5.7	93.7	1.5	1.5
Merton	66.2	2.1	3.2	65.5	0.7	1.0
Newham	80.8	3.9	4.8	79.6	1.2	1.5
Redbridge	85.9	3.0	3.5	85.1	0.7	0.8
Richmond	68.9	2.9	4.1	69.1	0.2**	0.3**
Southwark	89.9	6.1	6.8	85.9	4.0	4.5
Sutton	63.6	1.2	1.9	63.3	0.3	0.4
Tower Hamlets	57.2	3.1	5.4	55.1	2.1	3.7
Waltham Forest	87.6	3.5	4.0	85.9	1.7	2.0
Wandsworth	104.8	5.6	5.4	105.8	0.9**	0.9**
Westminster	96.2	13.3	13.8	91.0	5.2	5.4
Greater London	2669.5	132.5	5.0	2648.2	21.3	0.8

*   Includes second homes.

** Crude deficit of dwellings compared with households.

166

TABLE 102 Type of Accommodation: District

District	Type of accommodation						All household spaces
	Detached house	Semi-detached house	Terraced house	Purpose built flat or maisonette	Other flat or rooms	Other	
Birmingham	26.9	119.7	138.3	60.9	30.2	5.6	381.5
Bradford	14.4	62.0	69.7	15.7	8.3	1.6	171.6
Bristol	7.9	42.3	61.6	19.2	23.0	2.1	156.1
Dudley	17.6	59.2	17.3	11.3	2.3	1.7	109.4
Gateshead	4.4	34.4	23.1	18.1	2.7	0.2	82.9
Kirklees	18.8	47.6	61.0	9.5	3.0	1.4	141.2
Leeds	27.5	107.9	86.4	35.3	14.6	2.6	274.3
Liverpool	4.3	38.1	94.4	38.8	17.4	3.2	196.3
Manchester	4.3	48.9	67.7	35.2	16.8	2.6	175.5
Newcastle-upon-Tyne	4.2	34.7	31.3	35.5	7.1	1.1	113.7
Salford	4.0	29.7	36.1	20.9	4.6	1.9	97.2
Sandwell	5.9	48.9	37.0	20.7	3.0	1.5	117.1
Sheffield	17.6	72.4	70.7	34.5	8.5	1.8	205.6
Sunderland	3.2	47.3	36.5	14.3	4.6	1.6	107.5
Wakefield	12.6	53.9	32.8	6.9	1.6	1.0	108.8
Wigan	8.9	52.5	41.7	8.0	1.2	1.0	113.5

District	Type of accommodation						All household spaces
	Detached house	Semi-detached house	Terraced house	Purpose built flat or maisonette	Other flat or rooms	Other	
Birmingham	7.1	31.4	36.2	16.0	7.9	1.5	100.0
Bradford	8.4	36.1	40.6	9.1	4.9	1.0	100.0
Bristol	5.0	27.1	39.5	12.3	14.7	1.3	100.0
Dudley	16.1	54.1	15.8	10.3	2.1	1.5	100.0
Gateshead	5.4	41.4	27.8	21.9	3.3	0.2	100.0
Kirklees	13.3	33.7	43.2	6.7	2.1	1.0	100.0
Leeds	10.0	39.3	31.5	12.9	5.3	1.0	100.0
Liverpool	2.2	19.4	48.1	19.8	8.9	1.7	100.0
Manchester	2.5	27.9	38.5	20.1	9.6	1.5	100.0
Newcastle-upon-Tyne	3.7	30.5	27.5	31.2	6.2	0.9	100.0
Salford	4.2	30.6	37.1	21.5	4.8	1.9	100.0
Sandwell	5.1	41.7	31.6	17.7	2.6	1.3	100.0
Sheffield	8.6	35.2	34.4	16.8	4.1	0.9	100.0
Sunderland	3.0	44.0	34.0	13.3	4.2	1.5	100.0
Wakefield	11.6	49.5	30.2	6.3	1.5	0.9	100.0
Wigan	7.9	46.3	36.8	7.1	1.1	0.9	100.0

TABLE 103   Lowest Floor of Accommodation: District

District	Lowest floor of accommodation						All households
	Ground floor or lower	1st floor	2nd floor	3rd floor	4-9th floor	10th floor or higher	
Birmingham	309.0	26.7	12.7	2.4	9.5	4.5	364.8
Bradford	151.8	8.3	2.1	1.0	1.2	0.3	164.6
Bristol	125.3	13.6	5.8	1.6	2.5	0.8	149.6
Dudley	97.8	5.0	1.4	0.4	0.9	0.7	106.1
Gateshead	67.7	8.5	0.8	0.5	1.5	0.9	79.8
Kirklees	128.0	5.2	1.0	0.2	0.4	0.1	134.9
Leeds	237.0	16.5	4.8	1.4	4.7	2.1	266.4
Liverpool	153.7	14.4	10.3	3.0	4.4	2.0	187.8
Manchester	137.0	15.1	7.5	1.2	4.3	1.6	166.7
Newcastle-upon-Tyne	86.0	14.5	4.0	1.0	2.4	1.7	109.6
Salford	76.7	6.9	3.9	1.0	3.3	2.2	94.1
Sandwell	97.6	6.5	2.2	1.2	3.3	1.9	112.6
Sheffield	172.1	12.7	7.3	2.2	2.9	1.5	198.8
Sunderland	93.1	6.2	1.8	0.8	1.2	0.7	103.8
Wakefield	100.4	3.4	0.5	0.2	0.5	0.2	105.2
Wigan	103.8	3.8	0.7	0.3	0.5	0.2	109.4

District	Lowest floor of accommodation						All households
	Ground floor or lower	1st floor	2nd floor	3rd floor	4-9th floor	10th floor or higher	
Birmingham	84.7	7.3	3.5	0.7	2.6	1.2	100.0
Bradford	92.2	5.0	1.3	0.6	0.7	0.2	100.0
Bristol	83.8	9.1	3.9	1.0	1.7	0.5	100.0
Dudley	92.1	4.7	1.3	0.4	0.9	0.6	100.0
Gateshead	84.8	10.7	0.9	0.6	1.8	1.1	100.0
Kirklees	94.9	3.8	0.7	0.2	0.3	0.1	100.0
Leeds	89.0	6.2	1.8	0.5	1.8	0.8	100.0
Liverpool	81.8	7.6	5.5	1.6	2.4	1.1	100.0
Manchester	82.2	9.0	4.5	0.7	2.6	0.9	100.0
Newcastle-upon-Tyne	78.5	13.2	3.6	0.9	2.2	1.5	100.0
Salford	81.5	7.4	4.2	1.1	3.5	2.3	100.0
Sandwell	86.6	5.8	1.9	1.0	2.9	1.7	100.0
Sheffield	86.6	6.4	3.7	1.1	1.5	0.8	100.0
Sunderland	89.6	6.0	1.8	0.8	1.1	0.7	100.0
Wakefield	95.5	3.2	0.5	0.2	0.5	0.2	100.0
Wigan	94.9	3.5	0.7	0.3	0.4	0.2	100.0

TABLE 104 Household Size : District

Thousands

District	Number of people in household						All households
	1	2	3	4	5	6 or more	
Birmingham	81.9	116.3	60.3	55.4	27.3	23.7	364.8
Bradford	37.8	52.0	26.6	27.1	12.4	8.7	164.6
Bristol	35.1	49.6	25.1	23.8	10.8	5.2	149.6
Dudley	18.5	35.0	21.5	20.2	7.2	3.6	106.1
Gateshead	17.3	25.7	14.7	13.6	5.6	2.9	79.8
Kirklees	30.6	43.3	22.3	23.2	9.0	6.6	134.9
Leeds	61.0	84.1	43.9	46.2	19.2	11.9	266.4
Liverpool	45.1	54.8	31.5	27.6	15.6	13.2	187.8
Manchester	46.4	51.1	25.2	21.3	12.5	10.2	166.7
Newcastle-upon-Tyne	27.7	35.7	18.4	15.7	7.4	4.6	109.6
Salford	22.6	29.2	15.1	14.9	7.2	5.1	94.1
Sandwell	22.9	35.9	21.0	18.2	8.0	6.6	112.6
Sheffield	46.8	66.5	32.1	32.7	12.6	8.1	198.8
Sunderland	20.5	31.1	21.1	18.4	8.0	4.8	103.8
Wakefield	19.4	34.7	19.6	19.8	7.9	3.8	105.2
Wigan	21.0	34.2	21.7	20.4	7.7	4.4	109.4

Percentages

District	Number of people in household						All households
	1	2	3	4	5	6 or more	
Birmingham	22.4	31.9	16.5	15.2	7.5	6.4	100.0
Bradford	23.0	31.6	16.2	16.4	7.5	5.2	100.0
Bristol	23.5	33.2	16.7	15.9	7.2	3.4	100.0
Dudley	17.5	33.0	20.2	19.1	6.8	3.5	100.0
Gateshead	21.7	32.2	18.4	17.1	7.0	3.7	100.0
Kirklees	22.7	32.1	16.6	17.2	6.6	4.8	100.0
Leeds	22.9	31.6	16.5	17.3	7.2	4.4	100.0
Liverpool	24.0	29.2	16.8	14.7	8.3	7.0	100.0
Manchester	27.8	30.7	15.1	12.8	7.5	6.2	100.0
Newcastle-upon-Tyne	25.3	32.6	16.8	14.3	6.7	4.1	100.0
Salford	24.0	31.0	16.1	15.8	7.7	5.4	100.0
Sandwell	20.3	31.9	18.6	16.1	7.1	5.9	100.0
Sheffield	23.5	33.5	16.2	16.4	6.3	4.1	100.0
Sunderland	19.7	30.0	20.4	17.7	7.7	4.6	100.0
Wakefield	18.4	33.0	18.7	18.8	7.5	3.6	100.0
Wigan	19.2	31.3	19.8	18.7	7.0	3.9	100.0

TABLE 105   Type of Household: District

District	Married couple household	Lone parent household	One person aged under 60	One person aged 60 or over	Other household	All households
Birmingham	237.4	31.4	27.1	54.7	14.2	364.8
Bradford	109.8	12.0	11.0	26.8	5.0	164.6
Bristol	93.3	11.3	12.6	22.5	9.9	149.6
Dudley	78.9	5.6	4.7	13.8	3.1	106.1
Gateshead	53.2	6.9	4.4	12.8	2.5	79.8
Kirklees	92.3	8.1	6.4	24.2	4.0	134.9
Leeds	178.2	19.8	22.2	38.8	7.4	266.4
Liverpool	114.6	18.6	14.3	30.8	9.5	187.8
Manchester	94.3	17.2	17.8	28.5	8.9	166.7
Newcastle-upon-Tyne	67.1	9.1	9.8	17.9	5.7	109.6
Salford	60.5	8.0	6.4	16.2	3.1	94.1
Sandwell	77.8	8.4	6.1	16.8	3.6	112.6
Sheffield	134.5	11.1	12.4	34.4	6.5	198.8
Sunderland	72.5	8.0	5.7	14.8	2.9	103.8
Wakefield	77.1	6.3	4.9	14.5	2.5	105.2
Wigan	78.0	7.4	5.4	15.6	3.0	109.4

District	Married couple household	Lone parent household	One person aged under 60	One person aged 60 or over	Other household	All households
Birmingham	65.1	8.6	7.4	15.0	3.9	100.0
Bradford	66.7	7.3	6.7	16.3	3.0	100.0
Bristol	62.4	7.6	8.4	15.1	6.6	100.0
Dudley	74.3	5.3	4.4	13.0	2.9	100.0
Gateshead	66.6	8.7	5.6	16.1	3.1	100.0
Kirklees	68.4	6.0	4.7	17.9	3.0	100.0
Leeds	66.9	7.4	8.3	14.6	2.8	100.0
Liverpool	61.0	9.9	7.6	16.4	5.1	100.0
Manchester	56.6	10.3	10.7	17.1	5.3	100.0
Newcastle-upon-Tyne	61.2	8.3	8.9	16.4	5.2	100.0
Salford	64.3	8.5	6.8	17.2	3.3	100.0
Sandwell	69.1	7.5	5.4	14.9	3.2	100.0
Sheffield	67.7	5.6	6.2	17.3	3.2	100.0
Sunderland	69.8	7.7	5.5	14.3	2.8	100.0
Wakefield	73.3	6.0	4.6	13.8	2.4	100.0
Wigan	71.3	6.8	5.0	14.2	2.7	100.0

TABLE 106 Type of Household : District

District	One person household	Small adult household	Small family	Large family	Large adult household	Older small household	All households
Birmingham	81.9	50.8	61.1	41.4	67.3	62.4	364.8
Bradford	37.8	23.5	32.7	17.6	25.9	27.1	164.6
Bristol	35.1	23.2	25.8	12.6	27.8	25.2	149.6
Dudley	18.5	17.5	24.9	8.6	19.7	16.9	106.1
Gateshead	17.3	11.7	16.6	6.5	14.5	13.2	79.8
Kirklees	30.6	19.1	27.9	12.9	21.5	22.9	134.9
Leeds	61.0	39.8	55.2	25.4	43.2	41.8	266.4
Liverpool	45.1	21.6	30.6	20.9	38.4	31.1	187.8
Manchester	46.4	21.5	24.4	18.0	29.0	27.5	166.7
Newcastle-upon-Tyne	27.7	15.7	19.0	9.2	19.1	18.8	109.6
Salford	22.6	12.5	16.8	9.9	16.7	15.6	94.1
Sandwell	22.9	15.3	21.0	12.4	21.0	19.9	112.6
Sheffield	46.8	27.5	37.4	16.9	32.1	38.0	198.8
Sunderland	20.5	15.0	23.7	10.1	19.3	15.3	103.8
Wakefield	19.4	17.4	24.3	9.6	18.1	16.5	105.2
Wigan	21.0	16.4	26.9	9.9	18.1	17.0	109.4

District	One person household	Small adult household	Small family	Large family	Large adult household	Older small household	All households
Birmingham	22.4	13.9	16.7	11.4	18.4	17.1	100.0
Bradford	23.0	14.3	19.8	10.7	15.7	16.5	100.0
Bristol	23.5	15.5	17.2	8.4	18.6	16.8	100.0
Dudley	17.5	16.5	23.5	8.1	18.5	15.9	100.0
Gateshead	21.7	14.6	20.8	8.1	18.2	16.6	100.0
Kirklees	22.7	14.2	20.7	9.6	15.9	17.0	100.0
Leeds	22.9	14.9	20.7	9.6	16.2	15.7	100.0
Liverpool	24.0	11.5	16.3	11.1	20.5	16.6	100.0
Manchester	27.8	12.9	14.6	10.8	17.4	16.5	100.0
Newcastle-upon-Tyne	25.3	14.3	17.4	8.4	17.4	17.2	100.0
Salford	24.0	13.3	17.8	10.5	17.7	16.6	100.0
Sandwell	20.3	13.6	18.7	11.0	18.7	17.7	100.0
Sheffield	23.5	13.9	18.8	8.5	16.2	19.1	100.0
Sunderland	19.7	14.5	22.8	9.7	18.6	14.7	100.0
Wakefield	18.4	16.6	23.1	9.1	17.2	15.6	100.0
Wigan	19.2	15.0	24.6	9.1	16.6	15.5	100.0

TABLE 107 Number of Rooms:　District

District	Number of rooms								All households
	1	2	3	4	5	6	7	8 or more	
Birmingham	5.1	9.5	33.2	61.9	131.3	95.3	17.6	10.7	364.8
Bradford	2.8	7.2	17.7	40.8	54.5	30.1	6.7	4.8	164.6
Bristol	3.2	5.9	13.6	24.4	41.6	46.0	9.6	5.2	149.6
Dudley	0.5	1.7	6.9	18.1	42.2	31.8	3.7	1.1	106.1
Gateshead	0.2	1.2	7.6	26.3	26.4	14.6	2.2	1.3	79.8
Kirklees	1.1	5.6	17.1	38.9	38.3	26.9	4.5	2.4	134.9
Leeds	2.9	8.4	26.5	67.3	88.6	52.0	13.3	7.5	266.4
Liverpool	1.7	6.2	19.7	31.1	56.9	54.9	10.3	7.0	187.8
Manchester	4.6	7.6	17.9	31.6	53.7	40.7	7.1	3.5	166.7
Newcastle-upon-Tyne	0.8	4.5	9.0	32.7	33.4	20.8	4.3	4.0	109.6
Salford	1.4	2.5	9.9	21.5	31.8	21.4	4.0	1.5	94.1
Sandwell	0.5	1.7	9.7	20.4	43.3	33.2	2.9	0.9	112.6
Sheffield	2.3	4.4	20.5	50.6	72.2	39.0	5.9	3.8	198.8
Sunderland	0.4	2.0	12.5	28.1	33.5	21.6	4.1	1.7	103.8
Wakefield	0.3	1.6	7.0	29.8	42.6	19.7	3.1	1.1	105.2
Wigan	0.3	1.3	6.8	24.5	48.5	24.4	2.4	1.0	109.4

District	Number of rooms								All households
	1	2	3	4	5	6	7	8 or more	
Birmingham	1.4	2.6	9.1	17.0	36.0	26.1	4.8	2.9	100.0
Bradford	1.7	4.4	10.8	24.8	33.1	18.3	4.1	2.8	100.0
Bristol	2.2	4.0	9.1	16.3	27.8	30.8	6.4	3.4	100.0
Dudley	0.5	1.6	6.5	17.0	39.8	30.0	3.4	1.1	100.0
Gateshead	0.2	1.5	9.6	33.0	33.1	18.3	2.8	1.6	100.0
Kirklees	0.8	4.2	12.7	28.8	28.4	19.9	3.4	1.8	100.0
Leeds	1.1	3.1	9.9	25.3	33.2	19.5	5.0	2.8	100.0
Liverpool	0.9	3.3	10.5	16.5	30.3	29.2	5.5	3.7	100.0
Manchester	2.8	4.6	10.7	19.0	32.2	24.4	4.3	2.1	100.0
Newcastle-upon-Tyne	0.7	4.2	8.3	29.8	30.5	19.0	3.9	3.7	100.0
Salford	1.5	2.7	10.6	22.8	33.8	22.7	4.2	1.6	100.0
Sandwell	0.4	1.5	8.6	18.2	38.4	29.5	2.6	0.7	100.0
Sheffield	1.2	2.2	10.3	25.5	36.3	19.6	2.9	1.9	100.0
Sunderland	0.4	1.9	12.0	27.1	32.3	20.8	3.9	1.7	100.0
Wakefield	0.3	1.5	6.7	28.3	40.5	18.8	3.0	1.1	100.0
Wigan	0.3	1.2	6.2	22.4	44.3	22.4	2.2	0.9	100.0

TABLE 108 Number of Bedrooms: District

Thousands

District	Number of bedrooms						All households
	1	2	3	4	5	6 or more	
Birmingham	46.6	82.5	210.1	20.5	4.4	0.8	364.8
Bradford	23.3	53.5	74.6	10.7	2.1	0.6	164.6
Bristol	22.6	36.2	79.8	8.6	1.8	0.7	149.6
Dudley	8.8	26.4	65.9	4.6	0.3	0.1	106.1
Gateshead	7.7	32.7	35.8	2.9	0.5	0.1	79.8
Kirklees	17.5	51.8	57.8	6.6	1.0	0.2	134.9
Leeds	35.2	78.6	125.5	21.6	4.5	0.9	266.4
Liverpool	26.9	43.1	103.3	11.5	2.2	0.8	187.8
Manchester	29.0	49.1	78.6	8.3	1.3	0.4	166.7
Newcastle-upon-Tyne	14.9	38.8	47.6	6.1	1.4	0.6	109.6
Salford	13.5	33.3	42.1	4.6	0.5	0.1	94.1
Sandwell	11.7	29.2	67.9	3.4	0.3	0.2	112.6
Sheffield	26.6	66.6	94.7	8.6	1.9	0.4	198.8
Sunderland	13.5	39.4	45.4	4.7	0.6	0.2	103.8
Wakefield	7.7	35.9	56.5	4.6	0.5	-	105.2
Wigan	8.1	35.9	62.0	3.0	0.3	0.1	109.4

Percentages

District	Number of bedrooms						All households
	1	2	3	4	5	6 or more	
Birmingham	12.8	22.6	57.6	5.6	1.2	0.2	100.0
Bradford	14.1	32.5	45.3	6.5	1.3	0.3	100.0
Bristol	15.1	24.2	53.3	5.8	1.2	0.5	100.0
Dudley	8.3	24.9	62.1	4.3	0.3	0.1	100.0
Gateshead	9.7	41.0	44.9	3.7	0.6	0.2	100.0
Kirklees	13.0	38.4	42.8	4.9	0.8	0.1	100.0
Leeds	13.2	29.5	47.1	8.1	1.7	0.3	100.0
Liverpool	14.3	22.9	55.0	6.1	1.2	0.4	100.0
Manchester	17.4	29.4	47.1	5.0	0.8	0.3	100.0
Newcastle-upon-Tyne	13.6	35.4	43.5	5.6	1.3	0.6	100.0
Salford	14.3	35.4	44.8	4.9	0.6	0.1	100.0
Sandwell	10.3	26.0	60.3	3.0	0.2	0.1	100.0
Sheffield	13.4	33.5	47.6	4.3	1.0	0.2	100.0
Sunderland	13.0	37.9	43.7	4.5	0.6	0.2	100.0
Wakefield	7.3	34.1	53.7	4.4	0.5	-	100.0
Wigan	7.4	32.8	56.7	2.8	0.3	0.1	100.0

TABLE 109   Density of Occupation: District

District	Persons per room					All households
	Less than $\frac{1}{2}$	$\frac{1}{2}$ to $\frac{3}{4}$	Over $\frac{3}{4}$ to 1	Over 1 to $1\frac{1}{2}$	Over $1\frac{1}{2}$	
Birmingham	150.2	128.6	68.2	15.2	2.6	364.8
Bradford	59.5	64.2	32.0	7.0	1.9	164.6
Bristol	63.0	56.3	27.3	2.5	0.5	149.6
Dudley	41.9	41.6	20.0	2.4	0.2	106.1
Gateshead	28.9	33.4	14.7	2.5	0.3	79.8
Kirklees	45.8	57.0	25.1	5.6	1.4	134.9
Leeds	99.3	106.3	51.9	7.8	1.2	266.4
Liverpool	76.8	65.5	34.4	9.5	1.7	187.8
Manchester	67.8	58.6	31.2	7.6	1.4	166.7
Newcastle-upon-Tyne	42.7	45.4	17.9	3.1	0.4	109.6
Salford	36.4	35.7	18.0	3.5	0.6	94.1
Sandwell	45.0	41.2	21.0	4.6	0.7	112.6
Sheffield	80.4	74.7	35.9	6.8	1.0	198.8
Sunderland	34.3	44.3	21.1	3.7	0.4	103.8
Wakefield	37.5	42.1	22.1	3.1	0.4	105.2
Wigan	41.4	42.9	21.4	3.4	0.3	109.4

District	Persons per room					All households
	Less than $\frac{1}{2}$	$\frac{1}{2}$ to $\frac{3}{4}$	Over $\frac{3}{4}$ to 1	Over 1 to $1\frac{1}{2}$	Over $1\frac{1}{2}$	
Birmingham	41.2	35.2	18.7	4.2	0.7	100.0
Bradford	36.1	39.0	19.4	4.3	1.2	100.0
Bristol	42.1	37.7	18.2	1.7	0.3	100.0
Dudley	39.5	39.2	18.9	2.2	0.2	100.0
Gateshead	36.2	41.9	18.4	3.1	0.3	100.0
Kirklees	33.9	42.3	18.6	4.2	1.1	100.0
Leeds	37.3	39.9	19.5	2.9	0.5	100.0
Liverpool	40.9	34.9	18.3	5.0	0.9	100.0
Manchester	40.7	35.2	18.7	4.6	0.9	100.0
Newcastle-upon-Tyne	39.0	41.4	16.3	2.8	0.4	100.0
Salford	38.7	37.9	19.1	3.7	0.6	100.0
Sandwell	40.0	36.6	18.7	4.1	0.7	100.0
Sheffield	40.4	37.6	18.1	3.4	0.4	100.0
Sunderland	33.0	42.7	20.3	3.6	0.4	100.0
Wakefield	35.7	40.0	21.0	3.0	0.3	100.0
Wigan	37.9	39.2	19.5	3.1	0.3	100.0

TABLE 110 Difference from Bedroom Standard: District   **Thousands**

| District | Difference from bedroom standard | | | | | All households |
	2 or more below	1 below	Equal	1 above	2 or more above	
Birmingham	4.7	22.7	119.1	131.2	87.1	364.8
Bradford	1.8	9.0	58.6	65.1	30.2	164.6
Bristol	0.9	7.0	54.9	50.9	35.8	149.6
Dudley	0.5	4.1	31.8	44.1	25.7	106.1
Gateshead	0.6	4.1	29.1	34.2	11.8	79.8
Kirklees	1.4	7.7	48.3	55.9	21.6	134.9
Leeds	1.1	11.0	91.2	107.4	55.6	266.4
Liverpool	2.7	15.1	68.4	58.7	42.8	187.8
Manchester	2.4	12.6	65.0	55.3	31.4	166.7
Newcastle-upon-Tyne	0.7	5.0	41.0	43.6	19.3	109.6
Salford	1.1	5.9	37.4	34.4	15.4	94.1
Sandwell	1.1	6.5	38.1	41.5	25.4	112.6
Sheffield	1.8	9.3	69.8	77.7	40.1	198.8
Sunderland	1.0	6.4	41.9	41.2	13.4	103.8
Wakefield	0.6	4.9	32.3	46.3	21.0	105.2
Wigan	0.6	5.2	35.5	46.9	21.2	109.4

Percentages

| District | Difference from bedroom standard | | | | | All households |
	2 or more below	1 below	Equal	1 above	2 or more above	
Birmingham	1.3	6.2	32.6	36.0	23.9	100.0
Bradford	1.1	5.5	35.6	39.5	18.4	100.0
Bristol	0.6	4.7	36.7	34.0	23.9	100.0
Dudley	0.5	3.8	29.9	41.5	24.2	100.0
Gateshead	0.7	5.1	36.5	42.9	14.8	100.0
Kirklees	1.0	5.7	35.8	41.4	16.0	100.0
Leeds	0.4	4.1	34.2	40.3	20.9	100.0
Liverpool	1.4	8.1	36.4	31.3	22.8	100.0
Manchester	1.4	7.6	39.0	33.2	18.8	100.0
Newcastle-upon-Tyne	0.6	4.5	37.4	39.8	17.6	100.0
Salford	1.1	6.3	39.8	36.5	16.3	100.0
Sandwell	1.0	5.8	33.8	36.9	22.5	100.0
Sheffield	0.9	4.7	35.1	39.1	20.2	100.0
Sunderland	0.9	6.1	40.3	39.7	12.9	100.0
Wakefield	0.6	4.7	30.7	44.1	20.0	100.0
Wigan	0.5	4.8	32.4	42.9	19.4	100.0

TABLE 111 Households Sharing a Dwelling : District

District	Type of Sharing					All households
	Sharing rooms	Sharing circulation space	Bedsit	Self contained accommodation		
				in shared dwelling	not in shared dwelling	
Birmingham	7.4	3.8	2.1	0.5	351.0	364.8
Bradford	2.5	0.8	1.6	0.1	159.6	164.6
Bristol	2.7	3.5	2.0	0.4	141.0	149.6
Dudley	0.8	0.3	0.3	-	104.6	106.1
Gateshead	0.3	-	0.1	-	79.4	79.8
Kirklees	0.5	0.2	0.8	0.1	133.3	134.9
Leeds	5.4	1.7	1.6	0.5	257.3	266.4
Liverpool	2.5	1.9	1.0	0.3	182.2	187.8
Manchester	3.9	2.6	2.5	0.2	157.5	166.7
Newcastle-upon-Tyne	3.1	0.5	0.2	0.1	105.7	109.6
Salford	1.1	0.5	0.7	0.1	91.8	94.1
Sandwell	1.3	0.3	0.2	-	110.9	112.6
Sheffield	2.8	0.9	1.1	0.3	193.6	198.8
Sunderland	0.3	0.8	0.3	-	102.4	103.8
Wakefield	0.2	0.1	0.2	-	104.7	105.2
Wigan	0.5	0.2	0.2	-	108.6	109.4

TABLE Households Sharing a Dwelling by District

District	Type of Sharing					All households
	Sharing rooms	Sharing circulation space	Bedsit	Self contained accommodation		
				in shared dwelling	not in shared dwelling	
Birmingham	2.0	1.1	0.6	0.1	96.2	100.0
Bradford	1.5	0.5	1.0	-	97.0	100.0
Bristol	1.8	2.3	1.3	0.2	94.2	100.0
Dudley	0.8	0.3	0.3	-	98.6	100.0
Gateshead	0.3	-	0.1	-	99.6	100.0
Kirklees	0.3	0.1	0.6	0.1	98.8	100.0
Leeds	2.0	0.6	0.6	0.2	96.5	100.0
Liverpool	1.3	1.0	0.6	0.1	97.0	100.0
Manchester	2.4	1.6	1.5	0.1	94.5	100.0
Newcastle-upon-Tyne	2.8	0.5	0.2	0.1	96.5	100.0
Salford	1.2	0.5	0.7	0.1	97.6.	100.0
Sandwell	1.1	0.3	0.2	-	98.5	100.0
Sheffield	1.4	0.5	0.6	0.1	97.4	100.0
Sunderland	0.3	0.8	0.2	-	98.7	100.0
Wakefield	0.2	0.1	0.2	-	99.5	100.0
Wigan	0.4	0.1	0.1	-	99.3	100.0

TABLE 112 Use of Basic Amenities: District

Thousands

District	Use of basic amenities			All households
	Sole use of all	Some shared none lacked	At least one lacked	
Birmingham	327.2	11.2	26.5	364.8
Bradford	149.1	4.1	11.5	164.6
Bristol	134.3	6.9	8.3	149.6
Dudley	99.4	1.4	5.3	106.1
Gateshead	76.1	0.4	3.3	79.8
Kirklees	123.7	1.6	9.7	134.9
Leeds	250.7	8.7	7.1	266.4
Liverpool	158.4	5.4	24.1	187.8
Manchester	142.9	9.2	14.6	166.7
Newcastle-upon-Tyne	100.1	3.7	5.7	109.6
Salford	82.3	2.0	9.8	94.1
Sandwell	100.7	1.3	10.6	112.6
Sheffield	177.2	5.3	16.3	198.8
Sunderland	97.5	1.2	5.1	103.8
Wakefield	101.1	0.4	3.7	105.2
Wigan	101.1	0.8	7.5	109.4

Percentages

District	Use of basic amenities			All households
	Sole use of all	Some shared none lacked	At least one lacked	
Birmingham	89.7	3.1	7.3	100.0
Bradford	90.5	2.5	7.0	100.0
Bristol	89.8	4.6	5.6	100.0
Dudley	93.7	1.3	5.0	100.0
Gateshead	95.4	0.5	4.1	100.0
Kirklees	91.7	1.2	7.2	100.0
Leeds	94.1	3.2	2.7	100.0
Liverpool	84.3	2.9	12.8	100.0
Manchester	85.7	5.5	8.8	100.0
Newcastle-upon-Tyne	91.3	3.4	5.2	100.0
Salford	87.4	2.1	10.4	100.0
Sandwell	89.4	1.2	9.4	100.0
Sheffield	89.1	2.6	8.2	100.0
Sunderland	93.9	1.2	4.9	100.0
Wakefield	96.1	0.4	3.5	100.0
Wigan	92.4	0.7	6.9	100.0

TABLE 113 Use of Bath or Shower: District

Thousands

District	Use of bath or shower			All households
	Sole use	Shared use	None	
Birmingham	343.8	12.8	8.2	364.8
Bradford	155.0	4.6	5.0	164.6
Bristol	139.9	7.5	2.3	149.6
Dudley	102.6	1.5	1.9	106.1
Gateshead	77.7	0.4	1.7	79.8
Kirklees	126.3	1.6	7.1	134.9
Leeds	253.5	9.4	3.6	266.4
Liverpool	168.9	6.7	12.3	187.8
Manchester	152.7	9.9	4.1	166.7
Newcastle-upon-Tyne	103.7	3.9	2.0	109.6
Salford	88.7	2.4	3.0	94.1
Sandwell	108.3	1.5	2.8	112.6
Sheffield	184.1	5.5	9.2	198.8
Sunderland	99.6	1.4	2.9	103.8
Wakefield	103.5	0.4	1.3	105.2
Wigan	103.8	0.8	4.8	109.4

Percentages

District	Use of bath or shower			All households
	Sole use	Shared use	None	
Birmingham	94.3	3.5	2.2	100.0
Bradford	94.2	2.8	3.0	100.0
Bristol	93.5	5.0	1.5	100.0
Dudley	96.7	1.5	1.8	100.0
Gateshead	97.4	0.5	2.2	100.0
Kirklees	93.6	1.2	5.2	100.0
Leeds	95.1	3.5	1.3	100.0
Liverpool	89.9	3.6	6.5	100.0
Manchester	91.6	5.9	2.5	100.0
Newcastle-upon-Tyne	94.6	3.6	1.8	100.0
Salford	94.2	2.6	3.2	100.0
Sandwell	96.2	1.3	2.5	100.0
Sheffield	92.6	2.8	4.6	100.0
Sunderland	95.9	1.3	2.8	100.0
Wakefield	98.3	0.4	1.2	100.0
Wigan	94.9	0.7	4.4	100.0

TABLE 114 Use of Hot Water Supply : District

Thousands

District	Use of hot water supply			All households
	Sole use	Shared use	None	
Birmingham	345.8	8.7	10.3	364.8
Bradford	157.8	3.0	3.8	164.6
Bristol	140.1	4.4	5.1	149.6
Dudley	103.0	1.0	2.1	106.1
Gateshead	78.4	0.2	1.2	79.8
Kirklees	129.1	0.7	5.0	134.9
Leeds	256.3	6.8	3.3	266.4
Liverpool	171.4	3.3	13.1	187.8
Manchester	157.4	6.0	3.3	166.7
Newcastle-upon-Tyne	104.8	3.2	1.5	109.6
Salford	90.0	1.4	2.8	94.1
Sandwell	107.8	1.0	3.8	112.6
Sheffield	190.4	2.8	5.6	198.8
Sunderland	100.4	1.0	2.4	103.8
Wakefield	104.0	0.2	1.0	105.2
Wigan	105.7	0.3	3.3	109.4

Percentages

District	Use of hot water supply			All households
	Sole use	Shared use	None	
Birmingham	94.8	2.4	2.8	100.0
Bradford	95.9	1.8	2.3	100.0
Bristol	93.7	2.9	3.4	100.0
Dudley	97.1	0.9	2.0	100.0
Gateshead	98.2	0.3	1.5	100.0
Kirklees	95.7	0.5	3.7	100.0
Leeds	96.2	2.5	1.2	100.0
Liverpool	91.3	1.8	7.0	100.0
Manchester	94.4	3.6	2.0	100.0
Newcastle-upon-Tyne	95.7	2.9	1.4	100.0
Salford	95.6	1.5	2.9	100.0
Sandwell	95.7	0.9	3.4	100.0
Sheffield	95.8	1.4	2.8	100.0
Sunderland	96.7	1.0	2.3	100.0
Wakefield	98.8	0.2	0.9	100.0
Wigan	96.6	0.3	3.1	100.0

TABLE 115 Use of Flush Toilet: District

District	Use of flush toilet				All households
	Sole use inside building	Shared use inside building	Use of outside WC only	None	
Birmingham	329.7	12.6	22.2	0.3	364.8
Bradford	150.3	4.6	9.3	0.4	164.6
Bristol	138.3	7.3	4.0	-	149.6
Dudley	101.0	1.3	3.8	0.1	106.1
Gateshead	76.4	0.3	3.0	0.1	79.8
Kirklees	126.4	1.4	6.7	0.4	134.9
Leeds	251.6	9.3	5.4	0.2	266.4
Liverpool	160.3	6.9	20.4	0.3	187.8
Manchester	143.8	10.0	12.8	0.1	166.7
Newcastle-upon-Tyne	100.6	3.7	5.3	-	109.6
Salford	82.8	2.6	8.6	0.1	94.1
Sandwell	102.9	1.3	8.3	0.2	112.6
Sheffield	178.6	4.9	14.7	0.6	198.8
Sunderland	98.1	1.3	4.4	0.1	103.8
Wakefield	101.5	0.4	3.3	0.1	105.2
Wigan	101.7	0.6	6.8	0.2	109.4

District	Use of flush toilet				All households
	Sole use inside building	Shared use inside building	Use of outside WC only	None	
Birmingham	90.4	3.5	6.1	0.1	100.0
Bradford	91.3	2.8	5.6	0.2	100.0
Bristol	92.5	4.9	2.6	-	100.0
Dudley	95.2	1.1	3.6	0.1	100.0
Gateshead	95.7	0.4	3.8	0.1	100.0
Kirklees	93.7	1.1	4.9	0.3	100.0
Leeds	94.4	3.5	2.1	0.1	100.0
Liverpool	85.3	3.6	10.9	0.2	100.0
Manchester	86.3	5.9	7.7	0.1	100.0
Newcastle-upon-Tyne	91.8	3.4	4.8	-	100.0
Salford	87.9	2.8	9.2	0.1	100.0
Sandwell	91.4	1.1	7.3	0.1	100.0
Sheffield	89.8	2.5	7.4	0.3	100.0
Sunderland	94.5	1.2	4.2	0.1	100.0
Wakefield	96.5	0.3	3.2	0.1	100.0
Wigan	93.0	0.6	6.2	0.2	100.0

TABLE 116 Type of Central Heating: District

Thousands

| District | Central heating fuel | | | | | | All households |
	No central heating	Solid fuel	Gas	Oil	Electric storage heaters	Other*	
Birmingham	225.0	6.3	89.0	5.0	12.6	26.8	364.8
Bradford	101.4	3.7	40.1	3.3	8.9	7.2	164.6
Bristol	69.7	14.6	32.6	8.5	16.9	7.3	149.6
Dudley	56.2	3.1	35.5	0.8	6.8	3.7	106.1
Gateshead	29.0	8.8	33.1	1.6	2.1	5.2	79.8
Kirklees	84.7	3.6	34.1	1.5	5.4	5.6	134.9
Leeds	152.4	6.9	67.5	2.5	16.6	20.5	266.4
Liverpool	139.2	1.6	36.8	1.4	3.6	5.2	187.8
Manchester	99.9	2.5	36.8	4.7	6.9	15.9	166.7
Newcastle-upon-Tyne	45.6	8.7	40.6	1.8	5.4	7.4	109.6
Salford	43.7	4.2	30.1	3.8	4.6	7.7	94.1
Sandwell	69.5	2.2	27.0	0.5	5.4	8.0	112.6
Sheffield	107.8	7.8	62.8	2.3	6.6	11.5	198.8
Sunderland	39.7	16.1	39.2	0.9	2.4	5.6	103.8
Wakefield	51.8	21.5	22.8	1.1	3.0	5.0	105.2
Wigan	49.8	9.0	31.7	4.5	7.1	7.2	109.4

* Mainly other electric

Percentages

| District | Central heating fuel | | | | | | All households |
	No central heating	Solid fuel	Gas	Oil	Electric storage heaters	Other*	
Birmingham	61.7	1.7	24.4	1.4	3.5	7.4	100.0
Bradford	61.6	2.3	24.4	2.0	5.4	4.4	100.0
Bristol	46.6	9.8	21.8	5.7	11.3	4.9	100.0
Dudley	53.0	2.9	33.5	0.8	6.4	3.5	100.0
Gateshead	36.4	11.0	41.5	2.0	2.6	6.5	100.0
Kirklees	62.8	2.7	25.3	1.1	4.0	4.2	100.0
Leeds	57.2	2.6	25.3	0.9	6.2	7.7	100.0
Liverpool	74.1	0.8	19.6	0.8	1.9	2.8	100.0
Manchester	59.9	1.5	22.0	2.8	4.2	9.5	100.0
Newcastle-upon-Tyne	41.6	8.0	37.1	1.7	4.9	6.8	100.0
Salford	46.4	4.5	32.0	4.0	4.9	8.2	100.0
Sandwell	61.7	1.9	24.0	0.5	4.8	7.1	100.0
Sheffield	54.2	3.9	31.6	1.2	3.3	5.8	100.0
Sunderland	38.2	15.5	37.7	0.9	2.3	5.4	100.0
Wakefield	49.2	20.5	21.7	1.0	2.8	4.7	100.0
Wigan	45.5	8.2	29.0	4.1	6.5	6.6	100.0

* Mainly other electric

181

TABLE 117 Main Form of Room Heating: District

Thousands

District	Main form of room heating						All households
	Central heating	Open fire	Closed stove	Electric	Gas	Other*	
Birmingham	106.8	12.1	3.9	61.2	175.2	5.6	364.8
Bradford	46.0	13.0	2.8	18.5	83.7	0.6	164.6
Bristol	69.0	16.0	5.7	24.6	30.4	3.8	149.6
Dudley	38.8	9.3	1.4	11.8	44.3	0.6	106.1
Gateshead	44.2	13.4	1.6	5.9	14.2	0.5	79.8
Kirklees	37.3	19.1	2.2	11.0	64.6	0.6	134.9
Leeds	88.3	17.9	2.0	29.0	128.1	1.1	266.4
Liverpool	39.8	19.5	2.7	31.2	93.5	1.1	187.8
Manchester	52.8	13.2	2.4	23.8	73.0	1.4	166.7
Newcastle-upon-Tyne	54.0	7.5	2.3	11.7	31.1	0.9	109.6
Salford	42.7	5.5	1.6	10.9	32.8	0.7	94.1
Sandwell	29.9	11.6	1.1	18.7	50.5	0.8	112.6
Sheffield	75.6	17.5	2.6	21.7	30.5	0.8	198.8
Sunderland	56.3	22.6	1.1	5.0	18.0	0.9	103.8
Wakefield	42.6	36.7	1.2	4.2	20.4	0.2	105.2
Wigan	50.8	20.7	1.3	7.5	28.6	0.4	109.4

* mainly oil or paraffin

Percentages

District	Main form of room heating						All households
	Central heating	Open fire	Closed stove	Electric	Gas	Other*	
Birmingham	29.3	3.3	1.1	16.8	48.0	1.5	100.0
Bradford	27.9	7.9	1.7	11.3	50.8	0.3	100.0
Bristol	46.1	10.7	3.8	16.5	20.3	2.6	100.0
Dudley	36.5	8.7	1.3	11.1	41.7	0.5	100.0
Gateshead	55.4	16.8	2.1	7.4	17.9	0.6	100.0
Kirklees	27.7	14.2	1.6	8.2	47.9	0.5	100.0
Leeds	33.2	6.7	0.7	10.9	48.1	0.3	100.0
Liverpool	21.2	10.4	1.4	16.6	49.8	0.6	100.0
Manchester	31.7	7.9	1.4	14.3	43.8	0.8	100.0
Newcastle-upon-Tyne	49.3	6.9	2.1	10.7	30.2	0.8	100.0
Salford	45.3	5.8	1.7	11.6	34.8	0.7	100.0
Sandwell	26.5	10.3	1.0	16.6	44.8	0.7	100.0
Sheffield	38.1	8.8	1.3	10.9	40.5	0.3	100.0
Sunderland	54.2	21.8	1.1	4.8	17.3	0.8	100.0
Wakefield	40.5	34.9	1.1	4.0	19.4	0.2	100.0
Wigan	46.5	19.0	1.2	6.9	26.2	0.4	100.0

* mainly oil or paraffin

TABLE 118   Tenure: District

District	Owned out right	Owned with mortgage or loan	Rented from council	Rented from housing assoc.	Rented privately un-furnished	Rented privately furnished	All households
Birmingham	71.9	106.1	132.4	10.0	31.5	12.8	364.8
Bradford	48.2	58.4	37.8	2.2	12.8	5.1	164.6
Bristol	36.9	40.5	47.3	2.3	12.2	10.4	149.6
Dudley	22.0	37.0	40.5	0.5	5.5	0.8	106.1
Gateshead	11.8	17.9	38.5	2.6	8.4	0.6	79.8
Kirklees	37.5	43.8	37.2	0.7	13.9	1.7	134.9
Leeds	49.2	85.5	94.8	3.7	22.2	11.0	266.4
Liverpool	26.1	41.9	75.1	6.0	31.9	6.7	187.8
Manchester	27.2	29.8	75.2	3.5	19.7	11.3	166.7
Newcastle-upon-Tyne	15.6	24.3	47.8	2.0	14.2	5.6	109.6
Salford	17.9	19.9	41.3	1.9	10.5	2.6	94.1
Sandwell	19.6	26.1	57.6	0.3	8.2	0.8	112.6
Sheffield	36.8	47.3	88.5	1.3	18.8	6.1	198.8
Sunderland	15.8	22.2	56.9	1.8	5.6	1.5	103.8
Wakefield	17.7	30.4	44.9	0.5	11.1	0.6	105.2
Wigan	24.7	38.8	37.3	0.1	7.8	0.6	109.4

District	Owned out right	Owned with mortgage or loan	Rented from council	Rented from housing assoc.	Rented privately un-furnished	Rented privately furnished	All households
Birmingham	19.7	29.1	36.3	2.8	8.6	3.5	100.0
Bradford	29.3	35.5	23.0	1.4	7.8	3.1	100.0
Bristol	24.7	27.1	31.6	1.5	8.2	6.9	100.0
Dudley	20.7	34.8	38.2	0.4	5.1	0.7	100.0
Gateshead	14.7	22.4	48.2	3.3	10.5	0.8	100.0
Kirklees	27.8	32.5	27.6	0.5	10.3	1.3	100.0
Leeds	18.4	32.1	35.6	1.4	8.3	4.1	100.0
Liverpool	13.9.	22.3	40.0	3.2	17.0	3.6	100.0
Manchester	16.3	17.9	45.1	2.1	11.8	6.7	100.0
Newcastle-upon-Tyne	14.3	22.2	43.6	1.9	12.9	5.1	100.0
Salford	19.1	21.2	43.9	2.0	11.1	2.7	100.0
Sandwell	17.5	23.2	51.1	0.2	7.3	0.7	100.0
Sheffield	18.5	23.8	44.5	0.6	9.5	3.1	100.0
Sunderland	15.2	21.4	54.8	1.7	5.4	1.5	100.0
Wakefield	16.9	28.9	42.7	0.4	10.5	0.6	100.0
Wigan	22.6	35.5	34.1	0.1	7.1	0.6	100.0

TABLE 119 Households in Privately Rented Accommodation: Type of Landlord: District

Thousands

District	Type of landlord						All households privately renting
	Property company	Employer- company	Employer- person	Relative	Other person	Other	
Birmingham	9.3	3.9	1.8	2.4	25.4	1.5	44.3
Bradford	2.8	1.3	0.2	1.3	10.5	1.9	17.9
Bristol	2.1	1.0	0.9	1.2	16.3	1.2	22.6
Dudley	0.7	1.1	0.2	0.6	3.2	0.5	6.2
Gateshead	1.4	0.7	0.2	0.7	5.9	0.2	9.0
Kirklees	0.9	2.0	0.6	0.9	10.3	0.8	15.6
Leeds	4.6	2.4	0.6	1.6	20.4	3.6	33.2
Liverpool	12.8	1.3	0.6	0.6	17.8	5.6	38.7
Manchester	6.4	1.7	0.4	0.5	20.5	1.4	31.0
Newcastle-upon-Tyne	3.5	1.4	0.7	0.8	11.9	1.6	19.8
Salford	2.9	1.1	0.3	0.2	7.7	0.8	13.1
Sandwell	1.5	1.3	0.4	0.4	4.9	0.6	9.1
Sheffield	1.2	1.9	0.7	0.7	18.2	2.3	25.0
Sunderland	0.7	1.7	0.2	0.2	3.8	0.4	7.1
Wakefield	0.4	4.8	0.5	0.4	4.1	1.4	11.7
Wigan	0.8	0.9	0.5	0.5	5.1	0.6	8.4

Percentages

District	Type of landlord						All households privately renting
	Property company	Employer- company	Employer- person	Relative	Other person	Other	
Birmingham	21.0	8.8	4.1	5.5	57.4	3.3	100.0
Bradford	15.8	7.4	1.1	7.0	58.4	10.4	100.0
Bristol	9.1	4.5	3.8	5.2	72.0	5.4	100.0
Dudley	11.3	17.4	2.9	9.8	51.1	7.4	100.0
Gateshead	15.7	7.2	1.9	7.6	65.1	2.5	100.0
Kirklees	6.0	13.0	3.9	5.8	65.9	5.4	100.0
Leeds	14.0	7.1	1.9	4.9	61.4	10.7	100.0
Liverpool	33.1	3.3	1.5	1.5	46.0	14.6	100.0
Manchester	20.8	5.5	1.4	1.6	66.2	4.6	100.0
Newcastle-upon-Tyne	17.4	7.1	3.3	4.2	60.0	8.0	100.0
Salford	22.0	8.3	2.6	1.6	59.3	6.3	100.0
Sandwell	16.4	14.3	4.3	4.3	53.9	6.7	100.0
Sheffield	4.7	7.5	2.8	2.7	73.0	9.3	100.0
Sunderland	9.8	24.4	3.1	3.2	53.9	5.6	100.0
Wakefield	3.8	40.9	4.4	3.5	35.4	12.0	100.0
Wigan	9.7	10.6	5.8	5.8	61.3	6.9	100.0

TABLE 120   Individual Private Landlords: District

Thousands

District	Households renting from individual*			All households renting from individual
	Resident landlord sharing space	Resident landlord not sharing space	No resident landlord	
Birmingham	3.3	0.6	25.7	29.7
Bradford	1.3	0.4	10.2	11.9
Bristol	1.8	2.3	14.2	18.3
Dudley	0.3	-	3.7	4.0
Gateshead	-	0.2	6.4	6.7
Kirklees	0.3	0.1	11.4	11.8
Leeds	0.7	0.9	21.0	22.7
Liverpool	0.8	0.5	17.7	19.0
Manchester	1.6	0.5	19.4	21.5
Newcastle-upon-Tyne	0.4	0.2	12.8	13.4
Salford	0.5	0.2	7.6	8.3
Sandwell	0.2	0.1	5.4	5.7
Sheffield	0.6	0.1	18.8	19.6
Sunderland	0.1	0.1	4.1	4.3
Wakefield	-	0.1	4.9	5.1
Wigan	0.1	0.1	6.0	6.1

Percentages

Stress Areas	Households renting from individual*			All households renting from individual
	Resident landlord sharing space	Resident landlord not sharing space	No resident landlord	
Birmingham	11.2	2.1	86.7	100.0
Bradford	10.8	3.5	85.7	100.0
Bristol	9.8	12.4	77.8	100.0
Dudley	7.4	0.5	92.1	100.0
Gateshead	0.7	3.7	95.6	100.0
Kirklees	2.5	0.8	96.7	100.0
Leeds	3.1	4.0	92.8	100.0
Liverpool	4.1	2.8	93.1	100.0
Manchester	7.5	2.3	90.2	100.0
Newcastle-upon-Tyne	2.7	1.8	95.5	100.0
Salford	6.6	2.2	91.2	100.0
Sandwell	3.7	1.7	94.7	100.0
Sheffield	3.1	0.7	96.1	100.0
Sunderland	2.6	2.0	95.3	100.0
Wakefield	0.7	2.9	96.4	100.0
Wigan	0.9	1.5	97.5	100.0

TABLE 121 Person Registered on Council House Waiting List: District

Thousands

District	Member of household registered				All households
	Head of household	Other person	HoH and other person	No one	
Birmingham	22.5	4.3	9.6	328.5	364.8
Bradford	6.1	0.9	1.6	156.0	164.6
Bristol	5.0	0.5	2.3	141.8	149.6
Dudley	4.3	1.8	1.8	98.1	106.1
Gateshead	7.2	1.2	2.1	69.2	79.8
Kirklees	8.2	1.3	1.4	124.0	134.9
Leeds	15.1	3.4	7.4	240.5	266.4
Liverpool	10.3	2.3	4.5	170.8	187.8
Manchester	15.2	2.6	2.0	146.9	166.7
Newcastle-upon-Tyne	10.2	1.7	2.1	95.6	109.6
Salford	7.3	0.9	2.4	83.5	94.1
Sandwell	8.5	2.5	1.7	99.9	112.6
Sheffield	17.5	5.5	2.9	173.0	198.8
Sunderland	8.1	1.3	2.2	92.2	103.8
Wakefield	6.6	0.9	1.9	95.8	105.2
Wigan	5.6	0.6	1.4	101.8	109.4

Percentages

District	Member of household registered				All households
	Head of household	Other person	HoH and other person	No one	
Birmingham	6.2	1.2	2.6	90.0	100.0
Bradford	3.7	0.5	1.0	94.8	100.0
Bristol	3.4	0.4	1.5	94.8	100.0
Dudley	4.1	1.7	1.7	92.5	100.0
Gateshead	9.0	1.6	2.7	86.8	100.0
Kirklees	6.1	0.9	1.1	91.9	100.0
Leeds	5.7	1.3	2.8	90.2	100.0
Liverpool	5.5	1.2	2.4	90.9	100.0
Manchester	9.2	1.5	1.2	88.1	100.0
Newcastle-upon-Tyne	9.3	1.5	1.9	87.3	100.0
Salford	7.7	1.0	2.5	88.7	100.0
Sandwell	7.6	2.2	1.5	88.8	100.0
Sheffield	8.8	2.7	1.5	87.0	100.0
Sunderland	7.8	1.3	2.1	88.8	100.0
Wakefield	6.2	0.9	1.8	91.1	100.0
Wigan	5.1	0.6	1.2	93.0	100.0

TABLE 122 Satisfaction with Accommodation: District

Thousands

District	Satisfaction with accommodation					All households
	Very satisfied	Satisfied	Neutral	Dissatisfied	Very dissatisfied	
Birmingham	104.9	176.8	40.7	28.6	13.9	364.8
Bradford	54.3	78.7	16.0	11.4	4.3	164.6
Bristol	51.5	71.2	13.5	9.2	4.2	149.6
Dudley	33.7	55.7	8.6	5.4	2.7	106.1
Gateshead	27.9	35.4	6.8	6.2	3.5	79.8
Kirklees	44.1	65.6	12.6	9.7	2.9	134.9
Leeds	89.9	124.9	23.4	20.0	8.2	266.4
Liverpool	42.7	87.3	21.0	22.5	14.3	187.8
Manchester	42.0	74.2	20.0	18.5	12.0	166.7
Newcastle-upon-Tyne	35.1	47.1	11.3	9.5	6.5	109.6
Salford	30.0	41.1	8.2	9.2	5.6	94.1
Sandwell	25.9	61.3	10.2	10.8	4.3	112.6
Sheffield	67.0	91.5	19.0	14.6	6.6	198.8
Sunderland	31.7	47.6	10.7	9.7	4.2	103.8
Wakefield	32.1	51.5	10.2	8.2	3.2	105.2
Wigan	34.7	52.5	10.0	8.7	3.4	109.4

Percentages

District	Satisfaction with accommodation					All households
	Very satisfied	Satisfied	Neutral	Dissatisfied	Very dissatisfied	
Birmingham	28.8	48.5	11.1	7.8	3.8	100.0
Bradford	33.0	47.8	9.7	6.9	2.6	100.0
Bristol	34.4	47.6	9.0	6.2	2.8	100.0
Dudley	31.7	52.5	8.1	5.1	2.5	100.0
Gateshead	35.0	44.4	8.5	7.8	4.4	100.0
Kirklees	32.7	48.6	9.3	7.2	2.2	100.0
Leeds	33.7	46.9	8.8	7.5	3.1	100.0
Liverpool	22.7	46.5	11.2	12.0	7.6	100.0
Manchester	25.2	44.5	12.0	11.1	7.2	100.0
Newcastle-upon-Tyne	32.1	43.0	10.3	8.7	5.9	100.0
Salford	31.9	43.7	8.7	9.7	6.0	100.0
Sandwell	23.0	54.5	9.1	9.6	3.9	100.0
Sheffield	33.7	46.1	9.6	7.4	3.3	100.0
Sunderland	30.6	45.8	10.3	9.3	4.0	100.0
Wakefield	30.5	48.9	9.7	7.8	3.0	100.0
Wigan	31.7	48.0	9.2	7.9	3.1	100.0

TABLE 123 Satisfaction with Area: District

Thousands

District	Satisfaction with area					All households
	Very satisfied	Satisfied	Neutral	Dissatisfied	Very dissatisfied	
Birmingham	95.6	168.0	39.9	42.4	18.9	364.8
Bradford	52.0	75.7	15.1	15.2	6.6	164.6
Bristol	50.0	70.9	11.3	12.2	5.3	149.6
Dudley	35.6	55.3	6.9	6.2	2.0	106.1
Gateshead	29.2	35.6	5.5	6.0	3.6	79.8
Kirklees	44.5	66.1	9.9	10.7	3.7	134.9
Leeds	85.8	122.3	22.9	27.0	8.5	266.4
Liverpool	40.2	95.0	15.9	22.8	14.0	187.8
Manchester	33.3	77.1	19.5	22.1	14.8	166.7
Newcastle-upon-Tyne	32.2	50.7	10.5	10.2	5.9	109.6
Salford	26.4	44.1	7.7	9.9	6.1	94.1
Sandwell	23.5	62.8	8.9	12.3	5.2	112.6
Sheffield	73.5	91.6	12.0	15.6	6.1	198.8
Sunderland	33.4	50.4	7.3	8.7	4.1	103.8
Wakefield	31.5	53.5	7.4	8.8	4.0	105.2
Wigan	35.1	51.5	7.8	9.1	5.8	109.4

Percentages

	Satisfaction with area					All households
	Very satisfied	Satisfied	Neutral	Dissatisfied	Very dissatisfied	
Birmingham	26.2	46.0	10.9	11.6	5.2	100.0
Bradford	31.6	46.0	9.2	9.2	4.0	100.0
Bristol	33.4	47.4	7.5	8.1	3.5	100.0
Dudley	33.6	52.1	6.5	5.8	1.9	100.0
Gateshead	36.6	44.6	6.9	7.5	4.5	100.0
Kirklees	33.0	49.0	7.3	7.9	2.8	100.0
Leeds	32.2	45.9	8.6	10.1	3.2	100.0
Liverpool	21.4	50.6	8.5	12.1	7.4	100.0
Manchester	20.0	46.2	11.7	13.2	8.9	100.0
Newcastle-upon-Tyne	29.4	46.3	9.6	9.3	5.4	100.0
Salford	28.1	46.8	8.2	10.5	6.5	100.0
Sandwell	20.8	55.8	7.9	10.9	4.6	100.0
Sheffield	37.0	46.1	6.0	7.9	3.1	100.0
Sunderland	32.2	48.5	7.0	8.3	4.0	100.0
Wakefield	29.9	50.9	7.1	8.4	3.8	100.0
Wigan	32.1	47.1	7.1	8.3	5.3	100.0

TABLE 124 Satisfaction with Number of Rooms: District

Thousands

District	Satisfaction with number of rooms			All households
	Too few	Too many	About right	
Birmingham	48.8	32.6	283.4	364.8
Bradford	23.1	11.5	130.0	164.6
Bristol	22.8	9.8	116.9	149.6
Dudley	13.7	6.7	85.9	106.1
Gateshead	11.0	6.0	62.9	79.8
Kirklees	19.4	7.6	107.9	134.9
Leeds	40.0	16.6	209.8	266.4
Liverpool	32.4	15.0	140.4	187.8
Manchester	27.2	14.3	125.2	166.7
Newcastle-upon-Tyne	15.9	10.4	83.3	109.6
Salford	15.4	6.9	71.8	94.1
Sandwell	12.4	9.7	90.5	112.6
Sheffield	28.5	13.2	157.0	198.8
Sunderland	15.1	7.5	81.3	103.8
Wakefield	15.2	8.6	81.4	105.2
Wigan	15.5	8.4	85.4	109.4

Percentages

District	Satisfaction with number of rooms			All households
	Too few	Too many	About right	
Birmingham	13.4	8.9	77.7	100.0
Bradford	14.0	7.0	79.0	100.0
Bristol	15.2	6.6	78.2	100.0
Dudley	12.9	6.3	80.8	100.0
Gateshead	13.7	7.5	78.8	100.0
Kirklees	14.4	5.7	80.0	100.0
Leeds	15.0	6.2	78.7	100.0
Liverpool	17.3	8.0	74.8	100.0
Manchester	16.3	8.6	75.1	100.0
Newcastle-upon-Tyne	14.5	9.5	76.0	100.0
Salford	16.3	7.4	76.3	100.0
Sandwell	11.1	8.6	80.3	100.0
Sheffield	14.4	6.6	79.0	100.0
Sunderland	14.5	7.2	78.3	100.0
Wakefield	14.5	8.2	77.4	100.0
Wigan	14.2	7.7	78.1	100.0

TABLE 125 Satisfaction with Size of Rooms: District

Thousands

District	Satisfaction with size of rooms				All households
	All or some too small	All or some too large	All about right	Some too large, others too small	
Birmingham	65.2	8.1	284.9	6.5	364.8
Bradford	26.4	3.6	131.1	3.5	164.6
Bristol	23.7	3.0	119.4	3.5	149.6
Dudley	19.2	1.5	83.8	1.7	106.1
Gateshead	14.9	1.2	63.1	0.7	79.8
Kirklees	21.7	2.6	108.8	1.8	134.9
Leeds	49.8	5.3	207.6	3.8	266.4
Liverpool	37.0	4.2	141.0	5.7	187.8
Manchester	30.6	3.1	130.0	3.0	166.7
Newcastle-upon-Tyne	20.0	2.6	85.3	1.7	109.6
Salford	17.8	1.8	72.5	2.0	94.1
Sandwell	17.6	2.3	90.8	2.0	112.6
Sheffield	33.4	4.3	156.8	4.3	198.8
Sunderland	20.3	2.7	78.8	2.0	103.8
Wakefield	20.7	2.5	80.5	1.6	105.2
Wigan	20.0	2.1	85.4	1.8	109.4

Percentages

District	Satisfaction with size of rooms				All households
	All or some too small	All or some too large	All about right	Some too large, others too small	
Birmingham	17.9	2.2	78.1	1.8	100.0
Bradford	16.0	2.2	79.6	2.1	100.0
Bristol	15.8	2.0	79.8	2.3	100.0
Dudley	18.1	1.4	78.9	1.6	100.0
Gateshead	18.6	1.5	79.1	0.9	100.0
Kirklees	16.1	1.9	80.6	1.4	100.0
Leeds	18.7	2.0	77.9	1.4	100.0
Liverpool	19.7	2.2	75.1	3.0	100.0
Manchester	18.4	1.9	78.0	1.8	100.0
Newcastle-upon-Tyne	18.2	2.4	77.9	1.5	100.0
Salford	18.9	1.9	77.0	2.1	100.0
Sandwell	15.6	2.0	80.6	1.8	100.0
Sheffield	16.8	2.2	78.9	2.1	100.0
Sunderland	19.6	2.6	75.9	1.9	100.0
Wakefield	19.7	2.3	76.5	1.5	100.0
Wigan	18.3	1.9	78.1	1.7	100.0

TABLE 126 Availability of Cars and Vans : District

Thousands

District	Number of cars and vans available to household				All households
	0	1	2	3 or more	
Birmingham	188.9	144.9	27.2	3.8	364.8
Bradford	87.6	63.0	12.1	1.8	164.6
Bristol	67.1	68.1	12.6	1.8	149.6
Dudley	41.4	51.6	11.8	1.4	106.1
Gateshead	48.8	27.4	3.3	0.3	79.8
Kirklees	67.9	56.1	9.8	1.1	134.9
Leeds	135.7	108.3	19.9	2.5	266.4
Liverpool	123.3	56.3	7.3	0.9	187.8
Manchester	106.5	52.4	6.9	0.9	166.7
Newcastle-upon-Tyne	66.7	36.9	5.1	0.8	109.6
Salford	55.1	33.0	5.5	0.5	94.1
Sandwell	60.6	46.1	5.4	0.5	112.6
Sheffield	109.2	77.1	11.1	1.3	198.8
Sunderland	60.3	37.7	5.2	0.6	103.8
Wakefield	52.8	45.2	6.7	0.6	105.2
Wigan	51.8	49.5	7.4	0.6	109.4

Percentages

District	Number of cars and vans available to household				All households
	0	1	2	3 or more	
Birmingham	51.8	39.7	7.4	1.0	100.0
Bradford	53.2	38.3	7.4	1.1	100.0
Bristol	44.8	45.5	8.4	1.2	100.0
Dudley	39.0	48.6	11.1	1.3	100.0
Gateshead	61.2	34.4	4.2	0.3	100.0
Kirklees	50.3	41.6	7.3	0.8	100.0
Leeds	50.9	40.7	7.5	0.9	100.0
Liverpool	65.7	30.0	3.9	0.5	100.0
Manchester	63.9	31.4	4.1	0.6	100.0
Newcastle-upon-Tyne	60.9	33.7	4.6	0.8	100.0
Salford	58.5	35.1	5.9	0.5	100.0
Sandwell	53.8	41.0	4.8	0.5	100.0
Sheffield	55.0	38.8	5.6	0.6	100.0
Sunderland	58.1	36.3	5.0	0.6	100.0
Wakefield	50.2	42.9	6.3	0.6	100.0
Wigan	47.4	45.3	6.8	0.5	100.0

TABLE 127 Off Street Parking Provision for Households with Car or Van: District

Thousands

District	Off street parking provision			All households with car or van
	Yes for all cars or vans	Yes for some cars or vans	None	
Birmingham	137.2	4.6	34.1	175.9
Bradford	60.3	1.5	15.1	76.9
Bristol	54.3	2.7	25.5	82.5
Dudley	56.2	1.3	7.3	64.8
Gateshead	23.0	0.7	7.2	31.0
Kirklees	56.3	0.9	9.7	67.0
Leeds	103.5	2.5	24.7	130.7
Liverpool	36.3	1.0	27.2	64.5
Manchester	38.4	1.0	20.8	60.2
Newcastle-upon-Tyne	33.1	1.1	8.6	42.8
Salford	28.5	0.8	9.7	39.0
Sandwell	40.2	1.2	10.6	52.0
Sheffield	65.3	1.6	22.6	89.5
Sunderland	32.1	1.3	10.1	43.5
Wakefield	44.2	0.7	7.6	52.5
Wigan	47.9	0.9	8.7	57.5

Percentages

District	Off street parking provision			All households with car or van
	Yes for all cars or vans	Yes for some cars or vans	None	
Birmingham	77.9	2.6	19.4	100.0
Bradford	78.4	2.0	19.6	100.0
Bristol	65.8	3.3	30.9	100.0
Dudley	86.7	2.0	11.3	100.0
Gateshead	74.3	2.4	23.2	100.0
Kirklees	84.1	1.4	14.5	100.0
Leeds	79.2	1.9	18.9	100.0
Liverpool	56.3	1.6	42.1	100.0
Manchester	63.8	1.7	34.5	100.0
Newcastle-upon-Tyne	77.4	2.5	20.1	100.0
Salford	73.0	2.0	25.0	100.0
Sandwell	77.3	2.3	20.4	100.0
Sheffield	73.0	1.8	25.3	100.0
Sunderland	73.9	3.0	23.1	100.0
Wakefield	84.1	1.4	14.5	100.0
Wigan	83.3	1.6	15.1	100.0

TABLE 128 Age and Sex of Head of Household : District

Thousands

District	Male				Female				All heads of household
	16-29	30-44	45-64	65 or over	16-29	30-44	45-59	60 or over	
Birmingham	39.5	77.0	108.3	51.3	7.2	9.6	15.8	56.2	364.8
Bradford	19.7	35.9	48.2	22.0	2.4	3.7	6.5	26.3	164.6
Bristol	19.0	29.5	41.8	30.0	5.0	3.9	6.5	23.6	149.6
Dudley	11.2	28.4	32.6	14.2	0.7	1.2	3.2	14.5	106.1
Gateshead	9.0	16.4	24.2	11.3	0.9	1.4	3.3	13.3	79.8
Kirklees	14.3	31.2	38.6	20.0	1.7	2.7	4.0	22.5	134.9
Leeds	34.0	59.0	77.8	35.2	6.5	6.6	10.5	36.8	266.4
Liverpool	22.0	33.4	52.9	27.3	4.2	4.5	9.3	34.2	187.8
Manchester	19.3	27.4	47.8	22.4	6.1	5.5	9.1	29.2	166.7
Newcastle-upon-Tyne	13.6	19.8	31.1	15.4	3.4	2.4	5.2	18.5	109.6
Salford	9.6	19.1	29.3	12.2	1.7	2.1	3.7	16.5	94.1
Sandwell	11.0	24.4	36.3	16.8	1.4	1.9	3.7	17.0	112.6
Sheffield	19.8	42.2	59.9	30.6	3.6	3.0	6.4	33.3	198.8
Sunderland	13.7	22.8	32.3	12.9	1.3	1.9	4.3	14.6	103.8
Wakefield	12.7	26.2	32.9	14.0	1.1	1.7	3.1	13.5	105.2
Wigan	14.1	28.2	31.6	13.8	1.1	1.7	3.7	15.1	109.4

Percentages

District	Male				Female				All heads of household
	16-29	30-44	45-64	65 or over	16-29	30-44	45-59	60 or over	
Birmingham	10.8	21.1	29.7	14.0	2.0	2.6	4.3	15.4	100.0
Bradford	11.9	21.8	29.3	13.3	1.5	2.3	3.9	16.0	100.0
Bristol	12.7	19.7	28.0	13.5	3.3	2.6	4.3	15.8	100.0
Dudley	10.6	26.8	30.7	13.4	0.7	1.2	3.0	13.7	100.0
Gateshead	11.3	20.6	30.3	14.1	1.2	1.8	4.1	16.7	100.0
Kirklees	10.6	23.1	28.6	14.8	1.3	2.0	3.0	16.7	100.0
Leeds	12.8	22.2	29.2	13.2	2.4	2.5	3.9	13.8	100.0
Liverpool	11.7	17.8	28.2	14.5	2.2	2.4	4.9	18.2	100.0
Manchester	11.6	16.4	28.7	13.4	3.7	3.3	5.4	17.5	100.0
Newcastle-upon-Tyne	12.4	18.0	28.4	14.1	3.1	2.2	4.8	16.9	100.0
Salford	10.2	20.3	31.1	12.9	1.8	2.3	3.9	17.5	100.0
Sandwell	9.8	21.7	32.2	15.0	1.3	1.7	3.3	15.1	100.0
Sheffield	10.0	21.2	30.1	15.4	1.8	1.5	3.2	16.7	100.0
Sunderland	13.2	22.0	31.1	12.5	1.2	1.8	4.2	14.0	100.0
Wakefield	12.1	24.9	31.3	13.3	1.0	1.6	2.9	12.9	100.0
Wigan	12.9	25.8	28.9	12.6	1.0	1.6	3.4	13.8	100.0

TABLE 129 Marital Status of Head of Household: District

Thousands

District	Marital status					All heads of household
	Single	Married	Divorced	Widowed	Separated	
Birmingham	39.0	239.5	12.2	66.7	7.4	364.8
Bradford	16.1	110.8	5.8	28.0	3.9	164.6
Bristol	20.9	93.8	5.6	26.5	2.7	149.6
Dudley	5.8	79.2	2.0	18.0	1.2	106.1
Gateshead	5.8	53.1	2.2	17.3	1.4	79.8
Kirklees	10.2	92.7	3.8	25.7	2.4	134.9
Leeds	28.1	178.7	11.0	43.5	5.2	266.4
Liverpool	22.6	114.8	7.0	40.7	2.8	187.8
Manchester	26.8	94.3	7.2	33.3	5.1	166.7
Newcastle-upon-Tyne	14.4	67.4	3.6	21.6	2.6	109.6
Salford	8.0	60.6	3.9	19.3	2.3	94.1
Sandwell	7.8	78.2	3.1	21.9	1.7	112.6
Sheffield	16.4	135.1	4.9	40.2	2.2	198.8
Sunderland	6.9	72.6	3.3	19.5	1.7	103.8
Wakefield	5.9	77.5	2.8	17.3	1.7	105.2
Wigan	6.8	78.2	3.5	19.7	1.3	109.4

Percentages

District	Marital status					All heads of household
	Single	Married	Divorced	Widowed	Separated	
Birmingham	10.7	65.6	3.4	18.3	2.0	100.0
Bradford	9.8	67.3	3.5	17.0	2.4	100.0
Bristol	14.0	62.7	3.7	17.7	1.8	100.0
Dudley	5.4	74.6	1.9	16.9	1.1	100.0
Gateshead	7.2	66.5	2.8	21.7	1.8	100.0
Kirklees	7.6	68.7	2.8	19.1	1.8	100.0
Leeds	10.5	67.1	4.1	16.3	1.9	100.0
Liverpool	12.0	61.1	3.7	21.6	1.5	100.0
Manchester	16.0	56.6	4.3	20.0	3.1	100.0
Newcastle-upon-Tyne	13.1	61.5	3.3	19.7	2.4	100.0
Salford	8.5	64.4	4.1	20.5	2.5	100.0
Sandwell	7.0	69.4	2.7	19.4	1.5	100.0
Sheffield	8.3	68.0	2.5	20.2	1.1	100.0
Sunderland	6.6	69.9	3.1	18.8	1.6	100.0
Wakefield	5.6	73.7	2.7	16.5	1.6	100.0
Wigan	6.2	71.5	3.2	18.0	1.1	100.0

TABLE 130 Length of Residence of Head of Household: District

District	Length of residence (years)						All heads of household
	Under 1	1 but under 2	2 but under 3	3 but under 5	5 but under 10	10 or over	
Birmingham	38.6	27.5	28.1	31.2	63.7	175.8	364.8
Bradford	16.2	11.4	14.7	15.2	32.8	74.3	164.6
Bristol	19.1	11.2	12.3	11.3	22.4	73.3	149.6
Dudley	6.9	6.9	7.7	9.0	19.2	56.4	106.1
Gateshead	7.5	5.3	6.7	7.9	14.4	38.0	79.8
Kirklees	11.2	9.3	11.4	11.6	28.4	63.2	134.9
Leeds	31.4	18.6	22.9	25.5	50.3	117.8	266.4
Liverpool	17.1	10.3	14.8	17.0	31.2	97.4	187.8
Manchester	20.2	11.3	13.8	15.6	29.2	76.7	166.7
Newcastle-upon-Tyne	13.2	9.1	9.9	9.5	21.9	46.0	109.6
Salford	9.9	5.6	8.7	9.0	17.5	43.5	94.1
Sandwell	9.4	7.1	8.7	8.6	19.6	59.3	112.6
Sheffield	17.2	12.4	14.8	16.6	35.8	102.0	198.8
Sunderland	10.4	8.8	9.6	11.0	18.0	46.1	103.8
Wakefield	9.7	6.7	9.2	10.8	19.4	49.5	105.2
Wigan	9.2	7.3	7.9	10.3	21.1	53.6	109.4

Percentages

District	Length of residence (years)						All heads of household
	Under 1	1 but under 2	2 but under 3	3 but under 5	5 but under 10	10 or over	
Birmingham	10.6	7.5	7.7	8.5	17.5	48.2	100.0
Bradford	9.8	6.9	8.9	9.2	19.9	45.2	100.0
Bristol	12.8	7.5	8.3	7.5	15.0	49.0	100.0
Dudley	6.5	6.5	7.2	8.5	18.1	53.2	100.0
Gateshead	9.4	6.6	8.4	9.9	18.0	47.6	100.0
Kirklees	8.3	6.9	8.4	8.6	21.0	46.8	100.0
Leeds	11.8	7.0	8.6	9.6	18.9	44.2	100.0
Liverpool	9.1	5.5	7.9	9.0	16.6	51.9	100.0
Manchester	12.1	6.7	8.3	9.4	17.5	46.0	100.0
Newcastle-upon-Tyne	12.0	8.3	9.0	8.6	20.0	42.0	100.0
Salford	10.5	5.9	9.2	9.6	18.6	46.2	100.0
Sandwell	8.3	6.3	7.7	7.6	17.4	52.6	100.0
Sheffield	8.6	6.2	7.4	8.3	18.0	51.3	100.0
Sunderland	10.0	8.5	9.3	10.6	17.3	44.4	100.0
Wakefield	9.3	6.3	8.7	10.3	18.4	47.0	100.0
Wigan	8.4	6.6	7.2	9.4	19.3	49.0	100.0

TABLE 131 Employment Status of Head of Household: District

Thousands

| District | Employment status | | | | | | All heads of household |
| | Employed | | Unem-ployed | Retired | House-wife | Other | |
	full time	part time					
Birmingham	218.6	13.3	17.8	70.4	34.4	10.4	364.8
Bradford	98.5	5.1	7.3	32.7	14.6	6.4	164.6
Bristol	86.5	5.2	7.0	27.1	16.7	7.1	149.6
Dudley	70.5	2.8	2.7	18.1	9.7	2.3	106.1
Gateshead	44.6	1.5	4.1	14.6	11.6	3.3	79.8
Kirklees	81.6	4.6	4.4	27.1	13.8	3.4	134.9
Leeds	164.2	7.2	8.0	48.6	24.2	14.3	266.4
Liverpool	96.1	5.1	14.3	37.3	24.1	10.9	187.8
Manchester	85.3	7.1	10.8	34.8	16.6	12.1	166.7
Newcastle-upon-Tyne	60.0	3.2	6.0	19.7	14.7	5.9	109.6
Salford	54.1	3.1	4.7	18.4	9.3	4.5	94.1
Sandwell	69.0	3.4	4.4	22.7	9.6	3.4	112.6
Sheffield	115.7	6.1	6.9	36.7	25.6	7.7	198.8
Sunderland	59.4	2.2	7.9	15.3	13.7	5.3	103.8
Wakefield	66.3	2.2	3.1	19.5	10.4	3.7	105.2
Wigan	67.8	2.2	4.2	18.4	9.8	7.0	109.4

Percentages

| District | Employment status | | | | | | All heads of household |
| | Employed | | Unem-ployed | Retired | House-wife | Other | |
	full time	part time					
Birmingham	59.9	3.6	4.8	19.3	9.4	2.8	100.0
Bradford	59.9	3.1	4.5	19.9	8.8	3.9	100.0
Bristol	57.8	3.5	4.7	18.1	11.1	4.7	100.0
Dudley	66.4	2.7	2.6	17.0	9.1	2.1	100.0
Gateshead	55.9	1.9	5.1	18.3	14.5	4.2	100.0
Kirklees	60.5	3.4	3.3	20.1	10.2	2.6	100.0
Leeds	61.6	2.7	3.0	18.2	9.1	5.3	100.0
Liverpool	51.1	2.7	7.6	19.9	12.8	5.8	100.0
Manchester	51.2	4.2	6.5	20.8	10.0	7.3	100.0
Newcastle-upon-Tyne	54.8	2.9	5.4	17.9	13.4	5.4	100.0
Salford	57.5	3.3	5.0	19.6	9.9	4.7	100.0
Sandwell	61.3	3.0	4.0	20.2	8.5	3.0	100.0
Sheffield	58.2	3.1	3.5	18.4	12.9	3.9	100.0
Sunderland	57.2	2.1	7.6	14.8	13.2	5.1	100.0
Wakefield	63.1	2.1	3.0	18.6	9.9	3.5	100.0
Wigan	62.0	2.0	3.8	16.8	8.9	6.4	100.0

196

TABLE 132 Birthplace of Head of Household: District

Thousands

| District | Birthplace | | All heads of household |
	United Kingdom	Not in United Kingdom	
Birmingham	312.4	52.3	364.8
Bradford	148.4	16.2	164.6
Bristol	139.6	10.0	149.6
Dudley	102.9	3.2	106.1
Gateshead	78.7	1.1	79.8
Kirklees	125.0	9.9	134.9
Leeds	249.3	17.1	266.4
Liverpool	181.7	6.1	187.8
Manchester	143.5	23.2	166.7
Newcastle-upon-Tyne	105.6	3.9	109.6
Salford	89.6	4.5	94.1
Sandwell	103.9	8.7	112.6
Sheffield	191.3	7.5	198.8
Sunderland	102.3	1.5	103.8
Wakefield	103.2	2.0	105.2
Wigan	107.3	2.0	109.4

Percentages

| District | Birthplace | | All heads of household |
	United Kingdom	Not in United Kingdom	
Birmingham	85.7	14.3	100.0
Bradford	90.2	9.8	100.0
Bristol	93.3	6.7	100.0
Dudley	97.0	3.0	100.0
Gateshead	98.6	1.4	100.0
Kirklees	92.7	7.3	100.0
Leeds	93.6	6.4	100.0
Liverpool	96.7	3.3	100.0
Manchester	86.1	13.9	100.0
Newcastle-upon-Tyne	96.4	3.6	100.0
Salford	95.2	4.8	100.0
Sandwell	92.3	7.7	100.0
Sheffield	96.2	3.8	100.0
Sunderland	98.6	1.4	100.0
Wakefield	98.1	1.9	100.0
Wigan	98.2	1.8	100.0

TABLE 133 Age and Sex of Private Household Population: District

District	Age of Males					All males
	0-14	15-29	30-44	45-64	65 or over	
Birmingham	119.7	121.4	87.2	115.4	54.9	498.6
Bradford	53.0	52.0	39.2	50.0	23.4	217.5
Bristol	41.1	47.8	33.7	44.5	22.0	189.2
Dudley	33.5	29.9	31.6	34.5	15.2	144.6
Gateshead	23.5	24.7	19.0	26.0	11.8	105.1
Kirklees	43.5	38.6	33.6	39.9	20.9	176.6
Leeds	81.0	84.7	64.6	80.6	36.4	347.3
Liverpool	58.4	67.9	39.8	57.3	29.2	252.5
Manchester	49.3	56.4	32.8	51.3	23.9	213.7
Newcastle-upon-Tyne	28.8	34.9	22.9	33.5	16.3	136.3
Salford	29.8	28.7	21.8	30.7	12.9	123.9
Sandwell	36.7	34.6	28.6	38.8	17.6	156.2
Sheffield	58.0	54.3	47.5	63.2	31.5	254.4
Sunderland	33.8	34.6	25.5	34.4	13.5	141.8
Wakefield	34.1	31.4	28.4	34.2	14.7	142.7
Wigan	37.4	32.7	30.9	33.1	15.0	149.1

Thousands

District	Age of Females					All females
	0-14	15-29	30-44	45-59	60 or over	
Birmingham	107.9	111.7	87.5	92.3	115.7	515.2
Bradford	53.3	48.8	39.1	39.6	51.9	232.6
Bristol	38.1	47.8	33.3	36.1	48.2	203.5
Dudley	31.2	29.4	30.0	26.7	31.7	148.9
Gateshead	21.4	22.8	19.3	20.7	25.0	109.1
Kirklees	42.1	38.4	34.1	31.4	43.7	189.7
Leeds	85.3	82.5	66.3	64.9	74.9	373.9
Liverpool	52.1	66.5	40.5	48.3	64.8	272.2
Manchester	44.7	52.9	33.6	41.8	54.8	227.8
Newcastle-upon-Tyne	27.4	33.9	23.4	27.0	36.1	147.8
Salford	26.8	28.4	21.9	23.7	30.6	131.3
Sandwell	34.3	32.0	28.0	28.0	36.5	158.7
Sheffield	53.6	52.5	47.2	48.8	66.8	268.8
Sunderland	33.1	33.9	26.1	27.8	28.1	149.1
Wakefield	33.7	31.5	28.0	26.4	29.0	148.6
Wigan	34.6	33.3	28.1	25.8	31.8	153.6

TABLE 134   Age of Private Household Population: District

Thousands

District	All persons					All persons
	0-14	15-29	30-44	45-59/64*	60/65* or over	
Birmingham	227.7	233.1	174.7	207.7	170.6	1013.8
Bradford	106.3	100.8	78.3	89.5	75.3	450.2
Bristol	79.2	95.6	67.0	80.6	70.3	392.7
Dudley	64.7	59.2	61.6	61.1	46.9	293.5
Gateshead	44.9	47.5	38.3	46.7	36.8	214.2
Kirklees	85.6	77.1	67.7	71.3	64.6	366.3
Leeds	166.3	167.2	130.9	145.5	111.4	721.3
Liverpool	110.5	134.4	80.3	105.6	94.0	524.8
Manchester	94.0	109.3	66.4	93.1	78.7	441.5
Newcastle-upon-Tyne	56.2	68.9	46.3	60.5	52.4	284.1
Salford	56.6	57.1	43.6	54.4	43.5	255.2
Sandwell	70.9	66.5	56.5	66.8	54.1	314.9
Sheffield	111.5	106.8	94.7	112.0	98.3	523.3
Sunderland	67.0	68.6	51.5	62.2	41.7	290.9
Wakefield	67.9	62.9	56.4	60.5	43.6	291.3
Wigan	72.0	66.1	59.0	58.9	46.7	302.7

Percentages

District	All persons					All persons
	0-14	15-29	30-44	45-59/64*	60/65* or over	
Birmingham	22.4	23.0	17.2	20.5	16.8	100.0
Bradford	23.6	22.4	17.4	19.9	16.7	100.0
Bristol	20.2	24.4	17.1	20.5	17.9	100.0
Dudley	22.0	20.2	21.0	20.8	16.0	100.0
Gateshead	21.0	22.2	17.9	21.8	17.2	100.0
Kirklees	23.4	21.0	18.5	19.5	17.6	100.0
Leeds	23.0	23.1	18.2	20.2	15.4	100.0
Liverpool	21.0	25.6	15.3	20.1	18.0	100.0
Manchester	21.3	24.8	15.0	21.1	17.8	100.0
Newcastle-upon-Tyne	19.7	24.2	16.2	21.3	18.4	100.0
Salford	22.2	22.4	17.1	21.3	17.1	100.0
Sandwell	22.5	21.1	18.0	21.2	17.2	100.0
Sheffield	21.3	20.4	18.1	21.4	18.8	100.0
Sunderland	23.0	23.6	17.8	21.4	14.3	100.0
Wakefield	23.3	21.6	19.5	20.8	14.9	100.0
Wigan	23.7	21.8	19.5	19.4	15.4	100.0

* 59 for females, 64 for males

TABLE 135 Length of Residence: District

District	Length of residence (years)						All persons
	Under 1	1 but under 2	2 but under 3	3 but under 5	5 but under 10	10 or over	
Birmingham	118.0	84.1	87.9	103.8	207.4	412.6	1013.8
Bradford	54.8	35.7	45.2	49.3	98.1	167.1	450.2
Bristol	53.1	31.4	35.5	32.7	66.9	173.1	392.7
Dudley	22.1	21.7	22.7	29.2	62.9	134.9	293.5
Gateshead	23.9	14.8	20.0	23.1	43.1	89.4	214.2
Kirklees	38.1	28.7	33.8	37.5	85.5	142.7	366.3
Leeds	91.4	54.4	70.4	79.3	154.9	270.8	721.3
Liverpool	55.1	32.4	47.1	51.0	101.7	237.5	524.8
Manchester	58.2	32.4	38.0	45.2	88.5	179.2	441.5
Newcastle-upon-Tyne	35.6	25.0	28.2	27.9	63.7	103.7	284.1
Salford	29.9	16.9	26.0	27.7	53.2	101.5	255.2
Sandwell	30.3	22.6	28.3	28.3	65.0	140.4	314.9
Sheffield	51.6	35.6	44.3	48.9	106.5	236.4	523.3
Sunderland	31.7	26.8	30.0	32.8	58.5	111.2	290.9
Wakefield	32.1	20.0	27.3	32.7	61.8	117.3	291.3
Wigan	28.5	22.9	24.0	33.7	67.5	126.1	302.7

District	Length of residence (years)						All persons
	Under 1	1 but under 2	2 but under 3	3 but under 5	5 but under 10	10 or over	
Birmingham	11.6	8.3	8.7	10.2	20.5	40.7	100.0
Bradford	12.2	7.9	10.0	10.9	21.8	37.1	100.0
Bristol	13.5	8.0	9.0	8.3	17.0	44.1	100.0
Dudley	7.5	7.4	7.7	10.0	21.4	46.0	100.0
Gateshead	11.2	6.9	9.3	10.8	20.1	41.7	100.0
Kirklees	10.4	7.8	9.2	10.2	23.3	39.0	100.0
Leeds	12.7	7.5	9.8	11.0	21.5	37.5	100.0
Liverpool	10.5	6.2	9.0	9.7	19.4	45.3	100.0
Manchester	13.2	7.3	8.6	10.2	20.0	40.6	100.0
Newcastle-upon-Tyne	12.5	8.8	9.9	9.8	22.4	36.5	100.0
Salford	11.7	6.6	10.2	10.8	20.8	39.8	100.0
Sandwell	9.6	7.2	9.0	9.0	20.6	44.6	100.0
Sheffield	9.9	6.8	8.5	9.3	20.4	45.2	100.0
Sunderland	10.9	9.2	10.3	11.3	20.1	38.2	100.0
Wakefield	11.0	6.9	9.4	11.2	21.2	40.3	100.0
Wigan	9.4	7.6	7.9	11.1	22.3	41.6	100.0

TABLE 136   Employment Status : District

District	Employment status						All persons aged 16 or over
	Employed						
	full time	part time	un-employed	wholly retired	house-wife	other	
Birmingham	378.5	83.5	35.1	89.8	139.2	40.6	766.7
Bradford	162.5	36.0	12.3	41.9	62.7	20.2	335.7
Bristol	142.6	30.6	12.7	33.0	66.7	22.0	307.6
Dudley	115.4	26.0	5.3	22.7	45.4	9.2	224.0
Gateshead	77.2	15.4	8.8	17.4	37.8	8.6	165.1
Kirklees	132.4	31.0	8.4	33.3	56.0	13.6	274.8
Leeds	266.6	58.0	15.2	59.6	103.8	39.3	542.6
Liverpool	174.1	36.4	31.4	47.4	81.8	32.7	403.8
Manchester	152.7	32.1	19.4	44.5	58.6	31.8	339.1
Newcastle-upon-Tyne	102.5	22.0	11.5	23.4	47.6	15.9	222.7
Salford	95.4	19.8	8.5	23.4	34.0	12.8	193.9
Sandwell	120.1	24.9	8.4	29.7	44.5	10.8	238.4
Sheffield	188.8	44.6	12.3	43.4	91.5	23.0	403.6
Sunderland	98.8	21.1	15.7	17.5	51.7	13.7	218.5
Wakefield	108.0	23.1	6.2	23.3	47.5	10.6	218.8
Wigan	113.2	20.0	9.2	24.2	43.5	15.3	225.4

District	Employment status						All persons aged 16 or over
	Employed						
	full time	part time	un-employed	wholly retired	house-wife	other	
Birmingham	49.4	10.9	4.5	11.7	18.2	5.3	100.0
Bradford	48.4	10.7	3.7	12.5	18.7	6.0	100.0
Bristol	46.4	9.9	4.2	10.7	21.7	7.1	100.0
Dudley	51.5	11.6	2.3	10.1	20.3	4.1	100.0
Gateshead	46.8	9.3	5.3	10.5	22.9	5.2	100.0
Kirklees	48.2	11.3	3.0	12.1	20.4	5.0	100.0
Leeds	49.1	10.7	2.7	11.0	19.1	7.3	100.0
Liverpool	43.1	9.0	7.8	11.7	20.3	8.1	100.0
Manchester	45.0	9.5	5.7	13.1	17.3	9.3	100.0
Newcastle-upon-Tyne	46.0	9.9	5.2	10.5	21.4	7.1	100.0
Salford	49.2	10.2	4.4	12.1	17.5	6.6	100.0
Sandwell	50.4	10.4	3.5	12.4	18.7	4.5	100.0
Sheffield	46.8	11.0	3.1	10.8	22.7	5.7	100.0
Sunderland	45.2	9.6	7.1	8.0	23.6	6.4	100.0
Wakefield	49.4	10.6	2.8	10.6	21.7	4.9	100.0
Wigan	50.2	8.9	4.1	10.7	19.3	6.8	100.0

TABLE 137   Economically Active Persons : Socio-Economic Group : District

Thousands

District	Socio-economic group						All persons economically active
	Professional employers and managers	Other non-manual	Skilled manual	Semi-skilled manual	Unskilled manual	Other	
Birmingham	55.3	142.4	139.2	109.0	36.1	15.1	497.1
Bradford	28.3	56.9	59.1	47.5	14.3	4.9	210.8
Bristol	23.1	62.4	47.1	31.8	15.4	6.2	185.9
Dudley	20.4	39.2	46.5	29.2	9.5	2.1	146.8
Gateshead	8.6	30.5	30.5	19.1	9.8	3.0	101.4
Kirklees	22.3	43.2	54.0	36.9	11.4	4.1	171.8
Leeds	50.0	105.5	96.0	61.4	20.7	6.2	339.8
Liverpool	21.1	72.2	58.0	52.5	24.9	13.3	241.9
Manchester	20.0	58.2	54.1	47.4	18.6	5.8	204.2
Newcastle-upon-Tyne	17.6	45.5	33.8	22.4	12.3	4.4	136.0
Salford	11.9	35.4	34.1	28.1	10.4	3.7	123.6
Sandwell	11.4	36.0	54.3	36.4	11.8	3.6	153.5
Sheffield	27.6	71.8	77.5	42.4	20.4	5.9	245.7
Sunderland	12.2	36.1	43.5	25.9	13.6	4.3	135.6
Wakefield	13.7	34.5	49.1	27.8	9.3	2.9	137.3
Wigan	15.4	37.1	44.6	31.3	11.0	2.8	142.4

Percentages

District	Socio-economic group						All persons economically active
	Professional employers and managers	Other non-manual	Skilled manual	Semi-skilled manual	Unskilled manual	Other	
Birmingham	11.1	28.6	28.0	21.9	7.3	3.0	100.0
Bradford	13.4	27.0	28.0	22.5	6.8	2.3	100.0
Bristol	12.4	33.6	25.3	17.1	8.3	3.3	100.0
Dudley	13.9	26.7	31.7	19.9	6.5	1.4	100.0
Gateshead	8.5	30.0	30.1	18.9	9.7	2.9	100.0
Kirklees	13.0	25.1	31.4	21.4	6.6	2.4	100.0
Leeds	14.7	31.0	28.2	18.1	6.1	1.8	100.0
Liverpool	8.7	29.8	24.0	21.7	10.3	5.5	100.0
Manchester	9.8	28.5	26.5	23.2	9.1	2.9	100.0
Newcastle-upon-Tyne	12.9	33.4	24.9	16.5	9.0	3.2	100.0
Salford	9.7	28.6	27.6	22.7	8.4	3.0	100.0
Sandwell	7.4	23.4	35.4	23.7	7.7	2.4	100.0
Sheffield	11.3	29.2	31.5	17.3	8.3	2.4	100.0
Sunderland	9.0	26.6	32.1	19.1	10.0	3.2	100.0
Wakefield	10.0	25.1	35.8	20.3	6.8	2.1	100.0
Wigan	10.9	26.1	31.3	22.0	7.8	2.0	100.0

TABLE 138 Birthplace: District

District	Birthplace		All persons
	United Kingdom	Not in United Kingdom	
Birmingham	893.3	120.6	1013.8
Bradford	410.2	40.0	450.2
Bristol	371.4	21.3	392.7
Dudley	285.7	7.8	293.5
Gateshead	211.4	2.8	214.2
Kirklees	342.0	24.3	366.3
Leeds	681.1	40.2	721.3
Liverpool	512.7	12.0	524.8
Manchester	394.0	47.5	441.5
Newcastle-upon-Tyne	275.3	8.8	284.1
Salford	246.6	8.6	255.2
Sandwell	293.9	21.0	314.9
Sheffield	505.9	17.4	523.3
Sunderland	287.2	3.7	290.9
Wakefield	286.5	4.8	291.3
Wigan	298.2	4.4	302.7

Percentages

District	Birthplace		All persons
	United Kingdom	Not in United Kingdom	
Birmingham	88.1	11.9	100.0
Bradford	91.1	8.9	100.0
Bristol	94.6	5.4	100.0
Dudley	97.4	2.6	100.0
Gateshead	98.7	1.3	100.0
Kirklees	93.4	6.6	100.0
Leeds	94.4	5.6	100.0
Liverpool	97.7	2.3	100.0
Manchester	89.3	10.7	100.0
Newcastle-upon-Tyne	96.9	3.1	100.0
Salford	96.6	3.4	100.0
Sandwell	93.3	6.7	100.0
Sheffield	96.7	3.3	100.0
Sunderland	98.7	1.3	100.0
Wakefield	98.4	1.6	100.0
Wigan	98.5	1.5	100.0

TABLE 139 Ethnic Group: District

| District | Ethnic group | | | | | All persons |
	White	West Indian	African	Indian/ Pakistani/ Bangladeshi	Other	
Birmingham	878.6	48.2	2.3	64.5	20.3	1013.8
Bradford	404.3	2.7	0.2	34.9	8.1	450.2
Bristol	376.1	7.0	1.1	4.2	4.3	392.7
Dudley	282.8	2.1	-	4.9	3.8	293.5
Gateshead	212.0	0.1	0.2	0.3	1.6	214.2
Kirklees	334.7	5.3	0.4	21.4	4.6	366.3
Leeds	686.6	7.1	1.4	17.6	8.5	721.3
Liverpool	512.7	1.4	1.3	0.8	8.6	524.8
Manchester	400.3	11.1	2.0	13.7	14.2	441.5
Newcastle-upon-Tyne	277.6	0.1	0.1	3.5	2.8	284.1
Salford	251.1	0.3	0.2	1.2	2.3	255.2
Sandwell	283.4	9.5	0.5	18.1	3.4	314.9
Sheffield	504.7	5.9	0.5	7.7	4.5	523.3
Sunderland	287.2	-	0.2	0.5	3.0	290.9
Wakefield	289.1	0.1	-	1.3	0.8	291.3
Wigan	300.7	0.1	0.1	0.5	1.3	302.7

| | Ethnic group | | | | | All persons |
	White	West Indian	African	Indian/ Pakistani/ Bangladeshi	Other	
Birmingham	86.6	4.8	0.2	6.4	2.0	100.0
Bradford	89.8	0.6	-	7.8	1.8	100.0
Bristol	95.8	1.8	0.3	1.0	1.1	100.0
Dudley	96.3	0.7	-	1.6	1.3	100.0
Gateshead	99.0	-	0.1	0.2	0.7	100.0
Kirklees	91.4	1.4	0.1	5.8	1.4	100.0
Leeds	95.1	1.0	0.2	2.5	1.1	100.0
Liverpool	97.7	0.3	0.2	0.1	1.6	100.0
Manchester	90.6	2.5	0.5	3.1	3.2	100.0
Newcastle-upon-Tyne	97.7	-	-	1.3	0.9	100.0
Salford	98.4	0.1	0.1	0.5	0.9	100.0
Sandwell	89.9	3.0	0.1	5.7	1.1	100.0
Sheffield	96.4	1.1	0.1	1.5	0.9	100.0
Sunderland	98.7	-	0.1	0.2	1.1	100.0
Wakefield	99.2	-	-	0.5	0.2	100.0
Wigan	99.3	-	-	0.1	0.5	100.0

TABLE 140   Type of Family: District

Stress Areas	Main married couple	Main lone parent	One person HoH	Concealed married couple	Concealed lone parent	One person not HoH	All families
Birmingham	237.4	31.4	96.1	5.0	2.7	29.7	402.3
Bradford	109.8	12.0	43.0	1.5	1.4	11.3	178.9
Bristol	93.3	11.3	45.0	1.5	0.9	19.3	171.4
Dudley	78.9	5.6	21.6	1.5	0.4	6.3	114.4
Gateshead	53.2	6.9	19.7	0.6	0.7	4.9	85.9
Kirklees	92.3	8.1	34.6	1.3	1.0	7.5	144.7
Leeds	178.2	19.8	68.5	1.9	1.2	15.6	285.2
Liverpool	114.6	18.6	54.6	3.4	2.4	18.3	211.9
Manchester	94.3	17.2	55.2	2.3	2.2	16.6	187.8
Newcastle-upon-Tyne	67.1	9.1	33.4	1.0	0.9	10.5	121.8
Salford	60.5	8.0	25.7	0.5	0.7	6.3	101.6
Sandwell	77.8	8.4	26.4	2.3	0.7	6.3	121.9
Sheffield	134.5	11.1	53.2	1.8	1.5	12.9	215.0
Sunderland	72.5	8.0	23.4	0.6	0.9	5.9	111.2
Wakefield	77.1	6.3	21.8	0.5	0.8	5.0	111.6
Wigan	78.0	7.4	23.9	0.8	0.6	6.0	116.8

Percentages

Stress Areas	Main married couple	Main lone parent	One person HoH	Concealed married couple	Concealed lone parent	One person not HoH	All families
Birmingham	59.0	7.8	23.9	1.3	0.7	7.4	100.0
Bradford	61.4	6.7	23.9	0.9	0.8	6.3	100.0
Bristol	54.4	6.6	26.2	0.9	0.5	11.3	100.0
Dudley	69.0	4.9	18.9	1.4	0.4	5.5	100.0
Gateshead	61.8	8.0	23.0	0.7	0.8	5.7	100.0
Kirklees	63.8	5.6	23.9	0.9	0.7	5.2	100.0
Leeds	62.5	6.9	24.0	0.7	0.4	5.5	100.0
Liverpool	54.1	8.8	25.8	1.6	1.1	8.6	100.0
Manchester	50.2	9.1	29.4	1.2	1.1	8.9	100.0
Newcastle-upon-Tyne	55.1	7.5	27.4	0.8	0.7	8.6	100.0
Salford	59.5	7.8	25.3	0.5	0.7	6.2	100.0
Sandwell	63.8	6.9	21.7	1.9	0.5	5.2	100.0
Sheffield	62.6	5.1	24.7	0.8	0.7	6.0	100.0
Sunderland	65.2	7.2	21.0	0.5	0.8	5.3	100.0
Wakefield	69.1	5.6	19.6	0.5	0.7	4.5	100.0
Wigan	66.8	6.3	20.5	0.7	0.5	5.1	100.0

TABLE 141   Dwelling, Vacant Dwellings and Households: District

District	Total dwellings 000's	Vacant dwellings*		Households 000's	Crude surplus	
		000's	as % of all dwellings		000's	as % of all dwellings
Birmingham	369.8	13.6	3.7	364.8	5.0	1.4
Bradford	167.8	6.6	3.9	164.6	3.2	1.9
Bristol	150.9	6.1	4.0	149.6	1.3	0.9
Dudley	108.3	3.0	2.8	106.1	2.2	2.1
Gateshead	82.4	2.7	3.3	79.8	2.6	3.2
Kirklees	140.1	6.2	4.4	134.9	5.2	3.7
Leeds	267.7	7.6	2.9	266.4	1.3	0.5
Liverpool	192.9	8.5	4.4	187.8	5.1	2.6
Manchester	167.9	7.1	4.2	166.7	1.2	0.7
Newcastle-upon-Tyne	110.6	3.8	3.5	109.6	1.1	1.0
Salford	95.3	2.9	3.1	94.1	1.2	1.3
Sandwell	116.0	4.4	3.8	112.6	3.4	3.0
Sheffield	202.3	6.8	3.4	198.8	3.5	1.7
Sunderland	106.5	3.5	3.3	103.8	2.6	2.5
Wakefield	108.2	3.2	3.0	105.2	3.0	2.7
Wigan	113.0	4.0	3.6	109.4	3.7	3.3

* Includes second homes.

206

NOTES AND DEFINITIONS

AMENITIES The basic amenities are fixed bath or shower, plumbed
hot water supply, and WC with entrance inside the
building. Some shared, none lacked means that the
household had use of these three amenities but at
least one of them was shared with another household.
For further details of amenities see Interviewers
Instructions, page 271.

BEDROOMS See Interviewers Instructions, page 270.

BEDROOM STANDARD This standard has no statutory force, but has been
widely used in presenting survey results as a measure
of whether households are short of space or have spare
rooms. The standard number of bedrooms is:

(a) One for each married couple;

(b) One each for other men and women aged 21 or over;

(c) One for each two persons of the same sex aged
10-20;

(d) One for any person aged 10-20 and a child under
10 of the same sex;

(e) One for any person aged 10-20 not paired as in
(c) or (d);

(f) One for each two of any remaining children;

(g) One for any child remaining

CARS AND VANS See Interviewers Instructions page 275.

CONCEALED HOUSEHOLDS This is a married couple family with or without never
married children, or a lone parent family with never
married child of any age, which does not contain a
head of household.

COUNCIL HOUSE
WAITING LISTS This includes transfer lists and lists for old people's
homes. For further details see Interviewers
Instructions, page 274.

DWELLING This is a building or any part of a building which
forms a separate and self-contained set of premises
designed to be occupied by a single household. In this
survey estimates of number of dwellings have been based
on information about the number of households with which
a household shares circulation space. At properties
where no household shared circulation space, each household was counted as occupying a separate dwelling. At
all other properties households were ordered according
to the number of other households with which they shared.
The household sharing with the largest number, n, of

207

other households was assumed to occupy a single dwelling with the following n households in the list. Remaining households were treated in the same way. Any household that did not share rooms or circulation space and that had at least 3 rooms and exclusive use of all basic amenities (inc cooker and sink) was counted as occupying a separate dwelling. Any bedsits remaining after this procedure were together counted as a single dwelling. Where a household shared with more households than lived at the property sampled the property was counted as part of a dwelling.

EMPLOYMENT STATUS

Persons were recorded as wholly retired if the person had retired from a full-time occupation at the approximate retirement age for that occupation. A woman who had ceased paid employment at, say, age 25 would be coded as housewife even if she was aged 60 or over at the time of the survey. Unemployed means the person was seeking work, waiting to start a new job, or prevented by temporary sickness from seeking work. For further details see Interviewers Instructions page 280.

ETHNIC GROUP

The following 12 categories were listed on the showcard used in this question: White, West Indian, Indian, Pakistani, Bangladeshi, Chinese, Turkish, Other Asian, African, Arab, Other (please state), and Mixed Origin (please state). In the tables these have been grouped as follows:

> White: White and Turkish.
> West Indian: West Indian.
> Indian/Bangladeshi/Pakistani: Indian, Bangladeshi and Pakistani.
> African: African.
> Other: Chinese, Other Asian, Arab, Other and Mixed origin.

In some tables African has been combined with Other.

FAMILIES

See Interviewers Instructions page 278.

HEAD OF HOUSEHOLD (HoH)

See Interviewers Instructions page 265.

HOUSEHOLD

See Interviewers Instructions page 267.

ROOMS

This is the total number of rooms available to the household but excluding bathroom, toilets, kitchens less than $6\frac{1}{2}$ ft wide, garages and rooms used solely for business. (see Interviewers Instructions, page 270, for full list of exclusions). Shared rooms counted as $\frac{1}{3}$: $\frac{1}{2}$ rooms in the total number of rooms were randomly rounded up or down.

SATISFACTION WITH
ACCOMMODATION/AREA

Neutral means neither satisfied nor dissatisfied

SHARING

Four types of sharing are distinguished:

Sharing rooms: this applies if any of the rooms used by the household, other than bathroom, toilet, small kitchen and rooms used solely for business, were also used by another household.

Sharing circulation space: this applies if the household was not sharing rooms (as defined above) but in moving between the rooms of its accommodation (excluding bathroom and toilet) it had to use a passageway to which another household had unrestricted access.

Bedsit: this applies if the household had the use of only one room, other than bathroom, toilet and small kitchen, and did not have exclusive use of a bathroom.

Self-contained accommodation in a shared dwelling: this applies if the household did not fit into any of the previous categories but did not occupy a whole dwelling.

SOCIO-ECONOMIC GROUP

The basic occupational classification used was the Registrar General's socio-economic grouping "Classification of Occupations 1970" OPCS (HMSO 1970). A collapsed version of this classification has been used in the tables as follows:

Description	SEG numbers
Professional	3,4
Employers and managers	1,2,13
Intermediate and junior non-manual ('other non-manual')	5,6
Skilled manual (including foremen, supervisors and own account non-professional)	8,9,12,14
Semi-skilled manual (including personal service)	7,10,15
Unskilled manual	11

The 'other' category includes members of the armed forces, persons with occupation inadequately described, persons who had never worked, full-time students, persons permanently sick or disabled, and housewives. Persons unemployed were coded according to their last occupation, and retired persons were coded according to their previous main occupation.

TENURE

Rented from council: rented from local authority, Greater London Council or new town corporation.

Rented from HA: rented from housing association.

Rented privately unfurnished: includes partly furnished.

Rented privately furnished: includes squatters of whom 32 were interviewed in the national sample.

For further details see Interviewers Instruction's page 273.

TYPE OF ACCOMMODATION

In these tables this refers to the actual accommodation occupied by the household: where more than one household occupied a house all households have been included in "other flat/rooms".

TYPE OF HOUSEHOLD

Two classifications have been used defined as follows:

One person household -

Married couple household - A household containing a married couple with or without children. Other people may live in the household provided the head of household is either the husband or one of his never-married children.

Lone parent household - A household containing a lone parent living with one or more never-married children of any age. Other people may also live in the household, provided the head of household is either the lone parent or one of the never-married children.

Other household - Any household not falling into one of the previous categories. Examples are brothers or sisters living together, lone parents living with divorced children, and groups of unrelated persons.

One person aged under 60 -

Small adult household - 2 persons aged 15-59.

Small family - 1 or 2 persons aged 16 or over, and 1 or 2 persons aged 0-15.

Large family - 1 or 2 persons aged 16 or over, and 3 or more persons aged 0-15; or 3 or more persons aged 16 or over, and 2 or more persons aged 0-15.

Large adult household - 3 or more persons aged 16 or over with or without 1 person aged 0-15.

Older small household - 2 persons aged 16 or over, one or both of whom are aged 60 or over.

One person aged over 60 -

PART II

NATIONAL DWELLING AND HOUSING SURVEY:

THE SURVEY

CHAPTER 4. CONDUCT OF THE SURVEY

1.   The Department of the Environment commissioned a consortium (known as the Dwelling and Housing Survey Group) of three companies - National Opinions Polls Market Research Ltd, Research Surveys of Great Britain Ltd, and Social and Community Planning Research - to undertake the survey. This consortium dealt with all stages of the survey, from the conduct of interviews to the production of tabulations. However to ensure uniformity of standards various tasks were carried out by the Department itself; aspects of the work were also carried out by the Greater London Council Survey Unit (which worked to the Department). Overall responsibility for the conduct of the survey was vested in a steering committee chaired by the Department and consisting of representatives from the organisations involved, this committee met regularly to monitor progress on the survey.

THE SAMPLE

2.   The sampling frame used for the survey was the valuation lists maintained by the Valuation Offices of Inland Revenue. These are complete lists of properties in the country including most properties in the last stages of construction. In addition to a full address of all properties, the lists contain a description of the type of property so that obvious non-residential addresses such as "garage" could be excluded without a visit by an interviewer.

3.   The sample design was such as to generate a representative sample of addresses both in England as a whole and in each planning region and metropolitan county. In each London borough and metropolitan district a sample of one in 200 addresses was selected. The remaining districts in England were first grouped into planning regions with the South East region being split into two areas, the first consisting of the counties Bedfordshire, Buckinghamshire, Essex and Hertfordshire, and the second area being the rest of the region. This was necessary because the former area together with East Anglia form the DOE administrative region Eastern. Within each region, districts were allocated to one of four groups. The first group comprised seaside resorts, defined as districts with a coastline which were not predominantly industrial. Remaining districts were grouped according to their density of population as follows:-

    (a)   over 15;

    (b)   between 5 and 15;

    (c)   under 5 persons per hectare in mid-1976.

Within each of these groups districts were ordered alphabetically within their counties. A systematic sample of districts was then selected from each region in such a way that the probability of a particular district being selected was proportional to the number of domestic properties in that district in April 1977. The ordering of the districts ensured that (where appropriate) each region was represented by a selection of seaside, urban and rural districts and by districts from several counties.

4.   Within the selected districts in each region a sample of domestic properties equivalent to one in 200 of the total number of domestic properties in that region was required. Because districts were selected with probability propor-

tional to size the probability of any given address in a selected district being sampled had to be inversly proportional to the size of the district in order to give each address in the region an equal chance of selection overall. This meant that the same number of domestic properties was required from each sample district in a region. This number was expressed as a fraction of the total number of domestic properties in the district, and this sampling fraction was used when drawing the sample from the valuation lists in that district. The number of districts sampled in each region was such that the sample for each district contained about 600 domestic properties; the total sample in each district was greater than this because of non-domestic properties on the valuation lists. In all, 84 of the 297 non-metropolitan districts in England were included in the survey.

5.   In London boroughs and the 16 other areas intensively surveyed the sample drawn for the national survey was augmented to yield a total sample of approximately 6,500 domestic properties in each area.

6.   In planning the survey one of the objectives was to produce national and regional results in advance of results of the areas being intensively surveyed. This could be achieved by conducting interviews at a representative sample of one in 200 addresses in each of the areas being intensively surveyed, as well as at all addresses in the other sample districts. However, in order to minimise disruption of fieldwork in these areas, which would have led to delays in producing final results for these areas, it was decided that this sub-sample would be selected from one quarter of the wards in each area; the wards being selected in such a way as to be representative of the whole district. This was the model adopted and in London boroughs and the other areas intensively surveyed priority was given to conducting interviews in the selected wards. The tabulation system was designed on the basis that national and regional results would be produced using a sub-sample of addresses in London boroughs and the other 16 areas equivalent to one in 200 addresses in each of those areas rather than using results for all sampled addresses with appropriate weighting factors.

7.   In the event fieldwork in all wards in the intensively surveyed areas was completed concurrently so national and regional results were produced using a sub-sample equivalent to one in 200 addresses selected throughout these areas. Through using only a sub-sample of addresses in the national and regional results small differences arise between these and results based on the full samples: the most noticeable differences being those for Greater London based on the one in 200 sample and those based on the more extensive samples in each London borough.

SELECTION OF ADDRESSES

8.   In each area in the survey a systematic sample of addresses was drawn by staff working in the local Inland Revenue Valuation Offices. The detailed instructions for staff extracting the sample were agreed between the Valuation Office and Department of the Environment. Apart from the addresses and descriptions of the property, information, where available, was also supplied on the type, age, rateable value and floor space of the property. This information supplemented that collected in the survey interview and provided a core of information about those properties where the residents could not be contacted and properties that were vacant at the time of the survey. In total, 415,000 eligible addresses were selected, some of which contained more than one household space at which interviews were required.

9.   Completed lists of sampled addresses for each area were returned to the Department of the Environment by Inland Revenue during the period September to December 1977. Subsequently DOE staff went through these lists and deleted any properties that were obviously non-residential: this was based on a list of descriptions drawn up by the Department. All remaining addresses were numbered sequentially and 3 copies of these addresses were sent to the consortium.

10.   A separate exercise was mounted to ensure that blocks of addresses that were rated as a single unit were correctly represented in the sample. These addresses were mainly armed forces married quarters, where as many as 1,000 houses had been included as a single entry in the valuation lists. In each sampled district, the Valuation Office separately listed block addresses and provided details about number of residential properties included. These lists were then sampled at the sampling fraction appropriate to the district within which they were located.

11.   Addresses in London and the other areas intensively surveyed were coded to ward level. All London addresses were coded by the GLC Survey Unit, which had extensive experience of this type of work from its work with the 1974 GLC Transportation Study. Addresses in the other areas were ward-coded by the consortium with assistance from the Department. The wards used were those current at the time of the survey. This coding was undertaken both to facilitate the planning of fieldwork and to allow tabulations to be produced at below borough and district level.

12.   The Dwelling and Housing Survey Group allocated $\frac{1}{3}$ of the sample addresses to each company which was then responsible for conducting interviews at these addresses and editing the returned questionnaires. Each company dealt with 11 London boroughs, $\frac{1}{3}$ of the wards in each of the 16 other areas intensively surveyed, and $\frac{1}{3}$ of the other districts sampled in each region.

FIELDWORK

RECRUITMENT OF INTERVIEWERS:

13.   Outside London, the consortium generally had sufficient interviewers to cope with the survey, but in some of the areas intensively surveyed a small number of interviewers were recruited. In London, however, the scale of operation was so much greater than the normal level of interviewing in surveys that substantial recruitment of interviewers was essential for the job to be conducted in the time required. Accordingly during September and October some 450 persons were recruited as interviewers in the London area. Most of these new recruits continued to work for the companies throughout the autumn, but over the Christmas period a large number of them gave up interviewing. It was therefore necessary to recruit further large numbers of interviewers in January and February to make good this loss and maintain the tempo of the fieldwork. During the entire fieldwork period over 2,000 interviewers were employed by the consortium on the survey of which just over 1,000 were employed in London.

TRAINING AND BRIEFING OF INTERVIEWERS:

14.   All persons recruited to work as interviewers on the survey underwent rigorous training on the fundamentals of household interviewing and on the basic concepts employed in the survey. In addition, all new recruits and all experienced interviewers who worked on the survey attended a briefing session at which the finer details of the questionnaire were explained.

215

15.   The training and briefing programme developed was a joint effort by the consortium, the Department of the Environment and the GLC Survey Unit with considerable advice from the Social Survey Division of the Office of Population Censuses and Surveys. The objectives were to ensure that the interviewer was trained to an acceptable level of efficiency and that all interviewers would conduct the interview in a similar manner so that no inter-company variation would arise.

16.   In view of the large numbers of persons undergoing training it was necessary for each company to undertake its own training sessions. To ensure uniformity of standards, senior interviewers from the GLC Survey Unit were specially instructed to assist at all training sessions in London; each of the GLC staff participated in training sessions run by at least two of the companies.

17.   Following the training sessions all recruits and experienced interviewers attended a briefing session on the questionnaire. These sessions were administered by the three companies and were attended by staff from the Department of the Environment and/or GLC interviewers to ensure that common standards were applied. Briefing sessions in the provinces were identical to those conducted in London and were also attended by staff from the Department.

THE QUESTIONNAIRE

18.   Topics covered in the interview included the basic housing and household information collected in the 1971 Census, such as tenure, number of rooms, possession of basic amenities, sharing of space and amenities, and household composition including age, sex, marital status, length of residence at address, employment status, and occupation of household members. Questions were also included about main forms of room heating, satisfaction with accommodation and area, use of cars or vans and availability of off-street parking, and the ethnic group of members of the household.

19.   A set of interviewers instructions was issued to interviewers designed to cover all eventualities likely to arise in an interview, this is reproduced at Appendix B.

20.   The interview was directed to the head of household or housewife, but if neither of these could be contacted it was permissable to conduct the interview with any responsible adult member of the household. On average interviews lasted some 10 minutes. A separate questionnaire had to be returned for each household living at the given address and for each vacant household space at the address. The questionnaire had been extensively piloted in several areas.

INTERVIEWING

21.   Interviewing commenced in October 1977 and gradually built up to a peak 25,000 interviews per week in November. The rate at which interviewers could be deployed on the survey was dependent both on the availability of addresses and the speed with which new recruits could be trained to a sufficiently high standard.

22.   All new recruits were accompanied for their first day's interviewing by either a supervisor from the companies or one of the GLC interviewers. If the supervisor was satisfied that the interviewer had grasped the essentials of the survey and could conduct interviews courteously, the interviewer was then free to work on his/her own. If the supervisor was not satisfied, the interviewer was accompanied for a second day and in some cases attended another training session. If the interviewer was still unable to perform competently, he/she was withdrawn from the survey.

23.   In order to detect any cheating by the field force, a systematic sample of addresses was revisited by supervisory staff, including GLC interviewers. Interviewers were nominated for checking at given times and their most recently completed batch of questionnaires was revisited to check that the interviewer had called at the given address and had conducted the interview correctly and courteously. During the course of the survey about 6% of addresses were issued for recalls (see Chapter 5 for analysis of results of these recalls).

24.   Further details of the rate at which interviews were conducted and the response rates achieved are given in Chapter 5.

EDITING AND CODING

25.   The first batch of unaccompanied interviews returned by each interviewer was thoroughly examined by the editing staff to ensure that the questionnaires had been completed well and did not contain any significant omissions or obvious errors. Questionnaires that failed this check were returned to the interviewer for corrective action. Thereafter, all questionnaires returned by the interviewer were checked on the key questions and one in ten of all questionnaires were checked on all questions. Questionnaires failing these checks were returned to the interviewer for corrective action and if an interviewer persistently returned unacceptable questionnaires the interviewer was accompanied again by a supervisor.

26.   The answers that were checked on all questionnaires were questions 1 to 3, 5 to 10, 21 to 27 and 37. In addition to these, special attention was paid to addresses where more than one questionnaire was returned to ensure that the multi-household procedure had been properly followed. Any written comments by the interviewer were also taken account of at this stage.

27.   Editing was carried out by the consortium who were also responsible for transferring to the questionnaire information supplied by Inland Revenue. The Department monitored the desk editing throughout the survey to ensure uniformity of standards.

28.   Edited questionnaires were passed by each company to the GLC Coding Unit for coding of relationship to head of household, socio-economic group, address one year ago for persons who had moved in the previous 12 months, and whether the head of household or housewife had moved since July 1976. The last coding was required to generate the sample for the follow-up national survey on movers. The Coding Unit also listed questionnaires that contained details of households that rented their accommodation from other than a local authority or new town corporation: this list was used to generate the sample frame for the follow-up survey on the private-rented sector.

29.   Employing a single coding unit to undertake this work ensured consistent standards throughout the survey. This was particularly important in the case of socio-economic group coding as coding teams frequently adopt slightly different conventions.

30.   A copy of the coding and editing manual is reproduced at Appendix C.

31.   Two sub-contractors were engaged by the consortium to handle computing aspects of the survey. Cybernetics Research Consultants Ltd (CRC) was commissioned to carry out the computer edit of questionnaires and Computer Aided Marketing Ltd (CAM) was commissioned to design and implement a tabulation system based on the system successfully employed by the Department of Transport on the National Travel Surveys.

32.   All questionnaires from each of the companies had to pass a rigorous computer edit before being accepted for analysis. The full range of edit checks was agreed by the Department and the computer edit was run by CRC. At this stage checks were also incorporated to ensure that records existed for all addresses issued to interviewers even if no interview had been achieved. When all issued addresses had been accounted for, CRC produced three master computer tapes which were passed to CAM. The three tapes were for the national half per cent sample, London boroughs, and the other sixteen areas intensively surveyed. Questionnaires for addresses in London and the other sixteen areas intensively surveyed which were included in the national sample occurred on both the national tape and the London borough or other area tape.

33.   The tabulation system employed on the survey is based on a system of derived variables. From the basic interview record a computer tape of derived variables was prepared containing anonymous information about addresses, households, families and persons. Some of these variables were simply responses to questions asked in the survey, such as number of persons in the household, whereas others had a more complex derivation from responses to several questions, such as "bedroom standard".

34.   By April 1978 the basic tabulation system had been fully tested and was operational although a number of refinements to the system were still being developed. At that time provisional results for the London Borough of Lambeth were prepared to fully test and prove the operational facilities. This led to a number of refinements to the derivation of some of the variables and to some of the facilities in the system. The full system was operational by the time that fully edited computer tapes were available for analysis in summer 1978.

CHAPTER 5. FIELDWORK REPORT

INTERVIEWING PERIOD

1. Interviewing commenced in early October 1977 and continued until June 1978. At its peak some 25,000 questionnaires per week were being returned by interviewers. As noted in Chapter 4, priority was given to completing fieldwork for the national ½ per cent sample and virtually all interviews in the areas with small samples had been completed by the end of January 1978: so also had the majority of interviews in the quarter of the wards in the areas intensively surveyed that had, at that time, been selected for drawing the ½ per cent sample. Full details of interviewing periods are given in Table 5A.

TABLE 5A. ADDRESSES DEALT WITH: BY MONTH* AND AREA

Number

	London	16 Selected Areas	Other Districts
1977			
October	23,288	1,416	5,326
November	31,113	17,091	26,523
December	23,443	16,596	15,625
1978			
January	35,005	23,743	10,821
February	43,592	27,438	3,528
March	35,615	19,042	1,129
April	17,462	6,731	859
May	12,452	4,133	459
June	5,133	7,759	613
Total addresses issued	227,103	123,949	64,883

* At multi-household addresses the month of interview of household number one has been taken

2. The fieldwork period was extended by a decision to reissue addresses in areas where response rates failed to reach predetermined levels: addresses were reissued in 16 London Boroughs and in 8 other areas. The addresses reissued to interviewers were those where the first interviewer had failed to establish contact with a member of the household after at least 4 calls or where the member of the household contacted had refused to participate in the survey: many refusals to co-operate were found to have been due to the failure of an inexperienced interviewer to present the purpose of the survey convincingly and when this was done so properly many households who had previously refused agreed to participate.

3.   The response rate measures the proportion of households eligible for interview at sampled addressed from whom answers were obtained for at least the first 21 questions ie. answers to all questions relating to the accommodation and details of the household composition but not necessarily details about each member of the household. In practice there were very few cases where less than full information was obtained in the interview: persons willing to co-operate with the survey were, on the whole, willing to answer all questions in the survey.

4.   The overall response rate in the national ½ per cent sample was 85 per cent. Apart from Greater London, where the response rate was 76 per cent, there was little variation between regions: the lowest response rate was 85 per cent in Yorkshire and Humberside and the highest was 90 per cent in East Anglia. Excluding the areas intensively surveyed, the response rate at the district level also showed considerable consistency: 3 districts had a response rate below 80 per cent, 34 had a response rate between 80 and 85 per cent, 38 had a response rate between 85 and 90 per cent, and 29 had a response rate above 90 per cent.

5.   In the 16 areas intensively surveyed, response rates varied from 82 per cent in Manchester and Liverpool to 88 per cent in Sandwell and Gateshead.

6.   In London the overall response rate of 76 per cent is comparable with other similar surveys. The pattern of response between boroughs also mirrored what has generally been found in other surveys. In outer London response varied between 85 per cent in Bexley and 72 per cent in Brent, while in inner London it varied between 81 per cent in Newham and 61 per cent in Kensington and Chelsea. As usual interviewing proved to be especially difficult in Westminster and Kensington and Chelsea and these together with Camden and the City of London registered response rates below 65 per cent. The distribution of response rates for other boroughs was 7 boroughs in the range 70-75 per cent, 16 boroughs in the range 75-80 per cent, and 6 boroughs had response rates above 80 per cent. Full details of response rates are given in Appendix A.

7.   A small amount of information was collected about non-respondents as well as respondents to the survey: this is summarised in Table 3B, for the national sample. It can be seen that on these measures households not contacted and other non-respondents exhibit in aggregate slightly different characteristics to respondents: the implications of this for interpreting the survey results are discussed in the next chapter.

TABLE 5B. CHARACTERISTICS OF RESPONDENTS AND NON-RESPONDENTS: ENGLAND

Percentages

	Respondents	Households not contacted	Other non-respondents
Rateable value			
Up to £100	14.4	16.7	11.2
£101-£150	21.0	21.7	18.0
£151-£200	24.9	22.9	21.9
£201-£300	28.6	25.4	32.5
Over £300	11.1	13.3	16.4
Age of property			
Pre 1919	26.9	36.0	29.3
1919-1939	23.6	20.5	26.5
Post 1939	49.5	43.5	44.3
Type of accommodation			
Detached house	18.0	13.6	18.3
Semi-detached house	33.7	24.2	30.7
Terraced house	29.0	25.8	28.9
Purpose built flat	11.1	19.7	13.6
Other flat or rooms	7.0	15.2	7.2
Other	1.2	1.5	1.3
All households	100.0	100.0	100.0
Sample number	71,294	4,841	7,983

FIELDWORK QUALITY CONTROLS

8.   Fieldwork quality control procedures were designed to ensure that interviewers had understood instructions given at the briefing conferences and
that interviews were conducted correctly and courteously throughout the fieldwork period. These procedures, as described in the previous chapter, consisted of the following methods: interviewer accompaniment, visual examination
of the questionnaires, and personal recalls by supervisory staff including, in
London, GLC interviewers. The outcome of the personal recalls is described
below.

9.   In order to detect cheating or inaccurate completion of questionnaires
personal recall checks were made on the work of all interviewers during the
course of fieldwork. Personal recalls also enabled supervisors to ensure
that showcards had been used and that the interviewer had been polite. Certain factual items were checked at the recall stage including the multi-
household information, the number of people in the household, the working
status of the head of household and the age and sex of the original respondent. This information was summarised on a check form as supervisors were
not issued with actual completed questionnaires.

10.   A batch of fifteen questionnaires (twelve in Inner London) was the basis for checking, several batches of each interviewer who worked extensively being checked at intervals during the whole fieldwork period. Supervisors were instructed to call on as many addresses in the batch as seemed necessary to validate that interviewer's work. On completion of the checking of the batch a summary was made to indicate the number of questionnaires where inconsistencies were found at the time of recall.

11.   25,190 addresses were issued for recall by supervisory staff as part of the field checking: of these addresses 17,005 households were contacted and the results are summarised in Tables 5C and 5D. 31 per cent of recalls were conducted by GLC interviewers and the remaining 69 per cent by the Consortium's own supervisory staff.

12.   Care has to be taken in interpreting the results of these findings. Some negative responses were expected since the questionnaire was fairly short and it may not have made a lasting impression on the respondents. Moreover, any responsible adult in the household could be interviewed and this respondent may not have been present at the time of recall. Some discrepancies between the first interview and the recall might also have been due to inaccuracies in information supplied at one of the interviews rather than any fault of the interviewer.

13.   Taking into account the preceeding caveats the result of the field checking can be regarded as satisfactory. The most frequent interviewer error appeared to be not using the showcard. At 9 per cent of the addresses checked the respondent did not recall the showcard having been used.

14.   98 per cent of households recontacted said that the interview had been carried out. The level of inconsistencies on the number of persons in the household was 2 per cent and on each of questions 2, 3, 9 and 30 was 1 per cent. The sex and age of respondent appeared to show a larger proportion of inconsistencies, 3 per cent on sex of respondent and 4 per cent on age of respondent. (See Table 5C).

15.   Although supervisors were issued with a batch of 15 addresses (12 in inner London), generally between 8 and 11 of these addresses were recontacted. In total 1,857 batches were reissued. Few batches were found to have large numbers of inconsistencies. There were, however, a very few cases where almost all questionnaires checked were found to be inconsistent: in some of these cases the interviewer was found to have been cheating. In such circumstances the interviewer was taken off of the survey and all questionnaires that had been sent in by the interviewer were reissued for interview.

16.   A summary of the extent of field quality control checks is given in Table 5D. In total about 5 per cent of all questionnaires were completed with a supervisor present or the household was recontacted to check that the interview had been conducted correctly and courteously.

TABLE 5C. FIELDWORK RECALLS: TYPES OF INCONSISTENCIES

	Number	Percentage of total contacted
Questionnaires inconsistent on:		
Number of persons in household (Q1)	372	2
Number of other households at address (Q2)	211	1
Number of vacant flats/bedsits at address (Q3)	186	1
Sharing circulation space (Q9)	218	1
Employment status of head of household (Q30)	248	1
Sex of respondent	434	3
Age of respondent	682	4
Interview not carried out	310	2
Interviewer not courteous	59	*
Showcard not used	1,468	9
Total contacted	17,005	100

* Less than 0.5 per cent.

TABLE 5D.   FIELDWORK QUALITY CHECKS: SUMMARY

	Addresses	Percentage of total addresses
Interviewer accompanied	3,996	0.9
Issued for field recall check	25,190	5.9
Recontacted by supervisory staff	17,005	4.9
Accompanied or reissued for field recall check	29,186	6.8
Accompanied or recontacted	21,001	4.9

224

CHAPTER 6.   GROSSING OF RESULTS AND COMPARISONS WITH OTHER SURVEYS

1.   The survey was conducted in order to provide estimates, in absolute terms, of various aspects of housing characteristics and problems in each region and other areas intensively surveyed. Results in this report have therefore been presented in this form; they have been rounded to the nearest thousand for regional estimates, and to the nearest hundred for those of London boroughs and other districts. The procedure used to gross the survey results to provide estimates in absolute terms is outlined below. Much consideration has been given to the most appropriate way of grossing up the results and it is thought that the method described here produces estimates that most reliably reflect housing circumstances at the time of the survey. Grossing up the results of a survey such as this, however, presents a number of difficult problems and other procedures are being investigated; they are unlikely, however, to produce significantly different results.

2.   The following section describes the effect of the grossing procedure on the results and compares the national results of NDHS with those of the General Household Survey (GHS) for 1977 which was conducted by Social Survey Division, Office of Population Censuses and Surveys.

THE GROSSING METHOD

3.   The sample design of NDHS was such that, assuming the selection of addresses to have been carried out correctly, unbiased estimates of those attributes for which full information was obtained about all sample addresses would be achieved simply by multiplying results by the reciprocal of the sampling fractions. In the case of the national sample this would involve multiplying by 200, and in London boroughs and other areas would involve multiplying by the sampling interval used to select addresses from the valuation list in each area.

4.   For each sample address a questionnaire was returned for each household space identified by the interviewer recording at least the interview outcome, a description of the property and the lowest floor of accommodation of the household, and information on the number of calls made by the interviewer. Thus, for all sample addresses information is available on the type of address (ie whether it is residential, non-residential, demolished and so forth) and for non-institutional residential addresses information is available on the number of households living at the address, and the number of vacant household spaces at the address. Since all sample addresses are covered in this way multiplying by the reciprocal of the sampling fraction provides an estimate of the total number of non-institutional residential addresses in each area.

5.   Although interviewers were instructed to return a separate questionnaire for each household space at each address, at certain types of addresses it was impossible to carry out this task with complete accuracy. This was particularly so with completely vacant properties that were sub-divided internally, and addresses where more than one household shared self-contained accommodation but no information was obtained from any of the households. These omissions are likely to lead to a small under-estimate of total households and total vacant household spaces. However, from the quality control checks that were carried out, including revisits to properties recorded as vacant, non-residential and so forth, there is no evidence of substantial error in this respect so it has been assumed in presenting these results that interviewers correctly identified the number of household spaces at each address and also whether the household space was occupied or vacant. This means that in addition to providing an

estimate of residential addresses, multiplying by the reciprocal of the sampling fraction also provided an estimate of the number of occupied household spaces (and hence of households) and the number of vacant household spaces.

GROSSING FOR NON-RESPONSE

6.   Estimates on topics in the survey relating to households or persons are affected to some degree by the failure to obtain relevant information from some households at sample addresses. The main causes of this non-response were (a) a refusal by a member of the household contacted to participate in the survey, (b) the interviewer being unable to contact a member of the household despite repeated calls, and (c) failure to elicit the required information from a willing participant because the person was unable to understand the questions (for example, through deafness or senility).

7.   One way of dealing with non-response would be to assume that the "missing households" had the same pattern of characteristics as those which co-operated in the survey. In NDHS, however, as previously noted, some information was available about virtually all household spaces, irrespective of response. This was the type of accommodation, the lowest floor of accommodation, the rateable value, the age of the property and the number of calls made by the interviewer. Analysis of these characteristics for respondents and non-respondents indicated that respondents to NDHS may not have been a completely representative cross-section of households, and that it would be unwise to assume that non-respondents had the same pattern of characteristics as respondents in grossing the results.

8.   One obvious factor on which there were large differences between respondents and non-respondents was the number of calls made by the interviewer, since a large proportion of the non-response was caused by failure to contact a member of the household after at least four calls, whereas once contact had been established with a household no further calls were required. The distribution of the number of calls for respondents and non-respondents in the national sample is given in Table 6A. Non-response at calls 1-3 was due mainly to a refusal to participate or an inability to participate, whereas non-response at the fourth or later call was due mainly to failure to contact a member of the household.

TABLE 6A.   INTERVIEW OUTCOME BY NUMBER OF CALLS: ENGLAND

Percentages

	Number of calls made on household				Base (= 100%)
	1	2	3	4 or more	
Respondents	61	24	10	6	71,294
Non-respondents	31	18	9	42	12,824

9.   Now since an interview could be carried out with any responsible adult member of the household the probability of contacting a household in a specified number of calls would be expected to be related to the number of adults in the household, and hence the number of persons in the household. This, in fact, proved to be the case in this survey as shown in Table 6B.

TABLE 6B.   SIZE OF HOUSEHOLD BY NUMBER OF CALLS: ENGLAND

Percentages and numbers

Respondents	Interview carried out on call			
	1	2	3	4 or later
Number of persons in household:				
1	18.2	18.2	21.7	27.8
2	31.8	33.3	35.1	36.2
3	17.8	17.8	17.2	14.5
4	19.3	19.1	17.1	13.4
5 or more	12.9	11.6	8.9	8.1
All households	100.0	100.0	100.0	100.0
Average household size	2.84	2.78	2.61	2.42
Sample Base	43,267	16,939	6,907	4,181

10.   This table shows that the average household size was lower the larger the number of calls required to establish contact. Households interviewed on the first call had an average size of 2.84 persons whereas those interviewed on the fourth or later call had an average size of 2.42 persons. This suggests that households that were not contacted (after at least 4 calls) had a smaller average household size than did responding households. This hypothesis was further supported by comparing an estimate of total private household population derived from NDHS based on the assumption that non-responding households had exactly the same average household size as responding households with that based on the Registrar General's mid-year estimates. On this crude method of grossing, NDHS overstated total private household population by about 2.5 per cent.

11.   In order to make some allowance for the estimated lower average household size of non-respondents the grossing procedure incorporates an adjustment based on the number of calls made. Specifically, the assumption built into the grossing procedure is that within each area non-responding households that had each received n calls by the interviewer are assumed to possess the characteristics of households in that area that responded on the nth call. For the national sample this adjustment was applied separately for each metropolitan county, the rest of each region, inner London and outer London. Thus, for example, house-holds in the South Yorkshire metropolitan county with whom no interview had been carried out after at least four calls were assumed in aggregate to have the same characteristics as the aggregate of all households in South Yorkshire metropolitan county that were successfully interviewed on the fourth or later call.

227

12.   The effect of applying this adjustment to the national results was to reduce the average household size and consequently the estimate of total private household population. However, even with this adjustment the resultant estimate of total private household population was still 1.8 per cent higher than one based on the Registrar General's mid-year estimates.

13.   More detailed comparisons of differences between the two estimates revealed that NDHS estimates showed larger numbers of persons in the age groups under 15, and 25-44, and smaller number of persons aged over 60. These differences may have arisen because families with children where the mother was at home most of the day might have been easier for the interviewer to contact than other types of household. The apparent undercount of elderly persons, however, is more difficult to explain because elderly households are usually comparatively easy to contact. Possible explanations are that because interviewing was conducted in the winter months some elderly persons were temporarily in hospital, while others might have been disinclined to open the door to a stranger in the evening when most of the interviewing was carried out. However, there is no firm evidence to support these hypotheses as yet.

14.   In view of these differences compared with the Registrar General's estimates it was decided to make a further small adjustment to NDHS results for differential non-response to bring the NDHS national population estimates more closely into line with those based on the mid-year estimates. A weighting factor was applied at the individual person level in NDHS which was obtained by comparing the NDHS estimate of population in each 5 year age band for males and females separately with the equivalent estimate based on the Registrar General's mid-year estimates. For example, if the crudely grossed NDHS results showed that there were 1,753,000 males aged 15-19 and the estimate based on the mid-year estimates was 1,773,000 then each male aged 15-19 in NDHS was given a weight of 1,773/1,753. Where age or sex was not recorded in NDHS the person was allocated a weight of unity and account elsewhere was made for these cases.

15.   A final small adjustment to the weights in each region was made to bring the total number of households in each metropolitan county and region into line with the estimates of the number of households in each of these areas obtained by the procedure outlined in paragraph 5.

16.   Tabulations in this volume are largely based on households. The household weights applied to gross the results were the weights calculated for the head of the household using the foregoing procedure.

17.   In London boroughs, and the other areas for which grossed results are presented the grossing procedure was similar to that applied nationally: raw data were multiplied by the reciprocal of the sampling fraction appropriate to the area and the adjustment factors for number of calls made were calculated separately for each area. The adjustment for variations in non-response by age and sex of population were incorporated by applying the same factors that were calculated at the national level. As for the national data a final adjustment was made to bring the total number of households into line with that obtained by the procedure outlined in paragraph 5.

18.   Grossing results separately for each London Borough by this procedure and then summing the figures for each borough inevitably leads to a different set of results for Greater London than is obtained by grossing separately for inner London and outer London only. This arises because response rates vary between different London boroughs. The basic assumption in the grossing procedure was

that non-respondents, in various categories, had the same characteristics as respondents in other catagories. For the London region in the national sample the basic assumption was that non-respondents in inner London were like respondents in inner London, and non-respondents in outer London were like respondents in outer London (in fact, this was further complicated by incorporating the adjustment for number of calls but this does not affect the argument): for grossing individual London boroughs non-respondents were assumed to have the characteristics of respondents in that borough. For characteristics on which boroughs with low response rates differed markedly from boroughs with high response rates the two assumptions lead to different answers. Now response rates varied considerably in London and were substantially lower in Kensington and Chelsea, Westminster and Camden. This has meant that characteristics prevalent in those areas but not elsewhere in inner London are understated in the Greater London results based on the national $\frac{1}{2}$ per cent sample, and those characteristics prevalent in other parts of inner London but not in those areas are overstated in the Greater London results based on the national $\frac{1}{2}$ per cent sample.

19. Differences between the two sets of results for Greater London may also be due to basing the London results in the national sample on a subsample of the total interviews. (see Chapter 4 paragraph 7).

COMPARISON OF GROSSED AND UNGROSSED RESULTS

20. As outlined in the previous section, the main shortcoming in the ungrossed results appeared to be an overstatement of average household size (leading to an overestimate of total population). The grossing procedure was designed to adjust for this, so one would expect that there would be larger differences between the distributions of grossed and ungrossed results for this factor than there would be for other factors. This turns out to be so as shown in Tables 1-22. These tables also reflect the greater influence of London's data in the grossed results arising from adjusting for the higher non-response in London, especially in inner London. It can be seen that for most factors the grossing has made little difference to the distributions.

21. In Tables 1-4 the percentage distributions of the ungrossed results are based on (i) those households where an interview was conducted, and (ii) all occupied household spaces: these are contrasted with the distributions obtained by grossing the successful interviews.

22. None of the four factors - rateable value, age of property, type of accommodation, and lowest floor accommodation - were used in determining the grossing procedure but it can be seen that although the effect of the grossing was slight the changes that have occurred have brought the results closer to the distributions pertaining to all occupied household spaces in the sample. For example, the proportion of respondents with ground floor as their lowest floor of accommodation was 87.1 per cent: after grossing this proportion dropped to 86.3 per cent which is very close to the 86.2 per cent found for all responding households and non-responding households.

23. Tables 5-22 relate to household characteristics, so unlike Tables 1-4 there is no comparable information for households when no interview was obtained. Tables 5-7 on size and types of households demonstrate the main expected effects of grossing: in particular the average household size fell from 2.78 in the ungrossed data to 2.72 in the grossed results. In the grossed results both the proportions of 1 and 2 person households increased while the proportions of all larger households fell. The main change was the proportion of individuals aged

60 or over living alone which rose from 13.3 per cent in ungrossed data to 14.3 per cent in the grossed results; this was offset by a fall in the proportion of small family households from 21.8 per cent to 20.6 per cent and large family households from 9.7 per cent to 9.2 per cent.

24.   Examination of distributions on number of rooms and bedrooms (Tables 8 and 9) reveals an increased proportion of households with few rooms and a correspondingly decreased proportion of households with a large number of rooms, although the changes were not large. The largest proportionate change was the increase in the proportion of households with 1 bedroom from 11.0 per cent to 11.7 per cent. These changes reflect the larger grossing factors applied to small households which on average possessed a below average number of rooms.

25.   Possession of a range of household amenities is compared in Tables 10-13. The grossing factors had less effect on these distributions than they did on the distributions on number of rooms and type of household. The main effect was to increase the proportion of households which shared the use of basic amenities. Similarly with tenure the effects of grossing were small increases in the proportions of households renting accommodation privately, and owning outright - mainly small elderly households.

26.   The grossing procedure made little difference to the estimate of households living in overcrowded conditions or below the bedroom standard.

27.   Table 18 shows the distribution of the population by age and sex. This presents most clearly the effects of the grossing method. The proportions of persons aged under 15 and 30-44 decreased while the proportions in the older age groups, especially females aged 60 or over, increased.

28.   The 0.2 per cent upward adjustment in the proportion of heads of household born outside the United Kingdom in the grossed results (Table 22) was caused almost entirely by adjusting for the relatively higher level of non-response found in the conurbations.

29.   Overall, the effect of applying grossing procedures designed to adjust for any possible differential non-response has not been to change violently any of the distributions found in the survey. Rather the effect has been to modify those few attributes where the ungrossed results appeared to underestimate the true proportions through non-responding households exhibiting different characteristics to responding households. In the rest of this report all results quoted have been derived using the grossing procedure outlined in this chapter.

COMPARISON OF THE NDHS WITH THE GHS

30.   This section records the results of a comparison of the results of NDHS with those of the 1977 General Household Survey. The overall impression of the comparison is one of very close accord between the two sets of results.

31.   Both the NDHS and the English sample of the GHS were designed to provide estimates representative of the total private household population of England. However, as discussed in the previous section, non-response is likely to leave the samples of final co-operating households deficient in those with certain types of attributes and although it is likely that non-respondents in both surveys will have certain characteristics in common it is also likely that patterns of non-response will differ for several reasons, such as variations in field work practices. For example, in the NDHS it was usual for attempts

to contact households to cease after four unsuccessful visits to an address, whereas in the GHS any number of calls were permitted within a specified time period (a minimum of 2 weeks and usually 4 or 5 weeks). Other reasons why non-response patterns might differ are that although the two surveys had comparable response rates NDHS had a higher non-contact rate but a lower refusal rate, probably as a result of the much simpler subject matter and the need to contact only one member of the household.

32. The method used to gross the NDHS has been designed to adjust the results for some aspects of non-response but it does not necessarily adjust optimally for all household characteristics. By comparing survey results with independent estimates an indication of the total departure from representativeness is obtained. An example of such an exercise is a comparison of the results of the GHS in 1971 with those of the 1971 Census of Population (Chapter 3.5, General Household Survey: Introductory Report, HMSO).

33. A more direct way of examining the characteristics of non-respondents is to use information about the addresses containing non-respondents and the household resident at those addresses.*

34. Neither of these approaches could be carried out extensively for NDHS since the latest Census of Population was in 1971 and there are no sources other than the Census that provide sufficiently reliable estimates. Similarly, there were no sources from which details of household characteristics of non-respondents in NDHS could be ascertained. The main source of current data against which the NDHS could be compared was the GHS and these comparisons are shown in Tables 1-22 both for ungrossed NDHS data and grossed NDHS data.

35. In Tables 1-4 there is close accord between GHS and NDHS grossed results on the characteristics of occupied household spaces. The main difference being the higher proportion in NDHS of households living in properties with high rateable values and detached houses. The age of the property in NDHS was based on information supplied by the Inland Revenue Valuation Office and was thus probably more accurate than the GHS classification which was based on respondent or interviewer assessment: against this, however, information on age was available for only some 90 per cent of the NDHS sample and in some areas, such as Camden, very few properties were classified by age.

36. Comparison of types and sizes of households found in the two surveys reveals a higher proportion of 1 person households and lone parent households and a smaller proportion of large adult households in the GHS. In each of these cases the grossed NDHS results show a closer accord with GHS results than do the ungrossed NDHS results.

37. One curious feature found when comparing the number and type of rooms is the lower proportion in NDHS of kitchens reported as being less than 6'6" wide. In GHS the division was made at 6' wide rather than 6'6" wide which should, if anything, have reduced the proportion of such kitchens compared with NDHS whereas, in fact, twice as high a proportion was found. Since the interviewer personally inspected the kitchen in a high proportion of cases in the GHS it is likely that the GHS is more accurate on this measure.

---

* This approach has also been used for the GHS in comparison with results from the 1971 Census of Population (GHS Series No 8. The Census as an Aid in Estimating the Characteristics of Non-response in the GHS. R Barnes and F Birch).

38.   NDHS shows a higher proportion of households with exclusive use of a bath than GHS but the same proportion with exclusive use of an inside WC. NDHS also shows a higher proportion of households possessing central heating although a smaller proportion possessing electric storage heaters: this may be due to differences in the questions used in the two surveys and to the treatment of part central heating systems.

39.   In classifying tenure of households the GHS treated co-ownership as a form of renting whereas in NDHS these were classified as owner-occupied: this would account for some of the differences in renting from housing associations and in owned with mortgage. The proportion of households renting from a local authority or new town is higher in the GHS than in NDHS: part of the difference might be due to the practice whereby in the GHS local authority/new town was given preference over employer if the employer was a local authority whereas in NDHS employer was given preference and the household was classified as renting privately.

40.   Information on the occupation of persons in the GHS was obtained mainly from the person holding the job but in NDHS was, in many cases, obtained by proxy. Moreover, in GHS retired persons were asked for their last occupation whereas in NDHS they were asked for their last main occupation. Compared with GHS, NDHS recorded a higher proportion of persons in professional, managerial, other non-manual, and skilled occupations and a lower proportion in semi-skilled and unskilled occupations, but the differences are not large. A higher proportion of heads of household were recorded as unemployed in NDHS but some of this difference may be due to differences in timing of the surveys since unemployment is affected by seasonal factors.

41.   On length of residence at address NDHS found a much higher proportion of heads of household resident for less than 1 year. This is probably a more accurate reflection than the GHS since the GHS was based on the Electoral Register which tends to be less up-to-date than the Valuation List on which NDHS was based.

TABLE 6.1   RATEABLE VALUE

Percentages and Numbers

	GHS	NDHS Ungrossed		NDHS Grossed
		Respondents	Respondents and Non-respondents	
Up to £75	7.6	7.4	7.5	7.5
£76-100	7.6	7.0	6.8	7.0
£101-150	21.8	21.0	20.8	20.8
£151-200	25.6	24.9	24.5	24.7
£201-300	27.4	28.6	28.8	28.7
£301-400	6.7	7.1	7.3	7.2
£401 or over	3.3	4.1	4.3	4.1
Base (=100%)	10,208	70,583	83,045	-

TABLE 6.2   AGE OF PROPERTY/BUILDING

Percentages and Numbers

	GHS	NDHS Ungrossed		NDHS Grossed
		Respondents	Respondents and Non-respondents	
Pre 1919	26.4	26.9	27.6	27.3
1919-1939	26.0	23.5	23.7	23.7
1940-1964	26.6*	26.8	26.4	26.7
1965 or later	21.1*	22.7	22.2	22.3
Base (=100%)	10,419	65,439	76,819	-

* Includes an allowance for properties where the interviewer could not decide whether it was before or after 1965.

233

TABLE 6.3   TYPE OF ACCOMMODATION

Percentages and Numbers

	GHS	NDHS* Ungrossed		NDHS Grossed
		Respondents	Respondents and Non-respondents	
Detached house	16.7	18.0	17.8	17.6
Semi-detached house	33.4	33.7	33.0	33.0
Terraced house	29.1	29.0	28.8	28.9
Purpose built flat/ maisonette	12.2	11.1	11.8	11.8
Other flat/rooms	7.3	7.0	7.4	7.4
Other	1.3	1.2	1.2	1.2
Base (=100%)	10,150	70,656	82,188	-

* In NDHS the description of the rateable unit only was recorded. Where more than one household resided at an address each household has been allocated to 'other flats/rooms'.

TABLE 6.4 LOWEST FLOOR OF ACCOMMODATION

Percentages and Numbers

	GHS*	NDHS* Ungrossed		NDHS Grossed
		Respondents	Respondents and Non-respondents	
Below street level	⎫	1.8	1.8	1.9
Ground	95.5	87.1	86.2	86.3
1st floor	⎭	6.7	7.1	7.0
2nd floor	2.3	2.3	2.6	2.5
3rd floor	0.9	0.8	0.9	0.8
4th-9th floor**	1.1	1.0	1.1	1.1
10th floor or higher**	0.2	0.3	0.4	0.4
Base (=100%)	10,100	71,037	82,272	-

* GHS relates to main living part of the accommodation whereas NDHS is based on lowest floor of accommodation.

** GHS is 4th-10th floor and 11th floor or higher.

TABLE 6.5   NUMBER OF PEOPLE IN HOUSEHOLD

	GHS	NDHS Ungrossed	NDHS Grossed
Number of people in household:			
1	21.4	19.1	20.6
2	33.0	32.7	33.3
3	16.9	17.5	17.1
4	17.7	18.7	17.7
5	7.0	7.6	7.2
6 or more	3.9	4.3	4.0
Base (= 100%)	10,208	71,294	-
Mean household size	2.695	2.781	2.721

TABLE 6.6   TYPE OF HOUSEHOLD 1

	GHS	NDHS Ungrossed	NDHS Grossed
Married couple household	68.1	70.9	69.3
Lone parent household	7.0	6.3	6.3
One person household	21.4	19.2	20.6
Other household	3.5	3.6	3.8
Base (= 100%)	10,208	71,059	-

TABLE 6 .7   TYPE OF HOUSEHOLD 2

Percentages and Numbers

	GHS	NDHS Ungrossed	NDHS Grossed
Individual aged less than 60	6.8	5.8	6.3
Small adult household	14.5	14.9	15.3
Small family household	21.8	21.8	20.6
Large family household	9.4	9.7	9.2
Large adult household	15.4	17.3	17.1
Older small household	17.5	17.0	17.2
Individual aged 60 or over	14.7	13.3	14.3
Base (= 100%)	10,189	70,811	-

TABLE 6.8   NUMBER OF ROOMS

Percentages and Numbers

	GHS	NDHS Ungrossed	NDHS Grossed
Number of rooms			
1	1.2	1.1	1.2
2	3.4	2.4	2.5
3	8.8	7.8	8.2
4	20.8	20.8	21.2
5	33.6	33.2	32.6
6	23.9	24.8	24.5
7 or more	8.3	10.0	9.8
Base (= 100%)	10,167	70,450	-

236

TABLE 6.9   NUMBER OF BEDROOMS

Percentages and Numbers

	GHS	NDHS Ungrossed	NDHS Grossed
Number of Bedrooms			
1	11.3	11.0	11.7
2	27.3	28.3	28.7
3	52.1	50.8	49.9
4	7.5	7.8	7.7
5	1.2	1.5	1.4
6 or more	0.6	0.6	0.6
Base (= 100%)	10,125	71,287	-

TABLE 6.10   POSSESSION OF KITCHEN

Percentages and Numbers

	GHS*	NDHS Ungrossed	NDHS Grossed
Households with kitchen:			
At least $6\frac{1}{2}$* feet wide	86.5	92.6	92.4
Under $6\frac{1}{2}$* feet wide	12.8	6.3	6.4
Households with no kitchen	0.7	1.1	1.1
Base (= 100%)	10,168	70,766	-

* For GHS the division was made at 6 feet not $6\frac{1}{2}$ feet.

TABLE 6 .11   USE OF BATH OR SHOWER

Percentages and Numbers

	GHS	NDHS Ungrossed	NDHS Grossed
Use of fixed bath or shower:			
Sole use	93.4	94.6	94.3
Shared use	3.2	2.8	3.0
None	3.4	2.6	2.7
Base (= 100%)	10,163	71,260	-

TABLE 6 .12   USE OF FLUSH TOILET

Percentages and Numbers

	GHS	NDHS Ungrossed	NDHS Grossed
Use of flush toilet:			
Sole use inside building	92.9	93.1	92.9
Shared use inside building	2.7	2.5	2.7
No inside WC, sole use outside building	3.9	3.9	3.9
No inside WC, shared use outside building	0.2	0.2	0.2
None	0.3	0.3	0.3
Base (= 100%)	10,153	71,160	-

TABLE 6 .13   POSSESSION OF CENTRAL HEATING

Percentages and Numbers

	GHS	NDHS Ungrossed	NDHS Grossed
No central heating	48.6	46.8	47.2
Electric storage heaters*	9.1	7.0	7.1
Other forms of central heating	42.3	46.2	45.7
Base (= 100%)	10,160	71,033	-

* Multicoding of storage heaters and other central heating is attributed to the former in the GHS and is distributed between both in NDHS. In total in NDHS 7.1 per cent of households said that they had use of storage heaters.

TABLE 6.14   TENURE OF HOUSEHOLD

Percentages and Numbers

	GHS	NDHS Ungrossed	NDHS Grossed
Owned outright	23.1	23.1	23.4
Owned with mortgage/loan	30.1	31.8	31.0
Rented from local authority or new town	31.3	29.8	29.8
Rented from housing association	1.6	1.3	1.3
Rented privately unfurnished	10.1	10.7	10.9
Rented privately furnished	3.7	3.3	3.5
Base (= 100%)	10,109	70,951	-

239

TABLE 6.15   TYPE OF LANDLORD OF HOUSEHOLDS RENTING ACCOMMODATION

Percentages and Numbers

	GHS	NDHS Ungrossed	NDHS Grossed
Local authority	65.4	63.2	62.7
New Town Corporation	1.5	2.8	2.7
Property company	2.6	4.1	4.4
Housing association	3.4	2.8	2.9
Employer -	4.4	6.6	6.3
Relative	2.7	1.7	1.7
Other person	17.2	16.3	16.8
Other	2.6	2.4	2.4
Base (= 100%)	4,725	32,003	-

In GHS local authority/NT was given preference over employer if the employer was a local authority: in NDHS employers were given preference.

TABLE 6.16   DENSITY OF OCCUPATION OF HOUSEHOLDS

Percentages and Numbers

	GHS	NDHS Ungrossed	NDHS Grossed
Persons per room:			
Less than 0.5	39.4	38.1	39.6
0.5-1	57.0	58.7	57.4
Over 1-1.5	3.1	2.8	2.6
Over 1.5	0.5	0.5	0.5
Base (= 100%)	10,207	70,450	-

TABLE 6.17   HOUSEHOLDS BY DIFFERENCE FROM BEDROOM STANDARD

Percentages and Numbers

	GHS	NDHS Ungrossed	NDHS Grossed
2 or more bedrooms below standard	0.4	0.6	0.6
1 bedroom below standard	3.5	4.4	4.3
Equal to standard	31.3	32.7	32.7
1 bedroom above standard	39.8	39.8	39.5
2 or more bedrooms above standard	25.0	22.5	22.9
Base (= 100%)	10,207	70,902	-

TABLE 6.18   AGE AND SEX OF INDIVIDUALS

Percentages and Numbers

	GHS	NDHS Ungrossed	NDHS Grossed
Male			
0-14*	12.7	12.0	11.5
15-29*	9.6	10.8	10.9
30-44	9.3	9.7	9.4
45-64	10.9	10.9	11.3
65 or over	5.7	5.5	5.6
All males	48.2	49.0	48.8
Female			
0-14*	12.2	11.1	10.7
15-29*	9.4	10.7	10.7
30-44	9.3	9.7	9.4
45-59	9.3	8.7	9.1
60 or over	11.6	10.7	11.3
All females	51.8	51.0	51.2
Base (= 100%)	27,487	197,114	-

* In GHS categories are 0-15 and 16-29.

241

TABLE 6.19   SOCIO-ECONOMIC GROUP OF INDIVIDUALS*

Percentages and Numbers

	GHS	NDHS Ungrossed	NDHS Grossed
Professional occupations, employers, managers	14.2	15.9	15.9
Intermediate and junior non-manual	30.2	30.2	30.6
Skilled manual** and own account non-professional	26.8	27.7	27.4
Semi-skilled manual and personal service	20.4	18.9	18.9
Unskilled manual	7.0	6.7	6.6
Armed forces	0.4	0.6	0.5
Base (= 100%)	15,278	105,661	-

* Includes the economically active and the retired only, but not (NDHS only) full time students working in the reference week.

** Includes foremen and supervisors.

TABLE 6.20   EMPLOYMENT STATUS OF HEAD OF HOUSEHOLD

Percentages and Numbers

	GHS	NDHS Ungrossed	NDHS Grossed
Full-time work	60.7	63.1	62.4
Part-time work	4.9	3.1	3.2
All workers	66.6⌐	66.2	65.6
Unemployed*	2.3	3.6	3.5
Retired	18.2	18.0	18.2
Other	12.9	12.2	12.7
All non-workers	33.4	33.8	34.4
Base (= 100%)	10,058	71,184	-

⌐ Includes no answer to number of hours worked.

* Includes those waiting to take up a job or temporarily sick.

242

TABLE 6.21   LENGTH OF RESIDENCE OF HEAD OF HOUSEHOLD

Percentages and Numbers

	GHS	NDHS Ungrossed	NDHS Grossed
Less than 1 year	8.4	10.6	10.6
1 year but under 2	7.4	8.0	7.9
2 years but under 3	7.2	9.0	8.9
3 years but under 5	10.6	10.0	9.8
5 years but under 10*	25.8	19.0	18.7
10 years or over*	40.6	43.4	44.1
Base (= 100%)	10,201	71,196	-

* GHS 5-10 and 11+.

TABLE 6.22   COUNTRY OF BIRTH OF HEAD OF HOUSEHOLD

Percentages and Numbers

	GHS	NDHS Ungrossed	NDHS Grossed
United Kingdom	92.8	92.9	92.7
Not in United Kingdom	7.2	7.1	7.3
Base (= 100%)	10,055	71,147	

243

CHAPTER 7. SAMPLING ERROR

1.   The quality of survey results is dependent on all stages of the operation and failings at any stage can lead to errors in the results. For example, errors may be introduced if the sampling frame is incomplete, if questions are interpreted by respondents in a way not intended, and if respondents give incorrect answers for any reason. Errors can also be introduced when the questionnaires are edited and input to the computer. For this survey extensive efforts were made to minimise such errors as has already been described in previous chapters. These steps included testing the questionnaire in pilot surveys, training and briefing interviewers to a common standard, and checking the work of interviewers and editing staff.

2.   Another potential source of error in the results is response bias; respondents to a survey may differ in some respects from non-respondents, and thus may not form a representative sample. For this survey steps have been taken to reduce such errors through the grossing procedure which has been described in Chapter 6.

3.   Another source of error common to all sample surveys arises from the fact that only a sample of addresses was selected instead of all addresses, and those selected addresses might not have been completely representative of all addresses. Such errors are known as sampling errors and are dependent on both the size of the sample and the sample design. The remainder of this chapter is concerned with estimating the size of the sampling errors for this survey.

4.   A convenient way of presenting the sampling error attached to a survey estimate of a proportion is in the form of a range of values called a 95 per cent confidence interval. For example, the estimated proportion of lone parent households is 6.3 per cent and the 95 per cent confidence interval is 6.1-6.5 per cent. The meaning of this is that, if the survey could be repeated a large number of times with a different sample each time, but with the same sample design and with all other factors being the same, then in 19 out of 20 such surveys the 95 per cent confidence interval about the survey estimate would be expected to contain the actual proportion in the whole population.

5.   Sampling errors and related confidence intervals have been calculated for all of the major results of the survey. These are shown in Table 7A at the end of this chapter. The method used to calculate them is described in the following sections. Also included in Table 7A are estimates of the "design effect" associated with each of the results. A description of what this measures, how it is calculated and how it can be used to estimate sampling errors for characteristics not listed in Table 7A is given in the next section.

CALCULATION OF SAMPLING ERRORS AND DESIGN EFFECTS

6.   The design effect compares the sampling errors calculated for the survey with the theoretical sampling errors associated with a particular type of sample design - a simple random sample - for which sampling errors are easy to compute. Its use is both to examine the relative efficiency of the sample design, and to facilitate the calculation of sampling errors and confidence intervals for survey results not shown in Table 7A.

7. The design effect is different for different characteristics: for a proportion p it is measured by the formula

$$deff = \left(\frac{\text{estimated standard error of p with sample design used}}{\text{estimated standard error of p with simple random sample of same size}}\right)^2$$

Now the standard error of p (se(p)) with a simple random sample is easily computed using the formula

$$\sqrt{\frac{p(1-p)}{n}}$$

where n is the sample size. The 95 per cent confidence interval about the estimate p is estimated using the formula

$$p \pm 1.96 \ se(p)$$
which is equivalent to
$$p \pm 1.96 \ \sqrt{deff} \ \sqrt{\frac{p(1-p)}{n}}$$

8. For characteristics not shown in Table 7A the sampling error and confidence interval can be estimated using the above formula if an estimate of the design effect is available and the sample size is known. In general, the design effect can be approximated by selecting the design effect of a characteristic in Table 7A with a similar distribution and the same base (eg all households in England or all households in the North West). This is illustrated in the following example.

Example

Suppose that one wished to estimate the sampling error and the confidence interval for the proportion of households in England that had sole use of all basic amenities. This is not given in Table 7A but the value of $\sqrt{deff}$ for a percentage with a similar characteristic and the same sample base can be used to estimate it. A similar characteristic with the same sample base in this case would be the proportion of households in England having sole use of a bath or shower. $\sqrt{deff}$ for this is 2.12. The sampling error for the proportion p of households with exclusive use of all basic amenities would then be estimated by the formula $se(p) = \sqrt{deff} \ \sqrt{\frac{p(1-p)}{n}}$. In this case p = 0.914, n = 71,294, and $\sqrt{deff}$ is estimated as, say, 2.2. So the sampling error of p is 0.0023 and the 95 per cent confidence interval is 90.9-91.9 per cent. In fact the calculated $\sqrt{deff}$ for this characteristic is 2.19 and the 95 per cent confidence interval is as estimated.

9.   Table 7A gives estimated design effects and 95 per cent confidence intervals of selected characteristics at the national level. Table 7B gives a selection of design effects for regions, London boroughs and extensively surveyed districts. It should be noted that the design effects given are themselves subject to sampling error, which may explain some of the differences between areas. All design effects have been calculated on the ungrossed results of the survey but would be little changed by the grossing procedures adopted. Details of the sample sizes in each area for which results are shown may be found in Appendix A.

10.   The sample design used in the survey for each London borough and each of the 16 other extensively surveyed districts was a systematic sample and was generally more efficient than a simple random sample. However, for certain characteristics, such as sharing, which are clustered within addresses sampling errors are higher than would be associated with a simple random sample so the design effect is greater than unity. The design of the national sample was more complex and, in particular, only about one-third of non-metropolitan districts were sampled. This has resulted in sampling errors higher than those associated with a simple random sample of the same size drawn throughout the country. The design effects for the national sample are thus generally greater than unity. Design effects in the regions not containing metropolitan counties are generally higher than for regions containing metropolitan counties.

DIFFERENCE BETWEEN TWO PROPORTIONS

11.   A common requirement in using survey results is to establish whether the difference between two survey estimates of proportions, p_1 and p_2, is statistically significant. This will be so if the confidence interval about p_1-p_2 does not include 0. If p_1 and p_2 are based on samples of n_1 and n_2 and have design effects $deff_1$ and $deff_2$ respectively, an estimate of the 95 per cent confidence interval is

$$p_1-p_2 \pm 1.96 \sqrt{deff_1 \frac{p_1(1-p_1)}{n_1} + deff_2 \frac{p_2(1-p_2)}{n_2}}$$

This will generally overestimate the width of the confidence interval unless p_1 and p_2 are based on different areas.

Example

Suppose that one wished to estimate whether the proportion of households living at one bedroom below the bedroom standard was significantly higher in the North West than in the East Midlands. The design effects for this characteristic in these regions are given in Table 7B: they are 0.85^2 for the North West, and 1.23^2 for the East Midlands. The estimated proportions of households in the North West and East Midlands living at one bedroom below the bedroom standard are 5.2 per cent and 3.6 per cent respectively, and the sample sizes are 10,032 and 6,054 respectively. Applying the formula in the above paragraph gives

$$0.052-0.036 \pm 1.96 \sqrt{0.72 \times \frac{0.052 \times 0.948}{10032} + 1.51 \times \frac{0.036 \times 0.964}{6054}}$$

$= 0.016 \pm 0.0068$

or 0.0092 - 0.0228.

Since this range does not include the value 0 the difference between the two proportions is statistically significant ie the North West has a significantly higher proportion of households living at one bedroom below the bedroom standard than does the East Midlands.

METHOD USED TO CALCULATE SAMPLING ERRORS

12.   Because of the different sample designs in the non-metropolitan and metropolitan areas, the two parts of the sample had to be treated differently in the calculation of sampling errors. The proportion of cases (households, persons, etc) with a given characteristic is $r = \dfrac{x + y}{X + Y}$, where x and y are the numbers of cases with the characteristic in all sampled non-metropolitan districts and metropolitan districts (including London Boroughs) respectively, and X and Y are the corresponding total sample sizes. An estimate of the variance of r is given by the formula*

$$\text{Var}(r) = \frac{1}{(X+Y)^2}\;[\text{Var}(x+y)+r^2\text{Var}(X+Y)-2r\text{Cov}(x+y,X+Y)].$$

For this sample design this simplifies to

$$\text{Var}(r) = \frac{1}{(X+Y)^2}\;[\text{Var}(x)+r^2\text{Var}(X)-2r\text{Cov}(x,X)+Y^2\text{Var}(y/Y)].$$

Let x_{ij} be the number of cases with the characteristic in the jth non-metropolitan district in the ith region, where the districts are ordered as for drawing the sample, and let X_{ij} be the sample size in that district. $\text{Var}(x)$, $\text{Var}(X)$ and $\text{Cov}(x,X)$ are estimated by the formulae

$$\text{Var}(x) = \sum_i \frac{n_i}{2(n_i-1)} \sum_{j=1}^{n_i-1} (x_{ij} - x_{i,\,j+1})^2$$

$$\text{Var}(X) = \sum_i \frac{n_i}{2(n_i-1)} \sum_{j=1}^{n_i-1} (X_{ij} - X_{i,\,j+1})^2$$

$$\text{Cov}(x,X) = \sum_i \frac{n_i}{2(n_i-1)} \sum_{j=1}^{n_i-1} (x_{ij} - x_{i,\,j+1})(X_{ij} - X_{i,\,j+1})$$

where n_i is the number of non-metropolitan districts in the sample in the ith region.

13.   To estimate $\text{Var}(y/Y)$, the metropolitan sample was divided into ten equal subsamples, each subsample containing one tenth of the addresses from each district.

---

* For a fuller discussion see Kish, L., "Survey Sampling", Wiley (New York 1965), sec 6.

247

Let y_i be the number of cases with the characteristic in the ith subsample and Y_i the total size of the subsample. Var(y/Y) is estimated by the formula

$$\text{Var}(y/Y) = \frac{1}{90} \sum_i \left(\frac{y_i}{Y_i}\right)^2 - \frac{1}{900}\left(\sum_i \frac{y_i}{Y_i}\right)^2$$

14. Having thus estimated Var(r) the 95 per cent confidence limits were given by the formula $r \pm 1.96 \sqrt{\text{Var}(r)}$, and the design effect by

$$\text{deff} = \text{Var}(r) \Big/ \frac{r(1-r)}{X+Y}$$

The coefficient of variation of X, $\text{CV}(X) = \frac{\sqrt{\text{Var}(X)}}{X}$, was also calculated,

since the formula for estimating Var(r) is only suitable when CV(X) is less than 0.1; in addition the ratio estimate bias is negligible if this condition holds. For the whole national sample, CV(X) was 0.008 for households and 0.010 for persons. CV(X) was higher where the base was only part of the sample, but was less than 0.05 for all regional, London borough and district figures in this report.

TABLE 7A.   95 per cent confidence intervals and design effects for selected
             characteristics: England

Characteristic	% with characteristic		95% confidence interval (%) ±	Square root of design effect √deff
	Ungrossed	Grossed		
Type of property:*				
Detached house	18.43	..	1.41	5.39
Semi-detached house	33.41	..	0.97	3.05
Terraced house	30.47	..	1.32	4.24
Lowest floor of accommodation:				
Ground floor	85.71	86.29	0.64	2.76
1st floor	7.27	7.05	0.32	1.85
4th-9th floor	1.15	1.10	0.08	1.15
Type of household:				
Married couple household	70.89	69.27	0.66	1.96
Lone parent household	6.28	6.31	0.19	1.06
One person aged under 60	5.86	6.35	0.30	1.72
One person aged 60 or over	13.33	14.29	0.41	1.63
Other household	3.64	3.78	0.21	1.51
Number of rooms:				
3	7.78	8.23	0.33	1.68
4	20.80	21.17	0.51	1.72
5	33.16	32.60	0.71	2.03
6	24.78	24.48	0.53	1.65
Type of sharing:				
Sharing rooms	1.20	1.25	0.21	2.59
Sharing circulation space	1.05	1.13	0.11	1.44
Bedsit	0.54	0.59	0.09	1.69
Use of bath or shower:				
Sole use	94.57	94.29	0.35	2.12
Shared use	2.80	2.99	0.30	2.47
None	2.64	2.72	0.19	1.60
With central heating	53.25	52.76	1.24	3.39

* In this table property refers to the whole rateable unit, and not the space occupied by the household.

Characteristic	% with characteristic		95% confidence interval (%) $\pm$	Square root of design effect $\sqrt{\text{deff}}$
	Ungrossed	Grossed		
Main form of room heating:				
Open fire	14.96	14.76	0.91	3.46
Electric	11.97	12.50	0.53	2.24
Gas	25.76	25.86	1.06	3.30
Tenure:				
Owned outright	23.11	23.43	0.89	2.88
Owned with mortgage or loan	31.84	31.04	1.05	3.07
Rented from council	29.75	29.80	1.33	3.96
Rented from housing association	1.28	1.34	0.13	1.54
Rented privately unfurnished	10.71	10.88	0.48	2.11
Rented privately furnished	3.27	3.46	0.37	2.81
No one in household on council waiting list	92.50	92.47	0.33	1.68
Dissatisfied with:				
Accommodation	5.98	5.96	0.21	1.19
Area	7.76	7.82	0.30	1.53
Difference from bedroom standard:				
2 or more below	0.63	0.61	0.06	1.09
1 below	4.42	4.32	0.19	1.26
Length of residence of head of household:				
Less than 1 year	10.62	10.64	0.37	1.63
1 but under 2 years	7.96	7.90	0.27	1.37
10 years or over	43.45	44.06	0.76	2.10
Age and sex of head of household:				
Male aged 65 or over	14.48	14.33	0.41	1.57
Female aged 60 or over	13.11	14.09	0.42	1.69

	% with characteristic		95% confidence interval (%) ±	Square root of design effect $\sqrt{\text{deff}}$
	Ungrossed	Grossed		
Employment status of persons aged 16 or over:				
Employed full time	48.99	49.21	0.53	2.07
Employed part time	10.47	10.35	0.19	1.25
Seeking work	2.44	2.39	0.12	1.49
Wholly retired	10.71	10.92	0.32	2.06
Housewife	21.02	20.78	0.41	1.96
Full time student	3.42	3.41	0.25	2.75
Socio-economic group of persons:				
Employer or manager (under 25 employees) (SEG2)	8.37	8.44	0.24	1.47
Junior non-manual (SEG6)	20.45	20.75	0.36	1.50
Skilled manual (SEG9)	19.99	19.74	0.53	2.22
Semi-skilled manual (SEG10)	11.83	11.79	0.40	2.05
Unskilled manual (SEG11)	6.59	6.55	0.24	1.65
Persons born outside UK	6.24	6.45	0.29	2.71
Ethnic group of persons:				
White	95.48	95.36	0.30	3.25
West Indian	1.10	1.13	0.11	2.42
African	0.16	0.17	0.04	2.02
Indian	1.13	1.16	0.12	2.52

TABLE 7B. Design effects for selected characteristics: Regions, London Boroughs and extensively surveyed Districts

Characteristic	Square root of design effect ($\sqrt{deff}$)					
	North West	East Midlands	Greater London	Harrow	Lewisham	Birmingham
Type of property:*						
Detached house	3.46	4.03	0.40	0.58	0.81	1.28
Semi-detached house	2.98	4.08	0.91	0.66	0.80	0.71
Terraced house	4.47	4.45	1.22	0.67	0.88	0.74
Lowest floor of accommodation:						
Ground floor	1.81	4.76	0.88	0.98	1.08	1.25
1st floor	1.82	2.34	1.43	0.78	1.02	1.13
4th-9th floor	0.88	2.27	1.19	1.21	0.82	0.74
Type of household:						
Married couple household	1.30	1.84	0.88	1.40	1.07	1.33
Lone parent household	0.81	1.49	1.08	1.09	0.87	1.07
One person aged under 60	1.42	1.28	1.37	1.61	1.22	1.14
One person aged 60 or over	1.73	0.97	1.26	0.85	1.09	0.99
Other household	0.98	0.71	0.59	0.89	1.34	0.79
Number of rooms:						
3	1.64	1.64	0.46	1.05	1.05	1.27
4	1.97	2.13	0.43	1.09	0.98	0.97
5	1.32	1.85	0.80	0.82	1.20	0.93
6	1.29	1.80	0.54	0.65	0.70	1.05
Type of sharing:						
Sharing rooms	1.90	2.18	2.01	1.47	2.47	1.40
Sharing circulation space	0.88	2.44	0.98	1.37	0.90	1.62
Bedsit	2.06	0.69	1.32	1.42	1.57	1.97
Use of bath or shower:						
Sole use	1.43	3.13	1.03	1.65	1.43	1.67
Shared use	1.77	2.58	1.40	1.80	1.62	1.70
None	1.52	2.57	0.88	0.96	0.95	0.95
With central heating	2.37	3.85	0.83	1.20	0.93	0.82

* In this table property refers to the whole rateable unit, and not the space occupied by the household.

252

Characteristic	Square root of design effect ($\sqrt{\text{deff}}$)					
	North West	East Midlands	Greater London	Harrow	Lewisham	Birmingham
Main form of room heating:						
Open fire	2.79	3.85	0.89	0.92	0.91	1.20
Electric	1.23	2.28	1.31	1.24	0.95	1.16
Gas	2.49	4.50	0.81	1.07	1.39	0.94
Tenure:						
Owned outright	1.73	2.75	1.09	1.12	0.99	0.89
Owned with mortgage or loan	1.60	4.54	1.26	1.06	0.66	0.63
Rented from council	1.13	5.53	1.33	0.85	0.77	0.71
Rented from housing association	1.06	1.93	1.35	1.20	1.21	1.01
Rented privately unfurnished	1.29	1.87	1.16	0.89	0.98	1.30
Rented privately furnished	1.85	1.73	1.34	1.12	1.67	1.41
No one in household on council waiting list	1.13	2.40	0.66	1.34	1.31	0.88
Dissatisfied with:						
Accommodation	0.84	1.70	0.96	0.68	0.95	1.02
Area	1.51	2.92	1.12	1.02	0.84	0.58
Difference from bedroom standard:						
2 or more below	1.42	1.20	1.25	0.49	1.03	0.48
1 below	0.85	1.23	0.97	1.11	0.97	0.72
Length of residence of head of household:						
Less than 1 year	0.90	1.42	1.31	0.69	1.16	1.15
1 but under 2 years	1.20	0.92	0.68	1.01	0.98	0.94
10 years or over	0.98	2.33	0.85	1.13	0.85	0.78
Age and sex of head of household:						
Male aged 65 or over	1.02	1.68	0.76	1.03	0.74	0.83
Female aged 60 or over	1.51	1.31	1.35	1.10	1.03	0.71

253

Characteristic	Square root of design effect ($\sqrt{\text{deff}}$)					
	North West	East Midlands	Greater London	Harrow	Lewisham	Birmingham
Employment status of persons aged 16 or over:						
Employed full time	1.26	2.19	0.81	1.14	1.19	0.81
Employed part time	1.31	1.48	0.62	0.91	1.28	0.91
Seeking work	1.26	1.95	1.18	1.27	0.86	0.96
Wholly retired	1.98	2.10	1.03	1.17	0.73	0.92
Housewife	1.62	2.76	1.10	0.86	1.28	0.58
Full time student	0.72	2.03	1.31	1.47	1.07	1.13
Socio-economic group of persons:						
Employer or manager (under 25 employees)(SEG2)	1.09	1.83	0.59	1.08	0.90	1.00
Junior non-manual (SEG6)	1.43	2.57	1.06	0.92	1.05	1.18
Skilled manual (SEG9)	1.45	2.97	1.04	1.12	0.67	0.92
Semi-skilled manual (SEG10)	0.76	2.23	1.22	0.78	0.94	1.00
Unskilled manual (SEG11)	1.07	2.22	1.27	1.15	0.96	0.98
Persons born outside UK	1.88	4.62	1.35	1.93	1.40	1.80
Ethnic group of persons:						
White	4.12	7.59	1.69	2.23	2.50	2.43
West Indian	2.34	5.38	1.68	1.99	2.12	1.98
African	1.70	1.62	1.78	1.80	2.01	1.73
Indian	5.55	3.87	1.80	1.53	2.19	2.62

APPENDIX A   Sample Sizes and Response Rates

Region	Number of households identified	Number of responding households	Number of persons in responding households	Response rate %
North	5,601	4,910	13,607	87.7
Yorkshire/Humberside	8,707	7,414	20,614	85.1
East Midlands	6,856	6,054	17,166	88.3
East Anglia	3,389	3,039	8,336	89.7
South East	31,017	25,249	69,433	81.4
Greater London	13,299	10,127	27,699	76.1
Rest of South East	17,718	15,122	41,734	85.3
South West	7,914	6,886	18,928	87.0
West Midlands	8,958	7,710	21,974	86.1
North West	11,676	10,032	28,200	85.9
England	84,118	71,294	198,258	84.8

District	Number of households identified	Number of responding households	Number of persons in responding households	Response rate %
Birmingham	6,880	5,879	16,711	85.5
Bradford	6,860	5,776	16,166	84.2
Bristol	7,126	5,903	15,867	82.8
Dudley	7,075	6,088	17,148	86.0
Gateshead	7,982	7,015	19,290	87.9
Kirklees	6,745	5,768	16,006	85.5
Leeds	6,832	5,707	15,763	83.5
Liverpool	6,706	5,492	15,763	81.9
Manchester	6,945	5,687	15,454	81.9
Newcastle-upon-Tyne	6,849	5,688	15,075	83.0
Salford	6,726	5,705	15,788	84.8
Sandwell	7,040	6,203	17,723	88.1
Sheffield	6,623	5,601	15,064	84.6
Sunderland	6,921	6,040	17,222	87.3
Wakefield	6,574	5,744	16,199	87.4
Wigan	6,837	5,873	16,607	85.9

255

Sample Sizes and Response Rates

London Borough	Number of household identified	Number of responding households	Number of persons in responding households	Response rate %
City of London	205	103	201	50.2
Barking	6,333	4,840	13,482	76.4
Barnet	6,995	5,092	14,362	72.8
Bexley	6,522	5,570	15,904	85.4
Brent	6,798	4,881	14,113	71.8
Bromley	6,542	5,269	14,581	80.5
Camden	7,249	4,685	10,859	64.6
Croydon	6,954	5,505	15,573	79.2
Ealing	6,895	5,088	14,362	73.8
Enfield	6,489	5,169	14,494	79.7
Greenwich	6,126	4,809	13,583	78.5
Hackney	6,597	4,901	13,598	74.3
Hammersmith	6,669	4,955	12,306	74.3
Haringey	6,922	5,182	14,063	74.9
Harrow	6,658	5,315	14,814	79.8
Havering	6,617	5,204	15,218	78.6
Hillingdon	6,937	5,575	15,833	80.4
Hounslow	6,688	5,181	14,325	77.5
Islington	6,674	5,042	13,041	75.5
Kensington & Chelsea	7,048	4,281	9,560	60.7
Kingston-upon-Thames	6,705	5,383	14,049	80.3
Lambeth	6,546	5,111	13,457	78.1
Lewisham	6,249	4,905	13,594	78.5
Merton	6,548	5,041	13,569	77.0
Newham	6,124	4,972	14,433	81.2
Redbridge	6,551	5,121	14,394	78.2
Richmond	6,913	5,557	13,788	80.4
Southwark	5,729	4,343	11,524	75.8
Sutton	6,329	4,867	13,129	76.9
Tower Hamlets	6,124	4,569	12,526	74.6
Waltham Forest	6,607	5,061	13,936	76.6
Wandsworth	6,609	4,960	13,402	75.0
Westminster	6,066	3,701	7,955	61.0
Greater London	211,018	160,238	434,028	75.9

APPENDIX B.

INTERVIEWERS INSTRUCTIONS

CONTENTS

Background to the survey

Check list of documentation

Preparations

Introducing yourself to the household

THE QUESTIONNAIRE

General points

Front page of questionnaire

> The household
> Head of household
> Other households at the address/multi household procedure
> A building
> Accommodation/rooms
> Moving between your rooms
> Basic amenities
> Central Heating
> Own or rent
> Landlord sharing
> Council housing lists
> Satisfaction with accommodation incl. size
> Difficulties with steps/stairs
> Cars/vans
> Age
> Respondent
> Housewife
> Family units
> Sex
> Marital status
> Length of residence
> Movers
> Paid job last week
> Employee/Self employed
> Full time student/still at school
> Registered unemployed
> Those not working last week
> Occupation
> Country of birth
> Ethnic origin

Purpose of questions

BACKGROUND TO THE SURVEY

The Dwelling and Housing Survey has been commissioned by the Department of Environment. It is being carried out by three research agencies, (NOP, RSGB and SCPR), each of which is responsible for one-third of the fieldwork.

The latest detailed statistics about the housing situation were collected six years ago in the 1971 Census of Population and the Department needs up-to-date information on changes since then. This lack of up-to-date information was highlighted in the recently published Housing Green Paper and the need for a national housing survey was stressed there.

The survey will provide key information on housing conditions and household composition which will form the statistical basis for housing policies over the next few years. For example, it will provide information about the effects of the 1974 Rent Act and assist in the current review of the Rent Acts. It will also assist the Department in assessing housing needs in different parts of the country.

THE SAMPLE

The sample has been selected to provide information about the housing situation throughout England, and in areas where housing pressures are known to be especially severe. One out of every 200 addresses in England have been selected to provide the national and regional statistics, and about 7,000 addresses have been selected in each London Borough and other areas of housing stress.

THE INTERVIEWS

Interviews will take place between September 1977 and April 1978.

YOUR LIST OF ADDRESSES

The addresses on your list were selected at random from the rating lists for the area. You must investigate and return at least one questionnaire for each one. You must NOT replace any addresses with others not on your lists.

Information in the second and third columns of the left hand page of the sample address lists is to enable you to locate the address.

Information in the "Notes and Comments" column on the right hand page is to enable you to distinguish parts of the building where you should not be interviewing.

The remaining columns on the sample address lists need not concern you.

CHECK LIST OF DOCUMENTATION

Name	Description
Questionnaire	The main form in the survey, used and completed by the interviewer for each address and every household within the address.
Continuation Sheets	Continuation of questionnaire, to be used by the interviewer in recording information for households with more than 6 people.
Sample Address List	List of addresses to be called at by each interviewer.
Multi-household Envelope	Provided for addresses which contain more than one household, and for recording the whereabouts of each household.

Show Card which contains:-

Card 1	Satisfaction with accommodation. To assist respondents in answering Q.17(a) and (b).
Card 2	Employment Status. To assist respondents in answering Q.34.
Card 3	Ethnic group. To assist respondents in answering Q.37.
Interviewer's Instructions	Details on completing the questionnaire, question by question.
DOE Headed Letter	Letter for distributing to respondents after the interview, explaining in detail the purpose of the survey.
Interviewer Identity Card	For identification purposes if necessary.
Return envelopes	To return completed questionnaires to the office.

PREPARATIONS

1. Inform the local police that you will be interviewing in the area.

2. Before going out each day ensure that you have the following equipment:

    a) Sufficient blank questionnaires for the day, and continuation sheets.
Your Name and Interviewer Authority Number and the Rating Area number can be inserted on the questionnaire in advance.

    b) Any part-completed questionnaires for households you have previously seen but have arranged to call back on.

    c) Sets of part-completed questionnaires for any multi-household addresses which you intend to re-visit to obtain interviews with households not yet contacted.

    d) Your list of sample addresses.

    e) Show Card.

    f) Your Identity Card.

    g) A supply of multi-household envelopes.

    h) A supply of DOE headed letters (to leave with each respondent, explaining the purpose of the survey).

    i) Blue or black biros (or black felt-tip pens) for completing the questionnaires.
Never use red or green biro/felt-tip pens.
Never use pencil.

    j) Your Interviewer's Instruction manual.

INTRODUCING YOURSELF TO THE HOUSEHOLDER

1. Before commencing the interview you should make the following points:

   a)   The survey is being carried out on behalf of the Department
        of Environment.

   b)   The interview should take about 10 - 15 minutes.

   c)   The interview deals with questions about housing, amenities
        and households.

   If contact is still rather hesitant about co-operating, you can also tell
   them that:

   d)   Replies will be treated as strictly confidential.

   e)   Participation is voluntary, but it is important that everyone
        who is approached should take part.

   f)   The householder's address was selected at random from the
        rating list for the area.

2. Whom to interview:-

   You should ask to speak preferably to the Head of Household or his wife;
   otherwise a responsible adult (ie 16 or over). But you should try and
   interview one of the parents if a child aged 16+ answers the door.

   Where a person living alone is e.g. too old, too sick, too deaf to be
   interviewed and there is someone with whom you could do an interview on
   that person's behalf (e.g. relative, neighbour, health visitor) you may
   do so.

   If the parents do not speak English but a child does, that child may act
   as interpreter if he is approximately 14 or 15 or over and if you feel
   he is capable of understanding and interpreting the questions.

   When in doubt about whom to interview, contact your supervisor.

3. You must not ask for the respondent's name.

4. After each interview leave with each respondent a DOE headed letter,
   explaining the purpose of the survey and thanking them for participating.

   Do not leave the letter before the interview (e.g. when making an
   appointment to call back later) unless you are asked for it.

   Enter your Interviewer Number (which appears on your Identity Card)
   in the top right hand corner of each letter.

THE QUESTIONNAIRE

GENERAL POINTS

1.   References to CARD 1, CARD 2, CARD 3 in small boxes at the bottom
        of each page of the questionnaire relate to punched - CARD instruc-
        tions, and should be ignored by interviewers.

2.   Recording:

        a)   cross out codes by putting two parallel
                diagonal lines through a code.

        b)   write numbers clearly.

3.   If you are in any doubt as to how to code a question, write full
        notes.

4.   Make sure you provide an answer to every question that applies e.g.
        Q.20 - even if it is clear that the respondent household has no van,
        still put a '0' in the box at part (b).

FRONT PAGE OF THE QUESTIONNAIRE

I   For each household, transfer the following information from the
     sample address list to the top of Page 1 of the questionnaire:-

     1.   Rating Area Number (4 digits from top centre of address
           list)

     2.   Sample Issue Number (from first column of address list)
           N.B. This should be a 4-digit number and you may need to
           add zeros in front of the number you have been given. E.g.
           if the number of the address list is 37, you should enter
           0037 in the Sample Issue number boxes.

II   Then complete the Household Number as follows:

     Number the first questionnaire to be used at each address as 1. If
     you find more than one household at the address, number the additional
     questionnaires as 2, 3 etc., in the box for Household Number.

III LOCATION WITHIN THE ADDRESS: In multi-household addresses, give
     enough details at the top of each questionnaire for the address
     to enable someone else to carry out backchecks at the address. We
     want the precise location of each household.

IV   CALL RECORD: Enter details for each call made for each household at
     the address. At least four calls should be made before returning a
     questionnaire as a Non-contact; at least 2 of these calls should be
     in the evening or at weekends.

     If you have established at an early call that no one will be at that
     address until after the end of the interviewing period (e.g. because
     they are in hospital), there is no need to call at least 4 times.

V   TOTAL NUMBER OF CALLS: This should be completed after you have made
     your final call at the household.

     Do not forget to enter your name and authorisation number on the
     dotted lines.

VI   FINAL OUTCOME: This should be completed after your final call at
     the address.

     Vacant Accommodation: You must be sure that accommodation is not
     occupied before treating as vacant. Check with a neighbour wherever
     possible. Do not assume that because the garden is unkempt, the
     windows are unclean, there are no curtains etc., that the accom-
     modation is vacant.

NB: You should treat the accommodation as vacant as soon as you establish that fact and you should not recall at a later stage.

Most addresses will be entirely residential accommodation - houses, flats, maisonettes, rooms and so on.

The remaining addresses may be partly residential, entirely non-residential or institutions. You should find out if anyone lives there and deal with them as follows:

If it is partly residential, such as a school with a resident care-taker or an industrial establishment with a resident security officer, INTERVIEW SOMEONE FROM EACH HOUSEHOLD.

If no-one lives permanently in any part of the address (e.g. a lock-up shop, school without caretaker's flat, offices without living accommodation, church) code it "Property non-residential" (Code 9). NO INTERVIEW IS REQUIRED.

If it is a hospital, children's home, nursing home, hotel or boarding house with capacity for 5 or more guests, or any other establishment where there is communal catering such as a nurses' home, a boarding school or students' hostel, code it "Property is an institution" (Code 0). NO INTERVIEW IS REQUIRED.

If it is an Institution (e.g. Abbeyfield Homes) where there are some communal catering arrangements and where residents have their own individual cooking facilities, INTERVIEW SOMEONE FROM EACH HOUSEHOLD (subject to a maximum of 9 interviews - if there are more than 9 households, contact your Supervisor and await instructions).

If you cannot find an address when you visit the area, or are not sure to which building it refers, inform your supervisor as quickly as possible, after checking first with e.g. the local police station, fire station, post office etc. A property which is coded "TOR" in the "Notes and comments" column of your address list has been taken out of rating and may have been demolished. But do not assume it has been demolished: always check. If it has not yet been demolished, you should still seek to interview at the address.

VII   MONTH OF INTERVIEW: Do not forget to code this for each household at the address.

VIII   ADDRESS GIVEN IS:

"WHOLE HOUSE" includes "bungalow" i.e. one of codes 1 - 3 should be ringed for "bungalow"

"PURPOSE-BUILT FLAT OR MAISONETTE" includes purpose-built maisonette.

The "ADDRESS GIVEN" refers to the precise description of the address as stated on the sample address list. Thus, if the description of the address is "3, Smith Street" and this is a detached house within which the respondent has a room, then code 1 applies, not code 8; but if the description of the address is given as "Rooms at 3, Smith Street," then code 8 applies.

For multi-household addresses, every questionnaire for that address should have the same code at "ADDRESS GIVEN IS".

IX   LOWEST FLOOR:

Bear in mind we are using the British definition, not the European/ American one which refers to the ground floor as the first floor, whereas we define the first floor as the one above the ground floor.

This cannot necessarily be coded from observation (as stated on the questionnaire) since each household within a multi-household address may have the lowest floor of its accommodation on a different floor.

EXCLUDE garages, and communal accommodation such as a communal utility room. But a utility room that belongs solely to the house-hold's accommodation should be included.

MEMBERS OF THE HOUSEHOLD

Q.1   The number of people in the household should be entered in the two right hand boxes. If the number is less than 10, the first box should contain a '0'.

The relationship of each member of the household to the Head of Household should be entered on the dotted lines across the top of page 13. (HOH is pre-printed as Person number 1). It is important to record the relationships at this stage of the interview, because it will help you to:

a)   ensure both you and the respondent are clear about the composition of the respondent's household.

b)   ask the questions about the household's accommodation.

c)   ask the series of questions from Q.21 to the end.

HOUSEHOLD

A household is a group of people who all live regularly at the address given on the sample issue sheet, and who are all catered for, for at least one meal a day, by the same person.

This procedure requires slight modification when a interviewer encounters groups of students/young people sharing a flat. In such cases, all the occupants are included as one household if they have common catering arrange-ments in the sense of the food being purchased and stored communally, even though these people do not necessarily share "at least one meal a day". They should, however, eat the occasional meal together, but it does not have to be prepared by the same person each time. If, on the other hand, each person buys his own food and keeps it separate from that of the others, then each person forms a separate household.

Any other individual or group of individuals at the same address who has different catering arrangements forms a separate household.

"Living there regularly" means:

a)   for relatives and other persons, they are included if
      they spend at least 4 nights every week in this house-
      hold - even if they are regularly away from it for the
      remaining 3 or less nights. It is four nights every
      week which counts for household membership and not an
      average of 4 nights per week over a period of time.

b)   for married persons, they are included if they return
      to their spouse at this household at least one night
      every week. This covers spouses who work away from
      home and can only return home weekends.

Include in the household:

a)   People on holiday, away on a rare business trip or in
      hospital at time of interview, who normally live in the
      household (satisfying the rules above), unless they have
      been away for more than 6 months. (If it is precisely
      6 months on the day of interview, they should be included).

b)   Fishermen and any merchant seamen whose only shore address
      this is and who normally spend up to and including, but
      not more than, six weeks at sea on any one voyage.

c)   Children under 16 away at boarding or other schools.

d)   Boarders (i.e. people staying with the household who
      satisfy the 'catering' and 'regularity' rules) provided
      there are no more than 4 of them living as part of the
      household. (If there are 5 or more, the address is an
      Institution and no interview is required).

Exclude from the household:

a)   Members of the family of 16 years and over who live
      away from home and who only come home for holidays
      (this will cover persons away at school, or college,
      as well as those working away from home).

b)   Members of the Forces (and Merchant Navy) stationed
      permanently away from the address. (Of course, if they
      were stationed permanently at the address they would be
      included in the household).

c)   Temporary members of the household. Relatives who do
      not normally live there, and persons home on leave from
      abroad etc. They would only be included in the house-
      hold if they had been there for more than six months
      prior to the date of interview.

(NOTE: This 6 month's rule applies only to temporary members
          of the household. Anyone who has joined the house-
          hold within the last six months as a regular member
          i.e. someone with no intention of leaving the house-
          hold, is no longer considered a temporary member of
          the household).

266

d)   Lodgers (i.e. persons who reside at the address but who cater for themselves); each of these units form a separate household.

HEAD OF HOUSEHOLD (H.O.H.)

The Head of the Household must be a member of the household (by our definition). The Head of the Household is, in order of precedence, the husband of the person, or the person who either;

a)   Owns the household accommodation.

b)   Is legally responsible for the rent of the accommodation.

c)   Has the household accommodation as an emolument or perquisite.

d)   Has the household accommodation by virtue of some relation-ship to the owner in cases where the owner or lessee is not a member of the household.

POINTS TO REMEMBER

e)   The important fact to establish is in whose name the property is owned or rented. To obtain this infor-mation you should normally ask "In whose name is this house/flat owned or rented". Do NOT ask "Who is res-ponsible for PAYING the rent?" since the person who pays out the money may not be responsible for the house in name.

        If your informant is living in only part of the house, i.e. if there is more than one household at the address, you must make the point of the question clear by saying "For the part of the house in which you live (with your husband and your mother-in-law etc.) may I know in whose name it is owned or rented?"

f)   When the accommodation is in the name of a person who is not a member of the household (by our definition), you must establish another H.O.H. from within the household, taking the person within it who stands responsible for the house in the other person's absence. For example, if you are told the house is in the name of a husband who is stationed away from home, he is not a member of the household, and in this case you can take as the H.O.H. his wife who is living there.

g)   So long as the husband is resident he takes precedence over the wife in being H.O.H. This means if you have a married couple living together, even if the wife owns the property or has her name on the rent book, you count her husband as the H.O.H.

Where the household consists only of mother, father and children under 18 years, no questions as to who is the H.O.H. need be asked since, by the above rule, you take the father as the H.O.H. In all cases where there is any other adult (except boarders) living in the household you must ask "in whose name etc." since the house could be in the name of one of the other adults.

h)   When two persons of different sex have an equal claim to being H.O.H., i.e. if you are told ownership is joint, then you take the male of the two to be the H.O.H.

i)   When two persons of the same sex have equal claim to be H.O.H., i.e. if you are told ownership is joint, then you take the elder of the two as H.O.H.

OTHER HOUSEHOLDS AT THE ADDRESS

Q.2 & 3   The purpose of these questions is to ascertain whether other households live at the sample address, or, in the case of Q.3, whether an empty flat or bedsitter exists which could be occupied by another household at the sample address.

By 'address' we mean the precise address shown on the Sample Issue Sheet. To establish whether there are any other households or empty flats at the sample address, you must be sure to quote the exact address and description as given on the sample issue sheet.

e.g. if the address you are given is Flat 1, 23 Mill Lane, and the description is "Ground Floor Flat," then we need to know whether there are any other households at: Flat 1, 23 Mill Lane not just at: 23 Mill Lane. So if 23 Mill Lane is a house with 3 flats, (Flat 1 on the ground floor, Flat 2 on the first floor, Flat 3 on the second floor), then Flats 2 and 3 should not be included as they are not at the sample address.

However, if the address you have is 23, Mill Lane, and you obtain an interview at Flat 1 first, then Flats 2 and 3 are other households at the address and you should seek to interview at both of these.

If you establish that other households do exist, you should seek to obtain an interview with them after the interview with your present respondent. If you obtain information about empty flats/bedsitters at Q.3, you should always check to make sure the flat is empty; if it is, in fact, now occupied, you should interview the household living there.

At Q.2 and 3 obtain as much information as you can about the location of the other households. (You must repeat Q.2 and 3 for every household interviewed at one address).

The number of other households/empty flats should be entered in the box to the right of the appropriate question, or the code 0 ringed in that box.

A questionnaire should be returned for every household and empty flat/bedsitter at an address, whether or not an interview is achieved.

MULTI-HOUSEHOLD ENVELOPE

Where there is more than one household at the sample address, enter details of the precise location of each household space on the front of a multi-household envelope.

N.B.

1.   In the top right-hand corner of the multi-household envelope you should record the Rating Area number and the Sample Issue number of the address.

2.   Do not record the address on the envelope since we do not want the address to appear on any of the documents.

If you find there are 10 or more households at an address, contact your supervisor/team leader immediately after the interview you have been conducting and he/she will advise you as to whether these are in fact separate households within the address and if so at which household spaces to interview. You should give your supervisor as many details as you can of how these household spaces are arranged within the address e.g. "Flats 1, 2 and 3 on Ground Floor; bedsitters 4A, 4B, 4C, 4D, 4E on First Floor; 3 separate bedsitters un-numbered on Second Floor".

Q.4   BUILDING

         A building is:

         A house or bungalow (detached, semi-detached, or terraced):

         A block of flats or maisonnettes:

         Non-residential premises with living accommodation associated with them:

         A permanently sited caravan, chalet or shack.

         The purpose of the question is to establish whether the household occupies more rooms in the building than those at the sample address. This might happen, for example, where the sample address is part of a house that has recently been converted back to a single accommodation unit. Therefore, you may call at the first floor flat only to find that that household occupies the whole house.

Q.5 - 7   ACCOMMODATION

         Accommodation is the complete housing unit which the household either owns, pays rent for or occupies rent free.

         In recording the number of rooms care should be taken not to double count any rooms serving two purposes, e.g. if a living room is also used as a dining room it is to be counted once only; if a kitchen-dining room has been counted as a kitchen (because it conforms to the definition of a kitchen), do not also include it as a dining room.

A large room which can be divided by a sliding or folding fixed partition should count as two rooms. A room divided by curtains or portable screens into separate sections should count as one room. Rooms separated by an open archway count as only one room, not two.

Any rooms entirely sublet to a TENANT WHO IS NOT PART OF THE RESPONDENT"S HOUSEHOLD should be excluded, (and included when the tenant is interviewed).

Q.5   BEDROOMS

Record all rooms which are furnished as bedrooms, or regarded as such, whether or not they are slept in. Bed-sitting rooms count as bedrooms and not kitchens even if they have cooking facilities. Bed-alcoves are not "rooms" by our definition, and a bed-alcove does not therefore count as a bedroom, unless it is part of a bed-sitting room which is included at Q.5.

Q.6   KITCHENS

A kitchen is any separate room used for cooking and other terms may be used e.g. scullery.

ALWAYS ASK ABOUT THE WIDTH OF THE KITCHEN. If you can touch both walls with your arms outstretched you can be sure that it is less than $6\frac{1}{2}$ feet wide. In L-shaped or wedge-shaped kitchens take a mid-point and if in doubt count as over $6\frac{1}{2}$ feet and hence as a room. A hall or a landing with cooking facilities is not a kitchen and must not be included.

Q.7   ROOMS OTHER THAN BEDROOMS AND KITCHENS

1.   List all rooms the respondent mentions.

2.   The figure in the right hand box should be the total number of other rooms not counting the ones listed below.

3.   Even though you should not include in the total number of 'other rooms' bathrooms, toilets, etc. there is no need to tell the respondent that you are not including these.

Rooms to be excluded from total:-

-      bathrooms, lavatories, toilets, closets, laundry rooms, and drying rooms.

-      storerooms, pantries and rooms without windows.

-      rooms not usable all the year round.

-      rooms used solely for business purposes (such as offices or shops).

- halls unless they are used as living rooms.

- garages or summerhouses in the garden.

Q.8   SHARED ROOMS

This question establishes the number of rooms the respondent's household shares with other households.

The use of the phrase "Can I just check", before this question and Q.9, is necessary in cases where Q.2 and 3 have revealed that there are no other households at the address. It does not mean that Q.8 and 9 are check questions.

Part(a) The rooms which should be excluded from the total in the box also cover kitchens less than 6½ feet wide, as well as those covered at Q.7.

The same procedure applies as for Q.7.

NB: If after excluding bathrooms, toilets, etc. you have no rooms left on your list, enter code '0' in the box at (a).

Q.9   MOVING BETWEEN YOUR ROOMS

This refers literally to the space between the respondent's rooms and not to the access to his rooms. e.g. not hall and stairs to his accommodation.

Follow the filtering carefully e.g. if the answer to part (a) is "No", there is no need to ask part (b).

Q.9(c)   "Other" households means other actual households (i.e. exclude "empty flats/bedsitters").

Q.10   BASIC AMENITIES

SOLE USE/SHARED: If there is more then one household in the building and the respondent answers 'Yes' to any of the items (i) - (vi), you should ask "Do you share it with another household?"

The "SOLE USE" code has priority over the code for "SHARED" e.g. if a household has exclusive use of one bath but also shares a second with another household, code as "SOLE USE". If the household does not have sole use of an amenity, check that this answer corresponds with information at Q.8(a) e.g. if the household shares a bathroom (and provided they do not have sole use of another bathroom) then Q.10(iii) should be coded "SHARED".

"A flush toilet" - If there is SOLE USE of a flush toilet with an entrance inside the building (code 1 at item (v)), there is no need to establish whether there is a flush toilet with an entrance outside the building (i.e. do not ask item (vi)).

271

(ii)   A plumbed-in kitchen sink:

A sink counts if it has at least one water tap AND
a waste pipe to a drain.

Exclude wash basins even if they function as a
kitchen sink.

(iii)   A fixed bath or shower:

This must have at least one water tap AND a fixed
waste pipe.

(iv)   A piped hot water supply:

This counts even if it supplies water to only one
tap; thus a geyser over a bath, a sink water heater,
or a full supply from a boiler or immersion heater
all count. A hot water system temporarily out of
action should be included.

A piped hot-water supply is "shared" if more than
one household has access to the water at the point
at which it leaves the tap; if water is heated
for a number of households at a common source (e.g.
an oil-fired boiler in a block of flats) this does
not in itself constitute "sharing".

(v) & (vi)   A flush toilet:

A flush toilet is any toilet which can be flushed
into a sewer or cesspit, even if the system is
temporarily broken.

Earth and chemical closets do NOT count as flush
toilets.

The purpose of this question is to establish whether
members of the household need to go out of doors to
get to the toilet.

If the toilet has 2 entrances, one to the inside and
one to the outside, code as having an entrance inside.

Q.11   CENTRAL HEATING

Central heating includes any system where two or more rooms,
halls or landings in the building are heated from a central
source such as a boiler, a back boiler to an open fire, or
electricity supply (this excludes any appliance plugged into
the mains circuit at the wall).

Several households may share a central heating system.

'Solid fuel' means coal, coke, anthracite or other coal-
based products.

272

'Electric storage heaters' counts as central heating.

'Other electric' includes electric underfloor heating.

Gas includes calor/bottled gas.

Part (a): can be multicoded.

Q.12   If the answer is "SOLID FUEL" in order to decide which of codes
        1 or 2 apply, you will need to ask "Is it an open fire or a
        closed stove?"

        Code the main form of heating used. Emphasise the word "mainly"
        when you read out the question. If the respondent insists two
        forms of heating are used equally, code both.

Q.13   OWN OR RENT

        This question refers to the actual accommodation the household
        occupies, not necessarily the building in which it is located.

        "Owned outright/is buying" includes:

        (i)   Co-ownership

        (ii)   Leasehold property if the original lease was for a
                period of more than 21 years, or if it was extended
                to more than 21 years. If the lease was for less
                than 21 years, Q.13 should be recoded to "Rents/
                rent free".

        Part (b):

        "Mortgage" includes any long-term bank, insurance or private
        loan as well as a building society mortgage. If the owner
        is borrowing only temporarily, code as "owned outright" (e.g.
        if a bridging loan has been obtained until the owner sells
        another property).

Q.14   RENTED/RENT FREE

        If the answer to Q.13 is "Rent-free", then ask Q.14 as:
        "Is it provided furnished or unfurnished?" Similarly,
        at Q.14(c), use the word "provided" instead of "rented".

        Part (b) Whether house/flat goes with job:

        Code "YES" only if the household lives there because of the
        present job of one of the household. Code "NO" for an ex-
        employee allowed to stay on after retirement, or a widow of
        an employee allowed to remain after her husband's death.

        Part (c) From whom rented:

        If the accommodation is rent-free or goes with the job of a
        household member, the "landlord" is the person or company who
        provides the accommodation. e.g. police houses or school

273

caretaker's accommodation should be coded as "EMPLOYER" (code 6), and not as "COUNCIL" (codes 1 and 2); resident caretakers of private property should be coded as "EMPLOYER" (either code 6 or 8), and not any of the other categories.

The "landlord" excludes agents who collect the rent on behalf of a company or individual. Therefore, if the name of a company or firm is given, you will need to probe whether that company is the owner or the owner's agent. If the respondent deals exclusively with an agent and does not know who the landlord is, do not code "PROPERTY COMPANY" (code 4), but code as 'OTHER - GIVE DETAILS' (code 0).

NB Code 9 covers any individual who is not an employer or a relative, and is a code which you will use quite often.

Q.15   LANDLORD SHARING

See Q.4 for definition of 'building'.

A landlord who lives in a separate self-contained part of a converted house still counts as living in the same building as the tenant.

See Q.9 for definition of "moving between your rooms".

Q.16   COUNCIL HOUSING LISTS

If someone in the household has their name on a council house waiting list etc., you will need to ask the additional question to the left of the codes in order to establish whether it is the H.O.H. or another member of the household (or both) that has their name on the list.

Do not ring more than one code. Code 3 is provided for cases where both H.O.H. and another member (or other members) of the household are on a list.

Include 1) those on a list for a Council old people's home.

         2) people who have applied to go on to the transfer list but do not know whether they are actually on it.

Q.17   SATISFACTION WITH ACCOMMODATION/AREA

Hand Card 1 to the respondent so that they can answer parts (a) and (b) in terms of the categories listed on the card.

Part (b) If the respondent asks what is meant by "this area", you should say "whatever you choose to think of as this area".

Q.18   SIZE OF ACCOMMODATION

You should read out the words "your household" at the end of

274

parts (a) and (b) if there is more than one person in the household; the word "you" should be read out only if it is a single person household.

Part (b)   We want the respondent's overall view of the size of their rooms. But some of them may qualify their answers. Apart from using code 4 to cover "Some too large, some too small", you should deal with qualified answers as follows:-

        Code 1 includes "Some too small, some about right".

        Code 2 includes "Some too large, some about right".

Q.19   DIFFICULTY WITH STAIRS, STEPS ETC.

We want to know about difficulties people have regularly, and not just on isolated occasions. We are interested in parts of the building that cause them difficulties, regardless of whether that person is incapacitated or not. For some, e.g. elderly, sick people, the "getting about generally" code will apply.

Q.20   CARS AND VANS

If the answer to the main question is "YES", you need to ask (a) and (b) in order to make sure you have accounted for all vehicles.

A "Van" means a light van. It is a 3 or 4 wheeled motorised vehicle with no side windows to the rear of the driver's seat. Thus, Land Rovers and jeeps are 'vans'; Range Rovers and caravanettes are 'cars'.

Include all cars/vans normally available for private use by the household, but not necessarily owned by the household.

Exclude all cars/vans used solely for work or hire by other people.

Include: a)   cars/vans owned by an employer that the household has full use of

            b)   cars/vans on long-term (contract) hire

            c)   cars/vans temporarily out of action

            d)   cars/vans which are not taxed but are in road-worthy condition and are due to be taxed in the future

            e)   3-wheeled cars/vans

Exclude: a)   temporary hirings

            b)   cars/vans permanently untaxed or not road-worthy

            c)   motor cycles or scooters

Part (c)

If the answer is "Yes" and there is only one car/van, code "Yes, all". If the answer is "Yes" and there is more than one car/van, before you decide whether to code "Yes, all" or "Yes, some" you should ask "Is that for all the cars/vans, or only some of them?"

A garage or off-street parking space is a place, not on the public highway or verge, where a vehicle can be parked. e.g. car ports; lean-to garages; land in front of/behind the house; communal car park.

Include all garages available for parking the household's vehicles.

A parking space does not necessarily mean one specifically designated for the household, e.g. if a block of flats has a car park for the residents each household could park its car anywhere in this car park.

Q.21-37   From here to the end of the questionnaire, you have to code on the right hand pages answers to each question for each member of the household.

The relationship of each member of the household to the H.O.H. should already be recorded across the top of Page 13 so that it is clearly visible for the purposes of asking Q.21 onwards.

It is recommended that for Q.21-28 you work across the right hand page.

Interviewers may find the following procedure works best when dealing with the employment status questions (Q.30-35). Ask Q.30-34 down the page for the first person aged 16 or over, then turn over and ask Q.35A or B or C (as appropriate) for that person.

Turn back to Q.30 for the second person aged 16 or over, and repeat; continue in this way for each further person aged 16 or over.

Then ask Q.36 and 37 across the page.

N.B: Do not ask Q.36 and 37 before finishing Q.30-35 for all persons in the household.

Q.21   AGE

Enter the age last birthday for each household member in the boxes below "Relationship". These boxes are deliberately placed so that, when you come to ask Q.30 onwards and need to distinguish those aged 16 or more from the rest, the ages are clearly visible.

If the respondent refuses to reveal his age, enter your estimate and the letter 'E' beside it. For household members not seen whose age is not known to the respondent, probe for the approximate age; try at least to establish whether the person is 16 or more, or under 16, so that you know whether Q.30-35 apply.

Children less than 1 year old should be coded 00.

People over 99 years old should be coded 99.

Q.22   RESPONDENT

Ring the code 1 under the column for whichever person is the respondent.

N.B: Only one code 1 may be ringed.

Q.23   HOUSEWIFE

Each household must have a Housewife.

Ring the code 2 under the column for whichever person is the housewife.

N.B: 1)   Only one code 2 may be ringed.

        2)   It is possible for the housewife also
              to be the respondent and in cases of a
              single person household, that person
              will be H.O.H. Housewife and Respondent.

        3)   The Housewife can be a male member of the
              household.

The housewife is the person, other than a domestic servant, who is responsible for most of the domestic duties:

(a)   If these tasks are done by a paid servant, the
       servant is not the housewife. In such a case
       the housewife is the person responsible for
       seeing that the servant performs these tasks.

POINTS TO REMEMBER

(b)   The important fact is who is responsible for MOST
       of the domestic duties in the household.

       The point of the definition of housewife is lost if
       you single out separate items such as cleaning or
       cooking, therefore, ask:

       "Who is mainly responsible for the domestic duties?"

       or, for a multi-household:

       "Which of you is responsible for the domestic duties
       in this part of the house?"

The informant must be allowed to interpret "most of the domestic duties" for himself.

(c)   In cases of equal responsibility:

  (i)   Wife takes precedence over husband

  (ii)   female (e.g. sister) takes precedence over male (e.g. brother).

  (iii)   if both/all are of the same sex, older persons take precedence over younger persons.

Q.24   FAMILY UNITS

A family unit number must be entered in the box for every person in the household.

A family unit can consist of:

A married couple with or without never married children (natural or adopted, but not fostered). The marriage can be common-law.

or

A lone parent (single, widowed, separated or divorced, or married but not living with spouse/partner) living with never married children.

N.B: 1)   A brother and sister (whose parents are not part of the household) would form 2 separate family units.

  2)   In general, family units cannot span more than two generations, i.e. grand-parents and grand-children cannot belong to the same family unit. The exception to this is when it is established that the grant-parents are responsible for looking after the grand-children (e.g. while the parents are abroad etc.)

  3)   Where a couple who live together are not married but have children, treat them as one family unit if they regard themselves as a "couple". If they do not regard themselves as a couple but one of them has children, treat them as two family units with the children belonging to the same unit as the natural parent, or, if this is not clear, to the same unit as the mother.

Numbering of family units

Members of the H.O.H.'s family unit should be numbered 1; the next family unit 2, and so on.

278

EXAMPLES

1. PER NO.   Relationship to H.O.H.   Family Unit

        1   H.O.H.   1
        2   Wife   1
        3   Son (single)   1
        4   Mother   2

2. PER NO.   Relationship to H.O.H.   Family Unit

        1   H.O.H.   1
        2   Wife   1
        3   Son (single)   1
        4   Sister (widow)   2
        5   Brother   ) Married to   3
        6   Sister-in-law   ) each other   3
        7   Niece (single, daughter of person 4) 2

Q.25   SEX

        Code either 1 or 2 for each person in the household. There is
        no need to ask this question if the sex of each person is clear
        to you, but remember to code the appropriate numbers.

Q.26   MARITAL STATUS

        Code one of codes 1-5 for each person in the household.

        Ask this as a question and read out all the alternatives.

        Common-law marriages/couples living together as man and wife
        should be coded as married. If they do not regard them-
        selves as living together as man and wife, code them as
        single, divorced, widowed or separated - as appropriate.

        If someone says they are living apart from their spouse,
        code as "married" unless they are legally separated.

Q.27   LENGTH OF RESIDENCE

        This question is asked of everyone.

Q.28   DATE OF MOVING

        For each person who has MOVED within the last 2 years, obtain
        the month and year of their moving to their present address,
        and enter the answer on the dotted lines on the facing page.

        N.B: This question should not be asked about children born
        at this address within the last 2 years.

Q.29   ADDRESS 12 MONTHS AGO

        For each person who has moved within the last year, obtain their
        address one year ago, even if they have moved again since.

Q.30   PAID JOB LAST WEEK

This question, and those up to and including Q.35, are only
asked of those aged 16 or more.

Those to be regarded as working last week are:-

i)   Those who worked in private or public employment
        for wages, salary or any other form of payment, such
        as commission or tips.

        Casual or seasonal workers should be coded as "working"
        only if they were working during the week ending last
        Sunday.

ii)   Those who worked in his or her own business or firm
        for profit.

iii)   Those who were absent because of holiday, strike,
        sickness, temporarily laid off, or any other similar
        reason, provided he or she has a job to return to
        with the same employer.

        N.B: The distinction between the temporarily sick
        who should be included at Q.30 and the "Temporary
        sickness" code 3 at Q.34 is that in the former case the
        person has a job to go back to, whereas in the latter
        case the person has no job to go back to and would be
        seeking work were it not for illness.

Full-time/part-time:

Full-time means over 30 hours per week.

Part-time means 30 hours or fewer per week.

Include teachers as full-time if they work at least 25 hours
a week.

If someone has both a full-time and a part-time job, code for
the full-time one only.

Q.31   EMPLOYEE OR SELF-EMPLOYED

An employee is defined as someone who is not self-employed and
recognises that he/she has an employer (whether the employer
is a company or an individual).

Self-employment includes members of partnerships and work in
any kind of business for profit as opposed to the wages,
salaries, commission or tips earned by an employee.

If someone was both an employee and self-employed last week,
ask which job took up most time; do not code both answers.

Q.32   WHETHER FULL-TIME STUDENT/STILL AT SCHOOL

This should be asked about each person with a paid job last week,
even if the answer appears obvious. Some students may simply
have been in vacation jobs last week, or children still at school
may have worked on Saturday morning.

Those to be included in the 'YES' code are those aged 16 or over
who even though they were working last week, are still studying
full-time at a school, college, university, polytechnic or other
educational institution. This includes people on sandwich
courses.

Purely vocational training courses given by an employer as part
of the job do not count (e.g. nurses' training, police courses).

Q.33   WHETHER REGISTERED UNEMPLOYED

This is asked of those who did not have a paid job in the week
ending last Sunday.

Registered unemployed means registered as seeking work,
irrespective of whether they are registered to receive
benefit.

Q.34   THOSE NOT WORKING LAST WEEK

The question should read: "Please can you tell me which of
these descriptions apply to .... (PERSON)?" i.e. delete
the first line and a half of the question.

You should show the respondent Card 2 in order to establish,
for each person in the household, which of the descriptions
on the card apply.

More than one description may apply to a particular person, in
which case you should code only the first one on the list.

In general, you should accept the respondent's answer to this
question. The definitions below are guidelines to help you if
respondents query what we mean by the categories.

Seeking Work:

This category includes respondents who were not working during the
specified week but who were seeking work. "Seeking Work" means
actively seeking work e.g. being registered with an official body
such as the Employment Services Agency's Employment Office or Job
Centre, or at a private employment agency; answering advertise-
ments; advertising for jobs etc.

Also include being registered with the Professional and Executive
Register, the Youth Employment Service and the Careers Office.

People who are looking for work but are also receiving a retirement
pension should be coded as "seeking work" rather than as "wholly
retired".

Waiting to take up a job:

This category should include those who have already obtained a job but have not started it yet.

Temporary Sickness:

This category should include only those who were not working but who would have looked for work if they had not been temporarily sick.

Wholly Retired:

The Wholly Retired are those who retired from their full time occupation at the approximate retirement age for that occupation, and are not seeking further employment of any kind. Thus, for all women who answer "Wholly Retired", you must use the following probe: "Do you mean that you had a job from which you retired at the approximate retirement age for that job?" If the answer is "Yes", code as "Wholly Retired", if the answer is "No", code as "Housewife".

Housewife:

Again the informant's word should be accepted.

For this question, we are concerned about their ACTIVITY STATUS, not their HOUSEHOLD STATUS as at Q.23. Therefore, the person coded "HOUSEWIFE" at Q.23 will not necessarily also be coded "HOUSEWIFE" here e.g. that person may be working, or seeking work etc.

Permanently Sick or Disabled:

This category covers those who are unable to work because of some permanent sickness or disability, which has lasted for at least 6 months. Also they can have no job to go back to. Although you will need to accept the respondent's word for this in most cases, you should bear in mind that a person with a serious handicap may still have been looking for work and if so should be coded as "SEEKING WORK".

Full-time Student/Still at School:

See definition at Q.32.

This category includes students absent because of illness or injury.

During vacations, students should still be coded as "FULL-TIME STUDENT/STILL AT SCHOOL" unless one of the above categories applied to their situation in the last week.

Exclude those who are paid a wage or salary while attending school or college (they should be coded as 'working' at Q.30).

Q.35   OCCUPATION

What is required is: 1) The present occupation of those working
                          in the week ending last Sunday, apart
                          from those coded as full-time students/
                          still at school at Q.32.

                      2) The last occupation of those seeking
                          work, waiting to take up a job or
                          temporarily sick and with no job to
                          return to.

                      3) The last main occupation of the wholly
                          retired.

Record as full an answer as you can obtain, following the guidelines given below (see definitions). 6 spaces have been allocated
to you to record answers (3 on the left hand page and 3 on the
right). Do not be constrained by the space provided - if you do
not need all 6 spaces, continue to write in the next space. Otherwise use the space around the grid or on the back page.

As full a description as possible of the job and industry is
required.

Occupation: record the respondent's name for his job and a clear
description of the kind of work he does; the nature of the
operation performed unless it is self-evident from the job title;
the grade for jobs where this is relevant e.g. civil service,
local government, police, army.

If the respondent's description of his/her occupation is too tech-
nical or vague, ask:

"What kind of work is that?"

or

"What do you actually do in that job?"

N.B: Before being satisfied with the respondent's answer make
sure you clearly understand exactly what his job is.

───────────────

Industry: record a full description of the function of the respondent's employer. (We do not want the name of the employer.)
You should ask:

"What kind of firm do you work for?"
By "firm", we mean the place/establishment where the respondent
works, which may be only part of the firm.

283

You may need to ask:

"What is done at that part/branch of the firm in which you work?"
i.e. does the firm manufacture or process at the establishment,
and if so, what does it manufacture or process. If it is not
engaged in manufacturing or processing we want to know its fun-
tion e.g. whether it is engaged in insurance, banking, wholesale
or distributive trades, transport, civil engineering or some
other activity.

The 3 columns to the right of the grid, headed "If manager/self-
employed" should be used whenever the person is either a manager
or is self-employed in order to code the number of employees in
the establishment where the person works (e.g. in that branch of
Barclays Bank if he is a Bank Manager). Ring either code 0, or
1, or 2.

N.B: Code 0 can only apply if the person is self-employed, i.e.
he works for himself and employs no one else.

Q.36   COUNTRY OF BIRTH

Remember to ask this of every person in the household.

We are interested in the present boundaries of the United Kingdom,
thus someone born in Ireland before it was divided should only be
coded as born in the U.K. if he was born in what is now Northern
Ireland.

Q.37   ETHNIC ORIGIN

Show the respondent Card 3 and ask the question of every member
of the household. This is an opinion and you should accept
whatever the respondent says.

Enter the code for each person in the two boxes provided on the
right hand page.

REASONS FOR INCLUDING PARTICULAR QUESTIONS

You may find the following information useful if you are asked by respondents
why particular questions are being asked in a housing survey.

Q.1   The number of households of different sizes and types of
            household composition are basic pieces of information in
            assessing the number, type and size of houses required now
            and in future years.

Q.2-4   These questions are included to ensure that every household at
            the sample address is interviewed and every empty flat/bed-
            sitter is accounted for. If households are incorrectly omitted
            it will not be possible to produce meaningful results from the
            survey.

Q.5-9   Questions on number of rooms are clearly basic to a housing
         survey. Taken with the questions on the size and composition
         of the household they indicate the adequacy of our housing
         stock.

Q.10   Data on availability of basic amenities will help the
         Department to assess the need for improvement grants
         and indicate the areas where they are most needed.

Q.11-12 The answers to these questions will show the availability
         of various types of heating and show what, if any, types of
         central heating are available but not used by households.

Q.13-15 This information is required to monitor changing patterns
         of tenure and in particular to monitor the effect of the
         recent rent acts. It will also throw light on the likely
         future demand for mortgages.

Q.16   This question will provide comparable statistics throughout
         England on the number of persons on council house waiting
         lists, and the present housing circumstances of these people.

Q.17   This will enable the Department to identify the types of
         accommodation different types of household find unsatis-
         factory.

Q.18-19 These questions are being asked to find out whether sub-
         stantial numbers of households have accommodation which they
         consider to be unsuitable for their needs. This will assist
         in planning the types of houses/flats to be built in future
         years.

Q.20   Provision of appropriate car parking facilities with housing
         is, of course, a matter of concern to the Department. More-
         over, particularly in rural areas where public transport
         facilities may be scarce demand for housing is closely related
         to car availability.

Q.21-26 These questions will show the changing pattern of household
         formation which has implications for both the number and type
         of accommodation required.

Q.27-29 Information on population movement is essential in forecasting
         the future population of each area and hence the demand for
         housing in each area.

Q.30-35 It is being increasingly recognised that housing problems and
         employment problems are closely related, and that the housing
         problems of an area cannot be solved without tackling employ-
         ment problems. Information on employment is therefore being
         collected to enable well based policies to be pursued in each
         area.

Q.36-37 There are very few facts about the housing conditions of the
         various ethnic groups. The results of this survey will show
         what the real situation is.

APPENDIX C.

NATIONAL DWELLING AND HOUSING SURVEY, 1977

EDITING AND CODING MANUAL

INTRODUCTION

The approach to Data Preparation on NDHS. Three distinct stages are envis-
aged on NDHS, in the preparation of questionnaire data -

(i)   The first day's work of every experienced interviewer,
        and the first un-accompanied day's work of every newly-
        trained interviewer, will be inspected rigorously on
        receipt in the office. This check will be carried out
        in order to ensure that interviewers have understood
        instructions given at briefings, and have grasped the
        essential points of the questionnaire in administering
        the interview. Once an interviewer is regarded, on the
        basis of this edit, as having attained a satisfactory
        level of competence, similar checks will be conducted
        on approximately 10% of each interviewer's subsequent
        work to verify that standards are being maintained.

(ii)   A limited number of checks will be carried out on all
        questionnaires. These checks relate to items which the
        Department of Environment regard as vital to the conduct
        of the survey, and are separately described at the end of
        this appendix.

(iii)   As a final check on data quality, all punched cards will
        be subjected to a computer edit in order to rectify any
        internal inconsistencies that remain.

The function of the Editing and Coding Manual

This Manual is seen essentially as being the key document in achieving
Objective (i) above, as it contains all the necessary information which will
ultimately enable a judgement to be formed on the competence of individual
interviewers. It is vital that common standards are applied to that proportion of each interviewer's work which receives an exhaustive check, and
that identical criteria are employed by all clerical workers in their treatment of each aspect of the questionnaire. The Editing and Coding Manual is
the central reference document in which a formal record is kept of both the
general principles and the detailed conventions for handling individual
questions.

NATIONAL DWELLING AND HOUSING SURVEY

CODING AND EDITING MANUAL

GENERAL INSTRUCTIONS

1.   If a question (or dependent part) is blank and should have been answered, code it where an answer can be deduced, but refer to the instructions for that question first in case special corrective action applies (eg. notifying the interviewer of the error).

If the answer cannot be deduced, leave the question blank.

2.   If it is apparent by deduction that an answer is wrong:

either   a)   correct the answer if it is obvious what
               it should be

   or   b)   delete the incorrect answer if it is not
               obvious what the correct answer should be.

3.   If any question (or dependent part) has been asked in error, either delete the answer or amend the senior question, as appropriate.

4.   If an answer can be recoded from the "OTHER" code, delete the code for "OTHER".

FRONT PAGE OF QUESTIONNAIRE

Location within address

In multi-household addresses, enough details should be given about the location of that household within the address to enable someone else to recall at the address or household within the address.

Rating Area Number (columns 2-5)

This applies on every questionnaire. One digit should be entered in each of the 4 boxes. Thus, leading zeros should be entered where necessary. This number should be the same as the Rating Area Number on the sample address list.

Sample Issue Number (columns 6-9)

This applies on every questionnaire. One digit should be entered in each of the 4 boxes. Thus, leading zeros should be entered where necessary. This number should be the same as the Sample Issue number to the left of the address on the sample address list.

Household number (column 10)

This applies on every questionnaire. One digit should be entered in the box. For each address, there must always be a questionnaire with Household Number 1, even if "successful interview completed" is not coded under "FINAL OUT-COME". Thus, if it is left blank and there is only one household at the address, enter a code 1 in the box.

287

In multi-household addresses, each Household number should be different; the numbers should run consecutively from 1 upwards; the highest number should correspond to the total number of questionnaires received for that address. If the Household Number box is blank on any of the multi-household question-naires or in the case of any other kind of error (eg. Duplicate Household Numbers) consult the Coding Supervisor before sending the multi-household envelope and its contents back to the interviewer.

Transfer Coding (columns 12-37)

Into the horizontal row of "Office Use Only" boxes, codes should be trans-ferred from the sample address list. The headings of the boxes correspond to the headings on the sample address list.

Note that:

1. Alpha codes are permissible.

2. Enter leading zero(s) for each section, as necessary.

3. If on the address list there are no codes for a particular section, leave the appropriate questionnaire column blank - unless these are GV or RV (see below).

4. GV/RV: (i) GV/RV in excess of £999 should be coded as 999.

    (ii) Either GV or RV must always be completed. If GV is blank enter 001. If RV is blank, it should be left blank.

    (iii) The value in the GV boxes must be greater than or equal to the value in the RV boxes.

5. Ward Codes: 3-digit ward codes should be present for all GLC and all Stress Area addresses, but absent for all other areas.

6. Where two "T" codes have been given by Inland Revenue use the first code if it is an acceptable code; if the first is not an acceptable code use the other code.

7. Where the "T" code from Inland Revenue is just "H" "F" or "M" leave "T" blank.

8. Where the age code contains an "M" transfer it as an "O" eg. "M2" should be "02".

9. (i) M^2 boxes: ignore any figure that may appear after a decimal point. ie. just code the figure before the decimal point.

    (ii) Where the M^2 Section contains 2 figures, add them together and transfer the sum onto the questionnaire. eg. 67 and 112 should be transferred as 179.

CALL RECORD

This applies to every questionnaire.

Although this information is not to be punched, it should be checked for field quality control purposes:

If code 2 is ringed under "FINAL OUTCOME", at least 4 calls should be shown. These should include at least 1 evening call and 1 weekend call. The calls should be spread over at least 7 days. Refer to coding supervisor if there are discrepancies, as the questionnaire should be returned to the interviewer for further recalls.

The only exception to the 4 calls rule is if all adult members of the household are away on holiday, or away in hospital, until after the end of the fieldwork period - in which case it is possible for fewer than 4 calls to have been made.

Total Number of Calls (column 38)

This applies on every questionnaire.

Only one code should be ringed.

The code should correspond with the number of calls shown in "CALL RECORD".

If more than 6 calls have been made, code 7, 8 or 9 should be entered and ringed to the right of code 6 outside the coding box.

NB Code 9 means "9 calls or more".

If column 38 is blank, code from the Call Record.

If Call Record is also blank, code column 38 as follows_-

For successful interviews   (ie. column 39 is coded 1), ring code 1 in
                                  column 38

For unsuccessful interviews a) if column 39 is coded 3-9, 0 - ring code 1
                                in column 38

                            b) if column 39 is coded 2, X, Y - refer to
                                coding supervisor

Also check the following:

1.   If code 2 is ringed under "FINAL OUTCOME", one of codes 4-9 must be ringed, unless it is clear that fewer than 4 calls were necessary in order to establish that the adult members of the household would be away until after the end of the fieldwork period - in which case one of codes 1-3 may be ringed.

INTERVIEWER NAME   )
INTERVIEWER NUMBER) : These should be entered on each questionnaire.

If these are blank, it is only necessary to establish the interviewer's name and number if the questionnaire needs to be returned to her or if she needs to be notified of any errors.

Final Outcome (column 39)

This applies on every questionnaire.

Only one code should be ringed. Refer any case of multicoding to supervisor.

The rest of the questionnaire should be completed if code 1 is ringed.

Column 40 only should be completed if code 8, 9, 0, X is ringed.

Columns 40-42 only should be completed if code 2-7 is ringed.

Apply the following checks, according to which code has been ringed:

Code 2   "TOTAL NUMBER OF CALLS" is coded 4-9, "CALL RECORD" shows
                at least 1 call was in the evening and 1 at the weekend.

Code 3)
)   The interviewer should have recorded details (these
)   may appear on the back page of the questionnaire)
Code 4)

Code X   Refer all such cases to the supervisor.

Code Y   This covers incomplete/partial interviews. Information
                up to columns 46 only will be punched. Full questionnaires
                for multi-household addresses which contain one or more par-
                tial interview, may be accepted.

                If code Y is used in any other cases, back code where
                possible, otherwise refer to the coding supervisor.

A partial interview is one where one or more of the following questions is
blank AND there is a note on the questionnaire such as "Respondent refused
to go any further than this question":-

Q.1 - 3

Q.9

Q.22 - 26 for head of household.

If respondents refuse to answer any other questions, do not treat this as a
partial interview. Just leave those questions blank. Questionnaires where
there is a partial interview should be coded Y on P.1 column 39 and passed to
the coding supervisor.

Month of Interview (column 40)

This applies on every questionnaire.

Only one code should be ringed.

If column 40 is blank, code from the last date shown in the Call Record.

If column 40 is blank and there is no date shown in the Call Record, code
column 40 according to the month in which the work was received in the
office.

Address Given is (column 41)

This applies if one of codes 1-7 or Y is ringed in column 39 (FINAL OUTCOME).

Only one code should be ringed.

In multi-household addresses, the same code should appear on all questionnaires. Refer to the address lists where there are discrepancies. Also
refer these to the coding supervisor as the interviewer should be notified
of these errors.

Note the following:

Codes 1-3   include "bungalows"

             If "bungalow" has been recorded at code 0 ('other'),
             and there is not enough information to recode it to
             1-3, leave it as code 0, but refer to the supervisor
             as the interviewer should be informed of this error.

Code 6-7   These include maisonettes in converted houses.

Code 0   These should be recoded where possible.

All codes   These refer to the actual description of the address as
             given on the sample address list. Thus if someone has
             a room in a house described on the address list as "3 Smith
             Street", one of codes 1-3 will be ringed, not code 8. If,
             on the other hand, the description was "rooms at 3 Smith
             Street", code 8 should be ringed. It may be necessary to
             refer to the address lists if the interviewer records on
             the questionnaire details indicating that she is not sure
             how to code this column.

Corrective Action may be taken as follows:

If this column is left blank or if different codes are ringed on the
questionnaires for a multi-household address, the codes which appear in
the boxes headed "T" in the "OFFICE USE ONLY" boxes below the serial number
may be referred to and column 41 coded accordingly. Thus:-

Houses/Bungalows

        HD)   )
        DH) = Detached house   )   = code 1 in column 41
        BD   = Detached Bungalow)

        HS   = Semi-detached house   )
        BS   = Semi-detached Bungalow)   = code 2 in column 41

        HE   = End-terrace house   )
        BE   = End-terrace Bungalow)   = code 3 in column 41

        HT   = Mid-terrace house   )
        BT   = Mid-terrace Bungalow)   = code 3 in column 41

        HB   = Back-to-Back house   = code 3 in column 41

Purpose Built Flats/Maisonettes

1. The T boxes will contain the following codes if there is a lift:-

    FL, ML - Therefore column 41 can be coded 4.

2. The T boxes will contain the following codes if there is no lift:-

    FO, MD   -)
    FD, FS, FE, FT) Therefore column 41 can be coded 5.

Non-purpose-built Flats/Maisonettes

The T boxes will contain the following codes:

FC, FN, MC, MN

But if it is not possible to tell whether there is a lift or not, column 41 will have to be left blank.

In all other cases, column 41 will have to be left blank.

Lowest Floor (column 42)

This applies if one of codes 1-7 or Y is ringed in column 39 (FINAL OUTCOME). Only one code should be ringed.

In multi-household addresses, questionnaires can be coded differently.

Note the following:

1. It is the household's accommodation that is important here, not the address. Thus, if the address is 3 Smith Street, and there are 3 households within it - one in the basement, one on the ground floor and one on the first floor - then the three questionnaires returned for that address should be coded 1, 2 and 3 accordingly in column 42.

2. The following do not count as part of the household's accommodation:

    (i)   garages

    (ii) communal accommodation such as a communal utility room. But a utility room that belongs solely to the household's accommodation should be included.

Q.1 "How many people are there in your household ...."

This applies to all complete and partial interviews.

(Refer to Interviewer's Instructions for definitions of "Household" and "Head of household").

A number should have been entered in the box on the right.

If the number is less than 10, a leading zero should be entered.

The number should tally with the number of columns where "Relationship" has been recorded across the right hand back page. If there are moe than 6 people in the household, continuation sheets should be stapled to the back of the main questionnaire and the "Relationships" should continue across the top of the right hand back page.

If the number of people entered across the top right hand page is smaller than the number in the box at Q.1, return the questionnaire to field.

If the number of people entered across the top right hand page is greater than the number in the box at Q.1, alter the number at Q.1, provided the extra person obviously belongs to that household.

If there are 13 or more people in the household, refer to coding supervisor, as details can only be punched for 12 persons in accordance with the following order of precedence:-

Respondent/HOH

Spouse of HOH

Housewife (Q.23)

Full time working adults

Part time working adults

Someone forming a new Family Unit

Children from HOH's Family Unit

Other adults

Other children

All the continuation questionnaires will be stapled to the main questionnaire, but those relating to Persons 13 onwards will be marked "NOT TO BE PUNCHED"

Q.2   "Are there any other households living at ....?"

This applies to all complete and partial interviews.

Check that either the code 0 in the right hand box has been ringed or a number recorded on the dotted line in the box.

NB: If Q.2 is left blank, the questionnaire is to be sent back to the interviewer.

Q.3   "Does .... (address) include any flats or bedsitters where no-one is living at present?"

Check as for Q.2, (except for the "N.B")

Note the following:-

1.   The sum of the numbers entered at Q.2 and Q.3 PLUS ONE should equal the number of questionnaries you have for that address. Refer discrepancies to coding supervisor before sending the multi-household envelope and its contents back to the interviewer.

2.   The sum of the numbers entered at Q.2 and Q.3 should be the same on all questionnaires for that address (although each question does not have to contain the same number on each questionnaire). Refer discrepancies to coding supervisor.

3.   If Q.2 is coded 0 but Q.3 has been left blank, code Q.3 as 0. But the interviewer must be informed that she is omitting the answer at Q.3 (there is no need to return the questionnaire to the interviewer).

4.   If there are more than 9 households (ie. questionnaires) at an address refer to coding supervisor because:-

   a)   certain questionnaires should be withdrawn leaving the total number as 9. In such cases, the Household Numbers may require adjusting so that they run from 1-9.

   b)   the figure in the boxes at Q2 and Q3 may need adjusting since the maximum number possible in either box is 9 (although the sum of the numbers in the two boxes can exceed 9).

THE REMAINING INSTRUCTIONS APPLY TO COMPLETE INTERVIEWS ONLY

Q.4   "Does your household occupy any living rooms or bedrooms in this building other than those at ...... (address)?"

This only applies if column 41 "ADDRESS GIVEN IS" (P.1) is coded 6, 7 or 8. Only one of codes 1 or 2 should be ringed.

Q.5-7 Accommodation

Note the following:

1.   Interviewers should not have counted any rooms twice eg. if a living room is also used as a dining room it is to be counted only once at Q.7; if a kitchen-dining room has been counted as a kitchen at Q.6, it should not be included as a dining room at Q.7.

2.   Rooms which are separated by an open archway count as only one room, not more.

3.   Rooms divided by a sliding or folding fixed partition count as two rooms. Rooms divided by curtains or portable screens count as one room.

Q.5   "Firstly, how many bedrooms do you have, including bedsitting rooms and any spare bedrooms?"

This applies to all.

Check that a number from 1 upwards has been entered in the right hand box.

If the number is 10 or more, recode to 9.

Note the following:

1. All rooms which are furnished as bedrooms or are regarded as bedrooms should be included, whether or not they are slept in.

2. Bedsitting rooms count as bedrooms and not kitchens even if they have cooking facilities.

3. Bed-alcoves are not "rooms" by our definition, and a bed-alcove does not therefore count as a bedroom.

4. The number in the box can never be 0. Thus, if bedsitting room has been entered at Q.7 instead of at Q.5, delete it from the total at Q.7 and enter it as "1" in the box at Q.5.

Q.6   "Do you have a kitchen, that is a separate room in which you prepare and cook food?"

This applies to all.

Only one of codes 1 or 2 should be ringed.

Q.6(a)   "Is the narrowest side at least 6½ feet wide from wall to wall?"

This applies only if code 1 is ringed at Q.6 main.

Only one of codes 1 or 2 should be ringed.

Note the following:

1. A kitchen is any separate room used for preparing and cooking food.

2. Included are: Kitchen-diners.

3. Excluded are:-   Kitchens-in-cupboard

    Kitchens on a landing or in a hall

    Bedsitting rooms (already counted at Q.5)

Q.7   "What other rooms do you have?"

This applies to all.

Check that a number from 0 upwards is entered in the box on the right.

If that number is 10 or more, recode it to 9.

Note the following:

1. The number in the box does not have to correspond with the number of rooms listed on the dotted lines by the interviewer, since certain rooms are excluded from the total.

2.   Those rooms to be excluded from the total in the box are:

(i)   All rooms already counted in Q.5 and Q.6 (ie. bedrooms, bedsitters, kitchens).

(ii)   bathrooms, lavatories, toilets, closets, laundry rooms, drying rooms.

(iii) storerooms, pantries, rooms without windows.

(iv)   rooms not usable all the year round (eg. sunrooms) - (a note to this effect must have been recorded by the interviewer).

(v)   rooms used solely for business purposes (eg. as an office or shop).

(vi)   halls unless they are used as living rooms.

(vii) garages, summerhouses in the garden.

Therefore, read the rooms listed by the interviewer and correct the total if she has wrongly included or excluded certain rooms.

Q.8   "Do you share any rooms with another household?"

This applies to all.

Only one of codes 1 or 2 should be ringed.

Q.8(a) "Which rooms do you share?"

This applies only if code 1 is ringed at Q.8 main.

Check that a number from 0 upwards is entered in the box on the right.

(If Q.8(a) is '0', there is no need to change Q.8 to "NO").

If the number is 10 or more, recode it to 9.

Note the following:

1.   See notes 1 and 2 at Q.7.

But at Q.8(a), kitchens less than $6\frac{1}{2}$ feet wide should also be excluded from the total. (ie. if Q.6(a) is coded "NO" and "Kitchen" is listed at Q.8(a)).

2.   The number in the box must be the same as or smaller than the number of rooms coded at Q.5-7, ie. add the number of rooms entered in the boxes at Q.5 and Q.7, and add one if Q.6(a) is coded 'Yes'. This is the total number of rooms in the household's accommodation. Therefore, eg. if they share 2 rooms (Q.8(a)) they must have at least 2 rooms in their accommodation (Q.5 and Q.7 plus 1 if 'Yes' at Q.6(a)).

Q.9   "When moving between your rooms, do you have to use a hall,
       stairs, passage or landing that is also used by another
       household?"

This applies to all.

Only one of codes 1 or 2 should be ringed.

If neither code is ringed, code as 'no' (code 2) provided:

       (a) Q.2 and Q.3 are both coded '0'

and (b) Col. 41 on front page is coded 1-5 or 9.

But if neither code is ringed and either other households are recorded at
Q.2 or Q.3, and/or column 41 is coded 6, 7, 8 or 0 refer to the supervisor
as these cases should be returned to field.

Q.9(a)   This applies if code 1 is ringed at Q.9 main.

          Only one of codes 1 or 2 should be ringed.

Q.9(b)   This applies if code 1 is ringed at (a), not if
          code 2 is ringed at (a)

          Only one of codes 1 or 2 should be ringed.

Q.9(c)   This applies if code 1 is ringed at Q.9 main.

          Check that a number from 1 upwards has been entered
          in the box on the right.

          If that number is 10 or more, recode to 9.

Note the following:

1.   "Other" households means those households which are currently
      sharing the space in question. Empty flats, which would be
      sharing the space if they were occupied, should not be included.

Q.10   "Do you have the use of ...... (AMENITIES)?"

(Refer to Interviewers Instructions for definitions of each amenity)

Items (i) - (v): These items apply to all.

          Only one of codes 1-3 should be ringed.

Item (vi):   This only applies if code 2 or 3 is ringed
                  at item (v)

          Only one of codes 1-3 should be ringed.

Note the following:-

1. If, for any one item, both "Sole Use" and "Shared Use" have been ringed (ie. codes 1 and 2), delete code 2.

2. If any of items (i) - (vi) are coded 2 ("Shared Use"), then Q.8 main and Q.9 main must be coded "Yes"

    But the total at Q.8(a) will not include shared bathrooms or toilets (items (iii) - (vi)), nor shared kitchens less than 6½ feet wide (items (i) and (ii)).

3. If item (iii) or (v) is coded "Shared Use", then Q.9(a) should be coded "Yes"

Q.11   "Do you have any form of central heating, including electric storage heaters?"

This applies to all.

Only one of codes 1 or 2 should be ringed.

Q.11(a) This applies if code 1 is ringed at Q.11 main.

    One or more of codes 1-6 should be ringed.

    If code 6 is ringed, recode into one of codes 1-5 wherever possible.

    Code 1 includes: coal, coke, anthracite, other coal-based products

    Code 3 includes: electric underfloor central heating

    Code 4 includes: calor/bottled gas

Q.11(b) This applies if code 1 is ringed at Q.11 main.

    Only one of codes 1 or 2 should be ringed.

Q.12   "What do you mainly use for room heating in winter?"

This applies either if Q.11 main is coded 2
              or if Q.11(b) is coded 2

One or more codes 1-6 may be ringed, provided there is no interviewer's note indicating that one form of fuel is not used as much as the other - in which case, delete the appropriate code.

If code 6 is ringed, recode into one of codes 1-5 wherever possible.

Q.13   "Does your household own or rent this house/flat?"

This applies to all.

Only one of codes 1-3 should be ringed.

Code 1 includes:

(i)   co-ownership

(ii)   leasehold property if the original lease was for a period
       of more than 21 years, or if it was extended to more than
       21 years. If the original lease was for less than 21 years,
       Q.13 should be recoded to "Rents/rent free"

Q.13(a)   This applies if code 1 is ringed at Q.13

           Only one of codes 1 or 2 should be ringed

Q.13(b)   This applies if code 1 is ringed at Q.13.

           Only one of codes 1 or 2 should be ringed.

           Code 1 includes: any long-term bank, insurance or
                               private loan as well as a building
                               society mortgage. If the owner is
                               borrowing only temporarily, code as
                               "owned outright" (eg. if a bridging
                               loan has been obtained until the
                               owner sells another property).

Q.14(a)   "Is it rented/provided furnished or unfurnished?"

This applies if code 2 is ringed at Q.13 main.

Only one of codes 1 or 2 should be ringed.

Q.14(b)   This applies if part (a) applies.

           Only one of codes 1 or 2 should be ringed.

Note the following:

Code "Yes" should be ringed only if the household lives there because
of the present job of one of the household. If the "Yes" code is ringed
check that Q.30 is coded 1 or 2 for the head of the household. If it is
not, alter Q.14(b) to "No". Code "No" should be ringed for an ex-
employee allowed to stay on after retirement, or a widow of an employee
allowed to remain after her husband's death.

Q.14(c)   This applies if part (a) applies.

           Only one of codes 1-9, 0 should be ringed.

           If code 0 has been ringed, recode wherever possible.

Note the following:

1.   If the accommodation is rent-free or goes with the job of a
      household member, the "landlord" is the person or company
      who provides the accommodation, eg. police houses or school

caretaker's accommodation should be coded as "EMPLOYER"
(code 6), and not as "COUNCIL" (codes 1 and 2); resident
caretakers of private property should be coded as "EMPLOYER"
(either code 6 or 8), and not any of the other categories.

2.   If the household rents a business together with its accom-
      modation (and therefore "Yes" is coded at Q.14(b)) than
      Q.14(c) should be coded '0'.

3.   The "landlord" excludes agents who collect the rent on behalf
      of a company or individual. Therefore, if the name of a com-
      pany or firm is given, interviewers should have probed whether
      that company is the owner or the owner's agent. If there is no
      evidence of such a probe, refer to the supervisor. If the res-
      pondent deals exclusively with an agent and does not know who
      the landlord is, 'OTHER - GIVE DETAILS' (code 0) should have
      been coded.

Q.15   "Does your landlord live in the building?'

This applies if one of codes 7-9 has been ringed at Q.14(c)

Only one of codes 1 or 2 should be ringed.

Q.15(a) This applies if code 1 is ringed at Q.15 main.

         Only one of codes 1 or 2 should be ringed.

         If Q.15(a) is coded "Yes", check that Q.9 is also
         coded "Yes". If Q.9 is coded "No", alter it to "Yes".

         (If Q.15(a) is coded "No", Q.9 can either be coded
         "Yes" or "No").

Q.16   "Do you or does anybody else in your household have their
        name on a council house waiting or transfer list, or New
        Town Corporation list?"

This applies to all.

Only one of codes 1-4 should be ringed.

If both codes 1 and 2 have been ringed, delete them both and ring
Code 3.

Note the following:

1.   Include, in one of codes 1-3, those on a list for a Council Old
      People's home.

2.   Include, in one of codes 1-3, people who have applied to go on
      to the transfer list but do not know whether they are actually
      on it yet or not.

3.   If either code 2 or 3 is ringed, there must be more than one
      person in the household. If there is only one person in the
      household, recode to 1.

300

Q.17   "..... which of the phrases on this card best describes
        your feelings about .....

a)   your house/flat?

b)   this area in general?

Both parts apply to all.

Only one of codes 1-5 should be ringed at each part.

Q.18(a)   "In your view, does your house/flat have too few rooms,
          too many rooms, or about the right number of rooms for
          your household (you)?"

This applies to all.

Only one of codes 1-3 should be ringed.

Q.18(b)   "In general, are the rooms too small, too large, or
          about the right size for your household (you)?"

This applies to all.

Only one of codes 1-4 should be ringed.

If both codes 1 and 3 have been ringed, delete the code 3.

If both codes 2 and 3 have been ringed, delete the code 3.

OR If there is a comment written in, and no codes ringed, to the effect
that some rooms are about right but others are too large or too small,
code 1 or 2 have priority over code 3.

Q.19   "Do you, or anyone else in your household, regularly have
        difficulty coping with steps, stairs or other parts of
        this building?"

This applies to all.

Only one of codes 1 or 2 should be ringed.

Q.19(a) This applies if code 1 is ringed at Q.19 main.

         One or more of codes 1-4 may be ringed.

         If code 4 is ringed, recode into codes 1-3 wherever possible.

Note the following:-

1.   We are interested in where in the building the difficulty is
     experienced and not any other reason for the difficulty, such
     as old age or incapacity.

2.   But the code 3 will be used where there is nothing necessarily
     wrong with the building but the person just cannot get about
     easily anyway.

301

Q.20   "Is there a car or van normally available for private use by you or a member of your house?"

This applies to all.

Only one of codes 1 or 2 should be ringed.

Note the following:

1.   A van is a 3 or 4 wheeled motorised vehicle with no side windows to the rear of the driver's seat. Thus, jeeps are 'vans'; Range Rovers and caravanettes are 'cars'.

2.   A 'van' means a light van - thus lorries, even if used privately, are excluded.

3.   Include: (i)   cars/vans normally available for private use by the household but not necessarily owned by the household eg. cars/vans owned by an employer that the household has full use of.

              (ii)   cars/vans on long-term (contract) hire.

              (iii)   cars/vans temporarily out of action.

              (iv)   cars/vans which are not taxed but are in road-worthy condition and are due to be taxed in the future.

              (v)   3-wheeled cars/vans

4.   Exclude: (i)   cars/vans used solely for work or hire by other people.

              (ii)   temporary hirings.

              (iii)   cars/vans permanently untaxed or not roadworthy.

              (iv)   motorcycles or scooters

Q.20(a) and (b)   "How many cars/vans?"

These two parts apply if code 1 is ringed at Q.20 main.

Check that a number is entered in both boxes, even if it is '0' in one box.

A '0' cannot be recorded in both boxes.

If either or both boxes are blank, leave it/them blank.

If the number in the box is 10 or more recode to 9.

302

Q.20(c)   "Does your household have a garage or off-street
           parking space for the cars/vans?"

This applies if code 1 is ringed at Q.20 main.

Only one of codes 1-3 should be ringed.

If there is only one vehicle as recorded at (a) and (b), code 2 should
not be ringed. In such cases, accept the answers at (a) and (b) and
recode (c) to code 1.

Note the following:

1.   A garage or off-street parking space is a place, not on the public
      highway or verge, where a vehicle can be parked, eg. car ports;
      lean-to garages; land in front of/behind the house; communal car
      park.

2.   Include all garages available for parking the household's
      vehicles, wherever that garage is situated.

3.   A parking space does not necessarily mean one specifically
      designated for the household, eg. if a block of flats has a
      car park for the residents each household could park its car
      anywhere in this car park.

Q.21-37 These questions should be answered on the right hand page
         of the questionnaire for each member of the household to
         whom the question applies.

Q.21   "How old was each person last birthday?"

This applies to all members of the household.

For each person a two-digit figure for age should be entered in the
boxes below the Person Numbers.

Insert leading zeros if these have not already been entered for
children under 10.

Note the following:-

1.   Children less than a year should be coded 00.

2.   People aged 100 or more should be coded 99.

3.   If "E" is entered (for "Estimate") next to the age, accept
      the age given, but delete if simply marked "over 21".

4.   If "Ref/Refused" has been entered next to the boxes, leave
      the boxes blank for that person.

5.   Person No.1 should always be aged 16 or more (ie. the HOH).

Q.22   Respondent

This applies on all questionnaires.

Only one of the code 1s should be ringed on the right hand page (in line with the question).

Note the following:-

1.   The person in whose column code 1 is ringed should be aged 16 or more.

2.   If the interview was conducted with a non-member of the household, code as follows:

  a)   code 1 for the person answering through an interpreter e.g. HOH cannot speak English, son acts as interpreter - HOH should be coded 1.

  b)   code 3 in column 18 if someone outside the household is giving the answers eg. because the HOH is too old/ill.

3.   If Q.22 is blank and the household consists of only one person, ring code 1 in column 18.

4.   If Q.22 is blank, and there is more than one person in the household, return to the interviewer.

Q.23   Housewife

This applies to all questionnaires.

Only one of the code 2s should be ringed on the right hand page (in line with the question).

Note the following:-

1.   The housewife is the person, other than a domestic servant, who is responsible for most of the domestic duties. If these tasks are done by a paid servant, the servant is not the housewife. In such a case, the housewife is the person responsible for seeing that the servant performs these tasks.

2.   It is possible for the housewife also to be the respondent and in cases of a single person household, that person will be HOH, Housewife and Respondent.

3.   The Housewife can be a male member of the household.

4.   If Q.23 is blank and the household consists of only one person, ring code 2 in column 18.

5.   If Q.23 is blank and the household consists only of husband and wife (or husband, wife and their children of under 18 only), then code the wife as the housewife.

6.   If Q.23 is blank in any other circumstances, return to the interviewer.

Q.24 Family Units

This applies to every member of the household.

A family unit number must be entered in the box for every person in the household.

A family unit can consist of:

A married couple with or without never married children (natural or adopted, but not fostered). The marriage can be the commonlaw type.

or

A lone parent (single, widowed, separated or divorced, or married but not living with spouse/partner) living with never married children.

NB 1. A brother and sister (whose parents are not part of the household) would form 2 separate family units.

    2. In general, family units cannot span more than two generations, ie. grandparents and grandchildren cannot belong to the same family unit. The exception to this is when it is established that the grandparents are responsible for looking after the grandchildren (eg. while the parents are abroad, etc.)

    3. Where a couple who live together are not married but have children they should be treated as one family unit if they regard themselves as a "couple". If they do not regard themselves as a couple but one of them has children, they should be treated as two family units with the children belonging to the same unit as the natural parent, or, if this is not clear, to the same unit as the mother.

Numbering of family units

Members of the HOH's family unit should be numbered 1; the next family unit 2, and so on.

EXAMPLES

1. | Per No. | Relationship to HOH | Family Unit |
    |---------|---------------------|-------------|
    | 1 | HOH | 1 |
    | 2 | Wife | 1 |
    | 3 | Son (Single) | 1 |
    | 4 | Mother | 2 |

2.

Per No.	Relationship to HOH	Family Unit
1	HOH	1
2	Wife	1
3	Son (Single)	1
4	Sister (Widow)	2
5	Brother) Married to	3
6	Sister-in-law) each other	3
7	Niece (single, daughter of person 4)	2

Note the following:-

1. If the family unit coding is incorrect but there is enough information to enable you to amend it, do so. BUT ensure the interviewer is informed of the kind of errors being made.

2. If the family unit coding is incorrect and there is insufficient information to enable you to amend it (eg. details of relationships have been omitted), return to the interviewer.

Q.25   Sex

This applies to every member of the household.

For each person only one of codes 1 or 2 should be ringed.

Q.26   Marital Status

This applies to every member of the household.

For each person only one of codes 1-5 should be ringed.

Note the following:

1. Common-law marriages/a couple living together as man and wife should be coded as married. If they do not regard themselves as living together as man and wife, they should be coded as single, widowed, divorced or separated - as appropriate.

2. If someone says they are living apart from their spouse, they should be coded as married unless they are legally separated.

3. It is the person's present marital status that we are interested in. Thus, if they were married but are now divorced, only code 3 should be ringed.

Q.27   "How long has .... been living at this address?"

This applies to every member of the household.

For each person, only one of codes 1-6 should be ringed.

Q.28   "In what month and year did .... move to this address?"

This applies only to those members of the household coded 1 or 2 at Q.27, except for children aged under 2 years old who were born at this address (ie. the parents had not moved to the address since the birth of that child).

The month and year of each person's move, if within the last 2 years, should be entered on the dotted lines in the column for each person.

Q.29   This applies only to those members of the household coded 1 at Q.27 except for children under 1 year old who were born at this address.

Note the following:-

1.   Check that the person number of each person who has moved in the last 12 months is recorded on the left hand dotted lines (one person number on each line) and that these numbers correspond with the persons who are coded 1 at Q.27. If they do not correspond and are numbered consecutively from 1 upwards, alter according to the person numbers on the right hand page. If they do not corres- pond in some other way, refer to coding supervisor.

2.   Do not code "FULL POSTAL ADDRESS" (GLC to code)

Q.30   "Did .... have a paid job in the week ending last Sunday?"

This applies only to those members of the household aged 16 and over.

For each person, only one of codes 1-3 should be ringed.

Note the following:-

1.   Those to be regarded as working last week are:

    a)   those who worked in private or public employment for wages, salary or any other form of payment, such as commission or tips.

    b)   those who worked in his or her own business or firm for profit.

    c)   those who were absent because of holiday, strike, sick- ness, (including pregnancy), temporarily laid off, or any other similar reason, provided he or she has a job to return to with the same employer.

    d)   casual or seasonal workers should be coded as "working" only if they were working during the week ending last Sunday.

2.   Include teachers as "full-time" if they work at least 25 hours a week.

3.   If someone has both a full-time and a part-time job, code for the full-time one only.

307

Q.31   "Is .... an employee or self-employed?"

This applies to each person coded 1 or 2 at Q.30.

Only one of codes 1 or 2 should be ringed.

Note the following:

1.   An employee is defined as someone who is not self-employed and who
      recognises that he/she has an employer (whether the employer is
      a company or an individual).

2.   Self-employment includes members of partnerships and work in any
      kind of business for profit as opposed to the wages, salaries,
      commission or tips earned by an employee.

3.   If someone was both an employee and self-employed last week, the
      job which took up most time should be the only one coded.

Q.32   "Is .... a full-time student/still at school?"

This applies to each person coded 1 or 2 at Q.30.

Only one of codes 1 or 2 should be ringed.

Note the following:

1.   Include in code 1 ("Yes") those aged 16 or over who even though they
      were working last week, are still studying full-time at a school
      college, university, polytechnic or other educational institution.
      This includes people on sandwich courses. A person is classified
      as a full-time student only if (during normal term time) he/she
      attends classes/lectures for at least 15 hours per week and does
      NOT have a full-time job.

2.   Exclude from code 1 people on purely vocational training courses
      given by an employer as part of the job (eg. nurses' training,
      police courses).

Q.33   "Was .... registered last week as unemployed?"

This applies only to those coded 3 at Q.30.

Only one of codes 1 or 2 should be ringed.

Note the following:-

Registered unemployed means registered as seeking work, irrespective of
whether they are registered to receive benefit.

Q.34   ".... please can you tell me which of these descriptions
        apply to ....?"

(Refer to Interviewer's Instructions for definition of each category)

This applies only to those coded 3 at Q.30.

Only one of codes 1-8 should be ringed.

If more than one code is ringed, delete all except the top-most code.

If code 8 is ringed, recode into one of codes 1-7 wherever possible.

Q.35   Occupation

This question applies if:-

either Q.30 is coded 1 or 2 unless Q.32 is coded 1.

or   Q.34 is coded 1-4.

Q.36   "Was .... born in the United Kingdom?"

This applies to every member of the household.

Only one of codes 1 or 2 should be ringed.

Note the following:-

1.   We are interested in the present boundaries of the United
      Kingdom, thus someone born in Ireland before it was divided
      should only be coded as born in the UK if he was born in what
      is now Northern Ireland.

Q.37   "To which of the groups listed on this card do you consider
        .... belongs to?"

This applies to every member of the household.

A 2 digit code for the ethnic group of each person should be entered
in the 2 boxes at the bottom of the right hand page for each person.

Enter leading zeros if necessary.

If code 11 is ringed, recode into one of the other categories where
possible (ie. alter the code 11 in the 2 boxes to one of the other
2 digit codes).

The "other" group should be entered on the dotted line below the boxes
for the appropriate person.

NB: Whenever this question has been omitted, contact the supervisor
(as the interviewer needs to be informed of the omission, or accompanied
if she omits it more than once).

ADDENDUM TO EDITING AND CODING MANUAL

The following pages contain details of:-

1.   "Transfer Coding" (from address lists onto the questionnaire).

2.   The coding frames for questions coded by the GLC and not by the
     Consortium.

These details do not appear in the Editing and Coding Manual.

The "Transfer Coding" instructions contain not only lists of permissible
codes, but additional instructions on decisions that need to be taken at
the Computer edit stage.

I.   TRANSFER CODING

     GV/RV boxes:

     The value in the GV boxes must be greater than or equal to
     the value in the RV boxes. If this is not the case, refer
     to the address list; if it appears GV and RV have been
     reversed, alter them: otherwise leave the RV value blank.

G BOXES: "HOUSING GROUP" CODES

CODE

     Pre-1919

01   Rural cottages and farmhouses.

02   Country cottages and farmhouses, improved and modernised.

03   Small artisan-type houses and cottages.

04   Larger, more substantial houses and cottages.

05   Three or more storey terraced houses.

06   Small country houses of highest standard.

08   Small "villa" type houses.

09   Larger "villa" type houses, and farmhouses.

10   Large "family" houses, vicarages and farmhouses.

13   Substantial town houses of Georgian and Regency period.

14   Country houses in the "mansion" or "hall" category.

     Spanning First World War

19   Good quality dwellings, forerunners to GROUP 21.

310

1919-1939

20 Private and local authority "subsidy" dwellings.

21 Speculative builders' and local authority dwellings.

24 Better quality estate and individual dwellings.

25 Larger, architect designed "residences".

Post-1939

30 Small private and local authority dwellings built under licence.

31 Private estate and local authority dwellings.

32 Better quality estate and individual dwellings.

35 Larger, architect-designed "residences".

36 Town houses.

Flats and Maisonettes in converted houses

40 In GROUP 03, 04 and 05 houses.

41 In GROUP 08 and 09 houses.

42 In GROUP 10 houses.

45 In GROUP 13 houses.

46 In GROUP 19, 20, 21, 24 and 25 houses.

Flats and Maisonettes in purpose-built blocks or terraces

50 In two-storey terraces, from about 1880 to 1930.

51 In two-storey blocks, from 1930 onwards.

52 In three or more storey blocks, pre-1919.

55 In three or more storey blocks, 1919 to 1939.

56. In three or more storey blocks, post-1939.

Flats and Maisonettes in purpose-built, converted or adapted

60 Above (and rear of) shops and similar commercial premises.

Miscellaneous dwellings

70 Sub-standard, non-traditional dwellings.

71 Rateable caravans.

CODE

HD, DH	Houses	-	Detached
HS			Semi-detached
HE			End-Terrace
HT			Mid-terrace
HB			Back-to-back

BD	Bungalows	-	Detached
BS			Semi-detached
BE			End-terrace
BT			Mid-terrace

Flats (purpose-built, self contained, two storey residential)

FD			Detached block of two
FS			Block of four, semi-detached
FE			Terrace, at end
FT			Terrace, not at end

Flats (Other purpose-built, self contained, including those over shops, etc) -

| FL | | | With lift |
| FO | | | Without lift |

Flats (Non-purpose built) -

| FC | | | Fully self-contained |
| FN | | | Not self-contained |

Maisonettes (Purpose-built)

| ML | | | With lift |
| MO | | | Without lift |

Maisonettes (Non-purpose built)

| MC | | | Fully self-contained |
| MN | | | Not self-contained |

Note: (i) Where two 'T' codes are shown on the address list
            transfer the first code onto the questionnaire
            provided it is an acceptable code; if it is not

an acceptable code, transfer the second code (again, provided it is acceptable). If both are unacceptable, leave the 'T' columns on the questionnaire blank.

(ii) Where the 'T' code on the address list is just 'H', 'F' or 'M', then leave the 'T' columns on the questionnaire blank.

(iii) If the codes in the 'T' boxes conflict with that coded by the interviewer in column 41 and if the information under "Location within Address" agrees with the codes in the 'T' boxes, then the code in column 41 should be deleted and a code X entered instead.

If there is no information under "Location within Address", but other information on the questionnaire agrees with the 'T' codes, then the code at column 41 should be altered to X.

If there is no information under "Location within Address" nor elsewhere on the questionnaire, refer to the address list. If "Description of address" agrees with the 'T' codes, alter column 41 to X.

In any other cases, column 41 should be left as it stands, and columns 23-37 of the Transfer Coding should be deleted.

A BOXES: "HOUSING AGE" CODES

CODE	AGE
01	Pre 1900
02	1900 - 1918
03	1919 - 1929
04	1930 - 1939
05	1940 - 1954
06	1955 - 1964
07	1965 - 1972
73	1973
74	1974
75	1975
76	1976
77	1977
78	1978

Note: (i) If the first of these two boxes contains an M, it should be corrected to a zero when transferred onto the questionnaire. Thus, M2 should be 02.

313

Q BOXES: "HOUSING QUALITY" CODES

    Q.1

    Q.5

    Q.9

L BOXES: "HOUSING LOCATION" CODES

CODE

Urban

UI   Industrial area: mainly heavy and basic industries.

UC   Commercial locality where residential properties tend
to be in a minority and are adversely affected by their
close proximity to shops, offices, warehouses and similar
commercial premises and perhaps light industry.

UP   Poor, below average residential area of high density
dwellings possibly interspersed with a few commercial
and/or light industrial premises.

UA   Average urban residential area, regardless of age, in
both towns and suburbs: includes "estate" development
in such situations: generally made up of fairly non-
descript dwellings.

UG   Good residential locality: will include the better type
of more modern private estate development.

UB   Urban locality, better than UG, attracting high prices
and generally noted for its attractive or convenient
environment, where dwellings of some individuality,
style or architectural merit predominate.

Rural

RR   Remote rural situation where dwellings are widely scattered
or comprised only in small hamlets.

RV   Village situation typical of a rural area.

RD   Development in a rural setting, other than RR,
RV or RB.

RB   Best rural situation, outstanding for its natural beauty
(eg. sought-after coastal area or picturesque inland area
in a rural setting).

II QUESTIONS CODED BY GLC

CODING OF RELATIONSHIP TO HEAD OF HOUSEHOLD

1.   Person No.1 (Head of Household) is coded 1, in Card 3,
        Col. 34.

2.   Persons No.2-6 are coded in Card 3, Cols. 42, 50, 58,
        66 and 74 respectively (and Persons No.7-12 in Card 5,
        Cols. 34, 42, 50, 58, 66 and 74 respectively), according
        to the following code frame:

CODE	RELATIONSHIP TO HOH
2	Spouse
3	Son/daughter
4	Son-in-law/Daughter-in-law
5	Father/mother
6	Father-in-law/mother-in-law
7	Brother/Sister
8	Grandson/granddaughter
9	Other relation
0	Uncodeable
X	Unrelated
Y	Unknown

CODING OF ADDRESS 12 MONTHS AGO FOR MOVER GROUPS

CARD 2, COLS 48-68

Notes:

1.   Any group of persons (or single person) moving from the
        same address 12 months ago forms a "Mover Group". An
        arbitrary maximum of 3 "Mover Groups" has been set per
        household.

2.   The person number(s) of the first "Mover Group" are
        coded in Card 2, Col.48.

3.   The address from which the first "Mover Group" moved is
        coded in Card 2, Cols. 51-54, using the appropriate 4-
        digit code. Region Codes are used when the address is
        not sufficiently defined to allow an Area Code to be
        allocated. Code 9999 is used to denote "No Information".

4.   Where a Greater London Area Code is used in Card 2, Cols.
        51-54, the appropriate Ward Code (first 2 digits) is coded
        in Card 2, Cols. 49-50. Code 99 is used where the address
        details are insufficient to allow a Ward Code to be
        allocated.

5.   The second "Mover Group" is coded in Card 2, Cols. 55-61
        (and the third "Mover Group" in Card 2, Cols. 62-68),
        following the same coding practice as for the first
        "Mover Group".

DATE OF MOVEMENT OF HOUSEHOLD MEMBERS

CARD 2, COL. 69

CODE   DESCRIPTION

1   HOH and HW are separate persons, and both moved later than
         July 1976.

2.   HOH and HW are the same person, and that person moved later
         than July 1976.

3.   HOH moved later than July 1976, but HW did not.

4.   HW moved later than July 1976, but HOH did not.

5.   Neither HOH nor HW moved later than July 1976.

6.   Unable to decide whether HOH or HW moved later than
         July 1976.

7.   HOH moved later than July 1976, but HW uncodeable.

8.   HW moved later than July 1976, but HOH uncodeable.

CODING OF SOCIO-ECONOMIC GROUP

CARD 3, COLS. 35 & 36, 43 & 44, ETC.

1.   The 17 standard Socio-economic groups are coded, using
        codes 01-17 (where 17 = "insufficient information
        supplied"). No distinction is made between Sub-group
        1.1 and 1.2 (both coded 01); likewise 2.1 and 2.2 (both
        coded 02) and 5.1 and 5.2 (both coded 05).

2.   Persons 1-6 are coded in Card 3 Cols. 35-36, 43-44,
        51-52, 59-60, 67-68 and 75-76 respectively. Persons
        7-12 are coded in the equivalent columns in Card 5.

316

APPENDIX D: QUESTIONNAIRE AND SHOWCARD.

```
┌─────────────────────────────┐   ┌─────────────────────────────────┐
│                    Card 1   │   │                        Card 2   │
│                             │   │                                 │
│  1.  Very satisfied         │   │  1.  Seeking work               │
│                             │   │  2.  Waiting to start a new job  │
│  2.  Satisfied              │   │      (arrangements already made)│
│  3.  Neither satisfied nor  │   │  3.  Prevented by temporary     │
│      dissatisfied           │   │      sickness from seeking work │
│  4.  Dissatisfied           │   │  4.  Wholly retired             │
│  5.  Very dissatisfied      │   │                                 │
│                             │   │  5.  Housewife                  │
└─────────────────────────────┘   │  6.  Permanently sick or        │
                                   │      disabled                   │
                                   │  7.  Full-time student/still at │
                                   │      school                     │
                                   │  8.  Other                      │
                                   └─────────────────────────────────┘
```

```
        ┌─────────────────────────────────┐
        │                        Card 3   │
        │                                 │
        │   1.  White                     │
        │   2.  West Indian               │
        │   3.  Indian                    │
        │   4.  Pakistani                 │
        │   5.  Bangladeshi               │
        │   6.  Chinese                   │
        │   7.  Turkish                   │
        │   8.  Other Asian               │
        │   9.  African                   │
        │  10.  Arab                      │
        │  11.  Other (please state)      │
        │  12.  Mixed Origin (please state)│
        └─────────────────────────────────┘
```

Printed in England for Her Majesty's Stationery Office by Hobbs the Printers of Southampton
(64) Dd0596059 K16 2/79 G3927